THE SOUTH SINCE APPOMATTOX

THE SOUTH
SINCE APPOMATTOX

A Century of Regional Change

❧❧

THOMAS D. CLARK
AND
ALBERT D. KIRWAN

NEW YORK
OXFORD UNIVERSITY PRESS
1967

Copyright © 1967 by Oxford University Press, Inc.
Library of Congress Catalogue Card No: 66-22259
Printed in the United States of America

To Beth and Betty

The authors wish to acknowledge the following publishers who have graciously given permission to quote from their books: the University of North Carolina Press for Rupert B. Vance, *Human Geography of the South* and Howard W. Odum, *Southern Regions of the United States;* Harper and Row for Gunnar Myrdal, *An American Dilemma;* D. C. Heath and Company, for James G. Randall, *The Civil War and Reconstruction;* Alfred A. Knopf, Inc., for J. M. Dabbs, *The Heritage of the South;* Harcourt, Brace and World, Inc., for James M. Silver, *Mississippi: The Closed Society;* the University of Kentucky Press for Albert D. Kirwan, *Revolt of the Rednecks;* and the Louisiana State University Press for E. Merton Coulter, *The Confederate States of America* and *The South During Reconstruction,* and for C. Vann Woodward, *Origins of the New South.*

Contents

I   The New South—A Perspective in Change   1

II   Political Reconstruction   20

III   Agrarian Revolt   51

IV   Farmers on the Land   82

V   Demagoguery and Reform   108

VI   The Path to Industrialization   136

VII   Education, the Central Challenge   164

VIII   An Ever-Broadening Educational Challenge   187

IX   The Mightier Sword   202

X   Depression and the New Deal   229

XI   The South in the Electrical Age   244

XII   The Tide of Industrial Progress   269

XIII   The Great Crusade and After   286

XIV   The Negro   305

XV   Urbanization of the South   330

XVI   Enter the Supreme Court   347

XVII   Exit Jim Crow   362

XVIII   The Evolving South   378

Bibliography   395

Index   421

THE SOUTH

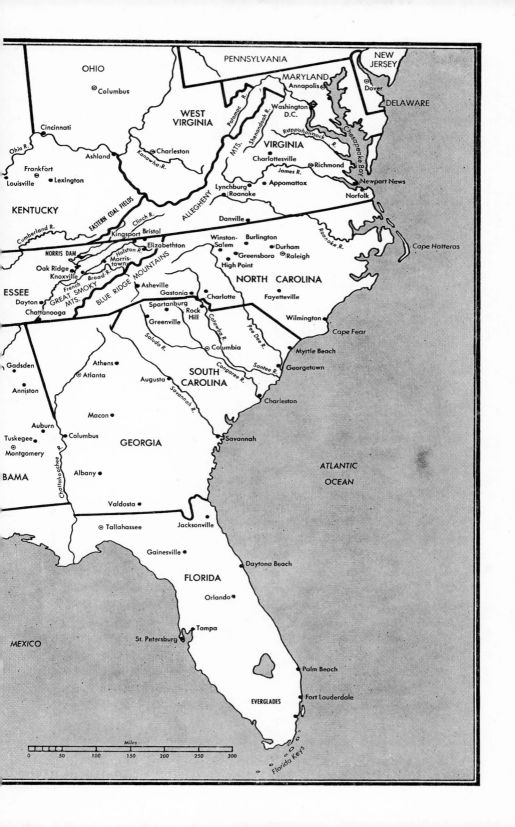

❧ I ❧

The New South—
A Perspective in Change

"Everywhere there is progress; in some regions such progress, that one may fairly call the South a new country. The population is indeed unchanged, for it is only lately that settlers have begun to come from the North, and no part of the United States has within the present century received so small a share of European immigration. Slavery was a fatal deterrent while it lasted, and of late years the climate, the presence of the negro, and the notion that work was more abundant elsewhere, have continued to deflect in a more northerly direction the stream that flows from Europe. But the old race, which is, except in Texas (where there is a small Mexican and a larger German element) and in Louisiana, a pure English and Scots-Irish race, full of natural strength, has been stimulated and invigorated by the changed conditions of its life. It has made great advances in almost every direction. Schools are better and more numerous. The roads are being improved. Cotton mills are rising in some places, iron-works in others. It sees in the mineral and agricultural resources of its territory a prospect of wealth and population rivalling those of the Middle and Western States. It has recovered its fair share of influence in the national government. It has no regrets over slavery, for it recognizes the barbarizing influence that slavery exerted. Neither does it cherish any dreams of separation. It has now a pride in the Union as well as in its State, and is in some ways more fresh and sanguine than the North, because less cloyed by luxury than the rich are there, and less discouraged by the spread of social unrest than the thoughtful have been there. But for one difficulty the South might well be thought to be the most promising part of the Union, that part whose advance is likely to be swiftest, and whose prosperity will be not the least secure.

"This difficulty, however, is a serious one. It lies in the presence of nine millions of negroes."

James Bryce, *The American Commonwealth*, 1888

The South is by no means unique in its history, or in its state of change and confusion. Other regions of the United States, and of the world for that matter, have experienced during the past century a social revolution which has shattered custom and tradition. Perhaps no Americans have experienced more penetrative change, however, than southerners. They started a century ago with at least two handicaps: they had to rearrange their economy and way of life, and to confront a new racial alignment in a land that had refused to believe such a thing could occur. The most direct thing that can be said to characterize this period in southern history is that it was one of uncertainties and confusion. Many conflicts arose further to complicate an already complex condition of life.

Above all the South has been confronted with stern reality, whether in economics, race matters, or partisan politics. At no time was this more dramatically clear than at the end of the Civil War. Not only did the region have to face up to old realities of a raw expanding frontier with its mixture of problems, an economy that was being reorganized in its many phases, a social system which was rendered in twain, the losses of a war, a race problem, and a manpower shortage, but it had to find its way back into the flow of national life in a world deep in technological revolution. The future which then confronted the region was one of blurred promises and uncertain objectives. Would the way of life of the so-called Old South be restored by new approaches to old problems? Would a new philosophy of social and political matters prevail, or would efforts be made to establish the all but unstated glories of the past?

Immediately it was clear that, aside from the physical damages of four years of military strife, the great emotional paradoxes created by a changing age were even more damaging. Groping in a decade of defeat, southerners of all conditions of society sought to overcome the past through acceptance of the challenges of the future. Some of them sought to deny that a hiatus had occurred in both the romantic dream and the southern system. Slavery was wrecked on the bars of national disdain and legality, nevertheless the former slaves were a source of highly subservient labor. Heavy participation by yeomen in the war made common cause between them and the so-called aristocratic planters. Too, the Negro and his former master found workable grounds on which to proceed. Traditions of the Old South, whether of culture, social privilege, or political leadership, now became common traditions of the two major social classes. Some way the past must be projected into the future, and the tenor of southern life restored to something approximating that of earlier years. In regional economy this was as true as it was in politics, social relationships, and labor. The old system was not so badly wrecked that there was not a burgeoning hope that it could survive. This hope blinded large numbers of southerners to the realities of the moment, and to future prospects of the South. Writers in *DeBow's Review*, for instance, gave more thought to the past as a living hope than to the future as a cold reality.

Some historians have contended with genuine eloquence that there was in fact little break between the Old and New Souths. Even with the destruction of slavery, both the method of labor and the plantation economy in many areas continued much as before. There was even continuity of the old political systems. There were areas, however, in which the chasms widened rapidly. For the first time the South was brought with full force into what of late has been called the mainstream of American history. However much of the past the South might try to redeem or live by, it could not live apart from the times. In trying to do so the region would certainly force itself into conflicts which could not be easily resolved. The web of nationalism might have been woven in crazy and uncertain patterns, but it was thick and unyielding, and it gathered the South more firmly into its folds in each succeeding decade.

Hinton Rowan Helper had introduced the Old South to the realism of statistics, a stern fact southerners neither fully understood nor wished to accept. This nevertheless was portentous of the future. The unbalanced burden of ignorance, human incapacity, superstition, and social blight of untrained poor whites and freedmen after 1865 added extra dimensions of adversity to the New South's history. Chivalry, the spirit of noblesse oblige, classical culture, and personal refinement were all precious values and highly cherished standards, but they added little of tangible worth to a society so heavily involved in searching out new directions, or in bearing the overweening burden of negative statistics. The new national society reckoned its advances toward the future in terms of production tables, crops grown, resources exploited, miles of rails laid, in the rise of cities, the establishment of banking houses, schools and colleges founded, and in social reform. For the South all of these things were important, but of more basic significance was education. There were dual demands in this area: the conditioning of freedmen and the training of the entire white population. Actually to compare educational efforts of the ante-bellum years with those after 1865 is to associate irrelevancies. This is not to say public schools were lacking. Public schools had been organized, but had not matured.

Education was the prime need of the New South. The crusade to build schools and to improve the quality of education in the region after 1865 was carried on with the fervor of a religious revival. The mass of southern population, however, remained indifferent to regional needs in this field. Many cultural heroes emerged from the crusade of the latter half of the nineteenth century to bring educational maturity to the South. Names of men in these hard years who sacrificed time and energy should be placed well ahead of even Confederate heroes as revered sons of the South. The bed was prepared by the pioneers in this century and the educational seed sown, but little mature fruit was borne. It was not until the turn into this century that results of the early educational drives could be clearly discerned.

The force of the twentieth century upon the South was all but staggering. Though cast against the backdrop of a past century fraught with controversy, conflict, and lingering crises, promises of the new age in the first decade seemed sparkling. Nowhere was this fact made more evident than in the Southern Commercial Congress which met in Atlanta in 1911. Delegates to this convention felt the strong impulse of the new age. The Panama Canal had been opened to trade, and once again foreign commerce beckoned to the South. Orators from many professions proclaimed not only the physical recovery of the South, but attempted to project the region forward with an enthusiasm which dazzled their listeners. G. Grosvenor Dawe wrote, "Nothing could have been more dramatic in its setting than this convention of the Southern Commercial Congress in Atlanta, surrounded by every evidence of prosperity." With the blare of a brass band playing *Dixie*, the southern state flags were paraded before President William Howard Taft, and dramatically a vast national banner was unfurled from the rafters of the hall to dominate the scene. In this setting of national unity the congress began an exploration of the South's future on the eve of World War I.

Each speaker added his bit of insight to the approach of the region into its new age. Eloquent southerners still paid compulsory tributes to King Cotton, while belaboring the traditional devils of lack of grains, meat, hay, livestock, and the drain of precious capital away from the South to purchase these things. Tributes to King Cotton, however, lacked the old ring of boastful assurance. New forces stirred in the South. Emotions were mixed, but clearly the Old South was rapidly fading away before a new one could burst into bloom. None was more specific on the needs of the new revolutionary generation than Henry S. Hartzog, secretary of the Arkansas Educational Commission. There was a central fact in southern history, and he proposed to face it squarely. "Ignorance," he said, "in the whole history of the world had never solved a single problem. Ignorance is not the remedy for any trouble of the white man or the black man. Ignorance has never lifted the burden from the backs of the world. Ignorance has never built a factory nor penetrated the jungle with a railroad; ignorance, I repeat, is a greater burden than taxation and the problem of the South is to increase the educational taxation in order to decrease ignorance." With bristling confidence the Arkansas educator assured his audience that a new day had dawned in the South. Education looked to the future, he said, and

> we educators of the South do not come to plead the disasters of 1864, to condone the educational shortcomings of 1911. We do not sit on a tombstone of John C. Calhoun, weeping over departed glories. We are not children in the darkness crying for light. We know what we want. We want in every community in the South a school building whose architectural lines will be an expression of parental love and whose modern conveniences will make it a factor for American manhood, and in that schoolhouse we will have every healthy child ten months in the year.

There was, nevertheless, to be much more weeping at "the tombstone of John C. Calhoun" before the South began to achieve the objectives of universal education. Two world wars and a biting depression made clear the fact that it took far more than prophetic oratory to mature an educational system. Even the jubilant prophets of 1911 could not foresee how formidable comparative statistics would become in the next half-century in showing the South its low position in relation to national achievement.

Eight years before Professor Hartzog delivered his prescription for a New South, William Garrott Brown scolded his homeland for its shortsightedness in his book, *The Lower South in American History*. While much of his study was apologetic, he saw clearly the course of the region's history. There was a restiveness discernible among southerners:

> As I have said, Southerners are restive under the restraints which keep them from entering actively and fearlessly into the larger political life of the Republic. Americanism is growing in the South. Pride in the flag, pride in the prosperity and prestige of the United States, is surely heightening. Industrial development has brought many regions, hitherto remote and separate, into close business relations with the North. Merchants and bankers are constantly visiting New York and other eastern cities. Metropolitan newspapers are active in every large town. The plantation no longer sets the standard of social usage and intellectual life. The whole South is too much alive to outer things, too cognizant of a civilization ampler than its own, not to feel keenly the limitations upon its participation in national political contests. Its political solidarity, once a source of pride, is now seldom vaunted; oftener, it is explained and apologized for. The Negro, is of course, the sole explanation, the sole apology. To get rid of him politically, and to do so by law, once and for all, is the only remedy proposed.
>
> But whenever there is discussion of specific plans the illiterate white man is bound to come in. Mississippi provides for him by permitting the registrars to decide that he understands the state constitution and the negro does not. The Supreme Court of the United States has sustained that provision, but obviously it merely transfers the task of suppressing the negro vote from the inspectors at the polls to the registrars of voters.

At stake in this issue was not only the political futures of managers of the southern vote, but likewise the crusade to provide universal education. The South, after the drafting of the new state constitutions, was so bound up in its effort to keep the Negro ignorant and disfranchised that it lost sight of the greater disfranchisement of the region itself in attracting and servicing industries. No matter how many southerners went to New York to confer with bankers, the poor quality of the human resource of the South still remained a great deterrent to economic expansion of the region.

In no field of vibrant human endeavor could southerners retreat into the past, even though they often dreaded to face the realities of the twentieth century. There remained only the future with its riddles; traditions and precedents had vanished in the face of national modernization. George W. Perkins, a New York capitalist, told the Commercial Congress that, "Whether we like it or not, whether it is good for us or not, the great, big, undeniable fact stares us in the face that the inventor brought us, by leaps and bounds, to the 'get together' age." This for the South was, he thought, an age when strong twentieth-century men should set about freeing their minds, and exploiting their resources intelligently.

These themes have been repeated annually in the South. Whether in regional congresses, governors' conferences, or in the daily press and conversation; the impact of the inventor, the scientist, the social reformer, the courts, and expansion of mechanization of the productive processes had brought change. A century of southern history had been marked by hills and valleys of crises. An agrarian society surrendered slowly to modernization. A farm-oriented economy definitely shaped the nature of constitutional government, the cast of politics, and largely explained the incapacities of state governments to confront the industrial and social revolution of mid-century. So far in the past century as there was a "New South," it has been only since 1930 that the region could truly lay claim to "newness," and it is only since 1945 that this has been really true. It is with the processes of change and transition that the following chapters are concerned.

Critics of every sort have upbraided the South within the past century, and many of them with good reason. Editors, bankers, travelers, statisticians, sociologists, and novelists have all written of the region as though it were truly backward or decadent. In times of depression the southern system stood exposed in its shallowness of purpose, and its failure to appreciate the opportunities of the region. It is an incredible fact of southern history that as late as 1930 the South was labeled a land of biting poverty. Much of the burden of modern southern history has rested on the failure of southern leadership to shock the people into a realization that they had failed to understand the potentialities of the South as one of the most dramatically productive areas of the world.

Poor educational training, however, weighed down hope of genuine progress in the South. Political leadership too often failed to look beneath the surface of emotional public reaction for answers to problems. Instead they helped the region to drift into a limited pattern of thinking, of narrow sectionalism, state-rights, and a tight binding of folk culture. Attacks on the intellect by bigots in and out of state legislatures in the first decades of the century handicapped, if it did not come near destroying, the intellectual spark so necessary to maintaining and advancing colleges and universities of higher quality. It was a paradox of broad significance that at the moment when the first impacts of American technology were being felt in southern life, reaction to higher education was so stultifying. As Howard W. Odum said:

> Before Hitler's Germany, parts of the South were revivifying an emotional culture through attack upon universities and intellectual life; through religious coloring of politics and statecraft; through appeal to sectional patriotism; through intolerance of criticism and opposition; and through continuing emphasis upon racial issues, Nordic superiority and one hundred per cent Americanism.

Southern politicians often cast their shabby image against a background of change. Campaigners promised progress and improvement. They proposed to perform miracles, but within the restrictive confines of traditionalism without disturbing the status quo. When southern politicians did strike at old political establishments and won, they did so because they promised to lead government back from some self-created brink of disaster. Modern southern political history since 1890 has been written largely within the framework of class and race conflicts, localisms, personalities, economic limitations, and political chicanery.

Noticeably lacking were crusades by southern politicians, or by the people themselves, to liberalize state constitutions, to revise antiquated state statutes, to finance the operation of vastly improved educational systems, or to reconstruct the industrial system of the South. In far too many instances the southern bloc in Congress has been highly conservative if not outright negative in its reactions to more liberal national measures. Instead of strengthening the South's leadership position in the nation as a positive force which would place the region in an effective position of national influence, this bloc has often maintained a position of flight from sectional reality.

A certain test of how positive southerners wished to reconstruct their region after 1877 as a vibrant economic and political force was to be found in constitutional revisions. It is doubtful that any of the new state documents contained as fundamental parts of their organization any philosophy that could be termed progressive in the context of modern industrial America. Quite the contrary, southern constitutions reflected not a progressive redirecting of the states toward a happier and more effective future, but rather to a series of conflicts involving the position of the races and the classes in southern society. They reflected more precisely an actual fear of the future. Specifically, there was fear of taxation and adequate appropriations to do more than sustain public institutions at the lowest possible level of operation. In a region where the per capita income was consistently not only in the lowest quarter of the nation, but dangerously below the national average, there was powerful resistance to agencies that fostered change. In discriminating against the Negro, delegates to the constitutional conventions contributed materially to handicapping further a major part of the South's white human resource.

Regional literature has been a fairly dependable measure of people and the maturity of their culture. Few if any of the regions of the United States have been written about so voluminously as the modern South. Novelists, economists, travelers, teachers, and politicians have all contributed to the mountain of pamphlets, reports, surveys, and books. In a great majority of these is recorded a history of crisis. Southern authors have often contributed precise descriptions of contemporary problems. Even more fundamentally they have understood the underlying forces of humanity and the times which shaped both the southern personality and the conditions of regional society.

The intensive search by everybody who has sought mature answers to regional questions has largely been directed toward the central forces which have shaped the South's history. Unhappily, much of the story of the past century has of necessity been written against a background of defeatism and limited accomplishments. In its more dramatic aspects the negative phases of southern history have all the absorbing and tragic characteristics of a Shakespearean drama in which the past haunts the present with enormous gloom. Howard W. Odum observed:

> The visible ends of this historical influence are manifest in a folk-regional culture of distinctive features, including many "special problems," a long catalog of crises, handicaps, and deficiencies, and a number of quality characterizations commonly assumed to be superior. The special problems and deficiencies constitute a separate category as do also the cultural distinctions of the past.

This has been true largely because transitions and changes have come hard for the southern people. These have often involved renunciations of traditions and folk loyalties which have had qualities of intimate personal bonds. If the land could have been settled from the start in the traditional way of the American frontier, it might have been true that the vastness of nature and southern geography would have shaped the personality of the region and conditioned its society by altogether different patterns. Slavery, and subsequently the race problem, was crisis enough, but secession, civil war, political conflicts, an inefficient regional economy, and a literal fundamentalist religion marked a century of change. The New South was born of crises at the end of the Civil War, and was christened in a long and bitter period of reconstruction. The ghost of the past stalked the land trying to reincarnate itself, while the spirit of conflict and revision blurred its vision. Two issues of these earlier years were of white-Negro relationships and power, and the foundations of a new southern economy. Unhappily settlement of the first problem was fraught with so much emotional confusion that no certain chart to the future could be drafted. No fact, however, was more important than that of making a positive clarification of its aims and objectives to Americans generally, to European critics, to social crusaders, and to politicians within and outside the region. On the surface the idealistic vision of the freed Negro to the poorly informed outsider was that of a semi-educated yeoman adapting himself quickly to conditions of Americans in urban society and to those of the West.

In the view of the ex-slaveholder the Negro was to be suspended between a condition of slavery and peonage; certainly he was not visualized as a responsible privileged person. Even more threatening to the Negro's welfare was the fact that he would quickly become a pawn of conflicting political interests. In the minds of southerners, the Negro was too backward culturally to permit him to enjoy immediately the privileges of a freedman; these were to come at an unspecified future time. As southerners looked to the past in efforts to relate themselves to the new age in America, they looked to the future for either amelioration or adjudication of the race problem. One thing they knew for certain, race conflicts had to be allayed, and they knew in this resolution they would suffer traumatic breaks with the past.

No single section in so affluent a nation as the United States promised to be after 1865 should have been involved in either emotional or material crisis by its economy. The South, however, was involved in many crises because of its peculiar agrarian economy; devotion to cotton culture embraced as many human elements as economic ones. A historian can cite a long list of abuses: tenantry, lien laws, soil butchery, falling prices, foreign competition, dependence upon a single crop, drainage of capital resources for fertilizer, racial competition, and recurring depressions.

It was significant indeed that southern yeomen never developed as part of their tradition the image of the revered common man as did the pioneers of the Northeast, Midwest, and Far West. Instead southern frontiersmen were submerged under the opprobrious labels of poor whites, hillbillies, rednecks, and peons of a single crop, and in competition with their Negro neighbors. The myth of King Cotton may well have symbolized in the minds of southern planters the supremacy of that staple, but simultaneously it cast the postwar farmer in the role of servitor rather than master of his principal crop. Thus, in public protest meetings of farmers in the latter decades of the nineteenth century, too many southerners complained, not as proud and independent yeomen but as impoverished apologists who often revealed themselves as absurd victims of their own folly. Crises of southern agrarianism went even deeper into what sociologists have called reference groups. Poor enslaved cotton farmers came to feel comfortable only within a vast reference group of their own kind, and that group lacked the inspired leadership necessary to shock it into breaking the bonds of economic enslavement. Diversification of crops required intellectual vigor, courage, and management ability and ingenuity. Because these qualities were at a premium in the agricultural South, the major crisis of the past century and the first decades of this one lay within class failures to correct their approaches to the future.

It can be seriously questioned whether the agricultural problems in the century after the Civil War could have been solved by any single formula. Prices, marketing, competition, the arrival of the boll weevil, mechanization of farming, and internal and external social forces all bore on the plight of the farmer. The thrust of agriculture after 1920 lay not in the mere improvement of the farming techniques so much as in the recognition that drastic revisions of economic procedures were necessary. For the first time in its history, southern agriculture was beginning to be co-ordinated with the wide-range potentialities of the land resource on the one hand, and with the expanding American and international industrial systems on the other. Once the South became industrially involved, the question of basic agricultural production ceased really to be central.

The so-called crisis of lack of capitalization was not really a primary issue within itself, even though in subsequent chapters this fact is given some positive emphasis. There were resources aplenty in the South to tempt capital into the region, and so they did, but their exploitation required capable human talents in the forms of technicians and daring industrial leadership. It was true that tobacco was manufactured in the region, and, from 1870 on, an increasing amount of raw cotton was processed. Forests were converted into lumber, and coal and iron were dug from the ground. Petroleum products increased both in supply and demand. Water power was first used to produce direct power and then to generate electrical current, and in time utilization of this source of energy brought a southern industrial revolution. There were, however, two major handicaps; unprocessed products were shipped away from the region to yield bigger returns for non-southern processors, and too many southerners looked to outside management to organize and bring industries to their region. In this way they could hardly escape an intra-national colonialism which subordinated both people and resources to the bidding of outside capitalism and management.

It was in the field of resources management and exploitation that the South experienced a break with traditionalism. It is an astounding fact that the South as a distinct region survived so long in a nation where the basic standards of progress depended largely upon the up-rooting of established institutions at least once every generation. The secret lay partly in southern geography. There is no doubt that the geography of the South went far to shape its economy and society. First there was spaciousness of land surface where soils were of fairly even quality, and which sustained for many generations a population of remarkable homogeneity; otherwise, it is doubtful whether a southern society could have survived. In this spaciousness there existed a surplus of fairly good quality virgin land which permitted a wastefulness of soil on the one hand, and the failure to develop an intelligent land-use policy on the other.

The symbol of southern agrarian poverty came to be "forty acres of land." This was an utterly ridiculous fact in southern life. Around the globe millions of people sustained themselves on as little as one-tenth this amount of land, and on soils vastly inferior to those considered poor even in the South. There were few acres in the South, except for dark swamp bogs and barren Appalachian rocky hillsides, where land was so unproductive as holdings in mountainous regions of the Near East, in India, or China—a fact that held true even for much of arid Texas, New Mexico, Arizona, Nevada, and California. Southern lands were highly responsive to fertilization, and to intensive management and cultivation.

Tragically, the modern South in struggling to balance its economy between agriculture and industry sought to do so by exploiting its resources of timber, minerals, fresh water, climate, and soil in a wasteful age in American history. In spite of the fact that traditionally the region was bound in the net of a "single crop" it had the resources to develop one of the most intensely diversified economies on the continent. This fact, not politics and the Negro, was ultimately to be the most serious threat to the established traditions of the Old South.

The paradox of the economic South was that most southern leaders believed that industrialization ultimately would help the region stabilize and expand its economy, yet they feared industrialization. They thought it would destroy their way of life. It would be impossible to estimate the amount of energy expended in orating, writing, and conferring on the subject. Seers predicted a revolution from industrialization that would be co-ordinated with agrarianism. Answering the critics, Harry Wise, editor of the *Tradesman* of Chattanooga, wrote in 1911:

> The industrial south is no less the garden spot because it has awakened the spirit of progressiveness. On the contrary, its beauty is enhanced, its desirability as a habitation has increased and its sphere of usefulness enlarged by this very thing, and as it grows and expands, its very environment will serve to add new dignity to labor and to rest. . . . The sun will never shine less brightly, the rivers flow less placidly, but in common with nature, will beckon all mankind to the coming manufacturing section of the country—the South.

Agriculture may have been the standby of the nineteenth century, but to the new planners it was industry that promised to keep the economic sun shining and the rivers flowing in the latter twentieth century.

Extremely conservative groups wished to resist the expansion of industry on the grounds that southern culture would be left baseless, and the people of the region would become either hirelings of the machines or money grubbers. Industrialism was a northern importation which further threatened the southern tradition. James McBride Dabbs said,

> Over the years, however, the South has been buying, mainly from the North, one *ism* so big, so attractive, so respectable, that for the most part we haven't recognized what we were buying. This is industrialism. To some degree, in both antebellum and postbellum days, Southerners did warn against industrialism as a threat to our way of life. But it has generally come with so little fanfare—except when we ourselves built the cotton mills—with so little statement of purpose—which was natural, the main purpose being to make money for the Northerners, and we Americans are a modest people when it comes to making money, especially out of somebody else—it came, as I say, so quietly, with here a smokestack and there a smokestack, saying nothing on the one important subject in the South, the race question—as it says nothing now—that as a rule southerners never recognized it as an *ism*, and indeed don't so recognize it today.

Mr. Dabbs was doubtless right in his characterization of the quiet way in which industrialism began to assume a leading role in the twentieth-century South. Sometimes industry came so subtly that it caught both people and institutions unready to receive it. Many changes had first to occur in the South before industry could thrive. The prevailing economic and social conditions of the nineteenth and early twentieth centuries subjected southerners to a tremendous amount of negativism, which ran counter to the eternal optimism of the industrialist. A horror of taxation by an agrarian society, for instance, denied adequate support to maintain necessary education and public service facilities. Too, somewhere along the line industry would be forced to meet the racial issue on terms of federal laws and court decisions.

It is possible that the area of greatest need for revision of the Southern system was in the field of government itself. The efforts by state constitutional conventions at the turn of the century to change the forms of government made the Negro, rather than southern economic and industrial progress, their central theme. These bodies were far more concerned in establishing white supremacy than in preparing the southern population for changes which many prophets were saying loudly would come to the South. In 1904 the Reverend Edgar Gardiner Murphy took a penetrating look at southern political issues, and at the leaders in the crusade to revise the southern state constitutions and institute "white supremacy." He regarded the loud outcries of the conventions, not so much appeals to protect white men's domination of politics as attempts "to arouse the white vote." In his view,

> "Negro domination" as a force of party control, as a weapon of political constraint, is fast losing its authority. Great masses of people are beginning to "know better." Its passing, as a party cry, will help both the Democracy and the South. The sooner the Democratic party comes to understand that, if it would hold the allegiance of the masses of our southern states, it must represent, not a futile programme of negation, animosity, and alarm, but a policy of simple ideals and constructive suggestions—a course which has given the party its historic position in our life—the better it will be both for the party and for the South. The South can then divide, and can make its division turn upon thought, fact, conviction. Every party and every section demands, in the interest of its broadest welfare, that there shall work within the regions, its traditions, and its ideas, the searching, sifting, divisive, regenerating forces of *truth upon its merits.* If this is not the privilege of the South, and if the masses of our people—through wanton provocation of the North, or through the failure of our own party leadership—are to be still possessed by the old benumbing and baffling error, then we shall have, as we have had in part already, a form of negro domination which we have least suspected. The soldier of old who bound his wretched captive to his wrist bound more than the wretched captive. If his slave was bound to him, he was hardly less in bondage to his slave. If the supreme apprehension of the South is to be the apprehension of negro domination, if our intensest effort, our characteristic and prevailing policies, our deepest social faiths, are to look no further than the negro, or to be even busied with the crude fiction of negro power, and ever-clouded by the outgrown demand for the negro's bondage, then at either end of this clanking chain, there is a life bound.

How prophetic was the Alabama minister! Howard Odum in *Southern Regions* presented in statistical tables the results of this southern policy. Later Benjamin U. Ratchford and Calvin B. Hoover in their survey of southern policies (*Economic Resources and Policies of the South*) discussed again the influence of government and governmental policies on the economic expansion of the South. Businessmen in states where racial conflicts and violence resulted after 1954 were quick to see that the old policies would leave them in ruin. In Arkansas, Alabama, and Mississippi especially, the results of violent racial upheavals had unfortunate economic results.

Historically, racial conflict and crises in this field existed continually. The shadow of Negro revolt from the bondages of the postwar South, from agricultural peonage, from political ostracism, from illiteracy, and from economic discrimination created so great a fear in much of the region as to cause white men even to condone murder by lynching, by armed attack, by ambush, and by miscarriage of justice in the courtrooms. The sordid crime of lynching alone was a stain far more ghastly than the lawlessness of frontier vigilantism. Its bestiality, hatred, shamelessness, and human depravity besmirched the honor of the South before 1930. As the course of history in the late nineteenth and the twentieth century has unravelled, the past was rapidly undone by social progress. The dominant element of the southern population had become firmly committed to modernization in every field, and there remained little room for the survival of the old and negative ways of life which could not be adapted to the present. Every outburst of violent resistance to inevitable changes brought the South nearer the central national objectives. The more positive the hand of the federal government in areas of decisions, the nearer the South has moved to conform with national patterns and objectives. It was not so much that mere barriers between men of differing races were being breached as it was that the whole fabric of the southern way of life was being rewoven.

There were loud pronouncements of negativism following the decision of the United States Supreme Court, May 17, 1954, and once again regional outcries in behalf of white supremacy had their effects. Islands of racial discrimination and racial violence were created to by-pass or nullify court decisions, but the heavier circumstance of national and international reactions worked too hard against such communities. This time the political impact of broad-gauged social revolution and Negro unrest had moved well beyond the sphere of influence of a southern state constitution, and even beyond that of a cluster of states and resisting political leaders trying to formulate a bloc of power that would neutralize the change. Not only was the matter of race relations deeply involved in local and domestic affairs, but it had become an enormously complex world-wide issue. Thus the South was caught not so much in change on a national scale, which it could resist directly, as in the tangled web of a world in social revolution.

Heavy rearrangements of the locale of the southern population in the scope of less than a half-century threw the old system out of balance. The historical tempo of modern regional society was so badly disrupted by internal movement and displacement that fresh beginnings were mandatory in every field of human activity. In a nation which had to consider its position and welfare in terms of advanced social and political theories, the modern South undertook to operate on realities, which, after all, involved no less the imprecisions of theory. James McBride Dabbs said that in dealing with the central fact of modern southern history the southerner has thrown realism to the wind.

> Your southerner [he wrote] is typically a realist. He will embrace practically anything life brings if it comes without benefit of theory; but if it comes waving a banner he is almost certain to grab his sword and, without further consideration, have at it. He's pretty short on theory, and what he is short on he's naturally suspicious of. How did he get that way?
>
> Check back on the *isms* he has feared most of all, radicalism and abolitionism. Both concerned the Negro. The Southern has feared *isms* most of all because they tended to disintegrate its own essential ism, the one abstraction upon which its massive, concrete life had been built. What was this abstraction? [Slavery]

The sociologists have been more successful than the historians in writing of the human element of southern life. This has been true in spite of the fact that no aspect of southern history since 1865 has been of greater importance than the region's folk culture. Southern history is basically that of many folk groups responding to traditions, customs, prejudices, and cultural limitations. The frame of reference and perspective of southerners have been formed according to how well they have broken restrictive barriers. Folk history of any people is complex, but that of the South was made even more complicated by the existence of two races, a deeply sectional social consciousness, a peculiar regional economy, and the influence of vast geographical variations and influences.

It matters little that much southern tradition is largely myth; it is the myth by which southerners have lived. Passage of time has reshaped if not shattered many myths. After all cotton was not king, and much of what southerners from the beginning of their history have said they understood about the Negro has been questioned if not refuted by anthropologists, sociologists, politicians, and judges of the federal courts. The South has had little historical continuity; the overwhelming Anglo-American population on the frontier did not exhibit all the civilizing virtues in daily living and all the ability to solve regional problems apologists have ascribed to it. This appeared to be true when this civilization was appraised in various terms: statistics of all sorts comparing it with other regions of the Union, respect for law, maintenance of a highly efficient and sustaining culture, and the production of a broadly based leadership of good quality.

The complexity of southern folk history reaches more deeply into the processes of regional decision-making. How, for instance, was progress instituted in the South in such fields as agriculture, education, industry, and race relations? A deep-seated Puritanism has kept southern religion unusually conservative. The rigidity of the folk mind has been reflected in the outlawing of the teaching of evolution in three states, belief in a literal interpretation of the Bible (both reflected in the famous Scopes evolution trial in Dayton, Tennessee, in 1925), and the subsequent support by organized religion of other threats to intellectual freedom.

In other areas folk culture was of the utmost historical significance. For three-quarters of a century the South maintained an economic system that could not be justified by any reputable economist or banker, yet many areas showed dogged resistance to change. In appraising the South's drift toward the future, Dabbs wrote:

> The South, fearful of *isms*, is accepting industrialism the father of most of the others. And we are doing it ignorantly. Industry is simply industry to us. That there might be an industrial way of life uncongenial to ours isn't deeply considered. The smoke from the factories is only smoke; it hasn't yet become the powerful genie released from the bottle. But it will. And whether the spirit is good or evil will depend upon the degree to which we understand both it and ourselves.

He might have added, and how fundamentally we change our folk culture.

The postwar South carried in its political and social systems germs which ultimately would destroy the older patterns of southern life. Among these were the race problem, the demands of industry as against an agrarian economy, utilization and conservation of natural and human resources, a shifting political system, increased urbanization, and the drive for universal education. It is with the evolution of these changes that historians of the modern South must primarily concern themselves. Whatever else may have played a part in the region's history during the past century these facts have remained central. They concern southern traditions on which people have patterned their folk mores and their society. All of these lay well within the main channel of national concern. As the century has unfolded, the South has had to struggle to keep abreast of the flow of American history itself, and at the same time retain as much of the peculiarly regional personality as possible. This conflict has taken place amid political conflict and change, a drive for better economic opportunities in the region, the problems of white and black men living within an integrated society, a rearguard action by Ku Klux Klansmen, citizens' councils, and bigots of every variety, and the constant crusade to reduce functional illiteracy. The region has had to face the problems that low per capita income, deficiencies in industrial development, poor agricultural output, human inefficiency, and other shortcomings that have held them back in relation to the rest of the nation.

What follows is a history of the South's breaking away from the past, and the reshaping of a southern image that was long ago cast in the mould of traditionalism and folk culture. Whatever the new image may finally become, there have been indications since 1920 that it will be a more positive one than much of the past proved to be.

❧ II ❧

Political Reconstruction

Confederate veterans returning to their homes in the spring of 1865, looked out upon a land ravaged and despoiled by war. On all sides they saw vestiges of the conflict resulting from their ill-fated rebellion. Union armies criss-crossing through the crumbling Confederate defenses left behind them a trail of destruction. Railroads, save only those needed to supply the invading armies, were completely destroyed. Tracks were torn up in all sections, the rails heated on fires made of the wooden ties, then twisted around trees into grotesque shapes called Sherman's neckties. Bridges were burned or dynamited. Streams were rendered unnavigable by obstructions sunk in channels. Ocean ports were made useless in like manner, and wharves and warehouses were burned. Principal cities were put to the torch. Jackson, Mississippi; Atlanta, Georgia; Selma, Alabama; Columbia, South Carolina, were almost completely destroyed; Savannah, Vicksburg, and Richmond only less so. Sherman's searing path through Georgia and the Carolinas has become the classic example of nineteenth-century "total war." Leaving Atlanta, Sherman's devil-may-care "bummers" went methodically about the business of devastating central Georgia. A southerner reported a bleak scene in Sherman's wake. "Dead horses, cows, sheep, hogs, chickens, corn, wheat, cotton, books, paper, broken vehicles, coffee mills, and fragments of nearly every species of property that adorned the beautiful farms of this country strew the wayside."[1] Even churches did not escape the "bummers." Confederate cavalry

(1) Augusta *Chronicle and Sentinel*, quoted in James G. Randall, *The Civil War and Reconstruction* (New York, 1937), 558.

burned property as they retreated before Sherman, so that the Union army might not make use of what the Confederates had to leave behind. Public buildings, food stores, livestock, draft animals, all were destroyed or removed.

Lessons learned in Georgia added to the "bummers'" efficiency in South Carolina, although there is reason to believe that Sherman had marked that state for special scourge. "Should you capture Charleston," General Henry W. Halleck had written him at the start of his Carolina journey, "I hope that by *some* accident the place may be destroyed; and if a little salt should be sown upon its site, it may prevent the growth of future crops of nullification and secession."[2] Sherman replied: "I will bear in mind your hint as to Charleston, and don't think salt will be necessary. . . . The truth is the whole army is burning with an insatiable desire to wreak vengeance upon South Carolina."[3]

Sherman would miss Charleston, leaving its destruction to other conquerors, but his army burned, in whole or in part, Robertsville, Grahamville, McPhersonville, Barnwell, Blackville, Orangeburg, Lexington, Winnsboro, Camden, Lancaster, Chesterfield, Cheraw, and Darlington. A correspondent of the New York *Herald*, traveling with Sherman, wrote: "The middle of the finest day looked black and gloomy, for dense smoke arose on all sides, clouding the very heavens. . . . As for the wholesale burnings, pillage, devastation . . . magnify all I have said of Georgia some fifty fold, and throw in an occasional murder . . . and you have a pretty good idea of the whole thing."[4] There is doubt as to whether the firing of Columbia was caused by Sherman or by Wade Hampton's retreating Confederates, but there is no question of the extent of the damage. Eighty city blocks, including 1386 buildings, were completely destroyed.

Destruction in other regions rivaled that of the Georgia and Carolina countryside. A visitor to the Shenandoah Valley after Sheridan's final campaign there reported that the upper valley was a scene of desolation. "From Winchester to Harrisonburg scarce a crop [or]

(2) *Senate Report No. 142*, 38 Cong., 2 Sess., Vol. I, 287.
(3) *War of the Rebellion: A Compilation of the Official Records of the Union and Confederate Armies*, Series I, XLIV, 799.
(4) Quoted in E. Merton Coulter, *The Confederate States of America* (Baton Rouge, 1950), 369.

fence . . . was in sight."[5] The country between Washington and Richmond was "like a desert." Members of the Congressional Joint Committee on Reconstruction visiting the valley in 1866 were assured that there was no danger to new crops from foraging cattle because Sheridan had had the foresight to remove all cattle and horses. Indeed, the lack of draft animals after the end of the fighting forced the people to resort to primitive methods of cultivation. Lone and blackened chimneys of once happy homesteads stood watch over the ruins of what had been rich forests of oak, hickory, chestnut, and pine. Entire villages, like Raccoonford and Stevensburg, disappeared, never to be restored.

What the regular armies overlooked, the guerillas took care of. In faraway Arkansas, in the autumn of 1865, Governor Isaac Murphy reported desolation beyond description in his state. Guerilla bands and scouting parties had pillaged almost every neighborhood north of the Arkansas River, and with winter coming on two-thirds of the counties of the state were desolate. Other regions were in similar plight; a northern newspaperman in Georgia reported 35,000 people in the counties around Atlanta dependent upon the United States government for food.

Northern soldiers returning home after the war would find prosperous communities and jobs awaiting them. But southern soldiers found impoverished and exhausted communities with no employment to offer: their homesteads destroyed, their farms devastated, their families in distress. Window glass in many places was nonexistent. Furniture was broken, dishes cemented, with only a few families able to set a complete table. Luxuries such as tea, coffee, sugar, and spices were absent; and even candles were replaced by cups of grease with a piece of cloth for a wick.

But even the desolate countryside failed to tell the full tragic story. This had to be seen on the faces of the people. "Everyone of them," wrote a northern traveler, "was a record of some phase of the contest, of its squalor and misery, of its demoralization, of its barbarism, of its ennoblement. Bright, fair faces that ought to have adorned happy rural homes, grown coarse and brassy, flaunted beside young officers. They were the transformation of the camps—the result

(5) J. B. McMaster, *A History of the People of the United States During Lincoln's Administration* (New York and London, 1927), 637.

of license and lax morality." Aimless young men in gray, ragged and filthy, seemed to have lost all object in life. "By the roadside, here and there, might be seen . . . a poor, half-starved, half naked white woman, gathering her little children about her, and cowering in the gray dawn over the dull embers by which . . . she had watched through the wretched night."[6]

In an agrarian society like that of the ante-bellum South, ravages of war are erased from the land more quickly than in urban, industrialized countries. Even so, it would be long years before physical reminders of the devastation disappeared from the southern countryside. An Englishman, traversing the Tennessee Valley in 1870, noted

> plantations in a state of semi-ruin, and plantations of which the ruin is . . . total and complete. . . . The trail of war is visible throughout the valley in burnt-up gin-houses, ruined bridges, mills, and factories . . . and in large tracts of once cultivated land stripped of every vestige of fencing. The roads, long neglected . . . in many places have become impassable, new tracts have been made through the woods and fields without much respect to boundaries.

He found less than one-third of arable land in cultivation.[7]

To the material destruction must be added the social disorder. Emancipation of the slaves had for the time demoralized the labor system. Able-bodied Negroes departed plantations for the towns and cities, leaving behind mostly those unfit for work. There were 3500 fewer Negroes in Alabama in 1866 than in 1860, yet Montgomery's Negro population had increased by 23 per cent, Mobile's by 25 per cent, and Selma's by 13 per cent. Refusal of freedmen to work the South Carolina rice fields in 1866 resulted in a harvest per acre planted of less than half that of 1860. A combination of bad weather and labor shortage reduced the Alabama corn crop of 1866 by half, and thousands were saved from starvation there only by federal rations furnished by General Swayne.

More portentous than property destruction was the loss in human resources. A quarter-millon of the youngest and ablest men of the region had their lives prematurely snuffed out, and countless others

(6) Whitelaw Reid, *After the War* (New York, 1866), 360; Walter L. Fleming, ed., *Documentary History of Reconstruction*, 2 vols. (Cleveland, 1906–7), I, 11.
(7) Robert Somers, *The Southern States Since the War* (London and New York, 1871), 114–15.

were maimed in body and spirit. Some ante-bellum leaders like Herschel V. Johnson, Alexander H. H. Stuart, Robert Toombs, and L. Q. C. Lamar remained to help lead their people. Others like Jubal Early, Matthew Fontaine Maury, and Judah P. Benjamin went into exile. Edmund Ruffin, distinguished agricultural scientist, implacable to the end, put a bullet through his heart. In a very real sense the war had turned time back for the South. It became once more a primitive society, a frontier region; and the violence that was a characteristic of earlier frontiers would become a familiar pattern in the postwar South.

With the close of hostilities the Confederate states were occupied for a time by northern armies, and southerners came to know what other Americans have yet to learn: what it means to lose a war. Yet it is doubtful if in the history of human relations any other vanquished people have been treated as generously as were southerners after Appomattox. No high official, either civil or military, was executed for treason or war crimes; some few were imprisoned, generally for only a few months. Within a half-dozen years all but those who would not request it were restored to full civil and political rights in the nation they had sought to dismember. A handful would suffer for a time confiscation of their lands, but eventually most secured full restitution. Although a small number went voluntarily into exile, no one was forcefully driven from his homeland.

Given the circumstances, it was inevitable that federally sustained governments should be imposed upon the Confederate states before they could resume normal relations. And these governments would attempt for a time to effect radical changes in the southern social and political order. Aggravating southern difficulties was the confusion accompanying the American constitutional division of powers, a division wherein executive, legislative, and judicial branches are frequently at loggerheads and where the powers of state and national government are as often in dispute. Under these twin handicaps it took several of the southern states almost a decade to work themselves back into an uneasy and unhappy relationship with the national government.

Because of the complexity of the federal system and of the rivalry that grew between Congress and President, there were fundamental constitutional questions posed by southern surrender. Just what was a state, and what were its rights after collapse of a rebellion it had promoted? Were the ex-Confederate states in or out of the Union? If out, were they in the position of unorganized territories, and therefore subject to the authority of Congress? Whose responsibility was it to see that their normal relations were resumed? Was secession an offense for which a state as a political entity could be punished? Were individual citizens of the seceded states guilty of treason for obeying dictates of their governments, or were those governments legitimate entities to which residents within their boundaries owed fealty? After surrender, what was the status of Confederate soldiers and civilians? Were they aliens, conquered rebels, or full-fledged citizens? What rights, if any, did they enjoy under either domestic or international law? What of southern Unionists? Should they be made to suffer whatever punishment might be imposed on secessionists? If not, how were they to be differentiated from the disloyal? Perhaps most difficult of all, what of the Negro freedman? Who would look to his wants, now that he was free but still dependent? Would he be a ward of the state, of the nation, or of no one? What were his rights? It would be years before answers would be worked out to most of these questions. Many lack solutions a century later. Political reconstruction, therefore, centered upon constitutional questions for which the Constitution had no answers. The founding fathers, not foreseeing secession, had made no provision for its sequel.

Mixed in with the constitutional confusion were partisan considerations. Congress had suffered diminution of power at the hands of the President during the war, and Congressional leaders were eager to retrieve the loss. Furthermore, the Republican party was clearly a minority and sectional party; and its avowed objective, the containment of slavery, had been more than achieved. Republicans well knew that a reunited Democratic party of North and South could easily win at the polls. To permit this "party of treason" to recapture political control of the nation was unthinkable to Republicans. Congress thus became a battleground between northern Democrats and Republicans, each struggling to restore the southern states under conditions which would guarantee control to themselves.

At the end of the war the people of the South, overcome by a feeling of bewilderment and well aware that their lives and property were at the very least matters of great uncertainty and possibly subject to forfeit, would have submitted to almost any conditions imposed upon them. "They expected nothing," wrote a visitor, "were prepared for the worst; would have been thankful for anything. . . . They asked no terms, made no conditions. They were defeated and help-less—they submitted."[8] Harvey Watterson, touring North Carolina a few months after Appomattox, wrote that North Carolina's loyalty was "as certain as that of any state in the Union." "Boston, today, is not more loyal than Newberne [sic]," he added. "The Rebellion has been ground into unpalpable powder. None can be found so insane as to think of further resistance to the authority of the United States. . . . The old secession leaders see that they are politically ruined . . . God be praised."[9]

Southern inclination to accept defeat was nurtured by extraordinarily liberal policies which Lincoln pursued until his death and Johnson thereafter. As early as 1862 Lincoln began appointing native leaders provisional governors in conquered states. Then on December 8, 1863, he announced his first formal policy on reconstruction. With relatively few exceptions, he would pardon all who would take an oath of future loyalty to the Union. Exceptions included high officers in the Confederate army and navy, those who had resigned commissions in the United States Army or Navy to take part in the rebellion, and those who had resigned seats in the United States Congress to go into the Confederacy. Even these, however, might, upon special application, obtain pardon. Whenever in any state a tenth of the number of voters of 1860 had taken a loyalty oath, a government might be formed which the President would recognize as soon as it repealed its ordinance of secession and agreed to emancipate its slaves. By early 1864 governments were organized on this plan in Virginia, Tennessee, Louisiana, and Arkansas.

Meanwhile, Congress, angered at Lincoln's generous reconstruction policy, and urged on by so-called Republican radicals, responded with the Wade-David bill of July 1864. By this act, Congress asserted its right to control procedures by which the Confederate states might be restored. In doing so, it proscribed many of the political leaders on whom Lincoln counted to lead the governments he wished to form. Lincoln's plan called only for a promise to be loyal in the future.

(8) Reid, *After the War*, 295-6.
(9) Elizabeth G. McPherson, "Letters from North Carolina to Andrew Johnson," *North Carolina Historical Review*, XXVII (July 1950), 336-63.

Congress demanded past loyalty as well, not of a small minority of the voters of 1860, but of a majority. Only those who had not voluntarily borne arms against the United States and those who had not held any civil or military office under the Confederacy would be permitted to participate in the formation of the new governments, and all civil officers in the Confederacy as well as military officers above the rank of colonel in the army or lieutenant in the navy would be prohibited from voting or from serving either in the legislature or as governor. New governments must also abolish slavery and repudiate the Confederate debt. The bill ordered the President not to recognize any reconstructed government until Congress had given its approval to it. Lincoln gave the bill a pocket veto, at the same time issuing a conciliatory statement giving the states the option to use the Congressional plan if they desired. The issue between Congress and President was now joined. Ignoring Congress, Lincoln continued his conciliatory reconstruction program, and when Congress reassembled in December it issued a manifesto charging Lincoln with usurping its authority. Already, in the election of 1864, Congress had refused to count the electoral votes from the Lincoln-reconstructed states.

Upon his succession to the Presidency, Johnson, after a brief flirtation with the radicals, continued Lincoln's policy. Completely ignoring the storm warnings of the Wade-Davis Manifesto, Johnson proceeded to appoint southerners provisional governors in the seven states not already organized by Lincoln and instructed them to call conventions of "loyal" citizens, chosen by all who would pledge future support of the United States Constitution. Conventions must repudiate secession, invalidate that part of the states' debts incurred in the war, and abolish slavery; but they were free to fix such qualifications as they chose for voting and office-holding. By autumn, 1865, civil governments had been organized and were functioning in all ex-Confederate states except Texas, and one would soon be established there. The new regimes were pretty largely dominated by former Whigs, who had as a rule been conservatives and Unionists in the ante-bellum period. Johnson had urged but had not insisted that the new constitutions, in order to "completely disarm the adversary," permit literate or property-owning Negroes to vote; but not one constitution did so.

By this time, too, there were indications that many ex-Confederates were somewhat recovered from the state of shock and humiliation into which their defeat had plummeted them. Carl Schurz, touring the South after the war in the service of the Congressional Joint Committee on Reconstruction, reported the changed attitude he thought he saw. "Treason does not appear odious in the South," he wrote. "The people are not impressed with any sense of its criminality." He noted an "utter absence of national feeling," and suspected that the people were merely assuming an attitude of co-operation with the government because they "could do no better."[10] This view was confirmed by other visitors. One of these, J. T. Trowbridge, thought the southerners were so embittered by their defeat and the loss of their slaves that they hated their conquerors. Their loyalty was of a negative sort, "simply disloyalty subdued. They submit to the power which has mastered them, but do not love it. . . . Many of them lately in the rebellion are . . . honestly convinced that secession was a great mistake. . . . Yet they do not feel much affection for the hand which corrected the error." A small fraction, he added, "would still be glad to dismember the country."[11]

Soon, former secessionists, encouraged by the liberality of Lincoln and Johnson, began speaking of their "rights" and arguing the constitutional questions of restoration of the Union. The southern press joined in to foment the spirit of disaffection among the masses that grew as the old Confederate leaders succeeded to positions of power in the new Johnson governments. Northern Congressmen were dismayed to learn that several of the state conventions had refused to permit the national flag to be flown over their sessions, that some had merely repealed their ordinances of secession, without declaring them unlawful. Some conventions had voted emancipation only after prolonged debate, and sometimes by a narrow margin. These errors were compounded when states elected to Congress men who were disqualified even under the liberal Presidential policy—the former Vice President of the Confederacy, six Confederate cabinet members, fifty-eight members of the Confederate Congress, four Confederate generals, five colonels.

If Republican Congressmen needed more evidence to persuade them that leaders of the late Confederacy were determined to restore as nearly as possible the conditions of the ante-bellum South, the John-

(10) *Senate Ex. Doc. No. 2*, 39 Cong., 1 Sess., 1–13.
(11) Quoted in A. A. Taylor, "The Negro in Reconstruction in Virginia," *Journal of Negro History*, XI (April 1926), 313.

son governments furnished it in the "black codes" soon enacted into law in all states of the deep South. As has been noted, emancipation disrupted both the social and labor systems of the states. Slaves by the thousands deserted the plantations and flocked to the cities, where, uninhibited by plantation discipline, many for a time revelled in idleness and petty vice, living from hand to mouth and placing additional strains upon the body politic. To relieve this situation the legislatures enacted codes applicable only to the freedmen and so harsh in some features that to northerners they seemed proof positive that their aim was to restore the old condition of slavery under a new name.

In general, the states with the most Negroes had the harshest codes, but even the milder codes were harsh enough. In all states the freedman enjoyed more rights than he had under slavery, but there can be little doubt that the codes were designed to, and did, make second-class citizens of all Negroes. All codes forbade interracial marriages but legalized slave marriages and legitimatized children born of such marriages. Freedmen could own property, make contracts, sue and be sued, testify for and against one another in court, but could not testify against whites. None gave the Negro the right to vote or permitted him to serve on juries. Some forbade free movement of Negroes from one community to another; some called for nightly curfews, forbade the carrying of firearms, and restricted occupations largely to farming and domestic work. Most required agricultural laborers to contract annually for employment early in each year and forbade the laborer to leave before the expiration of the contract. "Bad work," "impudence," "indecent language," were punishable by fines levied by the employer. Orphans or dependent females under eighteen and males under twenty were to be apprenticed, preference being given to former masters. Some codes made all unemployed Negroes over eighteen "vagrants" subject to a fine of fifty dollars and imprisonment for ten days. If the "vagrant" was unable to pay the fine, the sheriff was empowered to hire out the Negro to any person who would pay the fine and costs. The employers could then deduct the money paid from the Negro's wages. Mississippi empowered each county to impose a special poll tax of one dollar on every Negro, and if the tax was not paid the Negro was automatically subject to the vagrancy laws.[12]

(12) Fleming, *Documentary History of Reconstruction*, I, 301–2, 310, 275, 280–81, 284–6.

It is possible and even probable that these laws, like the ante-bellum slave codes were harsher in the writing than in their execution. A Negro politician in Florida, for instance, stated that "the great majority of the whites carried out their contract [with freedmen] to the letter," and did not take advantage of their workers.[13] Yet the laws made it possible to return the freedman to a condition of serfdom, and evidence is irrefutable that too often whites did defraud their Negro workers and deprive them of the meager fruits of their labors. It was certain, too, that an aroused North was in no mood after the war to accept even the possibility of a return to de facto slave conditions. As the editor of the Chicago *Tribune* wrote after passage of the Mississippi black code: "We tell the white men of Mississippi that the men of the North will convert the state of Mississippi into a frog pond before they will allow any such laws to disgrace one foot of soil in which the bones of our soldiers sleep and over which the flag of freedom waves."[14]

Unhappy with conditions they saw developing in the ex-Confederate states, radicals in Congress determined on a course of action. Under the leadership of Thaddeus Stevens of Pennsylvania, they set out to persuade their colleagues that the Johnson program was designed to dissipate the victory won in war. The only way to forestall the Johnson program was for Congress to control restoration of the seceded states. Accordingly, when the newly elected southern representatives of the Johnson governments appeared in Washington at the opening of Congress in December 1865, the Republican majority refused to admit them. Instead, a joint committee of both houses was set up to inquire into conditions in the former Confederate states. This committee would write the reconstruction legislation of the coming years.

Capitalizing on what appeared to be unrepentant attitudes of unreconstructed ex-Confederates, especially on the implications of the black codes, the radicals persuaded northern moderates that the South was unwilling to accept the finality of emancipation. In April 1866, Congress passed over the President's veto a civil rights act which nullified the black codes and guaranteed freedmen equal protection of the law under federal court supervision. To insure this act Congress

(13) *Ibid.*, 272.
(14) Issue of Dec. 1, 1865, quoted in John M. Mecklin, "The Black Codes," *South Atlantic Quarterly*, XVI (July 1917), 248-59.

passed a resolution submitting a Fourteenth Amendment to the Constitution. This Amendment declared freedmen citizens and prohibited state interference with fundamental civil liberties, or the denying any person equal protection of the laws. The Amendment did not compel Negro suffrage, but it penalized any state denying it by permitting reduction of the state's Congressional representation. It made most ex-Confederates ineligible for office-holding unless pardoned by Congress. It voided the war debts of the Confederate states and of the Confederacy and specifically validated the United States debt.

A year earlier, in the shock of defeat, southerners might have submitted willingly to such a measure. But the extraordinarily generous treatment they had received during the first year of peace had lulled them into a false sense of security. By the summer of 1866 southerners thought they had met conditions specified for their redemption, and that the Civil Rights Act and the proposed Fourteenth Amendment amounted to the imposition of new conditions on them. Their inclination to resist the new conditions was strengthened when Johnson questioned the constitutionality of the Amendment. They received additional encouragement when at the National Union Convention called in Philadelphia in the summer of 1866 to rally support for Johnson, ex-Confederates were warmly welcomed by Yankee veterans. Here, too, southerners learned of opposition in the North to the program of the radicals. By early autumn, southern backs were stiffened. In October 1866 the Texas legislature refused to ratify the Amendment by an all but unanimous vote. This set the pattern, and Georgia followed Texas's lead with only two dissenting votes. Soon all southern states as well as some northern ones had rejected the Fourteenth Amendment, and it failed of ratification.

But rejection of the Amendment was only a temporary setback for the radicals. In November, Congressional elections would be held, and Stevens and his followers determined that not only Republicans but radical Republicans must be elected. Few American elections have involved such portentous consequences. At the outset, moderate Republicans had grave misgivings concerning the unfolding radical program. But they faced a dilemma. The President's unyielding stubbornness, together with the questionable war records of many Democrats, made it difficult for them to support the latter. The northern press and clergy generally denounced Democrats and supported radicals, making much propaganda over recent race riots in Memphis and New Orleans. Financiers and industrialists were warned that a Democratic majority in Congress might well repeal tariff, railroad, and banking legislation passed during the war, and farmers were warned that it might also repeal homestead legislation so long sought and so recently won. The result was that many moderate Republican voters, faced with a kind of Hobson's choice, voted radical: returns showed 42 Republicans and 11 Democrats in the Senate, and 143 Republicans and 49 Democrats in the House, a safe majority to override Presidential vetoes. The radicals owed much of their victory to Johnson, whose unyielding attitude had recruited moderates to their cause, so that the early radical minority was now turned into a majority.

Soon this majority had Johnson in full retreat. When the Thirty-ninth Congress assembled for its final session in December 1866, the radicals, now in complete control, set up a dictatorship which soon stripped the President of all power to restore the seceded states. Usurping the President's authority to call a special session, the radicals pushed through a bill moving forward the opening date of the newly chosen Fortieth Congress from December 4 to March 4, thus depriving Johnson of a respite of nine months free of Congressional interference. On March 2 Congress passed the Tenure of Office Act, forbidding the President's removal of civil officers including cabinet members, without Senate consent. The same day it passed the Command of the Army Act, requiring all Presidential orders to the army to be issued through the General of the Army (Grant), who could not be removed from office nor even ordered from Washington without Senate consent. More important than either of these was the First Reconstruction Act, passed also on March 2.

This act, together with subsequent amendments, practically abolished the Lincoln and Johnson governments in the South. It declared that no legal governments existed in any of the ex-Confederate states except Tennessee. It divided the ten remaining states into five military districts, with an army general as governor of each. The generals were instructed to enroll an electorate which would include all Negro men and exclude all whom the proposed Fourteenth Amendment would disqualify for office. When his registration was completed, each military governor was to call for the election of a constitutional convention which must write into its constitution provisions for Negro suffrage and disqualification of ex-Confederate leaders. When these constitutions were ratified by the majority of qualified voters, when the legislature chosen under the new constitution had ratified the previously rejected Fourteenth Amendment, and when sufficient non-southern states had ratified it so that the Amendment had become part of the Constitution of the United States, Congress might by special act admit the state's Representatives and Senators. Not until then would the military be withdrawn and the state restored to civil government.

Meanwhile, during the process of reconstituting state governments on a basis of Negro suffrage, the military governors were given sweeping jurisdiction over all matters concerning freedmen. This arbitrarily took from state courts jurisdiction over nearly half the population—and in Mississippi and South Carolina more than half—and transferred this jurisdiction to military courts acting under regulations of the War Department, where fundamental civil legal guarantees were not provided. Under the amended act of July 1867, military governors could make arrests, suspend civil jurisdiction in any case, and order trials by military tribunals. They might permit state courts to try offenders, but if they deemed it necessary the governor could take jurisdiction from them. They might suspend any official, elected or appointed, state or local, and replace him with some other of their own choice. They could ignore the Johnson governments, or use them as they chose.

Under the reconstruction acts, governors of five states and hundreds of lesser officials were removed and replaced by Negroes, by immigrants from the North called carpetbaggers, or by local whites who were known as scalawags. Thousands of citizens were arrested by the military governor, and hundreds of them were tried by military tribunals. These trials were in defiance of a Supreme Court decision of April 1866 involving L. P. Milligan, a citizen of Indiana. Milligan had been sentenced to hang by a military court for engaging in a conspiracy to release Confederate prisoners in the Northwest in the autumn of 1864, but execution was postponed pending an appeal. The Court ruled that Milligan's trial by a military commission was illegal, and that martial law "can never exist where the courts are open, and in the proper and unobstructed exercise of their jurisdiction."[15] Despite

(15) 71 U.S. 127.

this, more than five hundred convictions by military tribunals went unchallenged in the Carolinas alone in the first fifteen months of radical reconstruction.

The generals meanwhile were proceeding with the process of constitution-making. The Reconstruction Act of March 23, 1867, called for registration of voters only by officials who could take the "ironclad oath," an oath that they had never willingly aided the rebellion. This oath most southern whites could not take; consequently, most registrars were Union soldiers, Freedmen's Bureau agents, or Negroes. These registrars disqualified tens of thousands of whites. In the end, a total of 703,000 Negroes and 627,000 whites were enrolled in the five districts. Registered Negroes outnumbered whites in Alabama, Florida, Louisiana, Mississippi, and South Carolina, despite the fact that only in the last two states were Negroes a majority of the population. Even in the five states where white voters were a majority, the margin was small, and for a time radicals would gain control there, too. This was according to plan. Wisconsin's Senator James R. Doolittle admitted that the purpose of all reconstruction legislation was to "put the Negro in power over the white race in all the States of the South and keep him there."[16]

By March 1868 new constitutions in all states except Texas had been formed. All provided for universal male suffrage, except for those disqualified under the proposed Fourteenth Amendment. Negroes were given full political and civil equality. Property qualifications for office-holding were abolished, and provision was made for popular education at public expense. Legislatures were reapportioned according to total population, the court system and local government were reformed, and women's rights were extended.

When the constitutions were submitted to the voters, conservatives, until then disorganized, united in many states to prevent ratification. Threatened with disfranchisement for the first time, many whites found that the right to vote took on new meaning and became the most precious of privileges. In a few states they delayed ratification, and in Virginia and Mississippi they were able to effect the removal of the harsher features of political disqualification. But generally their efforts were in vain, as most constitutions were ratified as written.

(16) *Cong. Globe*, 40 Cong., 2 Sess., 700.

Now began one of the most extraordinary proceedings of the entire reconstruction program—ratification of the Fourteenth Amendment under duress. There were thirty-seven states in the Union at the time, and before the Amendment could become a part of the federal Constitution, ratifications had to be received from three-fourths of them, or twenty-eight. Since by March 1867 only twenty-three, including Tennessee of the ex-Confederate states, had ratified, the Reconstruction Act passed that month required that each of the ten unreconstructed states must ratify the Amendment before Congress would consider it eligible to resume its normal place in the Union. This alone was a gross distortion of the Congressional prerogative. The Constitution presumed that each state would have the privilege of a free vote on such a matter, Congress's sole function in the amending process being the approval of a resolution by a two-thirds majority and passing it on for the state's consideration. Furthermore, the Reconstruction Act prescribed conditions—Negro suffrage and disfranchisement of certain whites—in the election of legislatures which would consider the Amendment, thus anticipating conditions which would only become fixed by the Fifteenth Amendment, at that time no more than a radical gleam in the Congressional eye. Paradoxically, the whole scheme of Congressional reconstruction was premised on the theory that the unreconstructed states were out of their normal relationship with the Union, a not unreasonable assumption but one in direct contradiction to the theory under which the federal government had prosecuted the war: namely, that only individuals were in rebellion and states had never left the Union. That states under such disabilities as Congress now presumed were competent to revise the fundamental law but incompetent to act on ordinary legislative matters was constitutional doctrine bordering on the grotesque.

Despite these irregularities, the legislatures of Arkansas, Florida, North Carolina, Louisiana, South Carolina, Alabama, and Georgia ratified the Amendment by late June 1868. Congress thereupon proclaimed the Amendment ratified and proceeded to admit the seven former Confederate states into the Union in time to count their electoral votes for Grant in the November election. The three states that had not completed the process, Texas, Virginia, and Mississippi, were not readmitted until 1870. By that time the Fifteenth Amendment, which extended suffrage to the freedmen, had been made a prerequisite, and

these three were forced to ratify it also before they could resume
their normal place in the Union.

The chronic contradiction between southern aims and southern
achievements was demonstrated in the adoption of the Thirteenth,
Fourteenth, and Fifteenth Amendments. Secession, resorted to in order
to preserve the rights of the states, brought on the war; and the war
brought the Amendments, the base upon which the greatly expanded
power of the national government would rest. In a very real sense,
therefore, the South was responsible for the concentration of power
in the national government that she was attempting to prevent and
which she so often protests against at the present time. It is noteworthy,
too, that the Civil Rights Act of 1866 and the Fourteenth Amendment,
which clinched its main features, were to reverse the relationship of
the citizen to his state and national governments. Prior to the Fourteenth Amendment, the state had posed as the guardian of its citizens
against a despotic national government; thereafter the national government would be armed to assume a protective role of the citizen against
state discrimination.

For several years after 1867 all of the southern states were under
radical control, and some did not re-establish "home rule" for a decade.
Meanwhile, they would be governed by carpetbaggers, scalawags, and
Negroes, supported by federal bayonets. As a rule, Negroes held only
the lesser offices. No Negro served as governor, although South Carolina, Louisiana, and Mississippi had Negro lieutenant governors, and
before the end of the century twenty-six Negroes would represent
southern states in the national House of Representatives. There were
two Negro Senators, both from Mississippi, and many Negroes were
chosen to the state legislatures and to local offices.

In the first elections under the new constitutions, four states chose
carpetbag governors: ten of fourteen Senators and twenty of thirty-
five Representatives were also carpetbaggers. Some of these, as for
instance, Negro Senators Blanche K. Bruce and Hiram R. Revels of
Mississippi, were high-minded, honorable men of more than average
ability. Other carpetbaggers like Henry Clay Warmoth and William
P. Kellogg, and Negro leaders like John R. Lynch and James Hill
of Mississippi and P. B. S. Pinchback of Louisiana were self-seeking
politicians tainted with corruption. Allied with both white and black
carpetbaggers were scalawags. Often former Whigs, some scalawags

were respectable and wealthy planters who had opposed secession, like Mississippi's James L. Alcorn. On the other hand, some were unscrupulous white southerners whose chief aim was self-enrichment by fair means or foul.

Recent scholars have shown conclusively that the stereotype of Congressional reconstruction, regimes devoid of all virtue, is greatly exaggerated. Nevertheless, it must be conceded that many officials of the radical governments were ignorant, others unscrupulous, and their administrations extravagant and corrupt. School funds were embezzled, tax rates quadrupled, and state debts increased by as much as 1400 per cent in a few years. Carpetbag officials came into the region penniless and quickly made fortunes. Henry Clay Warmoth, a native of Illinois, dismissed from the Union army by General Grant and subsequently indicted for embezzlement in Texas, settled in New Orleans and quickly rose to power. Elected governor in 1868 with a salary of $8000, he admitted making $100,000 the first year. At the close of his term in 1872 his fortune was variously estimated at a figure somewhere between $500,000 and $1,000,000. An eyewitness of the South Carolina legislative session of 1870 thought that body so generally corrupt that "the [few] honest and honorable members of either race had no more influence in it than an orchid might have in a mustard patch." Robert K. Scott, carpetbag governor of the state, sold pardons right and left and later admitted that he accepted a $15,000 bribe for approving a false printing bill. His successor, scalawag Governor Franklin J. Moses, Jr., used his contingent fund to bribe legislative committees that were charged to investigate reports of his misuse of that fund. As a result, Moses was exonerated by the legislature and his contingent fund increased. Conservative legislators were sometimes arrested in order to insure a radical majority when key measures were to be voted on, and in Florida a "smelling committee" was actually set up in the legislature to ferret out new schemes whereby dishonest legislators might enrich themselves.

There was much corruption of a comparatively petty nature. Booty in the form of state printing concessions was a favorite device by which legislatures rewarded their friends of the press. Florida's printing bill in 1869 was greater than the entire cost of the state government in 1860; Louisiana's under three years of Warmoth's administration grew almost tenfold, from $60,000 to $500,000. New offices were created to reward political henchmen, and salaries of others were raised. New counties were created in return for bribes paid by expectant county officials or by speculating landowners. An Arkansas Negro was paid $9000 to repair a bridge originally built for $500. The South Carolina legislature paid almost twice as much for the taking of a state census in 1869 as the Federal census would cost the following year. It also voted $1000 extra compensation to its speaker because he had lost that sum on a horse race. Westphalia hams, whiskies, and wines were purchased as "legislative supplies." A carpetbagger wrote from Raleigh, North Carolina, in the autumn of 1867: "I strayed down here and was appointed Register in Bankruptcy by Judge Chase and to use one of our Western *Phrases* am making it *pay*—"[17]

Thievery on a large scale was practiced through the use of the states' credit, generally by issuing bonds to promote railroads, some of which were never built. North Carolina issued $17,500,000 of railroad bonds, Arkansas more than $8,000,000, Georgia almost $6,000,000. Alabama had such confused records that it was never learned exactly how much she had pledged, but it was something more than $17,000,000. State debts rose to fantastic heights: in South Carolina, North Carolina, and Alabama, to about $30,000,000; in Louisiana to $50,000,000. Tax rates everywhere had to be raised sharply to meet obligations on these debts. Only in Mississippi, where the state constitution, written by "radicals," prohibited the pledging of state credit to support corporations, was the debt not drastically increased.

In all fairness, however, it must be pointed out that state debts and state taxes inevitably must have grown regardless of whether radicals or conservatives ruled. Physical rehabilitation of a war-devastated country called for extraordinary expenses by the vanquished in an age that knew no Marshall Plan. Besides, four million slaves, who had been dependent upon masters for all their needs, were now citizens and as such were entitled to all benefits accompanying citizenship: education, eleemosynary care, police protection, and access to courts of justice as well as penal care. Furthermore, a mere cataloguing of state debts left by radical regencies is misleading. As has been noted, much of the "debt" consisted of loans to railroads, and these were secured by mortgages on the assets of the railroads. Where the com-

(17) *North Carolina Historical Review*, XVIII, Part IV (Oct. 1941), 393-7.

panies defaulted, the state was obligated to creditors to the amount of the state's bonded obligation; on the other hand, the state would, in such cases, acquire the assets of the companies, which in many cases were considerable.

It must be noted, also, that this was an age when dishonesty and corruption ran amuck in all sections of the country, and that many high officials of the federal government—Representatives and Senators in Congress as well as cabinet members—did not come through the period with unblemished characters. Crédit Mobilier, Whisky Ring, War Department, and other scandals of Grant's administration would leave a trail of broken reputations in Washington, New York, Philadelphia, St. Louis, and other cities not subjected to reconstruction governments. Public money pilfered by the Tweed Ring in New York dwarfed anything that occurred in the South at this time. Nor was the bloc voting of the freedmen in southern states singular in its corruption of the ballot box. Illiterate aliens, whose unfamiliarity with democratic election processes was at least equal to that of the freedmen, were herded from polling place to polling place in northern cities by political bosses, and the votes purchased from them were counted as often as they were cast.

It is equally clear that responsibility for southern corruption and fraud should not be laid at the door of the Negroes. Even in the few brief instances when they constituted a majority of a legislative body, they were generally only pawns of white leaders who used them for their own ends. Besides, they were caught in an atmosphere so saturated with corruption that the honest and honorable members of either race had no influence. While some of the graft found its way into pockets of office-holders, great amounts went into coffers of railroad promoters. Of the $17 million of railroad bonds endorsed by the Alabama legislature between 1867 and 1871, the Louisville and Nashville and its affiliate got $7 million, while the Alabama and Chattanooga and its associates accounted for the rest. These two roads were involved in and dominated the political structure in the state throughout the period. Indeed, the chief issues between the Democratic and Republican parties in the state seemed centered upon support of one or the other of these two roads. With the panic of 1873 both roads, near bankruptcy, defaulted, leaving the state to settle the debt as best it could.

Side by side with fiscal dishonesty went election frauds. Opposition to the carpetbag-scalawag regimes existed from the beginning, and, in time, contests became close and bitter. Southern elections under the old regime had never been noted for their purity, but carpetbag and scalawag politics were to develop techniques of fraud which southern whites would employ with interest in post-reconstruction days. When conventions met in 1867 and 1868 under the Reconstruction Acts they were controlled by carpetbaggers and scalawags who managed bodies that in some states had a majority of Negroes and a minority of white conservatives. There was a tug-of-war between the conservatives and radicals for the votes of the Negroes, and when persuasion failed to win their support conservatives used force or intimidation to prevent the Negroes from participating in elections. Again and again, radical leaders in southern states were forced to appeal for federal troops to insure Negro voting and thus prevent defeat for their party. With Grant's re-election in 1872, the issue seemed settled for a time at least in favor of the radicals.

By that time, too, radicals were countering conservative violence with fraud of their own, and elections had become a travesty. According to James G. Randall, "blacks by the thousands cast ballots without knowing even the names of men for whom they were voting," and southern communities "were subjected to the misguided action of these irresponsible creatures directed by white bosses." Election laws were "deliberately framed to open the way for manipulation and fraud." Vote-buying "became so common that Negroes came to expect it." Union Leaguers, according to another authority, "voted the Negroes like herds of senseless cattle."[18] "We are entirely in the power of the radicals," wrote a southerner from Baton Rouge, "and there is a few low Whites Who Condescend to take the Negro by the arm to Get his vote. We are entirely at the mercy of the Negroe as there is four Negroes to one White registered. . . ."[19] A committee of Congress, investigating the Louisiana election of 1872, reported that the Republican returning-board juggled returns, accepted false affidavits, and merely "estimated what the vote ought to have been." In Alabama, radical bosses in 1874 distributed to thousands of Negro voters a

(18) Randall, The Civil War and Reconstruction, 847; Francis B. Simkins and Robert H. Woody, South Carolina During Reconstruction (Chapel Hill, 1932), 80.
(19) John D. Barnhart, ed., "Reconstruction on the Lower Mississippi," Mississippi Valley Historical Review, XXI (Dec. 1934), 393–4.

winter's supply of bacon and hams furnished by Congress for the relief of people in flooded areas of the state. In the same year, five hundred Georgia Negroes were marched across the Florida border on election day to Tallahassee, voting at each precinct en route under assumed names.[20] These tactics called for escalation of the political war, and white conservative leaders resorted to organized intimidation and violence. Most notorious of their organizations was the Ku Klux Klan.

Established as a social club at Pulaski, Tennessee, by a small group of Confederate veterans, the Klan took on political overtones after the beginning of radical control, and its growth thereafter was rapid but haphazard. Leading citizens joined, and by 1867 the sprawling chapters had been brought together under a formal constitution. The entire southland was designated as the Empire of the order and was ruled over by the famed Confederate cavalry leader Nathan Bedford Forrest, whose title was Grand Wizard. A council of ten Genii advised the Grand Wizard. The Empire was subdivided into Realms, ruled by Grand Dragons; Dominions, presided over by Grand Titans; Provinces, whose leaders were Giants; and Dens, governed by Grand Cyclops. There were also Hydras, Furies, Magis, Turks, Night Hawks, Scribes, Monks, and Sentinels.

Avowed purposes of the Klan were the protection of the weak from the lawless, the violent, and the brutal; the relief of the oppressed and the injured; the protection and defense of the Constitution of the United States and aid in the execution of all laws passed under it. As the radical program unfolded, however, Klan aims were directed not at enforcing the law but at its frustration. It sought to accomplish its purpose through suppressing Negro militia units and frightening Negroes from support of the radicals. Dressed in white flowing robes with tall, pointed hats, hooded horsemen rode through the country at night, bringing terror to Negroes, carpetbaggers, and scalawags. At first Klansmen sought to achieve their goals without violence, relying on their supernatural posture to strike terror into Negro hearts.

For a time such antics were effective. Inevitably, however, Negro militiamen fired at Klansmen, and when it was discovered that the hooded creatures bled and died, fear of their mystical powers vanished. Thereafter the Klansmen resorted to physical violence. Negroes were

(20) Fleming, *Documentary History of Reconstruction*, II, 83-6.

whipped, tortured, and sometimes killed; Union League councils were broken up, northern schoolteachers driven out. Warnings were issued, sometimes in doggerel verse, that support of the radicals at election would bring reprisals. The Greenville (South Carolina) *Southern Enterprise* in April 1868 published this warning:

> Niggers and leaguers, get out of the way,
> We're born of the night and we vanish by day.
> No rations have we, but the flesh of man—
> And love niggers best—the Ku Klux Klan;
> We catch 'em alive and roast 'em whole,
> Then hand 'em around with a sharpened pole.
> Whole Leagues have been eaten, not leaving a man,
> And went away hungry—The Ku Klux Klan;
> Born of the night, and vanish by day;
> Leaguers and niggers, get out of the way![21]

As the violence grew, the better elements of the Imperial Order withdrew in protest, and in 1869 Forrest formally disbanded the Klan. But the Klan's lawless activities had sown the wind, and the whirlwind must be reaped. Withdrawal of the more responsible members left the more brutal and ruthless in complete control. Masking their deeds under a false front of patriotism, these lawless ruffians, often motivated by greed or private grudges, went about their mischief-making. A federal judge in South Carolina observed that Klansmen in his court related the circumstances of cold-blooded murders they had committed as casually as if the killings were routine incidents of a normal day's work.

After the Klan's official ending in 1869, its work was continued under a multitude of local organizations: the Tennessee Pale Faces, the Louisiana Knights of the White Camelia, the North Carolina White Brotherhood, the South Carolina Council of Safety, the Alabama Men of Justice, the Mississippi Society of the White Rose, the Knights of the Rising Sun in Texas, the Red Jackets, the Native Sons of the South, the Knights of the Black Cross. So virulent was their activity that in 1870-71 Congress passed three civil rights acts for their suppression. A Congressional committee compiled thirteen volumes of testimony concerning southern disorders for which they were responsible.

(21) Quoted in E. Merton Coulter, *The South During Reconstruction* (Baton Rouge, 1947), 167-8.

As a consequence, more than 7000 indictments were returned, and martial law was declared in many sections. Federal government action was motivated partly by partisanship; but even southern conservatives, appalled at the lawless acitivity of their countrymen, supported the efforts of the Washington government to curb the Klan and its affiliates. In one county of Florida 163 Negroes were murdered in 1871, and in the same year more than 300 were killed in the parishes around New Orleans. It is estimated that at least 5000 Negroes were killed or driven out of southern communities during reconstruction, and countless other "troublemakers" were flogged or maimed. The greatest mischief, however, was committed in the hill counties of Tennessee and the Carolinas. Acting under authority of the Civil Rights Acts, President Grant imposed martial law in nine South Carolina counties in the spring of 1871. Hundreds of arrests and trials followed, and eighty-two Klansmen were convicted. By the end of 1871 Klan activities were effectively suppressed for the time.

Radical control was uniform, however, neither in severity nor in duration. The traditional view of Radical reconstruction as a period of universal unhappiness and pessimism needs revision. For despite the many acts of violence the relations between the majority of both races remained wholesome, and there is no evidence that in general their lives were less tranquil or less happy than were those of either their forebears or descendants. Misery, hatred, and repression there were, but they were not omnipresent. Fairs, camp meetings, parades, picnics, dances, and other simple social events brightened the lives of the people, even though poverty and political uncertainty sometimes cast shadows over the family hearth. Then, too, the legend of the Lost Cause with its heroic memories tempered with glamour and an air of nobility the drab reality of defeat. Nor were the people as preoccupied with politics as most historical accounts would suggest. As Howard K. Beale pointed out, most white southerners during the period "wanted nothing from politicians but a chance to live their lives undisturbed." Beale concluded that southerners supported those who restored white supremacy in the end not for ideological reasons or because of any personal preference but because "they were tired of the constant turmoil that was injurious to non-political pursuits."[22]

(22) Howard K. Beale, "On Rewriting Reconstruction History," *American Historical Review*, XLV (July 1940), 814.

Some of the states early fulfilled conditions for restoration prescribed by the Reconstruction Acts, and federal troops were
withdrawn. As soon as this happened, radical regimes were overthrown. Thus, Tennessee was recaptured by the conservatives in 1869,
Virginia and North Carolina in 1870, Georgia in 1871. Restoration
of white conservative control in North Carolina was featured by the
impeachment of scalawag Governor W. W. Holden, the first incident
of the kind in the history of the nation.

As the radicals sensed their waning influence, they redoubled their
efforts to maintain control in the other states. At each election radical
governors sent urgent appeals to Washington for additional troops
to maintain order and protect the Negro voter from violence and
intimidation. The intensifying of radical control resulted in a revival
of Klan-like activity. But this time there was a difference. In early
days a respectable minority of upper-class whites had co-operated with
the radicals; bitterness that had grown with radical repressive measures
made it no longer possible for them to do so. Planter joined hill farmer
in fomenting new terror. Hoods and gowns were now discarded for
red shirts, and mysterious night rides gave way to daylight parades
and demonstrations of armed strength. Republican rallies were broken
up by well-drilled companies of red-shirted rifle clubs, who made
no secret of their determination to overthrow the radical regimes at
any cost. Not only did these companies whip Negroes, they stood
up to Negro militia in open battle and easily defeated them. The
conservative cause was aided, too, when Congress passed a general
amnesty bill in May 1872 removing political disabilities from all but
a few of the 100,000 Confederate leaders disqualified from office-holding by the Fourteenth Amendment. These trusted leaders were now
in a position to rally all southern whites under the conservative political
banner of "white supremacy." They were further aided by the dissolution of the Freedmen's Bureau in 1872. The Negro was now left at
the mercy of the planter for his livelihood, and the planter often
insisted on the Negro's political submissiveness in return for his
patronage.

The classic example of the overthrow of radical rule by red shirt
activity took place in Mississippi in 1874-75. There, James L. Alcorn,
a wealthy Whig planter who had opposed secession, was chosen governor by the radicals in 1869 and then sent to the United States Senate.

As a Senator he opposed enactment of the bills to suppress the Ku Klux Klan, while his Mississippi colleague, Adelbert Ames, an incorruptible carpetbagger from Maine, supported the bills. Both men were candidates for governor in 1873, Ames supported by the radicals, Alcorn now by the conservatives. When Ames won overwhelmingly, carrying Negro candidates for lieutenant governor and superintendent of education into office with him, the conservatives started organizing for the legislative elections two years hence. Rifle clubs were formed and drilled in every county. Business was neglected as planters, lawyers, and merchants mobilized farmers and laborers for the final struggle. Companies paraded, bands played, men in red shirts astride prancing horses appeared everywhere, sometimes dragging field pieces and firing as they went. The conservatives were led by well-to-do lawyers, ex-Confederates Lucius Q. C. Lamar and James Z. George. General John B. Gordon came over from Georgia to aid them, and so did the old Kentucky abolitionist, Cassius Marcellus Clay, now exhorting Negroes to desert the radicals. Intimidation, threats, and violence were the conservatives' main stock in trade, but they also used milder forms of persuasion, promising the Negro that his rights would be better protected under conservative than under radical rule. In this way, by a judicious use of the carrot and the stick, the conservatives succeeded in dampening the enthusiasm of the Negroes upon whose votes the radicals were wholly dependent.

As the time of the election neared, there were sporadic acts of violence. Governor Ames had organized Negro militia to forestall conservative intimidation, but the Negroes were no match for their white opponents. Ames appealed to Grant for more troops, but by this time even northern Republicans were growing weary of the annual dispatch of troops during southern elections. Grant refused, and Ames was obliged to disband his Negro militia in exchange for promises from Lamar and George that they would prevent violence from their followers. As a result, the election went off in comparative calm. But preliminary work of the red shirts had been effective, and the Negro vote was greatly reduced, either through fear or bribery. The result was an overwhelming conservative victory. When the legislature met, Radicals were in a hopeless minority, and Ames and his Negro lieutenant governor resigned rather than face the impeachment proceedings which conservatives were preparing. John M. Stone, president pro tempore of the state senate, succeeded to the vacated governor's office.

By action of a similar but less dramatic nature, Alabama, Arkansas, and Texas had been "redeemed" from radical rule the year before. After 1875, however, the skillful employment of violence and intimidation of the Negro on the one hand and persuasion and bribery to win his support on the other became known as the Mississippi Plan, and was used in the remaining states to bring an end to the last vestiges of radical rule in the South.

By the autumn of 1876, only Florida, South Carolina, and Louisiana were still under Republican control, and it was clear by this time that only the presence of federal troops in those states insured the survival of the radical party. Unprecedented corruption in South Carolina under carpetbagger Scott and scalawag Moses had brought radical prestige to a low ebb by 1874, even though radicals were able to elect Daniel H. Chamberlain of Massachusetts as governor that year on a reform platform. Chamberlain was a man of great integrity whose honest administration was attested even by the conservatives, many of whom co-operated with him.

The political situation in Louisiana was complicated by a division within the Republican party. One wing, favored by the Grant administration, was led by Stephen B. Packard, federal marshal, and James F. Carey, collector of customs and Grant's brother-in-law; the other was led by former Governor Warmoth and his mulatto lieutenant governor, P. B. S. Pinchback. In 1872 the conservatives had joined Warmoth in support of John McEnery for governor, while the Packard faction had supported William P. Kellogg. Louisiana, like other southern states, had election "canvassing" boards whose duty it was to review the returns from the various election districts. These boards had legal authority to throw out all ballots they deemed fraudulent or returns they thought unfair. The Warmoth-appointed canvassing board reviewed the returns and declared McEnery elected, but the Packard faction refused to concede. With the aid of federal troops, and armed with a court order from a Grant-appointed federal judge, Packard seized the state house and had legislators loyal to him inaugurate Kellogg. Meanwhile, Warmoth called a special session of the legislature to meet at Mechanics Institute and inaugurate McEnery. Both governors held out through the summer. An uprising in September drove Kellogg from the state house and won his consent to resign, but when federal troops once more came to his support he changed his mind. In the legislative elections that fall the conservatives claimed a clear majority, but the canvassing board, now controlled by Kellogg, counted a majority for the Kellogg party. A Congressional investigating committee worked out a compromise giving the conservatives a legislative majority but permitting Kellogg to serve out his term.

The Presidential election of 1876 brought matters to a climax in all three states still under radical rule. It had become apparent before the election that choice of a President might well rest on the electoral votes of Florida, South Carolina, and Louisiana. In Florida, the corrupt carpetbag incumbent, Governor Marcellus L. Stearns, was opposed by former Whig George F. Drew. Chamberlain hoped for re-election in South Carolina on the strength of his honest attempt at reform, but the conservative party brought forward in opposition Lee's famed cavalry leader, Wade Hampton. In Louisiana, Packard himself was the radical candidate. Opposed to him was Francis T. Nicholls, representative of the planter class. If Nicholls's military reputation was not as eminent as Hampton's, he was the living embodiment of sacrifice for the Cause. He had lost an eye, an arm, and a leg fighting for the Confederacy.

The campaign was bitterly fought everywhere, but in the three southern states this was especially true. Hampton and his aide, Matthew C. Butler, who had lost a leg at Brandy Station, stumped the state of South Carolina, organizing red shirt rifle clubs in every county. So well had they done their work of intimidation that violence on election day was unnecessary. Thousands of Negroes, alarmed at red shirt demonstrations, stayed away from the polls. Both sides were guilty of gross irregularities, and there were more votes counted in the state than could have been honestly cast. The radical canvassing board, in what seemed on the surface like remarkable impartiality, declared Hampton the winner in the governor's race but also declared that Republican Rutherford B. Hayes had carried the Presidential electoral vote. Charging fraud, Chamberlain refused to concede, and he and Hampton set up rival governments in Columbia, each purporting to be the legitimate government of the state.

A similar situation developed in Louisiana, where the scandals of 1872 had turned many moderates, including the large German

colony in New Orleans, against the radicals. Mass meetings and barbe-
cues were punctuated by White League violence in the best traditions
of the Mississippi Plan. Conservatives intimidated Negroes and carpetbaggers, and federal troops arrested conservatives. It would strain the
imagination to attempt to judge which side was the greater transgressor
of the law, but the radical canvassing board declared for Packard
and Hayes. But now the conservatives refused to concede. Both Packard and Nicholls set up rival governments, just as did Chamberlain
and Hampton in South Carolina. In neither state would either side
give in, and rival governments existed side by side in both throughout
the winter and spring of 1876-77. In Florida, Drew's victory seemed
certain, but Stearns refused to turn over the state house to him until
an invading contingent of Georgians threatened the capital with armed
assault.

Meanwhile, in the Presidential race, Samuel J. Tilden had 184
uncontested electoral votes and Hayes, 165. In dispute were the four
votes of Florida, South Carolina's seven, Louisiana's eight, and one
from Oregon. If Tilden could secure only one of the twenty in question he would have a majority of the Electoral College. Hayes, on
the other hand, needed all twenty to win. The issue in Oregon concerned a Republican elector who was disqualified because he was a
federal postmaster. The Democrats did not make a determined fight
there, and the decision went to Hayes in Oregon almost by default.
But it was an entirely different matter in the three southern states.
There, radical canvassing boards had reported Hayes the winner in
all three, even though in South Carolina and Florida the same boards
had declared conservatives victors in gubernatorial elections. But conservative parties in all three states had sent returns into Congress claim-
ing victory for Tilden electors. This presented a dilemma for Congress
in the counting of electoral votes. The Constitution provided that
Congress should count the electoral vote, but it did not state how
disputed votes were to be counted. After great controversy, including
talk of armed rebellion if Tilden were counted out, it was agreed
that an Electoral Commission of fifteen—five from the Supreme Court,
five from the Democratic House, and five from the Republican Senate—should decide how the disputed electoral votes should be cast.
It had been hoped that the Commission would be composed of seven
Democrats, seven Republicans, and one non-party man, Justice David

Davis. But Davis, who was disqualified by accepting election to the Senate from Illinois, was replaced by Justice Joseph P. Bradley, a Republican. The composition of the Commission thus resulted in eight Republican and seven Democratic members. Thereafter, by a party vote of 8 to 7, the Commission determined that every one of the disputed votes should go to Hayes.

This was quite unsatisfactory to many Democrats, and there was renewed talk of civil war. But the seeds of compromise were present. To national leaders of the Republican party, victory in the Presidential election was of far greater value than was the maintenance of the shaky Chamberlain and Packard governments. On the other hand, the end of radical rule was the paramount aim of conservative leaders in the southern states. A secret understanding was reached whereby Louisiana, South Carolina, and Florida conservatives would consent to Hayes's election if Hayes would carry out a promise already made to withdraw federal troops from the South. Shortly after his inaugural, Hayes fulfilled his part of the agreement. Federal troops were withdrawn from the last of the southern states, and the Chamberlain and Packard governments collapsed, as it was known they would.

It is not often that abortive revolutions or faltering social ventures survive in myth and legend with the aura of nobility and defeated grandeur that has attached itself to the Lost Cause. More often such movements are branded as treasonous and unworthy and deserving of their fate. So it would be with radical reconstruction. The overthrow of the Congress-sponsored governments was overwhelming and final and would brand them ever after as failures. More than this, their overthrow would stamp as historical truth southern evaluations of those governments as the ultimate in corruption, fraud, and maladministration. Associated with this so-called truth is another, equally questionable: that all the evil fruits of reconstruction were the result of "Negro domination." That corruption and maladministration did occur too frequently in the radical governments has already been demonstrated. That they were of larger proportion or were more heinous than those perpetrated in northern cities at the time or in the South both before and after reconstruction is untrue. Equally false is the legend that prevailed that Negro "majorities" were responsible for the corruption, for as has been shown, there never was a Negro majority in any radical government. But the belief that radical reconstruction was dominated by Negroes and was characterized by corruption unparalleled in American history became myths that would not die.

Another myth that has prevailed over truth, especially for southerners, is the belief that nothing constructive was accomplished under the radicals. It was radical governments, however, that gave the South its first real taste of universal education at public expense; and constitutions drawn by radicals effected long-needed reforms in courts, in county government organizations, in election machinery, and in the tax system. That these constitutions gave general satisfaction to whites is borne out by the fact that they survived redemption for many years, years when conservative whites were in complete control. Indeed, new constitutions were not drawn until the end of the century, and then largely for the purpose of legalizing the de facto Negro disfranchisement already established.

Regardless of all this, it is certainly true that reconstruction produced a trauma in the southern psyche from which its people would not soon recover. The racial bitterness caused by pushing the Negro without preparation into political participation caused him ever after to suffer unjust deprivation of civil, economic, social, and political rights. In trying to establish a more democratic political system the radicals failed. Negroes were ignorant, and the ballot could not correct that. But even if the Negro had not been allowed to vote, the situation would have been little improved; for the poor whites who were forced to the center of political power by the revolution brought on by the war, were also ignorant. And those who overthrew the radicals were as unwilling to share power with poor whites as with poor Negroes. This, events would soon demonstrate.

⊰ III ⊱

Agrarian Revolt

The dark image of reconstruction that has emerged as a result of enduring myths is deepened by contrast with another myth: the myth of a utopian ante-bellum South, one where a legendary aristocracy was in undisputed control. That the region was, before the war, a crazy-quilt land of sophisticated culture among the few on the one hand, and of general backwardness and ignorance among a large segment of the people on the other, is well known to students: yet, the myth of an ante-bellum golden age persists today among southerners, and they contrast this image with the more sordid one, equally mythical, of radical reconstruction.

Not only has the South been misled by myths, but it has been governed for much of its history by ghosts—ghosts of a legendary past, of the Confederate dead, of religious orthodoxy, of Negro domination. C. Vann Woodward has observed that "One of the most significant inventions of the New South was the 'Old South'—a new idea in the 'eighties, and a legend of incalcuble potentialities."[1] It is as idle to suggest to a southerner today that there never was a time when Negroes "dominated" southern society as it is to intimate that the Cause was lost largely because the hearts of too many southerners were not in it. For in the decades after Appomattox the Lost Cause assumed a religious character. Newspapers filled with reminiscences and dying words of heroes propagandized it, and statues erected in village squares commemorated it. Indeed, few lost causes in modern history rival it for the blind devotion lavished upon the cause and

(1) C. Vann Woodward, *Origins of the New South* (Baton Rouge, 1951), 154-5.

the sanctification of its heroes. In the moment of death, according to Robert Penn Warren, "The Confederacy entered upon its immortality."[2] The heritages of civil war and its aftermath would have a lasting influence on the South. Its loss of self-confidence as a result of its humiliation caused it to accept a humbler position in the government of the nation than the Old South would have been content to accept. Woodward has pointed out that in the period from Washington to Lincoln, southerners had occupied the Presidency more than two-thirds of the time. For all but a dozen of those years the Chief Justice had been a southerner; and the South had furnished twenty of thirty-five justices of the Supreme Court, more than half the cabinet members, a majority of ambassadors to major powers, and a majority of speakers of the House of Representatives. In contrast, from Andrew Johnson to Lyndon Johnson no southerner would be nominated for President, and not until 1952 would any southerner even be nominated by either major party for Vice President. In the same period, the South would furnish only 14 of 133 cabinet members, only 7 of 31 justices of the Supreme Court, only 2 of 12 speakers, and barely a handful of diplomats to major powers. Nor would the region's representatives in Congress distinguish themselves during a large part of that period, little or no legislation of any importance being identified with southerners until the administration of Woodrow Wilson.[3]

The most striking political development of the South after redemption was the decline of the two-party system. In the Old South political behavior was not markedly different from that in other regions. Divisions along social and geographic lines and a lively participation in the mainstream of national political movements, even when it was attempting by nullification and secession to thwart majority decisions, had characterized southern politics. A vigorous yeomanry made up the backbone of the evenly divided political parties of the Old South, and the percentage of southern white participation in politics approximated that of other sections. Despite the presence of slavery, the paradox of which troubled the southerner, he did not regard himself as undemocratic. The Negro, as slave, was so clearly outside the political entity that his participation in politics was not even thought of. On the other hand, the yeoman of the hill country voted

(2) Quoted in Dewey Grantham, *The Democratic South* (Athens, Ga., 1963), 19.
(3) Woodward, *Origins of the New South*, 456.

as freely and as uninhibitedly as the northern farmer. He generally opposed secession, and might do so with impunity. He voted against it in 1860-61, and he filled the ranks and even led peace movements and other "disloyal" schemes during the war years.

For two decades before the slavery crisis of the 1850's political parties were almost equally divided, and Whig and Democrat had contested bitterly and on fairly even terms in most southern states: Whigs generally as spokesmen for business and planting interests, Democrats for the yeoman farmer. In the reconstruction period, former Whig and Democrat forgot their antagonism and united in opposition to radical reconstruction. At first Whigs distrusted their former adversaries and balked at accepting the name of their ancient enemy, and efforts were made to revive the Whig party, or else form a new conservative party. Unreasoning fear of Negro control eventually drove Whig and Democrat together, although their alliance was often referred to as the Conservative or White Man's party. It would be a decade or more before Whigs generally would consent to be known as Democrats.

When the old Whig leaders surrendered their historic name in making their new alliance with Democrats after redemption, however, they did not adopt their new allies' commitment to the farmer. Although in many ways they strongly resembled the oligarchy of the ante-bellum period, actually the new leaders were not as a rule primarily concerned with the planting interests. Some of them, like Wade Hampton, Alfred H. Colquitt, and Francis T. Nicholls, had been ante-bellum planters and would retain their planting interests in the postwar years; but they were the exception rather than the rule. The overwhelming majority of the people would continue to be occupied with agriculture, but there were richer rewards now to be found in other economic pursuits; for the war effected a revolution in the towns, where many returning soldiers took up banking, merchandising, railroad promotion, manufacturing, and other occupations. Even in the rural areas, the storekeeper soon replaced the planter as the dominant influence, and many an ante-bellum slave-owner turned merchant and furnished supplies to his former slaves as well as his yeoman neighbors.

By the 1880's the farmers' ante-bellum prominence had been taken over by merchant, banker, railroad promoter, and lawyer; and the unanimity with which spokesmen of the people had formerly championed the cause of agriculture was no more. The yeomen farmers were not unaware of the dichotomy between their interests and those of their political spokesmen, but, as Wilbur Cash pointed out, the hypnotic "Negro fixation" of the region demanded white unity. If the Negro was to be "kept in his place," the masses must be content to sacrifice any attempt at political factionalism which might improve their lot. Their leaders, on the other hand, secure in their positions because of the Negro bogey, came to regard the machinery of government as belonging to them and identified their own private interests with the public interest. For a generation after reconstruction, those who had led the redemption—the Lamars and Georges in Mississippi; the Joe Browns, Gordons, and Colquitts in Georgia; the Hamptons and Butlers in South Carolina; the Warmoths and Nicholls in Louisiana; the Comers in Alabama—sought to crush all opposition by calling up the phantom of Negro rule. When opposition to their rule arose, as it frequently did, they warned that division into political parties was a luxury which the South could no longer afford; for it would split the whites into factions which would compete for the Negro vote, and thus restore the Negro to power. The presence of the Negro thus became a great asset to so-called Bourbon politicians in crushing incipient revolts.

In these "Bourbon" governments that brought redemption, economy would be the watchword. Government expenditures, particularly for education, would at once be reduced drastically, in some places as much as fivefold. Generally the new governments would be hostile to all progressive or social legislation: prison reform, care of the deaf, the blind, the insane. There would be wholesale repudiation or else a readjustment downward of debts incurred during the radical period, perhaps $150,000,000 in all. Only Mississippi and Texas failed to readjust their debt in some degree.

On the whole, the redeemers would enjoy a reputation for restoring honesty to government which they hardly deserved. While state expenditures were being reduced, corruption on the part of officeholders was on an ascending scale over that of radical days. In 1879 a series of investigations in Georgia resulted in exposure and impeachment of the state treasurer, the comptroller, the commissioner of agriculture. Despite this, Governor Colquitt, who was somewhat tarnished by the scandals, was re-elected the following year, and the state treasurer, when he restored the stolen funds, went unpunished.

The Georgia scandals were not singular. In 1873 the Virginia state treasurer escaped trial for embezzlement when he pleaded insanity; yet, four years later there were additional embezzlements. In 1883 Marshall T. Polk, the state treasurer of Tennessee, cousin of Bishop General Leonidas Polk and adopted son of President James K. Polk, fled with $400,000 of state funds. About the same time, Isaac H. Vincent, the Alabama treasurer, escaped to Mexico, having embezzled a quarter of a million dollars. The state treasurer of Arkansas defaulted with $100,000 the same year; nine years later his successor was short $150,000 in his accounts. The Mississippi treasurer in 1890, William L. Hemmingway, was convicted of embezzling more than $300,000, and ten years later his successor was also exposed as an embezzler. In 1889 it was discovered that the former treasurer of Louisiana had escaped to Honduras after embezzling $1,750,000. All of this at a time when state services were cut to the bone and retrenchment on the score of poverty was a fetish.[4]

The penal system furnished one of the most fertile fields for corruption. Under slavery the plantation had been its own correction system, and in the first years after redemption no southern state had an institution prepared to cope with the great number of freedmen who ran afoul of the law. Leasing the convicts to employers who paid their keep and something more fitted the new order and was adopted everywhere. Instead of a liability, the convicts under this system became an asset. As numbers of convicts grew, fortunes were made from their labor; and the state, spared the expense of providing for them, received from five to ten cents per day for their labor. The convicts were worked on plantations in the delta country, in the coal and iron mines of Tennessee, Alabama, and Georgia, and in railroad and levee construction everywhere. Treatment accorded these convicts, most of whom were Negroes, would rival that of galley slaves of the Roman period or of heretics during the Inquisition. Having no property interest in the convict, the lessee intended to get the most work possible out of him while spending as little as possible for his care. If the convict became sick or disabled, he could be replaced by a healthy man. If he died, there would be another to take his place. A legislative committee in Mississippi called one convict labor camp a "nest of cruelty and graft," where drunken guards abused and sometimes murdered prisoners. At another camp, where a huge

(4) Woodward, *Origins of the New South*, 66-72.

shack served as a ward for the incurably ill, the committee found a dozen Negroes dying, all window glass broken and the "patients" exposed to the wintry blasts, some of them without bedding or cover of any kind. At about the same time, an official investigation in Georgia branded the system as "barbaric," "worse than slavery," and "a disgrace to civilized people."[5]

The system proved a bonanza not only for the lessees but also for unscrupulous politicians and contractors. Fortunes in Tennessee, Alabama, Louisiana, and Arkansas were based on fraudulent contracts between hirers of convicts and dishonest state officials. In 1886, Governor Robert Lowry and Attorney General Thomas Catchings, of Mississippi, falsely certified that the general contractor who sub-leased the state's convicts to planters and railroad builders had paid arrears of $80,000 to the state so that his contract could be renewed. Loose bookkeeping made it impossible to determine in many cases just how much was due the state under the lease. The Vicksburg *Herald* charged and submitted evidence to prove that the state of Mississippi had been defrauded of more than $400,000 during Anselm McLaurin's term as governor.

As undeserved as the redeemers' reputation for governmental integrity was the legend that they brought purity to political contests. C. Vann Woodward has pointed out that of 183 contested elections in the United States House of Representatives from 1875 to 1901, 107 came from twelve southern states, most based on charges of fraud. The governor of Alabama admitted at the turn of the century that "White men have gotten to cheating each other until we don't have any honest elections." A few years before, a Virginian admitted that he and his associates had been "preserving white civilization" by cheating. The president of the Mississippi Constitutional Convention in 1890 said fraud in elections had become so chronic between Mississippi whites that it had "excited nausea."[6]

As already noted, the redemption, although a counter-revolution in a social sense, continued to support the same industrial and commercial interests which had flourished during reconstruction. Generally there was an amicable relation between industrialists and planters, both

(5) Albert D. Kirwan, *Revolt of the Rednecks* (Lexington, Ky., 1951), 174; Woodward, *Origins of the New South*, 424.
(6) Woodward, *Origins of the New South*, 326-7; Kirwan, *Revolt of the Rednecks*, 58.

groups differing little from northern conservatives in the belief that salvation for their section lay in economic progress. Both southern industrialist and planter advocated reconciliation with the financial interests of the Northeast. While paying lip-service to laissez-faire governmental economy, the glories of the Lost Cause, and state-rights, they advocated subsidies for railroads and tax exemptions for industry. But when the philosophy of state-rights conflicted with practical benefits flowing from industrial growth, or if the principle of government economy forbade gifts of lands to railroads, they found ways to adjust both principle and philosophy to their economic advantage. It was not that they were anti-farmer in outlook: they simply neglected the farmer while bestowing great favors on corporations they represented as counsel or in which they held shares.

By 1890 millions of acres of public lands had been sold to lumbermen and speculators at bargain rates, or else were given away to railroads. Nothing in reconstruction equaled the generosity of the "Bourbons" in the gift of lands to corporate interests. In the years following the redemption, Texas granted more than 20,000,000 acres to twelve railroads, Florida sold an even larger amount to speculators for twenty-five cents an acre, and Louisiana sold 1,500,000 acres to English corporations at prices ranging from twelve and one-half to seventy-five cents an acre. Tax exemptions and special privileges went to all businesses, but railroads were the favorites. Alabama's redemption governor, George S. Houston, and his successor, Rufus Cobb, were closely allied with the Louisville and Nashville Railroad Company and worked out railroad bond settlement legislation that was highly advantageous to their client if not to the bondholders. In Tennessee, John C. Brown, first Democratic governor after redemption, was vice president of the Texas and Pacific Railroad and president of the Tennessee Coal, Iron, and Railroad Company. His successor, James D. Porter, was president of the Nashville, Chattanooga, and St. Louis Railroad. Both Brown and Porter were friends and business partners of Colonel Arthur S. Colyar, corporate lawyer, owner of the Nashville *American*, and director and general counsel of the Tennessee Coal, Iron, and Railroad Company. In Virginia, railroads and bondholders exerted great influence both under the regimes of Gilbert C. Walker and that of his successor, Confederate General William Mahone, leader of the move to readjust the state debt downward.

The most remarkable example of redeemer devotion to business interests of the New South is seen in Georgia. Joseph E. Brown had come out of a humble mountain home in north Georgia to lead his state as governor during the Confederacy. An extreme state-righter, his administration was marked by repeated disputes with the Davis administration over the limits of Confederate authority. For some years after the war he embraced the Republican party and was closely associated with radical Governor Rufus B. Bullock, who fled the state in 1870 following charges of corruption. But Bullock's downfall did little injury to Brown. Resigning from his judgeship to accept appointment by a Democratic governor to the presidency of the Western and Atlantic Railroad Company, he negotiated a contract, later denounced as fraudulent, leasing the state-owned railroad. But the railroad thrived and so did Brown, who later added a fortune in mining and Atlanta real estate to his railroad interests.

After the overthrow of radical rule, Brown became closely associated with John B. Gordon, Georgia's most distinguished Confederate hero, and with General Alfred H. Colquitt, a wealthy planter. Both Gordon and Colquitt were Democrats and had bitterly opposed Brown during his sojourn with the radical party. Colquitt was governor in 1880 when Gordon suddenly resigned his coveted seat in the United States Senate to succeed Brown as president of the Western and Atlantic and to become counsel for the Louisville and Nashville Railroad. Although Brown was still very unpopular in Georgia because of his political infidelity, Colquitt appointed him to Gordon's vacated seat. All three men were denounced for this "corrupt bargain," but they managed to survive the reaction and to share for almost two decades complete political control of the state. Gordon or Colquitt shuttled back and forth between the governor's office and one of the United States Senate seats during most of the period, while Brown occupied the other Senate seat. They also shared mine, railroad, steamship, insurance, and other business interests, and Brown and Gordon rose to positions of great eminence as southern industrialists. Through Gordon, the triumvirate maintained close ties with business leaders in other states: with Generals Jubal A. Early, returned from self-imposed exile in Latin America, and P. G. T. Beauregard in Louisiana, and with Confederate veterans Lamar and George in Mississippi. Beauregard and Early rose to political and business prominence in Louisiana when they lent their good Confederate names to the Louisiana Lottery. The Lottery was a creation of the radical regime and after redemption desperately needed identification with the Lost Cause. As has been seen, Gordon assisted Lamar and George in the overthrow of the Radical party in Mississippi, and thereafter kept close liaison with them in railroad and other business ventures. Lamar, George, and Lamar's protege General E. C. Walthall were corporate lawyers and particular friends of railroads. The three dominated politics in Mississippi as completely as Brown, Gordon, and Colquitt did in Georgia, defeating efforts of agrarian leaders for tax relief while dispensing tax concessions to corporations.

Another friend of Gordon and the Georgia triumvirate was Nathan Bedford Forrest, whose eminence as a Confederate hero was at least equal to Gordon's. Shortly after the redemption, Forrest organized the Memphis, Birmingham, and Atlantic Railroad and traveled the proposed route through Mississippi and Alabama taking subscriptions for capital stock from counties and towns as well as from individual farmers. Years passed without the building of the road, but when coal and iron fields were opened in north Alabama, Forrest secured permission of the Mississippi legislature to deviate from the agreed route without even returning subscription money. The Georgia triumvirate also had ties with South Carolina, where planters Wade Hampton and Matthew C. Butler controlled the state from 1876 until their defeat by Pitchfork Ben Tillman. During their regime, industrial and railroad interests in Columbia and Charleston fared well also in state concessions.

A few voices there were, here and there, pleading the cause of the once dominant but now forgotten agrarian interests: Isham G. Harris in Tennessee, Robert Toombs in Georgia, Ethelbert Barksdale in Mississippi. But their pleas generally were unheard. Harris won a fleeting victory in 1882 when his wing of the party succeeded in having some of the state's fraudulent bonds repudiated and a commission to regulate railroads established. Toombs was able to write antimonopoly clauses into the Georgia constitution of 1877, but after this one victory his influence waned before the power of the triumvirate of Brown, Colquitt, and Gordon. Barksdale, the voice of the Mississippi farmer through the 1870's and 1880's, never won a position of influence in the management of his state's affairs.

The overthrow of radical reconstruction was thus a revolution with limited aims. It turned out of office carpetbagger and scalawag. It effectively curbed the political ambitions of the Negroes, whose votes had made carpetbag rule possible. But other than that, the new regimes, for all their genuflections in the direction of the Lost Cause and the ante-bellum South, maintained a continuity with the programs of their predecessors. For a quarter of a century after the redemption, southern states would be a mecca beckoning ambitious industrial and railroad barons; and the lawyers who did their bidding would be as influential as in any northern metropolis.

Largesse presented to corporate interests while the farmer was being neglected soon dissipated the spirit of white unity purchased by the myth of Negro dominance during reconstruction. By 1880 cleavages began to appear in the white man's party, and during the next two decades these would grow ever wider. At the time, towns and cities were booming, while the rural areas were in a state of abject poverty. The number of small farms had increased notably since the war, but almost a third of them were operated by tenants on shares, and this ratio would increase during the next half-century.

The farmer's depressed condition was both caused by and reflected in the declining price of cotton. From an average price of fifteen cents in 1870-73, it fell steadily to little more than nine cents by 1884, to less than eight cents by 1890, and to an all time low of four cents by 1898. It cost the farmer seven cents a pound to produce cotton, but the declining price was not the sole cause of his grief. For the depressed cotton market was accompanied by a contraction in the currency and by steadily increasing tariff rates, which were raising prices of products the farmer bought. Inadequate banking facilities and high interest rates added to his woes. Furthermore, the new lien laws favored the landlords and the merchants to his disadvantage. All farmers lived on credit. If they owned land they mortgaged it and used the money to provide necessities. If they owned no land they mortgaged the next year's crop to the storekeeper and used up the proceeds.

The merchant was not the true villain in the play, however, for he was indebted to the wholesaler just as the planters were in debt to him and tenant and laborer to the planter; indeed, a pall of debt hung over the land. But the merchant, being part banker, part landlord, part storekeeper, in local circles had the power of a despot. Holding a mortgage both on the farmer's growing crop as well as on any personal property he might own, such as a mule and a wagon, he extended credit for all the farmer's needs during the summer and through the fall until the cotton was harvested and sold. He supplied the tenant with food, clothing, tobacco, and even medicine—all at a 50 to 100 per cent mark-up. The landlord and the merchant watched over the crop as eagerly as the tenant, for indeed their interest in it was as great as was his and their control even greater. When it was ready for market, the merchant took possession, sold it, paid the landlord his share for rent, deducted his bill, and, if anything remained, gave it to the tenant. Cotton thus became the currency of the rural South, and since landlord and merchant would accept rent or extend credit on no other crop, the system produced a surplus which depressed the price and held the tenant in all but perpetual debt. W. E. B. Du Bois reported that of three hundred tenant families in a black belt Georgia county in 1898, seventy-five made an aggregate profit of only $1600, while the remainder ended the year with a total debt of $14,000.[7] For more than half a century after 1865 both the number and the percentage of sharecroppers steadily increased from 30 per cent in 1880 to 61.5 per cent in 1930. V. O. Key attributes the decline of agrarian radicalism in the South after 1900 to the growth of farm tenancy and sharecropping. And it may well be that when a landowner lost his farm and slid into the ranks of tenantry, his intensified poverty caused him to lose hope in the future and interest in public affairs. This diminished the support of the fire-eating radical while at the same time it changed the former landowner into a dependent of his traditional enemy, the banker-merchant.

But depressed prices for the cotton he grew and usurious credit charges were not all the farmer's griefs. A multitude of trusts—in jute-bagging, in cottonseed oil, in tobacco, in fertilizer—held him in thrall. The worst of all trusts were the railroads. These, owned in the North and unregulated at the time by either state or federal government, charged "all the traffic would bear." Even where competing lines existed, they had learned to co-operate in fixing rates, and it was all but universal practice for local rates, where there was only one line, to be higher than through rates. Also, Midwest farmers

(7) *The Souls of Black Folk* (Chicago, 1928), 126.

at this time were benefiting from agricultural colleges and experiment
stations, but the conservative philosophy of "Bourbon" officials toward
anything that smacked of welfare prevented the creation of any of
these advantages for the backward southern farmer.

The southern farmer's anger against those who seemed responsible
for his lowly position grew, and he groped for some means to contend
with the forces holding him in poverty. If he acted sometimes in
an unreasoning and irrational manner, it was because he did not understand the nature of his problem. Oppressed by conditions which he
did not understand and which he could not control, knowing that
something was wrong without a clear understanding of what it might
be, he turned naturally enough to political action.

But efforts of the white farmer to secure political reform were
complicated by the presence of the Negro. The reconstruction constitutions still in force based legislative representation on total population
white and black, even though Negroes either ceased to vote in most
places after redemption or else voted only by leave of white political
bosses. Thus, the great number of Negroes in the black belt counties,
having practically no real voice of their own in political affairs, actually
contributed to the dominance in state politics of planters in the black
belt: men generally responsible for conditions against which the small
farmer railed. Mississippi farmers, for instance, protested in 1881 that
Warren County, with only twice as many white voters as Smith
County, had four times as many legislators; Lowndes County, with
fewer actual voters than Jackson County, had three times as many
legislators; and Washington County, with only a few more voters
than Harrison County, had twice as many legislators. The unfair representation in all cases was due to a large non-voting Negro population.
A decade later, fewer than 45,000 voters in Mississippi's plantation
counties chose sixty-eight legislators, while 71,000 in the white counties
chose only fifty-two. Nor was the inequity a simple controversy between white counties on one hand and black on the other. For most
counties, whether white or black, had reason to complain of the additional representation alloted some neighboring county because of its
Negroes, few if any of whom were voters. Of any two black counties,
or of any two white counties, the one with fewer white voters might
well have more legislators than its neighbor because of a larger non-
voting Negro population. Thus, DeSoto County had 200 more white

voters than Lowndes County in 1890. But Lowndes was given three representatives to DeSoto's two because it had 1000 more Negro residents than DeSoto. The injustice was not confined to representation in the legislature; for the same system was extended to state Democratic nominating conventions, where each county was alloted twice the number of votes it had in the lower house of the legislature.

The system employed in Mississippi applied in general to Alabama, Louisiana, Arkansas, Georgia, South Carolina, and Virginia, and in only a lesser degree to North Carolina, Tennessee, Florida, and Texas. In this way the black counties everywhere possessed more political influence than the number of actual voters entitled them to. White men were given representation in their state legislatures for non-voting Negroes, just as in ante-bellum days they were given federal representation for slaves. But the inequity was even greater in the later period; for representation had been allotted for only three-fifths of the slaves, while the post-bellum freedman was counted as a whole man politically. Thus it was that the plantation counties were able to control the state nominating conventions and to name candidates in August conventions who would win by default in November. And since governors chosen in conventions appointed state judges and many lesser officials, there was considerable truth in the complaint of white county residents everywhere that they were ruled by a small oligarchy in the black counties.

It was Georgia, however, that carried black county control to the extreme. There the state constitution prescribed a county-unit system for election of state officials. Each county was designated a unit vote similar to an electoral vote, and the candidate who received the majority popular vote in the county got its entire unit vote. Successful candidates must win a majority of the state's county-unit vote, or else have the election decided by the legislature. Rural counties with large non-voting Negro populations were given large unit votes in comparison to urban counties. Thus Fulton County (Atlanta) had only six unit votes for 130,000 voters, while Chattahoochie had two unit votes for only 309 voters. "As long as the representation in our Convention remains as it is now," wrote a southern editor in 1881, "a few white men in the Negro counties will name our candidates, and the white counties will have to elect them."[8]

(8) Brandon, Miss., *Republican*, quoted in Jackson *Clarion*, Aug. 4, 1881.

To correct this inequitable condition white farmers in the hills and piney woods agitated for legislative reapportionment and for reform in the convention system of nominating candidates for state offices. But the cards were stacked against the agrarians insofar as reform within their own party was concerned. The small oligarchy controlling the Democratic party in every southern state had no intention of surrendering power to rivals who made no secret of their determination to reverse policies established by the redeemers. In party-rigged conventions everywhere, farmers' advocates heard themselves denounced as "demagogues" when they pleaded for a return to the agrarian-oriented philosophy of the ante-bellum party. Rebuffed and frustrated, they denounced their opponents as "Bourbons" and sought other avenues of wresting control from them.

The first outward manifestation of agrarian discontent was the rash of "Independent" movements, which began to threaten Democratic solidarity about 1880. Often the Independents advocated liberal programs: more money, longer terms, and better pay for teachers in free schools; equal rights and free suffrage for Negroes; programs that were anathema to the orthodox laissez-faire conservatives who were advocating retrenchment both of the economy and of the electorate. If necessary to defeat the Independents, Democrats would not hesitate to resort to bribery, intimidation, or violence. Generally, the dominant party leaders, however, had as tight control over the machinery for conducting general elections as they exercised over nominating conventions. For a state board of election commissioners, composed of the governor and two or three members of his cabinet, appointed county election boards. The county boards appointed registrars and other officials who were the judges of the qualifications of voters presenting themselves at the polls. This made all things possible. The party-dominated election officials could locate voting places close to groups of friendly voters and distant from others. They could refuse registration or throw out any number of opposition votes on technical or fraudulent grounds. They could make false returns or stuff ballot boxes. True, the Republican party was entitled to a representative on the county election commission. But after redemption, the Republican commissioner had first to be approved by the Democratic county committee, and invariably subservient Negroes, "Uncle Toms," were appointed to represent Republicans. Consequently, only in unusual circumstances did the Democrats have to resort to violence.

The Republican party had ceased to be a threat in itself to Democratic rule after redemption, but the rise of Independent movements gave it new hope. For alliances between Independents with a large following of white farmers, and Republicans with Negro support might well challenge any but the strongest of state or local machines. It was only natural that self-interest would draw Independents and Republicans together in alliances against their common enemy, and fusion movements between them became common in the 1880's. Although they generally stood at opposite poles on economic questions, Republicans and agrarian Independents were driven together by corrupt practices of the regular Democratic machine, which stole elections from each of them with complete impartiality. "I am a hard-money national-bank man," wrote an Alabama Republican in 1881 in explanation of the Greenback-Republican fusion. But there were "questions of more vital importance in Southern politics than banking and currency." Among these questions were "fair elections, an honest count, free thought, free speech, free government itself."[9]

As Republican strength in the South waned, the national Republican party encouraged these Independent movements and urged southern Republicans to join in them. Republican Presidents, through generous patronage on the one hand and threats of intervention on the other, sometimes made the fusion movements truly formidable. Greatest success of all Independent ventures was the Readjuster movement in Virginia in the early 1880's. Ex-Confederate General William Mahone captured the legislature in 1879 on a program to "readjust" the state debt, which had grown prodigiously during reconstruction. Soon his faction won the governorship also, and he forced enactment of legislation that favored the poor: more equitable taxes, repeal of the poll tax, liberal appropriations for schools. Mahone had at least partial support of two Republican Presidents, Hayes and Garfield, and the full support of Garfield's successor, Arthur. Mahone's triumph raised hopes in the hearts of reform-minded Democrats in other states who aspired to emulate him. During Arthur's administration Independent movements appeared all over the South, and Republican aspirations grew for splitting southern Democrats and thereby regaining control of the section.

Fusion between Independents and Republicans posed a serious threat to oligarchical control in the southern states, and Democratic

(9) *Harper's Weekly*, XXV (1881), 302-3.

leaders brought out their heaviest artillery against it: the charge that dividing the white vote would lead inevitably to "Negro domination." Even when no threat of "Negro domination" loomed, however, the race question was used as a pretext to guarantee a solid white vote for the Democratic party. Nor did regular Democrats hesitate to make use of Negro voters whenever it suited their purpose, and they frequently put Negroes on local tickets in order to win Negro support for their candidates. James L. Chalmers, a Confederate brigadier and Democratic Congressman from the Mississippi Delta in 1880, refused to follow dictates of the party hierarchy. To discipline him, the Lamar-controlled legislature gerrymandered his district in a grotesque manner, a move that portended Chalmers's defeat in the next election. Thereupon Chalmers went into open rebellion and actually joined the Republican party. He won re-election as a Republican in 1882, but lost in 1884 when Lamar's lieutenants voted a large number of Delta Negroes in the contest against him.

The Independent candidate for governor in Georgia in 1880 charged that Negro ballots had enabled the Democrats to steal the election from him; and in Mississippi, Lamar and George consistently won Negro support by giving minor offices to Negroes. Even so, Democrats always raised the cry of "white supremacy and party regularity" whenever a strong Independent movement threatened their control. And identification of the Republican party with Negro voting during reconstruction struck fear in southern minds that an Independent victory might revive the old radical program. This proved embarrassing to Independents, who soon began to shun fusion with Republicans.

But southern Republican leaders were themselves split on the issue of a "black and tan" party or a "lily-white" one; indeed, many southern Republicans had urged Hayes in 1877 to abandon carpetbaggers and their Negro followers in an effort to make Republicanism respectable. In the years that followed, Republican administrations in Washington supported "black and tans" or "lily-whites" impartially. Chalmers, as a "lily-white" Republican in Mississippi in 1882, had Arthur's full support. But so did Thomas Clingman and J. M. Leach in North Carolina, who led an Independent movement calling for equal rights for all men regardless of color.

The abandonment of the Negro to the mercies of southern whites is a serious reflection on the integrity of national Republican leaders.

It was not, however, as much a reversal of philosophy as of tactics. For the enfranchisement of the Negro in 1867 was itself motivated less by idealism and more by the ambition to build a southern wing to the Republican party which would insure the party control of the national government. Abandonment of the Negro after 1877 aimed merely at the same result by a different route. Thereafter, most northern Republicans as well as Democrats were agreed that the South should be left alone to solve its problems of race.

Arthur's support of any and all Independents marked the high tide of Republican-Independent co-operation, and regular southern Democrats capitalized on this co-operation of their rivals by calling up the bogey of Negro rule whenever the occasion arose. The net result was to so discredit "black and tan" political amalgamation that control of the Republican party was seized by Negroes in many sections. This insured for them the dispensing of federal patronage in their states during the long years of Republican rule in Washington. On the other hand, Democratic leaders, while aiding Negro domination of the Republican party, could raise the cry of race treason against Independents who threatened to split the white vote. As a result, efforts of the national Republican party to "Mahonize" other states than Virginia were torpedoed.

The Independents were thus victorious only in Virginia, although they had been a threat everywhere. For the issues they stood for—readjustment of state debts, an expanded currency, more equitable systems of taxation, equitable division of school funds, opposition to convict leasing, unfair apportionment in party conventions and state legislatures, machine politics with all its evil connotations—were popular everywhere with yeoman farmers. Returning prosperity in the mid-1880's abated the Independent movements for a time. But the prosperity was short-lived, and within a few years renewed depression brought restiveness again to the rural areas in the South as in the rest of the country. While railroads, banks, manufacturing enterprises in towns and cities were experiencing unprecedented prosperity, agriculture was languishing. "There is a screw loose," wrote a North Carolina editor at the time, "the wheels have dropped out of balance."[10]

The cause of this imbalance, farmers now came to believe, was the amorphous, evil monster called the trust: the same trust that had

(10) Quoted in *North Carolina Historical Review*, II (April 1925), 164.

been the target of earlier Independent movements, only now grown stronger and more sinister. The trust controlled prices both of what the farmer sold and what he bought. In the earlier period the most menacing of all trusts had been the railroads. Fear and hatred of these were unabated, but a new monster had arisen to displace them as demons of the first order—the money trust. Knowing even less about the intricacies of finance than about other economic questions, the farmer, nevertheless, was able to see clearly that there was not enough money to do the business of the country, and he was convinced that this inadequacy both depressed the prices he got for his staple and caused interest rates to be unreasonably high. Furthermore, the supply of money was constant, not flexible according to needs of the season. The time of greatest need in the South was when the crop was thrown on the market, and since this came everywhere at the same time, there was not enough money to move the crops at fair prices. Then, too, the hub of the money control system was in the national banks, which made great profits for stockholders out of a government monopoly. Why, the farmers asked, should not the government issue its money directly rather than through these bank trusts, and why the discrimination in Treasury policy against state banks? "The one thing needed in the present condition of the people," said one of their leaders, "is a debt-paying system of finance, in comparison with which all other questions sink into utter insignificance."[11]

As spokesman for the southern farmer there came out of the Southwest in the late 1880's an organization designed to lay the foundation for a concerted agrarian political movement. Formed in Texas in 1875 the National Farmers' Alliance and Co-operative Union grew slowly until it absorbed a similar organization in Louisiana in 1887. Thereafter it swept through the South with remarkable speed. At first eschewing politics, it concentrated on educating farmers to improved methods of agriculture, and it succeeded in persuading legislatures to set up agricultural colleges in several states. It also engaged in co-operative buying and selling ventures, a few of which were successful but most of which were not. By 1890 the Southern Alliance claimed 3,000,000 members, with 1,250,000 others in a Negro affiliate. Except for the segregation of Negroes in the affiliate, the Alliance was remarkably free of class distinctions among agrarians: for planter

(11) *North Carolina Historical Review*, II (April 1925), 167–9.

and tenant made common cause against Wall Street, at least until the gold question came to divide them. Even there, however, the division was not on class lines, for tenants and croppers as a rule followed their old leaders, the "Bourbons," wherever they might lead on this issue, and some planters would advocate "free silver," while an equal number would be "gold bugs."

The Alliance program called for better support for public education, an end of convict leasing, improved roads, government regulation of railroads, repeal of the national bank act, a controlled currency inflation, prohibition of land ownership by aliens, more equitable taxation, and election reform both on the state and national levels. At first the Alliance tried to remain aloof from direct political action, but by 1888 it was throwing its wholehearted support behind legislative candidates pledged to its programs. The following year, under the leadership of Leonidas L. Polk of North Carolina, the Alliance became the dominant influence in the Democratic party in the South, and by 1890 no southern politican dared ignore its wishes. Throughout the section these were written unchanged into party platforms.

Not content with writing platforms, farmers insisted on electing their own kind to office, and a political revolution of a sort took place in the South in the early 1890's as veterans of state legislatures and of Congress were replaced by tillers of the soil. In 1891 the Democratic state convention in Tennessee resolved to "throw off the yoke of Bourbonism" and support farmers' candidates for state and national offices; and that autumn the Tennessee Alliance elected the governor, fourteen of thirty-three state senators, and forty of ninety representatives. Even though its candidate for governor was defeated in Alabama that year, the Alliance elected more than half of Alabama's legislature as well as a United States Senator. In Georgia it elected the governor and more than three-fourths of the legislature and defeated six incumbent Congressmen. In Mississippi it completely controlled the constitutional convention of 1890. In South Carolina it carried the election of Ben Tillman, and in Texas of James S. Hogg. It was no idle boast when a southerner wrote in 1890, "We took possession of the Democratic party."[12]

But some Alliance-elected officials refused to support the more

(12) Woodward, *Origins of the New South*, 201-4; John Ezell, *The South Since 1865* (New York, 1963), 161.

extreme Alliance demands. John B. Gordon, J. Z. George, Ben Tillman, Zebulon Vance, and James S. Hogg all professed support of Alliance platforms, but all refused to support such "radical" schemes as railroad ownership by the federal government, and none of them was enthusiastic about money inflation. Reuben Kolb, Alliance leader in Alabama, actually helped defeat bills in the legislature to increase the railroad commission's power and to reduce freight rates.

Even so, reforms of at least a limited nature followed in the wake of early Alliance victories: establishment of state railway commissions with rate-making power, the outlawing of rebates and unjust discriminations. Railroad property was reappraised, and tax increases imposed. As prosperity failed to follow in the wake of these limited reforms, Alliance men turned to schemes involving money and banking, free coinage of silver at a price above its market value. Most radical of all was their proposal of a "Sub-treasury plan" embodying both commodity credit and a flexible money supply.

These, however, were national programs: if they were to be enacted it must be by the national government. But the northern wing of the Democratic party, anchored in the commercial cities of the North and East, could not be persuaded to support such inflationary and radical schemes. Neither was there hope that the Republican party would do so, for conservative business interests controlled that party's councils, also. Thus it was that Alliance men began to look with favor, somewhat like drowning men clutching at straws, on the idea of a third party: a party which would unite workers whether on the farm or in the factory.

In May 1891, representatives of southern and western farmers, of Union and Confederate veterans' organizations, and of the Knights of Labor gathered at Cincinnati to formally launch the People's party. The Populist program was substantially an extension of that of the Alliance: fair elections, a national graduated income tax, an end to convict leasing, prohibition of child labor, extension of the public school system, lien laws to protect laborers and mechanics instead of only landlords and merchants, good roads, enlargement of powers of railroad commissions, revision of the tax system, a maximum legal rate of interest of 6 per cent, a ten-hour day for workers, expansion of the currency, an end to the money trust, and establishment of the Sub-treasury. The program was designed to appeal to all farmers.

But whereas planters had previously been allied with farmers in the Alliance, they now joined industrial and financial classes in southern towns in opposition to the new party. For with both Populists and Democrats competing for votes, the presence of great numbers of Negroes in their communities raised again for the planters the specter of "Negro domination."

It was generally expected that Leonidas L. Polk of North Carolina would be the Presidential candidate of the Populist party in 1892. Polk was president of the Alliance and one of the guiding spirits of the new party. But Polk died suddenly in June. Thereupon, the party convention at Omaha nominated Union General James B. Weaver of Iowa, who had been the Greenback candidate in 1880. To compensate in the South for Weaver, the convention nominated Confederate General James G. Field of Virginia for Vice President. Populist strategy called for a union of white and Negro farmers in the South and a union of farmers with workers in the cities everywhere. This conflicted with the philosophy of the New South as expounded by Henry Grady and his disciples. Grady's aim was to unite all southern whites into one party and then form an alliance with the financial and industrial powers of the East—in other words, to divide the very groups the Populists were attempting to unite.

Most difficult of all tasks the Populists assigned themselves was the projected union of white farmers with Negroes. This was made even more difficult by the Lodge Force Bill of 1890. The original Constitutional provision counting only three-fifths of the Negro population had been abolished during reconstruction, and thereafter the full Negro population was counted in apportioning representatives in Congress and in fixing a state's electoral vote for President. With the great decline in Negro voting after redemption, it was seen that the new apportionment proved a windfall to southern Democrats, whose representation in Congress was increased significantly. Furthermore, it was noted that with the decline in southern voting, southern Congressmen were generally chosen by a small fraction of the number voting in nothern Congressional elections. To terminate this inequity, Congressman Henry Cabot Lodge, in June 1890, introduced a bill calling for supervision of Congressional elections by federal supervisors who could control registration and decide disputed returns. The bill drove almost all southern whites together against the principle of federal interference in elections. The bill was defeated in January 1891, but it was unforgotten in the South for many years.

In the election of 1892 Democratic bosses throughout the southern black belt used Negroes to help defeat Populists, transporting the blacks from polling place to polling place, even across state lines, and voting them again and again. Subservient Negro orators were induced to urge their followers to vote Democratic. Even so, the Populists showed surprising strength. It was claimed that they actually polled a majority of votes in Alabama and Virginia; but a combination of violence, chicanery, and the clever manipulation of the Negro vote resulted in Democratic victory everywhere. In no state did the returns show a Populist vote of more than 37 per cent.

But the Populists were not discouraged, and they looked to the future with optimism. Distress caused by the Panic of 1893 added to their hopes, for Cleveland's refusal to favor relief measures brought the Democratic party in the South to its lowest ebb since the War. Local and state elections in 1894 found Populists reviving old fusion practices, as they co-operated with Republicans against the violence and corruption of local Democratic machines. The result that year was a significant gain for the Populists. Returns gave the party 44 per cent of the vote in Georgia, where it was probably defeated only by fraud. It actually elected Reuben Kolb governor of Alabama, only to have him counted out, and it won undisputed control in North Carolina by a majority of twenty thousand.

But 1894 would be high tide for the party, whose former bright prospects were now marred by a division within the Democratic party over the silver coinage question. Two irreconcilable leaders, Bryan and Cleveland, were contending for control of the Democratic party, with the South as the chief battleground. It would be one of the great battles of American political history, a contest between those favoring traditional economic and financial policies and those advocating more direct action on the part of government in the welfare of the people.

The silver forces won control of the Democratic national convention in 1896 and nominated Bryan for President. More important, the platform committed the party to free coinage of silver at $20.67 an ounce, a price considerably above the market, as well as to other reforms advocated by the Populists. Adoption of much of its program by the Democrats doomed the Populist party especially in the South. The decision to leave the Democratic party was a soul-searing one for the southerner to make, even when that party was led nationally by conservative easterners like Cleveland who did not understand or sympathize with the farmer's plight. In their neighbors' eyes such deserters were traitors to their region, apostates who would call back the horrors of reconstruction days just to win a new economic order of uncertain merit. But to leave the party of their fathers when that party had been captured by a leader of their own faction was doubly hard.

The demoralized Populists, meeting in convention at St. Louis, accepted Bryan as their candidate for President and then proceeded to nominate Tom Watson for Vice President. Heretofore, Populists in the South had urged fusion with Republicans in state elections. Now they were called on to fuse with Democrats nationally, a fusion repugnant to Negroes, upon whose support southern Populists had counted. Faced with these contradictory conditions the large Populist vote of 1892 and 1894 melted away, as the Democrats carried every state for Bryan. Only in North Carolina did the Populists win even local control. There, in a maneuver called the ultimate in political dexterity, the Populists endorsed Bryan, a Democrat, for President, an avowed Populist for governor, and fused with Republicans for other state offices. They won on all three fronts. Even in North Carolina, however, their victory was transitory, for Republican ascendancy revived unpleasant memories of reconstruction, and Democrats soon drove them from power.

Within a few years the Populist party was no more. Its brief surge, however, had shaken the Democratic party in the South to its foundation, and that party would never again be quite the same. Already a captive of the Alliance, the Democratic party managed to survive the Populist challenge in the South only at the cost of adopting the progressive program of the Populists. In state after state, laws they had advocated were passed after the party demise. But Populism did more than this: it created a cleavage in the Democratic party that would have lasting effects. It brought the downfall of the "Bourbons," as many of the old conservatives went into political retirement. A few of the more radical white Populists went into the Socialist party, but the great mass returned to the Democracy where they

added strength to the progressive wing. A few Negro members returned to the Republican party, now largely controlled by lily-whites
but most lost interest in politics altogether. They turned instead to
church, business, or fraternal organizations as outlets for their social
energies, vainly hoping that self-improvement through these agencies
might bring them into the main southern cultural stream.

But if Populism was the parent of progressivism in the South,
it also fostered a reaction in racial relations. The prospect of union
of Negroes and white yeomen farmers posed by the successive agrarian
movements had long aroused a profound fear in the hearts of the
conservatives. Populism had increased this fear to a frenzy. "The accident of color can make no difference in the interests of farmers, croppers, and laborers," said Tom Watson. "You are kept apart that you
may be separately fleeced of your earnings."[13] But the corrupt use
of the Negro vote by conservative leaders in the plantation counties
to bring about the defeat of the agrarians caused the farmers to turn
against the Negro. And black belt planters, eager to close the breach
in white unity, were willing to make some accommodation. The result
after the 1890's was a solid front of yeoman and planter dedicated
to the removal of the Negro once and for all from political participation. Once more, as during reconstruction, the race question became
an issue which transcended in importance all others. Once more,
farmers with grievances against the oligarchy that governed them
could be prevailed upon to support the Democratic party, provided
that Negro votes no longer were used to frustrate them.

Since the end of reconstruction, Negroes had suffered disfranchisement by illegal means—intimidation, violence, fraud. These practices
were clearly in violation of the Fourteenth and Fifteenth Amendments
and if continued threatened the South with loss of representation in
Congress and even with federal intervention. More disturbing to the
southern conscience, it was obvious that fraudulent election practices,
unless checked, would pollute the very sources of representative government. A prominent Democrat said on the floor of the Mississippi
constitutional convention in 1890: "It is no secret that there has not
been a full vote and a fair count in Mississippi since 1875—that we
have been preserving the ascendency of the white people by revolu-

(13) Thomas E. Watson, "The Negro Question in the South," *Arena,* VI
(1892), 541-8, quoted in Woodward, *Origins of the New South,* 257.

tionary methods. In plain words we have been stuffing the ballot boxes, committing perjury, and here and there in the state carrying the elections by fraud and violence until the whole machinery for election was about to rot down." The president of the convention agreed. "Besides the exercise of force," said S. S. Calhoon, "there was also brought into use fraud in the manipulation of ballot boxes . . . and it unfortunately became chronic. It began to be used as between the whites themselves."[14]

But fear of "Negro domination" was not the sole inspiration of legal disfranchisement. Side by side with it was the desire of voters in white sections to curtail the over-representation given the plantation counties for their non-voting Negroes. Not to be overlooked, too, was a genuine desire for democratic reforms—popular elections of judges, more equitable distribution of school funds, elimination of convict leasing, restrictions on monopolistic powers of corporations.

The first state to perfect a system of legal disfranchisement of the Negro was Mississippi. There in 1890 a convention adopted a scheme whose complex features would soon disqualify almost all Negroes and not a few whites. Within a dozen years all southern states had adopted the Mississsippi Plan with slight variations. Two years' residence in the state was a general requirement, as was also the poll tax, which had to be paid from four to nine months prior to the election. Conviction on any of a long list of crimes thought to be characteristic of the Negro would also disqualify a voter. North Carolina, South Carolina, Georgia, Alabama, Mississippi, Louisiana, and Virginia required all applicants to pass a literacy test. Most provided an escape for illiterate whites by either an "understanding" or else a "grandfather" clause. In the former, the applicant had to explain to the satisfaction of the voting registrar questions pertaining to the federal and state constitutions. The latter permitted those qualified to vote on January 1, 1867, together with their sons and grandsons, to vote despite illiteracy. Since no Negroes were eligible to vote at that time, none of them could qualify under the grandfather clause, while practically all whites could.

There was considerable opposition to the basic principle of disfranchisement, not only from illiterate whites, but from some who were both highly literate and financially solvent. The opposition was

(14) Jackson *Daily Clarion-Ledger*, Sept. 11, Nov. 1, 1890.

strongest in the hill and piney woods counties, where there were few Negroes. These were the same areas which had been least enthusiastic about secession and the Confederacy a generation earlier. Leaders of the disfranchisement movement were generally conservatives of the black belt who made impassioned appeals to their brothers in the white counties, appeals often with a hollow ring. "South Alabama raises her manacled hands in mute appeal to the mountain counties," wrote the Montgomery *Advertiser* during the constitutional convention of 1901. "The chains on the wrists of her sons, and the midnight shrieks of her women, sound continually in their ears. . . . Is there a white man in North Alabama so lost to all his finer feelings of human nature as to slight her appeal?"[15] The fact that the calling of the Alabama convention and the ratification of the resulting disfranchisement constitution were both carried by the overwhelming vote that poured in from the black belt, a vote many times more numerous than white voters there could legitimately account for, completely discredited the sincerity of the *Advertiser*.

In South Carolina and Georgia disfranchisement was accomplished without the co-operation of conservative leaders. Ben Tillman captured the Democratic party in South Carolina in 1890, and because his conservative opponent attempted to use Negro votes to defeat him he sponsored a constitutional convention to disfranchise the Negro. All through the period and well into the twentieth century, Negroes outnumbered whites, and the state was preoccupied with the prospect of "Negro domination" if Negro voting should become general and uninhibited. It was an issue which overshadowed all others. Even upcountry white followers of Tillman, however, were reluctant to support a movement which might be used to disfranchise themselves. Many of them joined Negroes and conservative whites in opposing the convention, and they all but mustered a majority against it. In Georgia, too, in 1906, disfranchisement was sparked by independent Democrats from the hill country with the help of Tom Watson. Together they elected governor an anti-corporation lawyer, Hoke Smith, on a disfranchisement platform.

The disfranchising conventions actually changed little for the Negro. They merely legitimatized practices which had prevailed

(15) Joseph H. Taylor, "Populism and Disfranchisement in Alabama," in *Journal of Negro History, XXXIV* (Oct. 1949), 410–27.

everywhere since the end of reconstruction. The new rules would not bring an absolute end to Negro voting, although they would greatly reduce the number of legally registered Negro voters. There were 147,000 Negro men, 37,000 of them literate, in Mississippi when the new voting rolls were made in 1892; but only 8600 of them were registered, and only 1500 voted for Benjamin Harrison that year. In like manner, Louisiana had 127,000 Negro men at the time of her disfranchising convention, but only 7000 of them registered. Alabama, with 130,000 Negro men, registered only 5000, and comparable results were obtained in other states. Notwithstanding the new regulations, however, unregistered Negroes would be permitted to vote in future as in past elections whenever interests of politicians dictated. A Mississippi editor "shamefully confessed" a decade after Mississippi's disfranchising constitution that Negroes were still voting freely there and that their vote was sometimes decisive. To add to the editor's humiliation, not only "democratic negroes" but also "republican negroes" were permitted to vote. But the voting had been in a Democratic primary, so at least the "republican negroes" had voted for a Democrat, even if not for the editor's choice.[16]

The Negro, then, would continue to vote in local and state elections whenever his vote was needed by those in control. He would cease to vote Republican, however, for two reasons. First, the reaction to Populism united practically all whites for a time, and the Republican party ceased to be a factor of any significance in the states of the deep South; while in the states of the upper South the Republican strongholds were in districts with few Negroes. Second, as we have noted, the Republican party nationally as well as in the South adopted a lily-white policy at the turn of the century; and the Negro despaired of working his political salvation through it. Mississippi Republicans, for instance, had cast 52,000 votes for Blaine in 1884, but could muster only 1500 ballots for Harrison in 1892, even though there were 8000 registered Negro voters in the state at the time. Thus, the Negro ceased to be a direct factor in southern politics at about the time of the disfranchising conventions, not just because of requirements written into the constitutions which many Negroes could not meet, but even more because there was no party in the South around which he might rally.

(16) Greenwood, Mississippi, *Commonwealth*, July 14, 1899.

But if the Negro ceased to exercise direct influence on southern politics after the disfranchisement conventions, indirectly he became the dominant influence. For his presence in the wings was a constant threat to "white supremacy" and ever since has largely inspired the extraordinary behavior of the white electorate. Equally important, the multiple-loaded franchise laws which disqualified him also struck from the rolls hundreds of thousands of whites. There were 120,000 qualified white voters in Mississippi in 1890, but only 68,000 were enrolled in the registration of 1892. More than 85,000 votes had been cast in the state for Cleveland in 1888, but he could garner only 40,000 supporters four years later. Despite Louisiana's grandfather clause, 80,000 whites fell from the registration lists of that state in the six years after her disfranchisement constitution became effective. In Virginia, the vote was cut in half in the first election after adoption of her disfranchising clauses. Negroes could account for only a small part of this decline, for they constituted only a third of the state's population, and it was well known that all but a few had ceased to vote prior to the disfranchising convention of 1901.

Although it had been generally promised that no white man would be excluded by the new constitutions, all whites were not in accord with that policy. "There are some white men," said the Alabama governor in 1901, "who have no more right and no more business to vote than a negro and not as much as some of them." A tidewater Virginian at his state convention admitted it was "not the negro vote which works the harm," but "the depraved and incompetent men of our own race." The editor of the New Orleans *Times-Democrat* wrote that all tests "must be applied with equal rigor in the case of poor or illiterate whites as in the case of poor or illiterate Negroes." The Charlotte, North Carolina, *Observer* said the disfranchisement movement in that state revolved around "the struggle of the white people . . . to rid themselves of the dangers of the rule of negroes and the lower class of whites."[17]

Whether or not the various devices, particularly the poll tax, were designed to disfranchise poor whites as well as Negroes is thus debatable, but the effect was not. The sharp reduction in voting that followed immediately after instituting the tax would continue. In 1942 it was estimated that well over eleven million voters in the eight south-

(17) Quoted in Woodward, *Origins of the New South*, 328–31.

ern states which retained the poll tax at that time were disfranchised through this requirement alone and that more than seven million of this number were whites. Voting participation in the nation that year was eight times as great in non-poll tax states as in those where the tax was a prerequisite.

That the poll tax would discourage white as well as Negro voters, however, is understandable. Cash incomes of southern farmers was notoriously low. A federal government report in 1938 revealed that sharecroppers earned from $38 to $86 annually, and even this sum often was expropriated by the lien-holding storekeeper without the farmer ever touching it. In most states the annual two dollar tax was cumulative for a number of years, in Alabama for the entire period between ages eighteen and forty-five; so that if the voter fell behind, the tax might be prohibitive. In addition, the tax had to be paid months before the election, before issues or candidates were known. This was "like buying a ticket to a show . . . months ahead of time and before you know who is playing or really what the thing is all about. It is easy to forget to do."[18]

The new constitutions resulted not only in the reduction of the electorate, they also continued the inequitable apportionment of legislative districts based on total population, white and black, even though it was universally understood that the Negro had long ceased to be an independent voter. Thus in Alabama, even though some reform in apportionment was effected in the 1901 constitution, twenty-one plantation counties with fewer than 190,000 whites were given thirty-nine representatives in the legislature, while three times as many whites in north Alabama counties were allotted only forty-five representatives. And a small minority of white voters in black counties in Mississippi after 1890 chose sixty-nine legislators, while the large majority who lived in the white counties chose only sixty-four.

As a result of the disfranchising conventions, a myth has grown that elimination of the Negro from voting in the South has had a purifying effect on the politics of the region. Nothing could be farther from the truth, for the record reveals as much debauchery, violence, and corruption since the conventions as before. A carload of firearms and fifty thousand rounds of ammunition were shipped into North

(18) George S. Stoney, "Suffrage in the South, Part I, The Poll Tax," in *Survey Graphic*, XXIX (1940), 4, 8–9.

Carolina from Richmond on the eve of the election of 1898. In Wilmington that year a mob led by a former Congressman fired a Negro newspaper office, killed eleven Negroes, and wounded many others. In Atlanta, for days following white supremacy elections there, mobs looted, lynched, and murdered. In South Carolina, three years after the disfranchising restrictions became effective, a dozen Negroes were killed in an election near Tillman's Edgefield district. In New Orleans two years after Louisiana's disfranchisement convention, white mobs roamed the streets, killing Negroes, looting, and burning. After a state-wide Democratic primary in Mississippi in 1899 a leading Democratic editor doubted if any of the officials chosen had "a really honest title to the offices which they are now holding." Prior to that election a professional ballot-box stuffer, willing to sell to either Democratic faction, wrote the governor of the state: "I will carry any box for you but you must assist me. . . . You understand what I mean. You write me what you will be willing to pay to carry a box." In some Mississippi counties election returns were reported where no election had been held; in others, votes recorded exceeded the total number of eligible voters. The leading Democratic paper in the state charged there had been "more swindlings and cheatings and ballot box stuffings" in 1899 than in all the years before.[19] Widespread election frauds in Alabama in 1897 caused the editor of the *Nation* to conclude that representative government had ceased to exist in the state. Cheating, he concluded, had become the rule, and it had spread far indeed from its original object, the Negro.

It was thought, too, that legal elimination of the Negro from active political participation would stimulate political activity among whites, who could then divide their votes in safety. Instead, the whites accepted their new security as an end in itself and proceeded to take far less interest in elections than before, when the Negro had always been a potential voter and sometimes a real one. The result was a surrender to party absolutism which produced an even tighter oligarchy than had existed before. Protest movements became extremely difficult to launch, for only within the Democratic party was there room for disagreement.

Elimination of the Negro from voting and establishment of the one-party system also had the effect of disfranchising to a high degree

(19) Vicksburg *Post,* quoted in Jackson *Weekly Clarion-Ledger,* Jan. 2, 1902.

the entire South in national politics. For on the national stage the Democrats could count on the South, and the Republicans had written it off. Henceforth, southerners had to vote en masse as whites, and this deprived them of individual political freedom. Over the years an understanding developed between southerners and northerners of both parties whereby the southerners renounced ambitions for national leadership in return for northern consent to disregard the provisions of the Fourteenth and Fifteenth Amendments. This gave the white southern oligarchy complete control on the state level, and they managed to keep it by legal and extra-legal disfranchisement of lower-class whites as well as Negroes.

In an effort to preserve this archaic system, therefore, the South dealt much injury to itself. Whether it was because he could not vote, or else in order to keep him from qualifying for the ballot, the Negro's education was sadly neglected. This resulted in a large population of illiterate or poorly educated people and kept the South impoverished and provincial. It also caused the South to use her energies in negative and unproductive efforts: in a frustrating struggle against the better instincts of the nation and the spirit of the age. It made the southerner peculiarly vulnerable to the emotional appeal of the racist, who never ceased to assail him either from the right or the left in the years to come.

The fact that the South succeeded for so long a time in preserving this political system against great opposition reflected the political skill and shrewdness of the white leaders in the black counties. First, by raising the myth of "Negro domination" they persuaded the white farmers concentrated in the hill and piney woods counties to put down the radical movements of Independents and Populists which were clearly working to the white farmer's advantage. Then, in order to present a solid front on the race issue, they foisted on the same people a scheme which would disfranchise half their own number. In these two maneuvers they achieved a victory which has few parallels in the struggle of minorities to preserve their own interests. Professor V. O. Key called it "the fundamental explanation of southern politics."[20]

(20) *Southern Politics* (New York, 1949), 11.

⪼ IV ⪻

Farmers on the Land

Whatever political and economic uncertainties faced the South in that dark April 1865, one thing was clear: farming was an occupation to which veterans of the war and ex-slaves could return with some assurance that they could earn a meager livelihood. No general statement could adequately describe conditions prevailing across the war-torn regions. In many areas, fields were gashed and leached by erosion, or matted with briars, scrub pines, and sassafras bushes. Fences, so necessary to keep animals away from growing crops, were rotted away, or had been burned as firewood. Livestock had strayed away or had been stolen and killed. Farm buildings showed the ravages of four years of neglect, if in fact they were still standing. Few men in the history of modern warfare ever returned to less promising scenes than did those ragged men who straggled home that desolate spring after Appomattox. They came back to pick up the pieces, to start their lives anew on the soil.

Contemporary observers and historians alike have published voluminous materials dealing with southern agriculture in the immediate post-Civil War years. Southerners were highly uncertain immediately after the war as to where their region stood. Cotton statistics, for instance, were unreliable and contradictory. Reporters in *DeBow's Review* attempted to determine the supply of cotton on hand, and to find out how much of the staple grown during the war years remained in farmer hands. Even more difficult was the making of crop predictions for the immediate growing season of 1865; labor efficiency had dropped to an unpredictably low level, and no one knew whether or not the new crop would be properly cultivated and harvested. The Atkinson cotton service and, much later, M. B. Hammond gave evidence of the lack of reliable information.

With something approaching anxiety southerners attempted to determine if cotton would recover its central place in regional agricultural production. Hammond was convinced that

> had the price of cotton been low in 1865–1866, the revival of the farming of the South would doubtless have been less rapid, but it probably would have taken a different direction, leading to the production of larger food crops and a more moderate increase in the production of cotton, and would thus have prevented many farmers from falling into that state of peonage to factors and merchants in which the majority of cotton growers are to-day to be found.

As much confusion prevailed in efforts to determine grain production and the number of head of livestock left on the farms. Deficits in food crops were as contributory to a state of peonage as cotton. The future of southern farming thus was clouded not only by disruptions of war and the revolution of the labor supply, but likewise by vast changes which occurred in agriculture in the rest of the nation and abroad. In viewing the future of southern farming from the perspective of 1865, a modern historian has reason to be severely critical of contemporary farmers who failed accurately to assess the promise of southern soil. Cotton myopia still blinded farmer, editor, traveler, and merchant alike. They believed that the staple would quickly fulfill its economic promise of regional crop supremacy for little and big farmers alike and they were anxious to bring annual production back to the level of 1860 as quickly as possible. This, however, was not to be realized until 1879.

Postwar faith in cotton was strengthened by high prices. There were, however, mitigating circumstances in the years immediately ahead which had not prevailed in quite the same form in 1850 and 1860. Lack of financial credit, displacement of labor supply, the limited understanding both of land capability and of the cotton plant, inadequate transportation facilities, competition from expanding American cotton fields and from cotton-growing regions elsewhere in the world, bore heavily upon the future of southern staple agriculture. Despite these problems there were positive conditions to be considered: Much of the cotton-growing South was abundantly blessed with fertile mineral soil, or with soil which could be made readily productive by application of chemical fertilizer. Rainfall was ample; no sharp extremes of temperature wrought major damage, and, most important of all, growing seasons were long and conducive to almost unlimited diversification of crops. Few, if any, other areas in the Union offered so great a combination of assets.

The challenge, however, of diversifying agriculture in the years following the Civil War was too great. It took long-range planning, calm-headedness and ingenuity, and efficiency well beyond that required for mere routine cultivation of a traditional staple. These were challenges which masses of southern farmers were intellectually and financially unprepared to meet. In an eloquent summary of conditions in the South in 1881, Henry W. Grady observed:

> In the cultivation and handling, under the new order of things, of the world's greatest staple, cotton, she [the South] is grappling with a matter that involves essentially her own welfare, and is of the greatest interest to the general public. To the slave-holder growing cotton was straight and easy, as the product of his land was supplemented by the increase of his slaves and he prospered in spite of himself. To the southern farmer of *post bellum* days, impoverished, unsettled, and thrown upon free labor, working feverishly with untried conditions, poorly informed as to the result of experiments made by his neighbors, and too impatient to wait upon his own experience, it is quite a different affair. After sixteen years of trial, everything is yet indeterminate. And whether this staple is cultivated in the South as a profit or a passion, and whether it shall bring the South to independence or to beggary, are matters yet to be settled. Whether its culture shall result in a host of croppers without money or credit, appealing to the granaries of the West against famine, paying toll to usurers at home, and mortgaging their crops to speculators abroad even before it was planted—a planting oligarchy of money-lenders, who have usurped the land through foreclosure, and hold by the ever-growing margin between a grasping lender and an enforced borrower—or a prosperous self-respecting race of small farmers, cultivating their own lands, living upon their own resources, controlling their crops until they are sold, and independent alike of usurers and provision-brokers—which of these shall be the outcome of cotton culture the future must determine.

The future did determine these issues in a highly negative way, and with social disaster.

Much has been made of the destruction of property on the southern farms during the war, but the fact that the average farmer had not kept abreast of technological improvements in farming and that there was no home capital with which to purchase tools and supplies to do so proved far more significant. In the long and gloomy period 1865-95, most cotton farmers worked with implements that were as primitive as those in use in the Balkans and India. Implements were too light and inefficient to permit more than the shallowest cultivation, and too clumsy to increase efficiency of farming in any way. In addition, the more modern sciences of soil chemistry, plant-breeding, and revised methods of cultivation remained both unknown and untried at the level of the small farmer, white and Negro alike. Unhappily the legacy of prewar cotton culture, with its wastage of land and its dependence on slavery, greatly affected the approach to famine. The Negro farmer has been severely criticized by southern agricultural historians of the latter quarter of the nineteenth century. Charles H. Otken of Mississippi, exhibiting a sharp racial bias, wrote:

> Their work today is inferior. It has depreciated in quantity and quality. When supervised, their work is entirely under their own control, it is very poor. It takes an average of two negroes of the old class to do as much as one did formerly, three of the class of young men to do the work that one did in a former period, and five women of this latter class to do the work of one in past time. There are worthy exceptions in these groups, but they are few. The equation resulting from the character of this labor may thus be expressed: the work of three negroes in 1860 equals the work of ten negroes in 1890. The result is equivalent to this: that if three do their full quota of reasonable work, seven are idle.

Otken apparently refused to recognize that during these years the rate of white tenancy was gaining an ascendancy. In his tables Matthew B. Hammond indicated that white tenancy was greater than Negro sharecropping. This author excused planter and tenants for their failures to adopt better means of cultivation. Negroes, he said, were accustomed to the old routine of cotton planting and were more reluctant to learn another. A lack of capital discouraged farmers from trying new methods of production. A plentiful supply of fresh land still permitted farmers to be wasteful of that precious resource already under cultivation. Finally, merchants had perhaps more say over what large numbers of planters grew than did farmers themselves. Effective agricultural education for the South was still a long way in the future, and there was so little communication among masses of farmers that even results of experimentation went unnoticed. A high rate of illiteracy prevented both white and Negro farmers from reading about new methods of farming or from learning about discoveries that could result from experimentation, even if these facts had been well published.

There remained the fact that for at least two decades following the Civil War the South was still frontier country. Despite emphasis which historians have placed upon the history of ante-bellum agriculture, vast areas of the region's landed domain remained untouched. The U.S. Commissioner of Agriculture reported in 1866 that approximately 300,000,000 acres were unimproved, less than 75,900,000 acres were only nominally improved, and only 13 per cent of the entire acreage open to cultivation. Not more than 5 per cent of this available land was cultivated annually. The editor of *DeBow's Review* observed in July 1866, "The primitive forests still cover the large part of the vast extent of land, the average density of the white population being a little over ten to the square mile."

At the outset of the new era in the South, its people sought immigrants, both northern and European, to come into the region. *DeBow's Review* carried much promotional material inviting exploitation of southern lands, and so did the weekly and daily newspapers. Immigrant associations were organized among the states, and bales of pamphlets, handbooks, statistics, and folders on all the states were sent North and abroad. Newspaper editors were diligent in their campaigns, because they believed that by successfully opening most of the land to cultivation, southern economy would be brought to a prosperous state. Too, they hoped to replace the Negro with thrifty Yankee and European farmers.

Conversely, there were other manifestations of the lack of labor and capital necessary to bring southern lands to maximum farming capacity. For instance, the advertisements of W. T. Withers of Jackson, Mississippi, in 1867 in *DeBow's Review* listed eighty-one plantations located in Louisiana and Mississippi for sale. In nearly every individual description of a plantation it was said that from half to two-thirds of the land was still under forest cover. Thus it must be considered that large areas of the South did not suffer nearly so much from war damages as from lack of capital to remove the heavy forest cover. This required a tremendous expenditure of energy to prepare for plow and hoe. Losses of slave labor, and of much white labor by attrition of battle and disease, struck a hard blow at the agricultural economy. There was no help from other sources, either, for foreign immigrants gave only a limited response to the states' propaganda campaign, and too few northerners came South. Native laborers, especially ex-slaves, were said to be no more than 50 per cent as efficient as they were in 1860.

On October 24, 1867, the editor of the Columbus (Georgia) *Enquirer* called upon fellow southerners to face the fact that conditions of life in the South were severely altered. This was especially true on the farm. He said:

> These we conceive to be the great essentials necessary to successful planting in the South under the free labor system, we of the South will have to act, in regard to the things, as the whole free labor world has and does still act, to succeed in making money by farming.
>
> First, then, economy is necessary. We must no longer expect to have thousands as the proceeds of our crops to spend extravagantly in dress, fine equipages, traveling at the North and in Europe, visiting watering places, etc.; to raise our children luxuriously, in idleness, and teach them, in too many instances, practices and habits that will unfit them for usefulness in society, in after life; but for years to come we must expect to husband our resources, buy but little, and only what we are compelled to have, and cannot raise or make. If we have no money to buy fine clothes, and carriages, and other fine things, and nothing to barter for them that is our own and can be spared, go without, until we have means to spare; do not go into debt unless it is to keep from actual suffering. Learn economy in all things; it may be a hard lesson for many of us to learn, but one we must learn, and that in the strictest sense, if we ever rise from the low estate of prosperity in which the war has left us. Humility is the royal road to exaltation. So surely is economy the first step to plenty and independence.

This editor set the theme for the region's comment on farming for the next three-quarters of a century. Though there was keen appreciation of changes which intervening years wrought, the admonition to stay out of debt was indeed whistling in an economic dark. Already individual farmers were becoming head over heels in debt. In 1866 some form of reasonable, readily available farm credit was an absolute necessity. Southern banks were few in number, and had too limited capital resources to meet more than a token part of the demand for credit. Even if banks had possessed capital funds to make loans, the capability of farmers to contract sound notes and to give assurances of their repayment was almost nil. Only the most reckless financier would have accepted lightly secured open-note loans from white and Negro tenants between 1865 and 1935. Yet agriculture in the South could survive only if some means of credit-granting could be geared to the uncertainties of small farm operation. On December 5, 1866, the General Assembly of Georgia enacted an agricultural lien law devised to protect landlords against the default of tenants, especially the new freedmen. Landlords and merchants were permitted to take liens against their tenants' crops to be planted during the forthcoming year.

The Georgia law was adopted in one form or another by other southern legislatures. Enactment of lien laws opened a new and highly devitalizing era of southern farm economics. One immediate result was the establishment of hundreds of small town and crossroads furnishing stores. If cotton growers needed further assurance of restoration of their staple in southern agriculture, the adoption of the lien laws was such a guarantee.

Lien laws and crossroads merchandising were inseparable parts of postwar southern agriculture. The new laws in fact only legalized the old system of credit through factors who supplied plantation owners prior to 1860, and country furnishing merchants in large part took up where the factors left off. Now they were near their customers, and served big and little farmers alike. Country stores became supply, marketing, and credit-granting agencies. Prior to 1920 major portions of agricultural credit in many areas were supplied by furnishing merchants.

Banking facilities in the South were severely limited. In 1870 there were 36 national banks in Virginia, North Carolina, South Carolina, and Louisiana with a combined capital of $7 million. In 1895 there were 417 national banks in the ex-Confederate states, with 214 of these in Texas. Georgia had 15 national banks in 1884 and 27 in 1894. For the same period there were 118 state banks located in 66 countries, while 123 counties had no banking facilities whatsoever. In more specific human terms there was one bank for every 58,130 southerners, as compared with one for each 16,000 in the nation. By 1905 there were 477 national banks in the old Confederacy, and capital assets had increased to more than $50 million, but this was still far too limited to permit major farm financing.

Small farmers and tenants were denied access to banking services not only because they lacked funds but because it was highly uncertain whether they could produce a proper return on their investment. Thus the furnishing merchants, living close to the soil, became substitute bankers. Functioning in an economy where cash wages were practically unknown, or extremely low if paid at all, and where farmers themselves saw little if any cash from one year to the next, merchants became experts on local farming conditions. Their stores, because of the diversity of their merchandise, and their functions as community centers, bore a kinship to the New England and midwestern country stores, but here the similarity ceased. By granting credit on lien notes, merchants became virtual overlords of their patrons' economic and social lives. Cotton, tobacco, and rice were cash crops which could be grown with some predictability by means of the most primitive modes of cultivation. Each of these commodities could be disposed of through an established regional market and handled successfully by the primitive transportation and warehousing systems.

Once a farmer signed a lien note he guaranteed to a merchant that he would plant enough of a cash crop to redeem his note at the year's end, and would deliver to his creditor the harvest of his fields. The merchant in turn delivered merchandise in small weekly amounts, depending upon the industry of the customer and his crop prospects. Critics of this system have freely condemned the merchant and his practice of charging excess prices, but they have overlooked the fact that it was not unusual for landlords to serve as middlemen between their tenants and merchants, and they also collected tribute from the tenants' incomes. Before a merchant would accept the note of a sharecropper or independent farmer, he demanded to know how much land he proposed to cultivate, what kind of work stock he had, how much labor force he had in his family, and whether he was a good worker. During the growing season creditors kept close watch over farming activities of their debtors, often riding through fields on inspection trips. At harvest time they purchased cotton for city brokers and forwarded it to warehouses and textile mills. There is no doubt that southern furnishing merchants were more influential than southern farmers, not only in perpetrating the evils of the one-crop system, but likewise in creating many of its more permanent abuses.

Merchants have been charged with all sorts of sharp practices. Among these were charging excessive prices for inferior merchandise, exacting usurious interest rates, dishonest bookkeeping and blocking agricultural progress. Some merchants were guilty of all these things. Nevertheless there were risks connected with a business that depended upon the frailties of ignorant human beings, the weather, and the uncertainties of national and world markets. Merchants, however, must share a preponderance of blame for this evil system. They and their customers were directly accountable for the shameless abuses of the soil. As agents for fertilizer companies, they sold ineffectual chemicals which only drive farmers deeper into debt and caused them to wreck their land. If the merchant sold high, he bought farm products at the lowest possible prices. The market seasons for cotton and tobacco came at the time when everybody was selling, and prices were at their lowest annual levels.

Yet after the criticism is made against the system it is a certainty that the cotton-oriented South after 1865 could not have carried on as well as it did without it. True, under the system millions of acres of land were farmed to absolute exhaustion. Erosion and soil wastage were high crimes which robbed the region of more wealth than a half-dozen Yankee armies marching to the sea. The higher cost, however, was reckoned in shabby homes, dilapidated farm buildings, worn and rusty implements, and the insufferable drabness of southern farm life itself. An examination of store records reveals discriminatory price structures, even though it is difficult to distinguish clearly between grades of merchandise sold.

There was a staggering mark-up in the price of goods to be sold to doubtful credit risks, and low-risk customers were penalized to make up the deficits. Losses always resulted from crop failures, disrupted family life, death, and tenants moving away in the midst of crop seasons. Interest rates were high, and were reckoned on an annual basis on notes, though merchandise was delivered throughout the year. Charles H. Otken observed in 1893:

> The cost of supplies on the time basis cripples the southern farmer. Whatever else may be fiction, this is history from 1865–1893. What is this credit cost above the cash cost? The evidence shows that

it is from *twenty-five to one hundred per cent* above a fair cash valuation. Some of the most successful and competent business men in the South contend that merchandise in the country stores and towns cannot be sold for cash at a profit less than twenty-five per cent. The credit cost to the customer ranges thus from fifty to one hundred and twenty-five percent.

A general charge against merchants seems not to have been made; there is little or no indication in their records that they willfully falsified accounts or manipulated bookkeeping to add further burden to their customers. There was a considerable amount of highly informal bookkeeping and record-keeping, but the merchant lost because of this as often as he gained.

The sinful mark of the primitive credit and furnishing system under the lien laws lay deep across the land. It was also revealed in illiteracy tables fattened by limited educational opportunities. Even history and religion reflected the evils of the lien laws and their self-perpetuating poverty. No more pertinent criticism was made of this system than by Benjamin R. Tillman when he spoke before the first meeting of the South Carolina Farmers Association on April 30, 1886:

> I discovered that not only "I do not know how to farm," but that very few of us in the hilly part of South Carolina do. We are land butchers, not farmers. We are overseers far worse than Irish landlords, and the Negroes are eating us out of house and home, while we follow the old ante bellum system, and strive after money to *buy* a living, instead of *making* a living at home. Our lands are going down the rivers and rapidly deteriorating.

The failures of the southern farm and land management and credit system prior to 1902 can be seen most clearly in the unfavorable balance appearance in the numerous index statistical tables of banking, food and livestock production, industrial development, per capita income, and support of public institutions. In many areas the South became a colonial appendage to industrial and grain-growing sections of the country. Dependence upon extra-regional capital and goods was the result, as Ben Tillman said, of farmers trying to "buy a living." Restraints imposed by outside economic interests upon the agrarian South were far more restrictive than federal laws. Not until the failure of cotton and tobacco markets in 1921, and the introduction of a larger cash-wage structure by industry into the region, did this ruinous

agricultural credit system break down. When critics of southern farming cast their barbs in the period after 1870, they were attacking
a system of financing which was primitive, like most southern agricultural practices.

The revolution wrought by the Civil War and the period following in agriculture reached much deeper than mere crop production
and finances. White and Negro were left stranded, and neither had
much choice but to farm the land as share tenants. In this connection
the term "tenancy" is almost too mild to describe the system which
actually developed. George K. Holmes labeled it "peonage" in an
article in the *Annals of the American Academy of Political and Social
Science*, (1890) which was perhaps a more precise description. A subsequent author, William H. Skaggs, labeled it an oligarchy. Whatever
it may be called, it contained all the elements of ultimate failure.

Some historians have at least implied that the Negro was responsible for inflicting tenancy upon the South because of his preference
for the simple routine of cotton cultivation. This was only partly
true. Every census report, 1870 to 1940, indicated a larger number
of white than Negro sharecroppers. After 1865 yeomen white farmers
were thrust into straitened circumstances, and plantation owners had
no other capital than land and livestock with which to operate on
an independent basis. Ex-slaves were wholly without capital resources
or proper guidance in the reordering of their economic lives. In 1860
four-fifths of southern cotton was produced by slaves, but in 1899
less than half the crop was grown by Negroes. The large turnover
of farm ownership in the South prior to the second decade of this
century was indicative of the instability of the white man's ownership
and tenure of much of the land in the South. One observer in 1936
wrote:

> Another view often advanced holds that southern tenancy is the
> normal development of abolition of slavery and the break-up of
> the ante bellum plantation. The shifting of former slaves into a
> matayer or share-cropping system was simply the method whereby
> large landholders made use of agricultural laborers lacking property
> in land, implements, and workstock.

Payment of cash wages to farm laborers at the outset in 1865
was most difficult, and in many areas all but impossible. Nevertheless
a considerable attempt was made the first year after the war to operate

farms on a low cash-wage basis. This proved difficult for the farm operator because he had little or no cash with which to pay wages, even though rates were ridiculously low. Wage hands barely existed on their earnings even when they received lodging and keep. Soon experience proved this plan unsatisfactory. Hands walked away from fields and left crops uncultivated and unharvested.

The sharecropping system brought both landlord and tenant into closer relationship to the land, and for the first time placed a burden of self-responsibility on the Negro. Thus it was that tenancy became a central fact in postwar farming. It was, however, by no means a new approach to farm operation; this practice had colonial beginnings. Sharecropping necessitated exchanges between landlords and tenants of housing, labor, use of draft animals, farm implements, fuel, and storage facilities. Tenants received in return half to two-thirds of the cotton and tobacco, and half the grain crops. The proportion of the crop surrendered by tenants depended upon the reasonableness of landlords and the supplies that they furnished.

Tenants grew mostly cotton and tobacco. They approached the land with the objective of getting from it as much income as possible in one crop season. It was an unusual tenant who looked upon his relationship to the land as more than a year's investment of labor. Tenants became so tightly bound in peonage that the only hope they had to free themselves was to produce several crops which would more than meet the cost of production. This was an economic treadmill which never ceased enslaving the tiller who did not own the land he worked. John H. Moore wrote:

> The tenant wears the soil out with his one crop, his one year lease, for his only concern is to secure a large yield. He wears himself and his family out with his inadequate teams and implements, and his yearly move. He wears his community out. He has only a passing interest in his neighborhood. The school and the church can do very little for him and his family, and they can do very little for the church and school.

(1) In 1880 there were in nine southern states, 301,758 farms operated by sharecroppers. By 1900 there were 785,000 tenant families in eleven of the southern states, a decade later, 1,393,355 tenant farms operated in twelve states and in 1920, there were 1,261,275 tenant farms. In another area, the failure of the staple crop system to keep the South abreast of national agricultural accomplishments was reflected in the value of land and buildings in 1910, which in twelve states were worth $2,193,774,898 as compared with a national evaluation of $16,082,267,689.

Staple-crop agriculture was a variable industry in the post-Civil War South. Historians have emphasized cotton culture as basic to the region, with tobacco, rice, and sugar cane treated incidentally. Tobacco did not influence the economic destinies of nearly so many people as cotton, nor did it become so emotionally intertwined with their lives. It was not so well suited to management by wholly unskilled and careless farm laborers. The crop, however, has a longer history in the South than cotton. In 1865 there were three general belts: Virginia and North Carolina, Maryland, and Kentucky and Tennessee west of the Appalachians. Up to 1865, tobacco farming was limited by lack of a good variety of plant, better means of handling raw leaf, inadequate manufacturing facilities, and proper promotion and advertising. The Civil War was in fact a boon in disguise to tobacco farmers. A tense nation with a large military force greatly increased consumption. Tobacco markets in Richmond, Louisville, and New York showed an increase in sales.

Just as cotton farmers after 1820 searched for new plant types, so did tobacco growers. North Carolinians discovered a close affinity between the quality of the tobacco plant and the soil on which it grew, and in the 1850's they introduced a light-leaf type which was subsequently to support a major manufacturing industry. Between the end of the war and the turn of the century, light-leaf-growing areas of North Carolina and Virginia spread to South Carolina, Georgia, and Florida. West of the mountains, tobacco types also underwent revolutionary changes. Up to 1870, Kentucky and Tennessee farmers grew a heavy dark-leaf variety better suited to use in plug, pipe tobacco, snuff, and cigars. Almost by accident the new light-leaf burley was introduced into the western belt.

Tobacco farming differed in many ways from cotton planting. Labor requirements, experience, land use, cultivation, harvesting and curing, and marketing required special care. Tenants were used in large numbers, but for the most part they were white, many of them coming from the Appalachian Highlands. Also, tobacco was traditionally a commodity which was sold upon prices on the international market. This was especially true of the heavier dark-leaf types such as those produced in western Kentucky and Tennessee. Prices of this crop fell below the cost of production in 1901, and continued near this level for almost a decade. This resulted in a farmer revolt called the "black patch war," which went on intermittently from 1904 to 1910. Farmers battled farmers in efforts to control production; they abused personal rights, destroyed seedbeds and growing crops, and burned storage warehouses. This outbreak, plus widespread dissatisfaction among burley growers, led to the organization of public auction sales, where farmers could at least see, if not understand, what went on in the disposal of their crops. The growing of tobacco was also regulated to some degree by farmers themselves, until the passage of the Agricultural Adjustment Administration Act in 1933. Immediately after the Supreme Court ruled this act unconstitutional in *U.S. v. Butler* in 1936, Congress enacted the Soil Conservation and Domestic Allotment Act, which not only rewarded farmers for reducing tobacco acreage but placed in their hands the power of decision over its application through periodic elections. Thus tobacco farming has since 1936 become a rather tight monopolistic industry in which growers jealously guard acreage allotments. As a result there are now far fewer persons in tobacco farming than there were in 1930.

Since 1950 the tobacco industry has been plagued by the cancer-from-smoking scare, but the industry appears to have suffered little if any loss of consumers. Attempts have been made by both manufacturers and growers to lessen the effects of this scare. Plant breeders have sought to develop a leaf which would contain smaller amounts of tar and nicotine. This they succeeded in doing just in time to get caught in the heavy manufacturing switch to production of filter cigarettes. The new type leaf did not produce a satisfactory flavor and strength of smoke through the filters, thus necessitating a return to use of stronger leaf types. Although acreage has been drastically reduced since 1933 by federal controls, the production of tobacco-leaf poundage has only fluctuated with the conditions of growing seasons. There has constantly remained in storage a generous supply of raw leaf for at least five years of projected manufacturing needs.

The warnings about cancer contained in reports of the U.S. Surgeon General seem to have had no readily discernible effect upon the reduction of cigarettes manufactured annually. In 1911 manufacturers produced approximately 27,500,000,000 cigarettes for a population of 107,436,441 persons. By 1963 the number of cigarettes had increased to 543,688,000,000, and the national population was 189,375,000. Thus it seems reasonable to conclude that the threat of cancer has had no appreciable effect on the southern tobacco industry. Likewise limitation on tobacco acreage and the threat to limit poundage do not offer a serious handicap to the growing and manufacture of tobacco products. Annually the Department of Agriculture is the largest single purchaser of tobacco in its efforts to maintain favorable prices for farmers.

By 1880 the postwar South was firmly stuck with the growing of staple crops. It became almost irretrievably a region of deficits so far as food and feed crops were concerned. This within itself was a paradox in southern economic history. The alluvial river bottoms of the South contained some of the best corn-growing land in the nation, yet southern history has been influenced by a shortage of grain. There were several reasons for this. First, much of the good corn land was still covered by forests until 1890 or 1900; second, no market facilities such as elevators and warehouses had been developed to handle corn as a commercial crop; third, a great deal more skilled labor and land management were required for growing cereals than for cultivating cotton. Yeoman white farmers and newly freed Negroes lacked both experience and facilities for handling grains. Corn was fairly easy to grow so long as it was kept free of grass, but small grains necessitated adaptations of seeds, arduous labor in the harvest, and costly machinery for threshing and grinding, most of which southerners lacked. After the grain was threshed it required fairly expensive storage to prevent spoilage through overheating and wastage by rats and insects.

Corn was the universal grain crop of the South, and in turn cornmeal was a major staple of diet. Between 1859 and 1899 the region showed an interesting shift in the growing of this crop. In the earlier year, southerners produced more than half the Indian corn grown in the United States. By the end of the century production had dropped to approximately 30 per cent of regional needs.[2]

The organization of experiment stations and the agricultural extension service helped increase corn production in the South. This in-

(2) Ten Confederate states, including Texas, produced in 1890, 401,923,447 bushels of corn, and excluding Texas, 301,953,097 bushels as compared with a national harvest of 2,666,440,279 bushels. Not only was the South behind in total bushels, its acre average approximated twelve bushels during the latter quarter of the century.

volved seed selection, better plant types, improved methods of cultivation and land management, and the application of adequate fertilizer. With the organization of boys' corn and pig clubs, Seaman A. Knapp was able to introduce a program of demonstration farming which stimulated cereal-growing. When Jerry Moore of Marlboro, South Carolina, produced 228 bushels of corn on his acre in 1910, he dramatically called attention to the values of careful cultivation and fertilization. That same year 142 other corn club boys in South Carolina topped the hundred-bushel mark, and elsewhere in the South boy farmers equaled the South Carolina achievements. The same year that Jerry Moore captured the attention of his elders, E. J. Watson, Commissioner of Agriculture in South Carolina, told members of the Southern Commercial Congress in Atlanta that his state was spending at least $80,000,000 of cotton income for oats, flour, corn, wheat, dairy products, bacon, beef, mules and horses, and other food products and draft animals which could be grown or raised at home. North Carolina, he said, bought annually 75 per cent of its food supplies at a cost of $80,300,000, or $4,490,847 more than the cotton crop brought in 1909. For the South as a whole the cereal bill was $324,000,000, or a third of the income from cotton. For all supplies and work stock, southern farmers paid out $720,000,000.

From 1868 to 1914 there was reluctance on the part of southerners to face the hard fact that their farm economy was one of deficits. They were troubled by the feeling that by growing cotton, tobacco, rice, and sugar cane, they sinned against nature and their land. There was virtue in balanced farming, but southern farmers were unable to arouse themselves sufficiently to break the bondage of one-crop farming. With pathetic delusion, stemming, it almost seemed, from the writings of Sidney Lanier and vague recollections of the Jeffersonian tradition, they clung to the same old one-crop economy. Not even the harsh admonitions of local editors awakened them. They still dreamed in a troubled way that they would ultimately realize the millennium of agrarian life by becoming self-sufficient farmers. Staple crops would supply the cushion for all other needs.

Speaking to sun-scorched and embattled cotton farmers at a Grange barbecue in Elberton, Georgia, June 29, 1889, Henry W. Grady drew for his audience a vision of Jeffersonian contentment, a condition none of them knew. After he had bent his oratorical sword against distant oppressors who extracted tribute from his hearers in the forms of inflated prices and escalated interest rates, Grady invited them to share the delights of:

> A modest quiet home sheltered by great trees and set in a circle of field and meadow, gracious with the promise of harvest—barns and cribs well-filled and the old smokehouse odorous with treasure— the fragrance of pink and hollyhock mingling with the aroma of garden and orchard, and resonant with the hum of bees and poultry busy clucking—inside the house, thrift, comfort and that cleanliness that is next to godliness—the restful beds, the open fireplace, the books and papers, and the old clock that held its steadfast pace amid the frolic of weddings, that had welcomed in company with the watchers of the sick bed, and ticked to solemn requiem of the dead; and the well-worn Bible that, thumbed by fingers long since stilled, and blurred by eyes long since closed, held the simple annals of the family, and the heart and conscience of the home. Outside stood the master, strong and wholesome and upright; wearing no man's collar; with no mortgage on his roof, and no lien on his ripening harvest; pitching his crops in his own wisdom, and selling them in his own time in his chosen market; master of his lands and master of himself.

Though redneck farmers stood captivated by Grady's eloquent description of an idyllic farm home, where there was no shadow of lien or mortgage, no smell of Ohio fatback, no failing cotton crop, and no deficits against their region for purchase of corn and fertilizer, they knew the hard contrary facts of their own lives. They were gripped in the realities of imbalances which held them in biting poverty—that is why they had gathered at Elberton. Grady, Otken, and Grange politicians were only a few of the articulate critics of southern farming. The Atlanta *Constitution*, like nearly every other southern newspaper, cudgeled farmers for their failures to diversify their crops, and for not living off their land. Even the densest sharecropper agreed with their contentions, but no one offered a plan to stop the treadmill of cotton peonage.

Furnishing merchants and their backers spoke in more immediately practical terms than editors. Farmers, though beset by woes, were hopeless optimists. They cherished the seductive hope that there would be one good crop year when high prices would square their accounts at the store, and they then could enjoy the Jeffersonian idyll of contented and self-sufficient agrarian life. This, however, was a treacherous mirage which beckoned desperate men deeper into the arid desert of lowering prices and rising production costs. In 1881 its fate was already clear to Henry W. Grady when he was preparing his essay for *Harper's Magazine*. He hoped a way through the morass of regional impoverishment lay in the location of textile mills in proximity to cotton fields to consume both the staple and surplus labor.

Promise for cotton peons was dashed on the rocks of adverse regional statistics. The National Cotton Planters' Association reported in 1881 that the southern states fell short of their needs by 42,252,244 bushels of wheat, 166,684,279 bushels of corn, 77,762,108 bushels of oats, and 86,689,632 bushels of other grain. Hay, in a land of abundant rainfall and grass, was short by 4,011,150 tons, and cotton-growers spent $32 million for ineffective chemical fertilizers. An observer said, "On this enormous amount the cotton farmer had to pay the usurious percentage charged by his merchant broker, which is never less than thirty per cent, and frequently runs to seventy per cent." This was the wrecker of dreams that rushed the South headlong into economic calamity.

From one historical perspective, southern change after 1880 was almost imperceptible, except for the creeping impoverishment of the region. Farmers were region- and folk-bound by their credit system. The threat in the 1880's of a minor revolution of farmers, expressed in the Farmers' Alliance movement, grew out of several causes: failure of masses of farmers to earn even modest livelihoods growing cotton and tobacco, greediness of brokers and suppliers, and wastage of resources.

Into this dormant economic period of southern agriculture came Seaman A. Knapp, Yankee-born-and-trained agriculturist who saw in the marshes of coastal Louisiana a slight glimmer of promise. He accepted the offer of the Louisiana Land Reclamation Company, a British syndicate, to attempt the reclamation of the Louisiana coastal marshes in Calcasieu Parish in 1880. Quickly he demonstrated that land which Louisiana cajuns believed to be utterly worthless could be reclaimed and profitably planted in rice and other crops. Not only did Knapp help transfer rice planting from the marshlands of tidewater South Carolina and Georgia, he began to improve the quality of the grain by selecting seed types, and by better handling and management. He

searched other rice-growing regions of the world for new varieties
which would increase southern yield and quality. Importations from
Japan, China, and other places led to the development of types far
superior to that grown by ante-bellum farmers from the seeds of
Madagascar.

Rice culture in the Louisiana marshes did not long hold the interest
of the restless New Yorker. Cotton offered a greater challenge. Migration of the Mexican boll weevil across Texas was an ominous threat
to cotton. Working with farmers along the Denver and Fort Worth
Railroad, which ran across the Texas cotton belt, Knapp saw that
if changes were not made by the farmers the railroad would suffer
loss of vital freight. He persuaded Walter Porter of Terrell County
to diversify his farm operations according to a plan which he would
supply. Porter was assured that he could produce greater return from
his land by diversification than by growing cotton alone. Sufficient
funds were procured to establish a bond to reimburse the farmer if
he failed; Knapp then outlined modern methods of cultivation and
management to be followed. Even suffering from boll weevil infestation
and a damaging storm, Porter more than reaped the harvest predicted.
And so began the demonstration farm movement in the South. As
promulgator of the Congressional act to establish experimental stations
and extension services, Knapp saw his idea applied nationally. By 1914
extension agents had begun to make an impression on southern farmers,
largely because agents worked through their sons and daughters.
Mightily chastened by the boll weevil, rednecks did less scoffing and
more listening to new ideas which promised delivery from ruin. This
was particularly true in livestock breeding, tick eradication, seed selection, and land conservation. The introduction of the dipping vat, with
its chemical baths so deadly to the fever tick, had a monumental effect
on restoring livestock raising in the South, even if ignoramuses did
blow many of the vats out of the ground with dynamite.

Terracing hillside fields and plowing furrow patterns that
followed contours of the land checked erosion at the eleventh hour,
but not before billions of dollars' worth of fertile top soil was washed
away. It is not to be inferred that masses of southern farmers and
their tenants rushed to accept changes; quite the contrary, they remained stubborn and ignorant, clinging to old ways of dredging the

soil and making profligate use of all other resources until it was observed by a special Presidential committee in 1938 that:

> Sixty-one per cent of all the Nation's land badly damaged by erosion is in the Southern States. An expanse of southern farm land as large as South Carolina has been gullied and washed away; at least 22 million acres of once-fertile soil has been ruined beyond repair. Another area the size of Oklahoma and Alabama combined has been seriously damaged by erosion. In addition, the sterile sand and gravel washed off the land has covered over a fertile valley acreage equal in size to Maryland.

There was evidence in the first quarter of this century that southern farmers misinterpreted the word "diversification" to mean largely the growing of vegetables and fruits. Newly established agricultural and mechanical colleges began to return boys and girls to family farms in the first decade who had received training in scientific agricultural procedures. Too, the progress of the boll weevil no doubt did more to initiate acceptance of change than did arguments of experimental and extension service agents. In 1909 Alfred H. Stone of Mississippi wrote:

> Wherever the weevil appears it creates the necessity for a revolution. . . . The measure of the Negro's ability to grow cotton under the conditions likely to confront him in the territory east of the Mississippi will be his adaptability to these changes and his capacity to become part of the industrial revolution.

He could have written the same thing about white owners and tenants. It was clear by 1910 that forces of change were astir in the South, and that old farm practices had failed miserably.

Another fact of extensive background was evident in the cotton belt in the first decade of this century. Geneticists were tampering with the cotton plant itself. Plant breeders and selectors like A. D. Mebane of Texas, John Griffin of Greenville, Mississippi, and Caleb and James Lide Coker of Hartsville, South Carolina, sought to develop improved types of cotton which would meet the challenges of the time. Scientists in experimental stations in North Carolina, Mississippi, Texas, and Louisiana applied themselves to plant research in seeking better strains of cotton. Commercial plant breeders of the Delta Pine Land Plantation at Scott, Mississippi, became important producers and distributors of seeds of improved varieties, which they sold throughout the South. They shipped stock abroad to India and other cotton-growing areas of the world. This breeding activity has gone on continuously, resulting in the accumulation of an enormous body of scientific knowledge about cotton, its nature, and production which ante-bellum planters, who crowned the crop king, never suspected.

By the middle of the great depression of the 1930's plant breeders were experimenting with all other major field crops grown in the South. They took advantage of the experience and knowledge of scientists and growers in the Middle West and introduced both hybrid and open-pollenated types of corn. By independent experimentation southerners made important adaptations of northern seed types which produced plants with characteristics adaptable to southern soils and climate conditions. In 1910 Southern corn farmers produced approximately 12 bushels per acre; in 1963 the regional average approximated 42 bushels, as compared with a national average of 67.3 bushels.

Equally dramatic changes were made in tobacco types as in corn and cotton. By 1935 the southern tobacco crop, in both the light and burley belts, faced calamity from bacterial and parasitic infection and plant deficiencies. Plant geneticists in Kentucky and the Carolinas were able by the time of World War II to introduce disease-resistant plants possessing physical qualities more adapted to soil chemists, and fertilizer manufacturers were able to modify conditions on the land by use of fertilizers which supplied nutrients for maximum production. Sugar-cane types were greatly improved by plant breeders, who saved sugar production from virtual extinction by developing disease-resistant plants. Following the pioneering work of Dr. Knapp, rice growers have sown new types of grain which have revolutionized both yield and quality of their crop. Small grains and grasses are now being grown as profitable southern crops. Oats especially have helped to close the gap of grain deficits. Importations of new grasses and extensive experimentation with native types have boosted hay production, and helped materially to convert worn and exhausted cotton fields into profitable cattle ranges. The tragedy resulting from clean tilth of cotton has largely been concealed if not erased in two generations. No longer do areas of the South, once notorious for their ghastly scars of erosion, present their fields in the deep scarlet hues of sin against the land.

The disastrous market season of 1921 was a shattering blow to the old way of life of the small farmer. The early recession of the 1920's gave momentum to a revolution started by the coming of the boll weevil, and the depression added further impetus to change. By 1932 southern farmers faced almost total frustration and ruin. In an admirable summary of conditions in this era, Howard W. Odum wrote in *Southern Regions of the United States*:

> The picture of the cotton agrarian South may almost be described as a landscape of dilemmas. The tenant type bordering on poverty and hopelessness is only one. The human factors of waste, product of a single crop system, had already been enumerated, as had the waste lands and forests. The instability that comes from great mobility and lack of purpose on the part of millions of citizens is another problem. Disgracefully low standards of housing follow a logical shiftlessness and impersonality. Instability of prices and income, speculation and tragedy of lost fortunes, lack of capital for efficient farm management and machinery, the low standards of wages due partly to the Negro, the debtor character of the southern economy— these and others cry out for more adequate analysis and long-time planning.

Analysis and long-time planning were already underway. President Franklin D. Roosevelt, sometime hill-country Georgia farmer, had appointed Lowell D. Mellett, director of the National Emergency Council, and a special committee to make an analysis of the troubled South. This committee published its findings, June 22, 1938, in a slender pamphlet which had a tremendous effect on both southern farmer and politician. Never before had the failures of the cotton-tenant farming tradition been presented so nakedly and graphically. In a brief summary statement on the "Ownership and Use of Land," the committee observed:

> The farming South depends on cotton and tobacco for two-thirds of its cash income. More than half of its farmers subjected year after year to risks which would apall the average business man. All their eggs are in one basket—a basket which can be upset, and often is, by the weather, the boll weevil, or the cotton market.
>   The boll weevil can be conquered, and weather hazards tend to cancel themselves out as good seasons follow bad; but the cotton market is a sheer gamble. On this gamble nearly 2,000,000 southern families stake their year's work and everything they own. Their

only chance of making a living is tied up with the fluctuations of the world price of cotton.

No other similar area in the world gambles its welfare and the destinies of so many people on a single crop market year after year.

Within the region in 1938 there were 1,838,000 tenant families, of whom two-thirds were white. This large number of tenants fed a constantly moving stream of migrants, involving an annual economic loss of $25 million in the cost of moving alone. These startling revelations came at the moment the agrarian hold on the South was being broken for the first time by massive departure from farms, the rise of industry, the introduction of mechanized agriculture, and the spread of cotton growing from east to west.

Down to 1940 the South still had a great deficiency of livestock of every variety. In a land which could produce grain, grass, and forage in inexhaustible abundance, there was a great shortage of farm animals. Before the tractor supplanted the mule in the fields, this animal was imported by thousands of head annually from Kentucky, Missouri, and Illinois. Horses in large numbers came from Wisconsin, Minnesota, and the Dakotas. Actually the shortage of these animals was never really checked by home breeding. In 1920 the tractor in the South was still a mechanical curiosity. Farmers contended that it could not be operated on sandy hill land, or sticky delta soil for that matter. The mule was in the South to stay, no matter what implement manufacturers created. It was not until 1940 that machines began to compete forthrightly with the mule.[3]

Once the South was a favorite cattle range for those carefree men, fugitives from civilization, who pushed herds and families a jump ahead of settlement from Virginia to Texas. It took three-quarters of a century after the Civil War for the region to recover its momentum in cattle production. At the depth of the depression there was a serious lag in cattle-raising, with only some 8,200,000 head of cattle on farms in 1932. This number increased in the next three decades to 18,260,000 head. But this differential in numbers does not

(3) In 1920 there were 246,000 tractors on American farms, and in 1950 the South Central States alone reported 325,000 tractors on 251,000 farms, and in the whole South there were 1,425,000 tractors, and 1,046,000 motor trucks. Horse and mule numbers were reported in inverse ratio. Their rate of disappearance was indicated in the decline from 827,000 horses and mules in the four South Central states in 1954 to 518,000 in 1958. This latter number included pleasure and sporting horses, and marked a decline from 3,256,000 since 1932.

reflect the heart of change. There was not only revolutionary increase in number of head, but the quality of animals had been greatly increased by improved breeding. Criticisms of the Southeast made by Howard Odum in *Southern Regions* in 1936 pertaining to cattle-raising ceased to be valid in 1950.

Phenomenal changes have occurred in cattle-grazing since 1920. Many facts contributed to the revival of this ancient pioneer industry. Control of the Texas fever ticks and other parasites and insects marked the end of an era of debilitating infestations. For instance, destruction of the screw worm by the release of sterile male flies made it possible to conduct profitable cattle-grazing in large areas of the Gulf coastal states. Retreat of cotton from both the hills and black belts resulted in the reconversion of millions of acres to hay and pasture lands. Better roads and improved means of transportation improved the organization of local markets where higher nation-wide prices were paid for beef cattle and hogs. A widespread breeding of both beef and dairy-type cattle changed Southern livestock farming from an atmosphere of backwoods indifference to a fairly sophisticated business. Enormous attention was given the growing of grasses by southern experimental stations and the United States Department of Agriculture, and thus the old contentions that southern lands could not sustain sufficient grass cover during the hottest summer months to supply herds of cattle have been successfully refuted.

Today cattle sales days throughout the South attract crowds which once flocked into towns to attend monthly court days. Pick-up trucks mounted with cattle cages line roads and sales-barn parking lots, and auctions stimulate almost as much excitement as do rodeos. Men and boys dressed in sharp-pointed shoes, tight-fitting blue jeans, and wearing huge Texas hats, all symbols of the shift of much of the grazing industry away from the western plains, flock about sales pens. Cattle shows in Baton Rouge, Dallas, Lexington, Tallahassee, Kissimmee (Florida) and Auburn (Alabama) attract exhibitors and breeders from everywhere in the Union. These sales and shows have contributed materially to the breeding and growing of much higher quality animals. Use of artificial insemination has also greatly advanced the development of pure-bred animals on farms where once scrub cattle depleted pastures without producing appreciable amounts of beef.

The ultimate diversification of southern crops had far-reaching ramifications in regional agriculture. In the semi-tropical areas of Florida and Texas, an increasingly larger proportion of the national citrus crops was grown. As California orange and lemon groves were absorbed by expansion of urban communities, Florida and Texas faced less competition for eastern growers. At the same time farmers in several southern states turned more and more to growing vegetables, fruits, and melons, North and South Carolina and Georgia produced large annual crops of peaches in competition with Michigan and California, while Virginia apple growers competed with those in Washington and Oregon. A number of southern states grew large quantities of cantaloupes, watermelons, and vegetables. A large part of the winter and early-spring supply of fresh vegetables for the eastern part of the United States have come from the Gulf coastal states. This type of specialized farming has for a long time displaced older staple crops, and involved a more highly capitalized venture. In human terms, fruit and vegetable farmers came to depend upon transient and seasonal workers for harvesting crops rather than upon share tenants. This fact created anew some of the old problems of the South. These transients bore little or no direct relationship to the land, and practically none to southern institutions such as schools and churches.

Southern farmers no longer sign lien notes or write store orders for the delivery of shoddy merchandise in piddling weekly installments. The ancient and hackneyed phrase "live at home" has little or no pertinency to modern farmers. They, however, owe considerable sums to banks and loan companies for machinery bought on installment plans, and for automobiles, trucks, and automatic household equipment. There is really no longer a serious shortage of either capital or credit. Unlike their forebears, southern farmers now seek the most recent advice, and some of them are eager to live out beyond even the experimentations of plant breeders and chemists.[4]

(4) Ranks of southern farmers are sinking phenomenally, but the average size of their farms is increasing. In 1900 in twelve states there were 2,749,514 farms which averaged from 67.6 acres in Mississippi to 269.1 in Texas. There were 1,466,922 farms in 1959 ranging from 102 acres in Tennessee to 631 in Texas. In fifty-nine years the South lost 1,282,494 farms, and had gained an average of 35 to 362 acres in size per farm. Too, the rural population, by the old method of counting, numbered 17,840,471 in 1900, and in 1960 there was a farm population of 5,460,000. While there is a discrepancy between the two counts it is not of major significance since the rural non-farm population in 1900 was

Mechanization of the southern farm has brought both economic and social changes in depth. Families which once depended upon farming for a livelihood have been forced off the land. The purchase of every new tractor and a complement of automatic farming equipment displaces from six to ten farmers. The mechanical cotton picker, a machine that was almost three-quarters of a century in creation, has, since its perfection by the Rust brothers of Memphis in 1936, displaced directly at least a million and half farm laborers, and has affected the lives of seven or eight million more. There is no way of estimating how many more farm laborers have been released by the availability of cheap rural electricity and the machines which it drives, or the vast improvement in the chemical composition of fertilizers now applied to southern soils. Farming as a way of life in the South has moved much nearer the midstream of American economic life than at any other time in the nation's history.

Social upheavals in the South in the field of race relations, political realignments, and vain attempts by state legislators to legislate a status quo are direct manifestations of changes which have occurred on Southern farms. The time has already arrived when the income from industry in the South is almost eight times greater than that from agriculture. Farmer and federal government are so firmly knitted in a partnership of management and finance that if public controls and supports were withdrawn there would be further shrinkage of number of farms and farm population, a fact which some economists say would not necessarily injure farming in the South as a business.

---

relatively small. Tenancy and subdivision of farms seemed in 1930 incurable blights on the land, but they no longer are matters of primary concern. Even more startling are the projections for 1975, when statisticians estimate there will be only 5,500,000 people on southern farms, and the number of farms will shrink to 500,000. Profound changes in the old cotton economy had occurred by 1945, but it was clear that cotton as a crop had not failed. Its production by tenants under the share-cropping, lien mortgaging system had failed, and so had primitive methods of growing and marketing farm products. These gave way before the onslaught of the boll weevil, soil exhaustion, and human inefficiency.

❧ V ❦

Demagoguery and Reform

Eliminated from effective political participation at the end of the nine-teenth century, the Negro would continue to be the biggest factor in southern politics; his presence would determine the political history of the region, and no major issue would arise that would not be decided largely in the light of its relation to him. In maintaining the exclusion of the Negro from politics, therefore, the South actually was domi-nated by the Negro. It was the one and only factor that preserved the one-party system. It determined the South's position on woman suffrage, on Prohibition, on child labor, on compulsory school laws. It would determine the southern position on the reforms of the New Deal and the Fair Deal, on the New Frontier as well as on the Great Society. Southern states dared not enforce compulsory school attendance laws for fear of the necessity of providing an education for the Negro. They would not liberalize the suffrage laws for whites for fear that the Negro would become too influential. On these as well as on hundreds of other questions of public policy the Negro stood as "an ever present shadow across the door of political councils."[1]

The barriers erected against Negro voting would survive legal scrutiny until near the middle of the twentieth century. The "grand-father clause" was invalidated by the Supreme Court in 1915, but by that time it was no longer needed. The literacy clauses, on the other hand, had been upheld by the Court in 1898, as were the "under-standing" clauses. Together and if applied impartially, these could

(1) Quoted in Gunnar Myrdal, *An American Dilemma: The Negro Problem and Modern Democracy* (New York, 1944), 1310.

108

have disqualified hundreds of thousands of whites as well as Negroes in the early decades after their enactment. In later years, as Negroes became more literate, the tests, if fairly administered, would not have served their purpose. Consequently, additional requirements had to be sought: in some states, "good character"; in others, either long-term residence or else property qualifications.

Most effective of all devices to disfranchise the Negro was "the lily-white primary." Beginning with South Carolina in 1896 and ending with North Carolina in 1915, state after state adopted laws requiring that nominations for all offices be made in primary elections. Only party members could participate in the primary, and party rules everywhere excluded Negroes from membership. Under the one-party system that prevailed in the South, the primary became the real election, for Republican opposition in the November general election was either non-existent or else nominal. It was the white primary, therefore, that from the time of its adoption became the great obstacle to Negro voting, more effective than all others combined. For even though the Negro met all other qualifications of literacy, good character, poll-tax payment, and was actually permitted to vote in November, the outcome of the election had already been determined in the white primary several months before. After adoption of the primary laws, therefore, the poll tax was a negligible factor so far as Negro voting was concerned, and in practice it operated to disfranchise only whites. The legality of the white primary went unchallenged for several decades; it was generally regarded as extra-legal, a decision made by private party action, and thus not in violation of the Fifteenth Amendment.

Aside from its practical disfranchisement of all Negroes, the primary would work profound changes in southern politics. Under the convention system of nominating candidates, the black counties, as already noted, had control. A state-wide primary, however, by giving every voter in the state an equal voice, could wrest dominance from the black counties, save in Georgia, where, as noted, the county unit system greatly weighted votes in the black counties. Despite the paradox of its disfranchisement of Negroes, therefore, the primary must be considered a democratic reform. For it broadened the political base: the choice of officials rested with the mass of voters, and when they were sufficiently stirred they might wrest control from the small oligarchy. And even if hundreds of thousands of whites were barred from the primary by failure to pay poll taxes, those who paid could vote and could determine the selection of their officials. Since the primary could break the stranglehold which the black counties had held over the nominating process, its introduction called for new and ingenious strategy on the part of their leaders if they were to maintain control. On the other hand, the primary would not diminish the unfair representation which black counties had in the legislatures.

One of the expectations of advocates of the primary was that it would bring an end to the swindling, trading, and frauds of the nominating conventions. In this they would be disappointed, for fraud and corruption were too ingrained in the southern body politic to be eliminated merely by a new elective device. Listening to wholesale charges of dishonesty in the aftermath of a Mississippi election in 1907, an editor who had long advocated the primary concluded that it had proved a failure and should be replaced by the old convention system. "More evils," he said, "occurred in the late primary than in all conventions ever held in the state."[2]

The primary would also revolutionize campaign techniques. Under the convention system, candidates contended for the support of a select group who controlled local politics in the predominantly rural South: prospective legislators, county committeemen, prospective delegates to the county and state conventions. If they could but win the support of these, the popularity of the candidate with the voters was of small concern, for the contest was won or lost in the convention. The primary, however, changed all this. Support of local leaders was still important because of the influence they might wield with voters. But if leaders now brought forth candidates whom the voters did not welcome, appeals to the masses by rejected candidates might prove effective. And since the masses generally were less educated and more parochial than the leaders, they would be responsive to a different kind of appeal. It is not surprising, therefore, that, with the institution of the primary, stale aphorisms gave way to impassioned appeals to class and racial prejudices. Oratorical ability and platform style henceforth became inportant characteristics of the more successful candidates and, unless some deep issue stirred the people, they frequently would be decisive. "Generally speaking," wrote one editor after a lifetime of political observation, "the men who can shake hands best,

(2) Jackson *Clarion-Ledger*, Aug. 9, Sept. 12, 1907.

wear the broadest smile, know the most people, and tell the funniest stories, have the best chance to win."[3]

Under the primary system of nominations there emerged at the beginning of the twentieth century in the South a remarkable group of politicians, progressive and reform-minded on social issues other than that of improving the lot of the Negro. Charles B. Aycock, Josephus Daniels, and William B. Kitchen in North Carolina; Hoke Smith in Georgia; Braxton B. Comer in Alabama; Andrew Montague in Virginia; Ben Tillman in South Carolina; Napoleon B. Broward in Florida; Charles A. Culberson and James Hogg in Texas; Jeff Davis in Arkansas; James K. Vardaman and Theodore G. Bilbo in Mississippi; Robert Love Taylor and Benton McMillan in Tennessee; and later Huey P. Long in Louisiana—these men all were opposed to monopolies and to the niggardly economy of the redeemers that had frustrated earlier clamor for social reform. When these neo-Populists came to power, they sought with some success to bring into the backward-looking southern states the progressive reforms then sweeping other sections of the nation. They believed in public education, in factory employment and safety regulation, in penal and child-labor reforms. In working toward these ends they stimulated a new dichotomy in southern politics, a bi-factionalism in the Democratic party based on intelligent planning for social improvement rather than the all-but-blind struggles of the agrarians seeking to solve complex economic problems they did not comprehend. Although they generally neglected the Negro and ignored the growing problem of farm tenancy; and although too often they won popular support for their reforms through Negro-baiting; nevertheless, they presented the voters in the primaries with a choice between progressive and conservative candidates.[4] They carried forward the Populist program after the Populist party had disappeared, fighting the farmers' battle in state and nation. In doing so they used extravagant and ruthless methods, never hesitating to arouse racial and class prejudices in the masses to achieve their purposes.

The southern progressive movement fed on itself, each victory adding strength for the next encounter. The first great breakthrough

(3) *Ibid.*, Nov. 17, 1910.
(4) For a more thorough discussion of this subject see Grantham, *The Democratic South*, 52–6.

was the establishment of the primary itself which, as we have seen, broadened the base of the election process, bringing the mass of voters into the choice of candidates and freeing them from the domination of an oligarchy led by planters, bankers, railroad officials, and corporate executives. Almost invariably the establishment of the primary was a prelude to reform, despite the paradox that many of the progressive leaders whose election was made possible by the primary were racial extremists like Vardaman, Smith, Tillman, Bilbo, and Aycock. Yet these same racists took the lead in terminating the leasing of convicts, the overwhelming majority of whom were Negroes, and in using the power of the governor's office to prevent lynching.

James K. Vardaman, Mississippi's first governor chosen in a primary election (after having twice been defeated under the convention system), brought convict leasing to an end there in 1906. Hoke Smith, another racist chosen governor by way of the primary, ended convict leasing in Georgia in 1907. Texas followed in 1910 under James E. Hogg, and Arkansas in 1912, when the governor pardoned 360 convicts at one time. By 1918 it was ended everywhere but Alabama. To replace the outmoded system, states established government-owned-and-managed penal farms. These proved economically more profitable to the states than leasing the convicts had been, but rehabilitation of the prisoners rather than pecuniary profit was the watchword of the new system. Prisoners were segregated by sexes, young convicts were separated from confirmed criminals, and a parole system was instituted. A policy of suspended sentences for first offenders was soon adopted, and prison libraries and educational programs were established. Cruel punishments were also abolished as a matter of policy and time off for good behavior was generally established by 1920.

One of the earliest sequels to the primary was the strengthening of the powers of the railroad commissions, whose regulatory authority was by no means limited to railroads but extended to all corporate affairs. The South led the nation in this respect, and southerners became leaders in the movement for national regulation. Only in the Midwest were commissions given nearly as much power. In the South they reduced freight and passenger rates, sometimes to a figure that companies complained was confiscatory; they prohibited rebates and rate discrimination, restricted the issuing of passes, reduced hours of labor of employees, required safety devices, and forbade pools and traffic agreements. Often the rulings of the commisssions prevailed, despite numerous appeals by the carriers to the federal courts. Insurance and oil companies and the tobacco trust were also objectives for reform, although here the reform record is less impressive. For despite legislative and commission efforts, the trusts continued to thrive and were stronger at the end of the period than at the beginning.[5]

Working conditions in southern industry at the turn of the century, particularly in the textile mills, was another object of progressive attack. Laws had been passed in the 1890's limiting the work week in South Carolina and Georgia mills to sixty-six hours, and when North Carolina set the limit at sixty hours in 1911 it was claimed the industry could not survive the blow. The most damning feature of the textile industry was the fact that the manual dexterity of women and children was at least as facile as that of men in directing the work of the spindles, and as a consequence women and children made up a large portion of the labor force. Seizing on the spirit of the progressive movement to dramatize the evils of child labor, Edgar Gardner Murphy of Alabama formed the National Child Labor Committee in 1904. This organization not only joined North and South in the movement but attracted southern politicians of liberal views such as Hoke Smith and Ben Tillman. In 1907 Congress, after investigation, reported that conditions were bad everywhere but were worst in the South. Three-fourths of the North Carolina textile mills, where conditions were better than elsewhere in the South, employed children under twelve, in isolated instances children of six or seven, and worked them on night shifts. Almost one-fourth of Mississippi's textile workers were under sixteen. In North and South Carolina more than half the working children under fourteen could neither read nor write; in Virginia the figure was 70 per cent.

Under the lash of the progressives, improvement was steady if not spectacular. By 1909 the ratio of children to adults in the North Carolina mills had dropped from 23.9 per cent to 18.9 per cent, although this compared poorly with 5.7 per cent in Massachusetts. By 1912 all southern states had adopted laws limiting ages, hours, and night work for children. But the age limit was twelve, and the work week was still sixty hours, with exemption provisions permitting even longer hours. The difficulty of enforcement led to a federal law in

(5) Woodward, *Origins of the New South*, 384–90.

1916, the vote on which divided the southern Congressmen almost evenly, forty-one for with forty-three against. The states in which the mills were located were almost solidly against the bill. But the law, together with one taxing profits of employers of children, was declared unconstitutional. It was not until the 1930's that a combination of the Great Depression, the New Deal, and the introduction of machinery which children could not operate prepared the section for effective curtailment of child labor. By that time all southern states prohibited the labor of children under fourteen, except that in some states children of twelve could work in canneries in the summer months, and farm labor was exempted. All prohibited night work for children under sixteen. Meanwhile, the South would continue to be the most backward section of the country in other labor legislation: in workmen's compensation laws, employer liability for hazardous machinery, and in programs for conciliating and mediating labor disputes. In 1938 in the South a larger proportion of women was employed than in any other section.

Prohibition was another target of the progressives. Puritanism in the South had grown steadily since the passing of the liberal Jeffersonian tradition. A growing number of blue laws aimed at gambling, drinking, and prostitution seemed to accompany the expansion of the fundamentalist doctrines of Baptist and Methodist sects which dominated the section at the end of the nineteenth century. The South's extraordinary emphasis on local autonomy furthered the so-called temperance movement, and long before the Civil War most southern states had permitted elections whereby cities and towns might ban saloons. In the 1880's there was a second wave of temperance and prohibition crusades, and the right to extend prohibition beyond municipal lines was granted counties in most states. The prohibition movement was given a great impetus by the progressives after the turn of the century. By 1907, it is reliably estimated that four-fifths of all southern counties had gone dry through the exercise of local option laws. That summer, Georgia adopted state-wide prohibition, and soon Alabama, Mississippi, North Carolina, and Tennessee followed. By 1910, ten of the former Confederate states had adopted state-wide prohibition, and when the Eighteenth Amendment was submitted in 1918, all eleven promptly ratified it. The prohibition sentiment was much stronger in the rural

than in the urban areas, and southern city folk continued during the
1920's to be as hard drinking as those in any other section.

Another facet of progressive politics, the movement for women's
rights, which had flourished in the North since the Civil War, had
little effect in the South. Perhaps this was because so much of the
southern effort at the time was aimed at eliminating the Negro from
the franchise rather than at extending its provisions. And women were
so dedicated to aiding their men regain and retain political control
they suppressed any ambition they may have had for enlarged opportunities outside the home in favor of this larger objective. Emboldened
by this attitude of their women, an attitude that continued well into
the twentieth century, southern politicians were outspoken in their
opposition to woman suffrage. Only six southern representatives—three
of them Republicans—supported the Nineteenth Amendment when
it passed in Congress in 1919.

The mythical threat of Negro domination had caused the South
to close ranks and remove the possibility of a two-party system in
which the Negro vote might be bargained for. With sanction of this
system by time and tradition, the Republican party lost respectability:
Republicanism became a term to be associated with desecration of
ancestors and even treason to the region, and identification with it
might invite social and economic reprisals. As a consequence, for a
half-century and more after redemption, the eleven ex-Confederate
states were completely dominated by the Democratic party. And the
near solid front which the section would maintain in national politics
until the middle of the twentieth century would have important consequences in the states and in the nation.

One-party domination had its advantages as well as its disadvan-
tages for those who exercised political control in the South. We have
already noted that the decline in southern leadership in national affairs
coincided with the emergence of the one-party system in the region.
Since there was no likelihood of the Republican party's carrying any
of the southern states in national elections, neither party was concerned
about catering to southern interests in the selection of its Presidential
candidates. It would be futile for Republicans to do so and needless
for Democrats. On the other hand, absence of an opposition party
organization to oppose incumbent Congressmen resulted in unusually

long tenure for southerners. The seniority they achieved gave them legislative influence far beyond their numbers and often in excess of their capacity to use it in the best interests of the nation; they moved to chairmanships of key committees, which gave them the power to bottle up legislation or to clear it for floor action. This power was used by most southern chairmen as a means of obstructing legislation that was undesirable to the section. Of the fifty-three standing committees in the House of Representatives in 1916, thirty-one were chaired by southerners and only twenty-two by Representatives from other sections. Forty years later in the Eighty-fifth Congress, the speaker of the House, the majority leader of the Senate, eleven of twenty chairmen of House standing committees, and ten of sixteen Senate committee chairmen were southerners.

Another disadvantage resulting from the one-party system was the absence of concerted state programs. Only in their customary attachment to Democratic Presidential candidates and their commitment to white supremacy were the factions in southern states united. With the possible exceptions of Virginia, North Carolina, and Tennessee, there was no semblance of a united Democratic party. In the other eight states there was only a multitude of factions which had no continuity save where a strong leader like Vardaman in Mississippi, Gene Talmadge in Georgia, or Huey Long in Louisiana was able to develop a personal organization. The multiplicity of candidates in the first primaries for every office, each put forward by local factions to promote local or personal interests, gave the people no opportunity to vote on major state-wide issues, and resembled more nearly a primitive four- or five-party system. Each candidate was for himself, and in a state-wide primary contest none could expect aid from a neutral central organization. Legislative candidates would be aligned in the primary with transient factional candidates for governor and other state offices. Since victory in the primary was tantamount to election, successful candidates went to the legislature often without any commitments to a program which the successful candidate for governor might have. Thus, when Huey Long, for example, was elected governor of Louisiana in 1928 on a liberal program, he found himself opposed by a large majority of the legislators elected with him. Had these legislators been forced to run in the general election against candidates supported by an opposition party, they would have had to pledge support to a party program. The newly elected governor might then have looked to them with confidence to support him in the legislature.

The great number of candidates in the primary, poorly organized and poorly financed, could not provide the army of precinct watchers and challengers organized parties are able to furnish in order to insure reasonably honest elections. In this respect, therefore, the one-party system contributed to fradulent elections. Furthermore, since the successful candidate in the Democratic primary won by default in November, there was no opposition candidate to appeal to the independent voter in an effort to insure better government.

In this kind of disorganized politics the advantage always lay with the conservative upper economic classes who were striving to prevent taxation for welfare programs and improved education. Their strategy, calling for preservation of the status quo, could be achieved by obstruction and needed no organization to accomplish its end. It followed from this that it was the great mass of underprivileged who lost in one-party political systems. Out of power and without influence, they had no mechanism whereby to elect their friends. They could but follow transient "demagogues" in fitful rebellion, and even when victorious, their leaders often lacked either the political skill or the moral character to carry through their reforms. Considering the handicaps of the one-party system, the reforms the progressives achieved were all the more remarkable.

Such continuity as did exist in southern politics was often the old alignment of the Populist, fighting the battle of the poor white farmer, against the planters and industrialists. This struggle was frequently associated with geographical divisions: in Mississippi the Delta against the hill counties, in South Carolina the coastal plain against the piedmont, in Alabama the black belt against the white counties to the north and south, in Louisiana the bayou parishes against the northwestern hills whence came Huey Long's strength. There was an alliance, too, as we have seen between the planters and the financial and industrial leaders of the cities and larger towns.

Despite common historical experience growing out of civil war and reconstruction the southern states, each possessed unique characteristics, as V. O. Key observed. Florida, for instance, had a fourfold population increase in the first four decades of the twentieth century and was the most highly urbanized of southern states. More than half her people lived in five urban centers in 1940. Floridians had the highest per capita income in the South, and her people were on the average older than those of other southern states. This, together with her urbanization, resulted in a comparatively mild attitude on the race question, and rustic "demagogues" won no state-wide contests. Because almost half her citizens were not native-born, her social structure was less rigid and her politics less traditionally southern. Because of her peculiar social structure there were more political factions than in other states, and sometimes a dozen candidates were in the first guber-natorial primaries. Alabama, on the other hand, is a more rural state and has a larger percentage of native-born citizens. The Farm Bureau is the spokesman for the well-to-do farmers of the black belt, who are allied with big business interests in Birmingham. But Alabama's one-party political system also has shown an inconsistent strain. In 1946, for instance, Jim Folsom and John Sparkman were nominated for governor and United States Senator respectively. Both were from north Alabama, and both were identified as progressives. Yet their sup-port came from different regions of the state, some counties giving Folsom a vote ten times the size of Sparkman's, while others went as heavily for Sparkman. This suggests that personal following took precedence over political issues or principles in both contests. Indeed, in one-party states, personality and local issues are more often than not decisive.

One of the arguments advanced to secure adoption of the primary in southern states was that in the one-party South the primary would afford an opportunity for all whites to vote, and that the degree of voter participation in the primary would be comparable to the regular election vote in two-party states. Such expectations, however, would not be realized. From 1920 to 1946 fewer than 30 per cent of adult southerners voted for governor in Democratic primaries; in Virginia, Tennessee, Georgia, and Alabama fewer than 20 per cent did. In strong two-party states like Ohio and New York, on the other hand, par-ticipation in general elections reached 75 and even 80 per cent. Nor can the low voting participation be laid only to Negro disfranchise-ment, for it was rare that as many as 15 per cent of adult whites in Virignia voted in primaries. Even within the South there were inconsistencies in voting behavior that defied explanation. Why, for instance, would twice as large a percentage of whites vote in Mississippi and South Carolina as in Alabama and Georgia? Why would a much smaller percentage of southern whites vote for United States Senator than for governor? In 1928, for instance, Kenneth McKellar was nominated for the Senate in Tennessee with only 120,000 votes, less than 10 per cent of the adult white population. Likewise, in 1944, Walter F. George won a landslide victory in Georgia with 211,000 votes, about 14 per cent of the adult population. In contrast, even one-party northern states like Maine and Vermont outvoted southern states by almost as much as did Ohio and New York. In 1932 only 255,000 Georgians out of 1,500,000 of voting age, cast ballots for President. This was 17 per cent of the adult population of the state, yet only slightly more than a third of Georgia's population was Negro at the time. Probably the insulation from national issues provided by the one-party system was largely responsible for poor voting participation in the South.[6]

On the other hand, the reduced electorate in the South, especially since the disfranchising conventions, gave the whites who did vote a weighted influence in national elections. Mississippi's 76,742 registered voters in 1892 chose nine representatives to Congress, while 335,747 Massachusetts voters chose only fifteen. Thus the Mississippi voter had approximately three times as much representation in Congress as the Massachusetts voter. But this was only the beginning. In the decade between 1892 and 1902 the average vote cast for Congressman declined 80 per cent in Georgia and Louisiana, 75 per cent in Arkansas, 69 per cent in Florida and Mississippi, 60 per cent in Alabama, 56 per cent in Virginia, 50 per cent in Tennessee, and 34 per cent in North Carolina. The city of Los Angeles cast more votes for President in 1924 than Georgia, Alabama, and Mississippi combined, but these southern states had thirty representatives in Congress, while Los Angeles had only two. Rhode Island in 1942 elected two Congressmen with 314,000 votes from a population of 687,000, while Mississippi, Alabama, Georgia, and South Carolina chose thirty-two Congressmen with 264,000 votes from a population of 9,300,000. This pattern would continue and would have significance in establishing political longevity for southern Congressmen.

Southern politics was thus caught in the predicament of trying to prevent corruption in a one-party system, the very cornerstone

(6) Key, *Southern Politics*, 492-7.

of which was "Negrophobia," and with even the whites indifferent
to fraud so long as the Negro was "kept in his place" and prevented
from voting. The resulting oligarchic regime consisting of planters,
businessmen, and industrialists tended to obliterate healthy, democratic
politics both on the local and national levels. In the words of
W.E.B. Du Bois, it "compels the white man to disfranchise himself in
order to take the vote away from the Negro."[7] And the party machinery was unable to meet the need of settling issues without an
opposition to raise them.

It is argued that the agrarian revolution, together with the institution of the primary election, brought demagogues for the first time
into southern politics, but they had been present since the redemption
and even before. Pleas for "white solidarity" so insistently urged by
"gentlemanly" leaders of the redemption were pleas to prejudice and
passion, just as were later crusades of so-called demagogues. Indeed,
so long as the South retained a one-party system, no politician could
avoid the agitation of racial discord. It was an issue on which the
most rational of voters would react emotionally, and a challenger attempting to unseat an incumbent office-holder could resort to Negro-
baiting, confident of its mass appeal. Nor was the seemingly secure
office-holder any more eager to see the racial issue resolved. For if
it should be, a two-party political system could be anticipated, new
issues would arise, and his position might be threatened by a newcomer
with new ideas. So long as he had the race issue to fall back on,
all others could be ignored.

The "Bourbon gentlemen" of the earlier period urged exclusion
of the Negroes from the polls so as to insure their own control, just
as later "demagogues" denounced Negroes in order to gain office.
In neither case was there actually danger of "Negro domination."
The "demagogues" were more vitriolic in their strictures on Negroes.
But L.Q.C. Lamar, Joseph E. Brown, John B. Gordon, and other
"gentlemen" made their appeals generally to smaller and more select
groups than did the "demagogues," they appealed to executive committees and party conventions which were the center of political power
in their day. Even so, when an opposition Republican ticket threatened
their control, these "gentlemen" never scrupled to paint the threat
of "Negro domination" in the most lurid colors. The "demagogues,"

(7) Quoted in Myrdal, *An American Dilemma*, 455.

living in a political milieu where the masses selected their candidates, and knowing the people better than did the "gentlemen," simply made more effective appeals. Denounced by their enemies as would-be destroyers of the social order, the "demagogues" resorted to vivid and dramatic appeals to the ignorant masses.

And it was the character of their rustic followers rather than what the rebels said that earned them their sobriquet. Thus, Tom Watson was denounced as a demagogue in his early period when he championed Negro voting just as he was later when he publicly advocated lynching to prevent Negro suffrage. Frank Burkitt and James K. Vardaman were both denounced as demagogues in Mississippi in the 1890's: the one for advocating Negro suffrage, the other for urging greater safeguards against it. The common denominator of all "demagogues" was that they were appealing to the same class, and all posed threats to the conservatives.

The typical "demagogue" is portrayed as an insincere opportunist without moral or political conviction. He is thought to be a man of limited ability bent upon securing political office by deceiving and misleading the voters and by appeals to their passions and prejudices. Many charged with demagoguery seemed to fill this prescription. On the other hand, many who passed for "gentlemen" and "statesmen" seem upon close examination to fit the description of the demagogue. Actually, "demagogues" were individuals with strong and colorful personalities, often with programs that went beyond Negro-baiting. It was a time of crying need for social reform which had long been ignored by the conservative leaders of the redemption. Those oligarchs, while paying lip-service to the majesty of the people, were, as we have seen, actually allied to the new business interests which the farmer regarded as his nemesis. The "demagogues" reawakened the social consciousness of the people, which had grown lethargic through long neglect. Had it not been for their racist extremism, some of them would deserve to rank with the great progressives of the nation: with Robert M. La Follette, or George W. Norris. The new election procedures gave them their chance and they made the most of it.

James K. Vardaman, for instance, was twice defeated for the gubernatorial nomination in Mississippi under the convention system. He was opposed by most party leaders, especially those in the Delta, and by almost all the press of the larger mercantile centers. He was

denounced as a dangerous radical for advocating repeal of the Fourteenth and Fifteenth Amendments. He campaigned throughout the
state, advocating also the division of school funds among Negroes and
whites according to the amounts of taxes paid by each race. The
state, Vardaman claimed, was paying half a million dollars a year
to educate the Negro in order to fit him for the higher duties of
citizenship, when actually the Negro, as everyone knew, would not
be permitted to rise above his lowly position. Consequently, the money
spent for his education was wasted and only made him dissatisfied.

But Vardaman did not argue his case dispassionately. Instead, he
launched into an emotional attack on the black race. The Negro was
"a curse to the country," "an industrial stumbling block," "a political
ulcer," "a social scab," "a lazy, lying, lustful animal which no con-
ceivable amount of training can transform into a tolerable citizen."
He urged lynching as the only antidote for the Negro's supposed lust
for white women, even though it occasionally resulted in punishment
of an innocent Negro. "We would be justified," he said, "in slaughter-
ing every Ethiop on the earth to preserve unsullied the honor of one
Caucasian home." Up and down the Magnolia state Vardaman went,
preaching the gospel of hate. He was a master showman. Clad in
white linen, with long hair flowing to his shoulders, he would enter
Mississippi backwoods towns in a farm wagon drawn by oxen. None
of his peers, at least until Theodore G. Bilbo emerged as his heir,
could match his malevolent eloquence. The hill farmers loved and
trusted him. For almost two decades Vardaman was the "Great White
Chief" of Mississippi, and no aspiring politician there who did not
have his approval could hope for preferment.

Elected governor in 1903, Vardaman's administration produced
social reforms long overdue in Mississippi. He brought an end to convict leasing, as we have seen, and improved vastly the conditions on
the state penal farms. In a time of general agricultural depression in
an overwhelmingly agricultural state, he increased common-school appropriations by 20 per cent and teachers' salaries 30 per cent. He
created a state textbook commission which broke the monopoly of
the American Book Company. He obtained legislation providing for
the regulation of insurance companies, railroads, banks, utilities, and
manufacturers. He sought but was unable to win legislative support
for child-labor laws, the building of a state school for the deaf and

dumb, aid to cripples and unfortunates, creation of a state highway commission, and a reduction of the legal rate of interest from 10 per cent to 8 per cent. At the same time, he vetoed measures permitting corporations to acquire vast real estate holdings and a bill permitting merger of railroad lines within the state. He also vetoed a bill creating a central bureau for fire insurance companies because it would establish a monopoly.

Bilbo, Vardaman's lieutenant, developed a new technique which made him the equal if not the superior of his master. He lacked Vardaman's impressive physical appearance, and his eloquence too, but he had an earthy humor that captivated his rural followers. Vardaman's private life was above reproach, whereas Bilbo was a notorious frequenter of bawdy houses and an associate of "fallen women." He was several times charged with accepting bribes while a member of the legislature. Nevertheless, Bilbo built a career on the discovery and exposure of moral laxity in his political opponents. In 1910 he was tried before the Mississippi senate for accepting $645 as a bribe to vote for Delta planter-lawyer Leroy Percy in a legislative caucus to choose a United States Senator. Bilbo admitted accepting the money but claimed he did so only to catch the evildoers. Four years later Bilbo was indicted for soliciting a bribe to create a new county in the Delta. Again he admitted the deed but contended he was acting only to entrap "criminal elements" who were corrupting the halls of government. The Mississippi senate resolved that Bilbo was "utterly unworthy of belief" and "unfit to sit with honest, upright men in a respectable legislative body." Percy denounced him as "a low-flung scullion, who disgraces the form of man," " a vile degenerate," and "a moral leper." But the farmers from the hills and piney woods gave Bilbo their votes, electing him governor twice and United States Senator three times. According to one observer, the people supported him not because they thought him innocent of the misdeeds of which he was charged but despite his guilt. They identified themselves with him as victims of the planter-merchant-industrialist oligarchy.

But whatever virtue his private life may have lacked, Bilbo's political career was not devoid of accomplishment. As governor he instituted notable tax reforms: establishment of a central board of equalization with power to revise assessments throughout the state so as to tax property at full value and equalize the burdens of government.

In its first year the board was able to add $300 million of property to the tax rolls and to reduce the tax rate commensurately. Bilbo obtained legislation establishing a new state tuberculosis sanatorium, the erection of a new state charity hospital and enabling legislation for three more, a hog-vaccination law for the elimination of cholera, the creation of a state highway commission with projected plans for a network of modern roads, establishment of a state board to systematize and regularize the granting of pardons, passage of a uniform negotiable instrument law, abolition of the fee system to support county offices, creation of a state board of legal examiners, enactment of a "blue sky" law to prevent the marketing of worthless stocks, and abolition of public hangings. On the other hand, he demoralized the state with his scandalous private behavior, and he discredited the state's colleges by discharging staff members who displeased him.[8]

A "demagogue" who aroused the rural masses in South Carolina much as did Vardaman in Mississippi was Ben Tillman, rustic, one-eyed farmer from Edgefield. Tillman was forty years old before the agricultural depression drove him into politics as the champion of the common man against the "aristocracy." He defeated Wade Hampton for governor in 1890, and for a dozen years thereafter he was undisputed political boss of South Carolina and served either as governor or Senator until his death in 1918. He had an earthy style of speech: his nickname grew from his promise that if the voters would send him to Washington he would stick his pitchfork into Grover Cleveland's ribs. He advocated force if necessary to keep the Negro disfranchised, and he justified lynching as ardently as Vardaman ever did. He lacked the dignified bearing of Vardaman, on one occasion actually engaging in fisticuffs with Anselm J. McLaurin in the United States Senate; but he was a match for Vardaman in pandering to the baser emotions of his poor white constituents. But like Vardaman, Tillman, for a time at least, devoted his energies to improving conditions of the white farmers: bringing them more actively into government through the compulsory primary, revising the tax system for their benefit, and establishing the state agricultural college at Clemson.

A politician of a different stripe, one without Tillman's redeeming virtues, was Cole Blease, whom Tillman brought to power and who was elected governor of South Carolina in 1910. Blease had the private

(8) Kirwan, *Revolt of the Rednecks*, 146-7, 152, 196-7, 211-2, 270-2.

morals of a Bilbo, although his administration was marked by none of the progressive legislation which Bilbo's achieved in Mississippi. A handsome man, flamboyant in dress and speaking style, he rose to political influence as a disciple of Tillman. He improved on Tillman's demagogic technique, however, making himself the pretended champion not only of the farmer but of the mill workers of the towns as well—the latter a group Tillman despised. Blease was continually attacked by "respectable" politicians and by the city press; and like Bilbo he turned this to his advantage, identifying himself with the common man as the victim of the oppression of the rich. Vardaman, Tillman, and Bilbo all could point to constructive measures they sponsored, but Blease's administrations were marked by his opposition to reform bills of all kinds: labor bills, including child-labor laws, even anti-trust legislation. In the end even Tillman turned against him, although by that time Blease had grown so strong Tillman was unable to prevent Blease's re-election. The people seemed to follow Blease because he, better than anyone else, expressed their hatred of two opposite groups, the down-trodden Negroes on the one hand and the well-to-do respectable leaders of white society on the other.

Rivaling Blease in his tirades against the Negro was Ellison D. "Cotton Ed" Smith. Smith hardly pretended to be more than he was, spokesman in the Senate for the planter and industrial interests of South Carolina, but he won election after election by whipping up the people through vague appeals to shibboleths of state-rights and by his attacks on the Negro. In campaigning for the United States Senate in 1908 Smith dressed up in a farm hat and rode about the state on a farm wagon loaded with cotton, all the time denouncing Wall Street and the Cotton Exchange for their abuse of the poor, hard-working, God-fearing cotton farmer.

Tom Watson of Georgia was another of the so-called demagogues. He began his career as a fiery champion of the small farmer, both white and black, in the 1880's and soon became one of the Independents of that period, fighting against the oligarchial rule of the triumvirate, Brown, Gordon, and Colquitt. In this early period, Watson risked his life to protect his Negro followers from severe beatings and worse. Elected as a Democrat to Congress in 1890, he switched to the Populist party. He supported all agricultural and labor reform bills and introduced a resolution which passed the House calling for rural free delivery of mail. Meanwhile, the Georgia legislature, controlled by the triumvirate, gerrymandered his district; and in the election of 1892 he was defeated by a Democrat in a bloody election contest in which he felt that the Negro vote was corruptly manipulated by his opponents to effect his defeat. Embittered, he turned savagely against his former black friends and henceforth was the most vitriolic of race-baiters. In countless speeches and writings he portrayed the Negro as ignorant and debased, incapable of intellectural or moral improvement and in a biological state somewhere between the simian and the human. Like Vardaman, Tillman, Blease, and others, he openly advocated lynching as punishment for Negroes charged with raping white women.

In 1896 Watson was candidate for Vice President on the Populist ticket with William Jennings Bryan, and in 1904 and 1908 he was the party's candidate for President. Then Watson's character underwent a great change. He rejoined the Democratic party, and, switching his support from faction to faction, he became the balance of political power in his state, although he himself was twice defeated for re-election to Congress. Meantime, he kept up his denunciation of the Negro, coupling it with tirades against Jews, Catholics, American intervention in the First World War, and against the League of Nations. Elected to the Senate in 1920, he turned full circle to his early position as a champion of labor, the farmer, and of civil rights. Although he possessed great talent, at the end of his career there was nothing that could be pointed to as a substantial contribution that he had made either to his state or his nation.

Most extraordinary of all the so-called demagogues and the one with by far the greatest ability was Huey P. Long of Louisiana. Born in the north-central parish of Winn, Huey grew up under the influence of Populist and socialist ideas which were strong there. Winn Parish had been anti-secessionist in 1860 and contributed little to the Confederate cause; indeed, Huey's father later claimed that both he and Huey's mother were Union sympathizers. The fact that Huey later made few sentimental appeals in his campaign speeches to the memories of the Lost Cause may be a reflection of his early environment. It is equally notable that Huey never relied on that other oft-repeated theme of embattled southern politicians—race-baiting. Instead of talking about the Negro, Huey discussed economics: the oil trust and other monopolies which were extracting an enormous toll on the wealth of the state.

In 1918, at the age of twenty-five, he was elected to the three-man railroad commission which had regulatory powers over all public service corporations. Here started his long feud with the Standard Oil Company when he persuaded the commission to rule that oil pipelines were common carriers and thus subject to regulation. Four years later, as chairman, he obtained reversal of a telephone rate increase and forced a refund to subscribers of excess rates collected over a two-year period. He followed this by persuading the legislature, over the opposition of the governor, to increase the severance tax charged oil companies on petroleum extracted from Louisiana wells.

Elected governor over the opposition of the Democratic party regulars in 1928, he set about building a political machine the like of which had never been seen in the South before. By his own admission, in order to enact his program, he bought legislators "like sacks of potatoes." The legislature was, he said, a "deck of cards" which he shuffled at will. He claimed, and perhaps truthfully, that he was only fighting fire with fire: that his opposition was bribing legislators to oppose him. When Long was under impeachment trial in 1929, one previously hostile senator voted for acquittal. Asked how he had effected the switch, Long replied, "Just the same way they got him. . . . I bought him."

Long started out as a supporter of Franklin D. Roosevelt and, indeed, helped swing southern support to him in the fight for the Presidential nomination in 1932. But Long soon broke with the New Deal over the NRA and over such programs as the destruction of crops to sustain prices. "There is," he once said, "no need of hunger in the land of too much to eat; no need of people crying for things to wear in the land of too much cotton and wool; no need of homelessness in the land of too many houses."

More than any other of the so-called demagogues, Long had a program. He was truly concerned with the social and economic welfare of the mass of people, especially the farmers, and his attention was never long diverted from his objective. The record of accomplishment in his brief career is truly remarkable. Between his inaugural in 1929 and his death in 1935, Louisiana's hard-road mileage grew tenfold, from 331 to 3750, while its gravel roads grew from 5728 to 9629, and the three major bridges within the highway system had become forty. Improvement in public education was equally noteworthy: free textbooks, increase of 20 per cent in school attendance, increased appropriations for higher education, free night schools for adult illiterates of both races. State hospitals were built and the most modern treatment and care provided. These improvements were instituted largely by increasing the bonded indebtedness of the state from $11 million to $150 million. But the funding of bonds was provided by new taxation which fell largely on corporations, especially the Standard Oil Company.

Long's program as governor was progressive, but hardly as radical as his opponents claimed. Nevertheless, he alarmed conservatives by his efforts to consolidate patronage in the hands of the governor and particularly by his success in rooting his power in the loyalty of the mass of voters. By 1934 he had created "the most thorough state dictatorship known in twentieth century America." It was this which changed the basic pattern of politics in Louisiana and made it difficult for the upper classes, the union of planters and industrialists, to regain the control they had held since reconstruction. Probably his most significant contribution to Louisiana politics was the creation of a bi-factionalism in which distinct groups supported the rival factions and displayed consistent political attitudes. Dirt farmers were aligned against planters, and the rural population against the urban.

Moving on to the United States Senate, Long launched his Share-the-Wealth program in March 1932. This truly radical program called for the confiscation of all personal fortunes in excess of $3 million and distribution of $4000 or $5000 (Long was not specific as to the amount) to every poor family to purchase a home, an automobile, and a radio. Monthly pensions of $30 or $50 (again he was not specific) would be paid to persons over sixty-five. Minimum wage laws would place a floor of $2500 (or $3000) a year under the income of each worker. Hours of labor would be limited to balance production with consumption, and agricultural surpluses would be purchased and stored by the government. Payment of a cash bonus to veterans and college scholarships for talented boys would also be provided. On this program Long probably hoped to win the Presidency in 1936, but an assassin's bullet brought his career to an end when he was on a visit to a special session of the Louisiana legislature in September 1935.

Despite Long's legislative achievements, his support of labor and of education was somewhat restrained. Actually of the total state expenditures, the proportion for education declined during his administration, although the amount spent increased greatly. He made large appropriations for the state university, but he interfered with the freedom of the institution, and he placed a corrupt and incompetent man in its presidency. He opposed the sales tax as regressive, but his graduated income tax had only a small spread between high and low tax brackets.[9]

Long used dictatorial methods to achieve his ends. Certainly, however, the label "dictator," at least with its European connotations, did not apply to him; although he was a powerful and ruthless political boss. Even after he left the governor's office for the United States Senate he continued to direct affairs in Baton Rouge. He would return to sessions of the Louisiana legislature, where he gave direct orders to his followers whether in committee room or from the floor of the legislative halls. On one occasion he forced passage of forty-four bills in twenty-two minutes. A total of 463 bills were passed in seven special sessions in the last year of his life.

As we have seen, many of the "demagogues" were race-baiters; others lacked a program, or the ability to put one through once they gained office. Some, with good intentions, were hopelessly confused as to what needed to be done. Some were charlatans and scoundrels who once they gained office sold out to the interests who opposed them. But the best of them—Long, Vardaman, and even Bilbo—worked for the best interests of the people whom they represented and who trusted them. Southern political history, confusing at best, is hopelessly confounded by too free usage of the term demagogue. It would be better to forget the word altogether and to classify politicians, if indeed they must be classified, as reformers or non-reformers, as progressives or conservatives. For although these terms are sweeping and subjective too, they do avoid evaluation of motives, a thing not often possible, and permit judgments on the politicans' accomplishments rather than on their supposed beliefs.

Throughout the first half of the twentieth century the Republican party made sporadic efforts to break the stranglehold of the Demo-

(9) T. Harry Williams, "The Gentleman from Louisiana," *Journal of Southern History*, XXVI (Feb. 1960), 3-21.

cratic party on the South. Its efforts were supported by southern intellectuals who saw the need for two parties, if the South was to regain a voice in national affairs, and also by industrialists interested in tariffs, ship subsidies, and the gold standard. One manifestation of Republican resurgence in the South was the "lily-white" movement, an effort to make Republicanism respectable by minimizing Negro influence and making it similar to the all-white Democratic party. The lily-whites were stronger in the upper South, but they existed in the deep South, too. Even before the Negro was legally disfranchised at the turn of the century, the lily-whites urged abandonment of him, repudiation of federal intervention in elections, and the appointment of white men to federal offices in the South.

Theodore Roosevelt, in his eagerness to break the Solid South, vacillated in his attitude toward the lily-whites. "Really, if I could carry one of the eleven ex-Confederate States, I should feel as though I could die happy," he wrote.[10] He even appointed respectable white southern Democrats to office, but when this policy threatened his control of the large number of Negro delegates to the Republican convention in 1904, he backed down. Thereafter, he removed lily-whites from office in the South and appointed Negroes in their place, a Negro collector at the port of Charleston and a Negro woman postmaster at Indianola, Mississippi. Roosevelt's efforts to win white southerners to his party finally went aground when they accused him of inviting Booker T. Washington to dine at the White House. But Roosevelt was disgusted by the undemocratic and corrupt Negro leadership of the Republican party in the South. He regarded the hand-picked Negro delegates to Republican national conventions as "rotten-borough delegates" who had no interest in building strong state parties but who, on the contrary, wished to keep the party small so that they might continue to exercise monopolistic control of federal patronage. He called them "black and white scalawags . . . whose venality makes them a menace to the whole party."[11]

Roosevelt's strictures were generally true but exaggerated, for there were some "genuine" Republicans as distinguished from "Presi-

(10) Quoted in Arthur S. Link, "Theodore Roosevelt and the South in 1912," *North Carolina Historical Review*, XXIII (July 1946), 313-24.
(11) Quoted in Henry F. Pringle, "Theodore Roosevelt and the South," *Virginia Quarterly Review*, IX (January 1933), 14-25.

dential" Republicans in the South in his day. His charge was particularly applicable, however, to Mississippi where, after the Populist revolt, almost all Republicans were Negroes. They were dominated by Negro leaders, first James Hill and John R. Lynch, and later Perry Howard. These men had the support of the national leaders of the Republican party, and all efforts by the few southern white Republicans to oust them proved abortive. Carrying Mississippi in Presidential elections was not possible in the first place, and the important thing to national party leaders was the control of the state delegation at nominating conventions; and despite contests, delegations headed by Lynch and Howard were seated at Republican conventions throughout the first half of the twentieth century.

The same situation existed elsewhere, only to a lesser degree. Everywhere in the South—even in the mountainous districts of Virginia, North Carolina, and Tennessee, the traditional Republican territory—growth of the Republican party was frustrated by selfish leaders, willing and eager to keep the party weak locally so that they might dispense patronage when a Republican occupied the White House. These leaders actually resisted efforts to build a party which might win state elections, for fear that strong leaders might then unseat them.

In 1908 Taft revived Roosevelt's early "lily-white" program, and Republicans showed marked gains that year in the South. Indeed, a few thousand additional votes would have swung both North Carolina and Tennessee to his banner. Almost all Taft's southern votes were cast by white men, too, for Negroes had by that time practically ceased to vote in the region. Encouraged by these results, Taft redoubled his efforts. In a speech in Atlanta he told Negroes their best friends were southern whites, and he said that he saw no inconsistency between southern suffrage laws and the Fifteenth Amendment. Taft might have accomplished much in rebuilding a southern Republican party, but his plans went sour when southern farmers turned against him for his support of the Payne-Aldrich tariff, which they regarded as a betrayal. In the end, the "lily-white" movement proved a failure on all counts. Herbert Hoover paid his respects to it in the early 1930's, but in 1940 the Republican national convention established a rule that Congressional districts casting fewer than a thousand Republican votes in the preceding election would lose representation in succeeding conventions. This rule again encouraged the recruitment of

Negro voters, for at this time large numbers of southern whites could not afford to desert the Democratic party.

Meanwhile, southern Democrats were all but ignored in the national councils of their party. Desperate to regain lost influence, they traded back and forth between eastern and western factions of the party. Embracing Bryan and free silver in 1896 and in 1900 in an alliance with the West, in 1904 they turned their backs on the Great Commoner and joined easterners in support of Alton B. Parker and the gold standard. But the new alliance did no better than the old, and the South was driven back to support of Bryan and the western alliance in 1908. With Bryan's third failure that year, the section found itself once more cut off from influence in national affairs.

This wandering in the political wilderness would receive at least a temporary respite in 1912, for in that one year would the southern voice be decisive in the choice of a Democratic nominee. Woodrow Wilson was backed by the progressive wing of the party in the South as elsewhere, while the conservatives of necessity rallied behind Oscar W. Underwood of Alabama. It was Wilson's native southern leaders at the Baltimore convention—Albert Burleson and Thomas W. Gregory of Texas, Luke Lea and William G. McAdoo of Tennessee, and William F. McCombs of Arkansas, urban progressives all—who held his southern delegates firm for him during forty-six ballots. This southern vote, together with that of New Jersey and Pennsylvania, was the rock upon which Wilson's ultimate victory was built.

But Wilson's strong southern support was unable to overcome southern apathy. Despite the fact that the general election that year was one of the most exciting in the history of the nation, with three attractive and colorful candidates, the South again lagged far behind other sections in voter participation. For one reason or another—one party, poll tax, literacy requirement—only 20 per cent of registered southern voters went to the polls as compared to 60 per cent for the nation as a whole.

With Wilson's election in November, a "revolution" not unlike those of 1800 and 1828 took place. The South returned to a position of influence in national affairs for the first time since 1860. Five of the new cabinet were either southerners or New Yorkers of southern background. In addition, Walter Hines Page of North Carolina was appointed Ambassador to England, Thomas Nelson Page of Virginia

ambassador to Italy, and Hugh L. White of Louisiana Chief Justice.
Thomas S. Martin, a Virginian, became majority leader of the Senate,
and Underwood of Alabama party leader in the House. Fifteen chairmanships of seventeen important House committees were taken over
by southerners, and almost as many in the Senate.

The 1920's brought a second resurgence of Republicanism in the
South. There was social unrest in the aftermath of the First World
War not unlike that of the Populist period three decades before. A
simultaneous growth of industry, urbanization, tenantry, and crop-
sharing had produced a class consciousness similar to that of the Old
South, but which lacked the paternalistic humanism of the earlier
period. Mill workers and farm tenants grew resentful over the depressed conditions of their existence. Their restiveness coincided with
the growth of a vigorous labor movement in the country, much of
it far to the left of the highly conservative American Federation of
Labor. Fear of the "red menace" was general throughout the country;
it struck particular terror in the heart of the southern millowner,
who equated all labor organizers with Communists. Southern patriotism
at the time was dedicated to progress, progress meant new industry,
and industry in the South was based on cheap labor. Thus, labor
unions were anathema to the established order, so much so that even
working men themselves were generally antagonistic to unions.

Coincident with labor unrest and closely associated with it was
a southern antagonism to aliens, who were competitors for workers'
jobs on the one hand and who were unburdened with a reverence
for "the southern way of life" on the other. Although many of these
aliens were Catholics, they too were equated with Communism. To
add to the unrest, there was always the Negro who, though generally
docile, was regarded with suspicion by the white men who exploited
and abused him.

As an antidote for this witches' cauldron of social unrest, there
grew up in the early 1920's the new Ku Klux Klan, whose name
was its only link with the Klan of reconstruction days. It was not
limited to the South, being particularly strong in the Midwest; but
the South was its spiritual home and the region where it exercised
greatest power and influence. The masses of the order were lower-class
whites, but its leaders were small-business and professional men. Industrialists and planters kept close liaison with its leaders, and even

the clergy were in it in great numbers. Politicians either joined it
or sought its support. Qualifications for membership were: twenty-one
years of age, white, gentile, Protestant, and membership in "a respectable profession." Asked what his profession was, one Imperial Wizard
who was an unemployed salesman replied, "Ku Klucking." The Klan
was, Wilbur J. Cash pointed out, "anti-Negro, anti-alien, anti-com-
munist, anti-Catholic, anti-Jew, anti-Darwin, anti-Modern, anti-Lib-
eral." It was militantly Protestant and fundamentalist. By terrorism
and by public exposure of personal sin it attempted to make itself
the chief instrument of preserving the moral status quo. It whipped
Negroes, prostitutes, adulterers, drunkards, ne'er-do-wells, child
deserters, non-churchgoers, and by so doing hoped to restore orthodoxy
both in religion and in morality. It tarred and feathered labor organizers or teachers who departed from fundamentalist doctrine. It
paraded through towns, terrifying Catholics, Jews, and aliens. The
Klan flourished through the mid-1920's and was on the decline when
the election of 1928 rejuvenated it for a time.[12]

The nomination of Al Smith by the Democrats at Houston faced
southern politicians with a dilemma. Smith was a Catholic and a wet,
and abhorrent to the Klan on both counts; on the other hand, Hoover,
the Republican candidate, was dry and Protestant, characteristics
which appealed to the rural South in general and to the Klan in particular. But many southern politicians feared to bolt the Democratic
party because of the dire effect desertion would have on their own
political futures. On the other hand, support of Hoover might in many
sections swing enough Democratic voters into Republican ranks to
defeat local Democrats. In the end, many compromised by supporting
the state Democratic ticket but refusing to vote for either Smith or
Hoover. They became the "anti-Smith Democrats."

The result was that the Solid South was broken for the first time
since 1876; Tennessee, Virginia, North Carolina, Florida, and Texas
all went for Hoover. Had it not been for the presence of Arkansas'
Joseph Robinson on the ticket with Smith, probably that state, too,
would have bolted. As it was, only Arkansas and the deep South
states of Alabama, Mississippi, Louisiana, Georgia, and South Carolina
remained loyal to the Democracy, and Alabama was saved for them
by only a slim margin. Hoover's victory in the upper South was a

(12) Cash, *The Mind of the South*, 335-42.

landmark in southern political history and demonstrated that no longer could southerners be counted on to support any Democrat to the exclusion of all other considerations. This election, too, fully revealed the decided shift in policies of the two great parties nationally. The Republican party, whose base was the great rural regions of the North and West, had grown conservative with political prosperity; while the Democrats, whose strength in the North lay in the great cities, had become increasingly progressive. The South, being rural, had a natural affinity for the Republican party, which only history and tradition and the fear of once more bringing the Negro into active political participation kept apart. Henceforth, the South would be Democratic nationally only in a nominal sense, in Presidential elections, and even there with an ever-decreasing consistency. Racist and nativist, its primaries would prove more and more embarrassing to northern Democrats, who more and more were forced to court the northern Negro and foreign vote. In the North, too, the Democratic party was becoming more closely allied with organized labor, while the plantation ideology still dominated southern thought, despite the prevalence of tenant farming and sharecropping. True, industrialization was making inroads in the South, but workers there were still far from the proletarian attitude.

Many southern whites voted Republican in 1928, but the returns show that whites in the black belt were most loyal to the Democratic party, while those regions with fewest Negroes gave Hoover his greatest support. Hoover's smallest vote was in Mississippi and South Carolina, the two states with the highest percentages of Negro population. Of 191 southern counties with more than 50 per cent Negro population, 184 gave Smith a majority. Of 266 counties with less than 5 per cent Negro population, only 79 gave him a majority, and 21 of these were in Arkansas where Joseph Robinson's influence was strongest. Thus, the whites in the black belt again demonstrated their traditional loyalty to the Democracy, bound to the party by their anxiety over the Negro. On the other hand, whites outside the black belt could afford the luxury of voting on issues other than the Negro.

❧ VI ❧

The Path to Industrialization

The Confederate soldier who turned homeward from Appomattox in 1865 not only had the farewell message of General Robert E. Lee ringing in his ear; his troubled mind was also fixed on going home to make a new economic beginning for himself and his region. Obviously the war had been ruinous to the South, and the region was in deep economic trouble. Most industries which were organized before 1860 were destroyed or so badly disorganized that they awaited new capital investment and fresh management. Young southern management talent which might have given southern industry new impetus was now either rotting in soldier's graves or so poverty-struck and frustrated that it was incapable of offering aggressive leadership. One of the costliest consequences of the war was the discouragement of southern industrial aggressiveness, which would have made the region competitive with the East and Northwest in the years of rapid industrial rise and expansion. Southerners lacked capital necessary to organize any sort of a major industry, and no one could be certain which direction the South would go in its political and social efforts to recover from the war. Whatever happened, however, it was clear that it would of necessity be placed in secondary positions in the building of a new industry.

Contemporary travel accounts and other descriptive material revealed a South held down from 1865 to 1882 by political and economic frustration. In 1873 and 1874 Edward King traveled in the former states of the Confederacy. There he saw drabness of surroundings, lack of hope, and little inclination toward industrial organization and progress. George A. Sala and his wife toured the region in 1879-80 and saw a land caught in the net of backwardness, ignorance and shiftlessness of the Negro, and agrarian poverty. Scores of other visitors in the two immediate postwar decades found the South a sharp contrast to the rest of the country. They recorded a sense of movement in which young and ambitious whites, along with large numbers of Negroes, were on the move to the North and the expanding West.

The brightest spot in the postwar South was the fact that the basic natural resources were still intact. Defeatists, who have constantly bemoaned the ruin of the South in the war, have overlooked the importance of southern natural resources. Both southerners and outsiders (northern and European capitalists) had before them the broad promise of wealth in the exploitation and utilization of these resources. The postwar South's advance into the future depended on three facts: How quickly would the significance of natural resources, other than land, be recognized? How far would exploiters go in perceiving a certain unity in the resources? How much would the South be held back by a feeling of defeat on the one hand, and by the lingering impact of traditionalism on the other? The region was very uncertain about the role the emancipated Negro was to play in southern affairs.

Many important resources awaited development. Labor, water, timber, minerals, petroleum, and land all existed in abundance, and all were largely in a raw and unexploited state in 1865. With the exception of cheap labor, the southern resources required the expenditure of enormous energy and capital to bring them into profitable production.

The years 1865-1920 were tragic ones in the South not because political reconstruction with all its deep-seated political inanities and social failures, had created deep emotional scars, but because natural and human resources which could have given the region new economic direction were ignored. Failure to use some degree of intelligence in producing great sources of natural wealth was really a national scandal. The policy of many promoters, inside and outside the South, and exploiters during the earlier postwar years amounted to "get in and get out" full-handed, no matter what permanent damage was done. There were limiting facts of the times which, of course, must be considered. Lack of capital, lack of venturesome native economic leadership, lack of transportation facilities, and a woeful lack of native skill were all serious deterrents.

It is no doubt true that resources everywhere yielded greater returns when they were utilized in conjunction with other resources. No place was this fact more eloquently revealed than in the economic history of the South after 1865. To exploit one resource without consideration of all the others produced shameful waste.

The basic southern resource has always been land. From 1865 to 1930 it was viewed largely in terms of its agricultural and timber-producing qualities, and the two were almost always considered separate from each other. Land was viewed largely as a resource for the production of cultivated crops, while timber was treated as an inexhaustible resource, exploited with no thought of future needs or of the nature of soils that grew good quality trees. In the same way water was something to drink to satisfy a momentary thirst, something to feed a fishing stream, a source of power for small and inefficient grain mills or cotton factories, or a bearer of steamboats. Missing from the economic approaches of the period between the Civil War and the end of World War I was a developed sense of conservation.

Land usage is treated more fully in the discussion of agriculture. Here it is considered in its broader relationship to other resources. The failure of southern land was due not so much to abusive modes of cultivation as to ignorance of its physical properties and deficiencies. No one prior to 1910 had an adequate knowledge of the chemical analysis of most of the southern soils, or of the chemical additives necessary to bring them into maximum production. The waste of soils which occurred at a frightening rate was due as much to ignorance as to a ruinous credit system or one-crop agriculture. When crusaders and editors pleaded for diversification in use of the land as a means of increasing income, they often asked for the same exhaustive exploitation of the soil.

Land and water use were inseparably associated. Before water appeared as a stream or as a lake it fell first on the land. How much silt and debris it transported depended to a large extent on land use itself. Water has been one of the most important resources in the development of the New South. Its importance ranged from the growing of timber to the generation of industrial power.

From the Potomac to the thick rim of eastern Texas, the South has grown heavy stands of timber of many varieties, and many of them have high commercial value. No other region of the United

States produced so great a variety of trees; over 150 species, or was crowned by finer stands of virgin stock. There were two major pine belts, the long leaf, or slash pine, which stretched around the coastal area from eastern Virginia to coastal Texas, and the short-leaf pine-deciduous belt, which covered the South from the ridges of Maryland to the Ozarks in Arkansas. From the long-leaf belt came a high percentage of the processed lumber shipped out of the early postwar South to northern and European markets, and all the turpentine gum.

The swamps of the coastal belt grew cypress, red gum, oaks of several varieties, hickory, and ash. While the ridgeland and mountain South yielded the loblolly and Virginia pines in heavy stands, poplar, maples, oaks, walnut, chestnut, hemlock, white hickory, and beech. This resource was one of the earliest exploited by Anglo-American settlers. From the casting of the first English settlement in the tidelands of Virginia, pine and hardwoods were used for ship timbers, building materials, household furnishings, and farm implements.

As settlers advanced across the South, they cut holes in the forest as patches and plantations. They cut tunnels through the vast woods to form trails and roads; they scarcely had force enough to sweep the forest itself away. In the opening of the seventeenth century there were approximately a million square miles of unbroken forest lands in the South. A ride through this area would have revealed a monstrous arcade of trees stretching more than 2000 miles in length and 400 in width. In 1865 perhaps a minimum of 65 per cent of the surface of the South was covered by forest growth. By 1923 no more than 260,000 square miles were left in second-growth merchantable forests.

In less than sixty-five years the South's timber resources had been butchered. The lumbering industry repeated below the Ohio the reckless "cutting and getting out" that had laid waste to the vast northern timber belt from Maine to Washington. One of the first industries to revive in the South following the Civil War, the lumber industry capitalized on the great demand for lumber in rebuilding the South and other parts of the expanding nation. On the New Orleans market the output of the Mississippi coastal mills returned twenty-five to thirty million dollars in 1865, a market which had been opened with the federal occupation of that city in 1863. Almost every year after 1870 saw the southern lumber industry expand its output.

Technological changes were necessary before the full development of southern lumbering could take place. Mills of sufficient power and capacity had to be developed and built before the heavy virgin saw logs could be handled, and band saws and high-speed carriages, more efficient edgers, and off-bearing or conveyer beds greatly facilitated sawing of lumber. In order for the larger companies to organize and operate the big all-purpose mills, it was necessary to secure access to large stands of timber, by both purchase of lands or procurement from private owners. Once mill owners embarked upon the procurement and extensive exploitation of far-flung stands, they were forced to go into the steamboat and railroad business. "Mud" lines were built through the forests, and donkey or "dummy" locomotives were used to push strings of log cars deep into the virgin woods, where ox wagons and lumberjacks met them with logs.

Southern raw lumber also became more desirable through the introduction of planning and matching mills, which processed lumber for a more profitable market. The swamps yielded millions of feet of cypress, oak, poplar, maple, and ash that brought top prices when converted into paneling, flooring, and furniture stocks. Creosoting and pressure treating of heavy timbers and poles after 1900 likewise increased profits. Despite the fact that a great deal of southern lumber was cut, planed, matched, and sometimes treated before it was started off to the ultimate consumer, most of it was sent away from the South to be converted into machine parts, ship timbers, building materials, furniture, and other commercial products.

Small mills scattered throughout the South converted large quantities of hickory, oak, and chestnut into tool handles and beams, spokes, felloes, hubs, barrels, tubs, and tannic acid for tanning purposes. Until the advent of the metal wheel in the manufacture of the automobile, and the introduction of the motor truck and tractor onto the American farm, there was a flourishing market in the manufacture of wheels and wood frames for farm implements. The automobile displaced the horse-drawn carriage; trucks and tractors displaced wagons and carts. Thus a wood-consuming industry that once flourished in the South was destroyed.

In 1870 the South produced 9.4 per cent of the timber cut in the nation as a whole. Near the end of the nineteenth century this figure had advanced to almost a third of the national cut, and in the peak decades, 1910-30, it was just under 50 per cent. Louisiana,

Mississippi, Arkansas, and Alabama were among the top lumber producers. Nine of the southern states in 1929 produced more than a billion feet of lumber, and there was an estimated stand in these states of 424 billion feet still in the woods.

The lumber industry was to have a profound influence on the New South. Timber was an elementary natural resource which could be processed even by use of the most primitive tools. There was a rising demand both at home and abroad for lumber and heavy timbers. Sawmill companies were organized in large numbers, with mills ranging in size from the small stationary steam rigs located in the midst of virgin stands to the large band mills which were fed by stream flotation and by railroad. These large operations, surrounded by their village shacks of workmen, became raw industrial communities which broke with the old southern social mores in almost every aspect of life. From manager to "sawdust doodler," lumbermen were socially and morally uninhibited, and according to the lights of southern rural society, wicked and blasphemous.

For the first time the South had a wage-paying industry which employed ignorant and unskilled labor for much of its operation. For thousands of common men, lumbering broke the dependence upon the meager returns from cash crops. For many southerners it was a highly satisfactory calling, because, next to farming, it was the closest of all modern American industries to the frontier. Men spent today what they hoped to make on the morrow, while their masters lived by an even harder philosophy. They believed in cutting and getting out with as much profit as they could. To them, men, mills, cattle, and mules were always expendable. The virgin stand of timber which had taken a century or more to mature seemed to wait their coming. Companies bought land by the hundreds of thousands of acres for ridiculously low prices per acre. Residual landholders were unable to see in the waiting forests the great profits which could be garnered by proper management.

Behind most of the mills the southern forest lands were left stripped of timber. This was especially true of the great long-leaf pine belt which stretched around the Atlantic and Gulf coasts. When the big mills had taken their toll of the prime trees, they ceased operation and left the field to the smaller operators, who removed the remaining stand; thus there were left millions of acres of sterile and compacted cutover land incapable really of re-seeding itself and of once again becoming productive. Conservation of forest resources of the South had to await further exhaustion of timber and the fright of the depression.

In the Appalachian Highlands at the end of the war there were soul-inspiring tracts of virgin hardwoods which had been centuries in maturing. Companies like the English Corporation at Newport, Tennessee, and Middlesboro, Kentucky, slashed this timber to the ground with a vengeance. In the Cumberland, Tennessee, Kentucky, and Big Sandy valleys the streams were jammed in freshet seasons with rafts of hardwood logs which had been rolled down and assembled on stream banks in the hills. Throughout the Appalachian South the land and timber speculator worked overtime to gain possession of the forests from naive hill-country natives who were incapable of imagining their lands stripped of forest cover or the value of their timber. The ridges, however, were left stripped of trees in a remarkably short time, and bleeding gores in the land poured down millions of tons of silt to clog streams and rivers, and to menace the lowlands with flash floods. No effort was made at selective cutting, at forest management, or in the grading of logs cut from the stands. Only as nature healed over the ugly wounds of wasteful exploitation were portions of the pine and hardwood stands restored, and some of them were never recovered.

By 1926 the South was cutting about fifteen and a half billion feet of lumber annually, a rate which promised to exhaust its timber supply within thirty-two years. The disaster of complete, or even near, exhaustion never occurred to forest owners. The great depression, with its accompanying panic of unemployment, led to the organization of the Civilian Conservation Corps, which concentrated its efforts upon restoring forest resources. This organization planted millions of trees, and otherwise conditioned much marginal land for forest production.

An even more dramatic stimulus was given to the forest industry in the pine-growing South by Dr. Charles T. Herty, who discovered means of neutralizing the heavy rosin content of pine to permit its use in the manufacture of paper. The census report of 1930 makes no appreciable listing of pulp-paper manufacture in the South, and Howard Odum in *Southern Regions* in 1935 did little more than make a prophecy what would happen to industry. By 1960 the South received almost a half-billion dollars annually from the sale of pulp and paper stock, and there were slightly more than 200 million acres of lands in young forests.

The tobacco industry also took on new life after the Civil War. Tobacco could be grown and processed by even the most primitive methods. It was an indigenous product, and the industry was not a new one—in fact, it was one of the oldest in the South. Since 1774 the southern tobacco belt had moved westward and southward from its old tidewater locations. In the passing of years the handling and manufacturing tobacco products became an important industry.

In many respects the Civil War had been a boon to southern tobacco growers and manufacturers. There was an increased demand for smoking tobacco, chewing plug, and snuff. The ante-bellum industry was a highly individualistic one. Many farmers pounded their leaf into pipe crumbs, or pressed it into licorice and fruit-ladened plugs. In 1860 the manufacture of tobacco was confined largely to Virginia, North Carolina, Kentucky, and New York. The war years, paradoxically, increased the demand for tobaco in its several forms, and at the same time saw a disruption of both the growing and manufacture of tobacco. Conservation of much of the military activity in Virginia brought disruption and pillage of the industry. Perhaps no southern product, with the possible exception of food, was considered a fairer spoil of war than tobacco.

No southern activity of industrial importance made a quicker or more extensive recovery than the manufacture of tobacco. An interesting result of the disaster of war was the experience of tobacco farmers and processors about Durham Station, North Carolina, when Sherman's army swept through in April 1865. Both northern and southern foragers pillaged barns and factory storage bins of their light tobacco stock. The vandals, however, were not unappreciative, for they went home and wrote back to North Carolina seeking to purchase new supplies.

By the time war broke out, farmers in Caswell County, North Carolina, had grown and learned to cure the bright tobacco which was to make the product of that state and southern Virginia famous. As is the case with other new plant types in this period, little is known about the origin of the bright tobacco. It was a product no doubt of varietal breeding and improvement, and of soil conditions on which the crop was grown.

Across the mountains in Kentucky, tobacco farmers were still growing the heavy-leafed dark type which they had carried west with them as pioneers. Their leaf had been used for pipe, cigar, chewing, and snuff. In 1866 George Webb of Brown County, Ohio, secured seed from G. W. Barkley of Bracken County, Kentucky, and the Kentuckian in turn had received seed from a Congressman. There appeared among Webb's plants some light lemon-colored broad-leafed variations with light midveins and slender stalks. These were strains of Maryland tobacco, and in a remarkably short time this new burley was grown in a wide belt which included southern Ohio, Kentucky, eastern Tennessee, and western North Carolina. With the rise of the cigarette industry these two new tobacco types had major significance.

Though the areas producing tobacco were widely distributed across the South, manufacturing centers were largely confined to Virginia and North Carolina. Immediate postwar manufacturing was largely restricted to the production of chewing and pipe tobacco. The tobacco industry was characteristic of southern industrial beginnings, for it consisted of dozens of small enterprisers who used their own particular principles of production. There was no standardization of products, and only a limited amount of mechanization during these years. Many early manufacturers, including George Washington Duke, R. J. Reynolds, and P. H. Haynes, traveled over parts of the South peddling their products. In time there were literally hundreds of brands of plug chewing tobacco on the market, the products of almost as many farmer-manufacturers. Brand names reflected the personal interests and sentimental views of their owners as well as the fashions of the times.

Almost from the beginning after 1865, the tobacco industry was to experience mechanical advances which in time were to be central to its growth. Machines were introduced to sweeten, flavor, and condition the leaf for compression into plugs or squares. Grinding and sacking machines were introduced to increase the output of smoking tobacco. Even the manufacture of sacks, packages, labels, tags, and wood caddies for packing the finished product was to become a mechanized operation. In later years the cigarette machine invented by James A.

Bonsack, 1879-81, was to expand the industry to enormous proportions. It is interesting to note that nearly all of the new machines were the handiwork of southern inventors, many of them rural southerners.

The story of the rise of the big commercial tobacco industry in the New South has many beginnings, but none more entrancing than that of John Ruffin Green's Bull Durham, a bright smoking tobacco. In 1865 Green brought to tobacco manufacturing a sense of quality, the importance of a standardized labeled product, and, in partnership with William T. Blackwell, a successful sales program. Blackwell subsequently purchased Green's interest from his estate, and in 1870 brought in Julian Shakespeare Carr as a partner. They set to work to mass-produce their product, and to sell it in the growing national market. At the same time they were called upon to defend their famous Bull of Durham trade mark against infringers, chief of whom was Wesley A. Wright. In 1875 the United States Supreme Court awarded Blackwell and Carr exclusive possession of the trade mark.

The balance in tobacco manufacturing between 1865 and 1885 shifted from Virginia to North Carolina. The old Virginia manufacturers, like Allen and Ginter, and Cameron and Cameron, in time found more than their match in Blackwell and Carr, P. H. Haynes and Company, R. J. Reynolds, and W. Duke and Sons. The last-named company soon dominated the American cigarette market. Washington Duke, an ex-Confederate, who for a short time had been confined in Libby Prison in Richmond, returned to his small hill farm near Durham Station in 1865 to begin his life anew as a farmer. He found stored away in an outbuilding a small quantity of bright tobacco which he and his sons granulated. He then set out in a wagon to peddle it under the brand name of *Pro Bono Publico,* and accepted sugar, bacon, and money in exchange. This was the beginning of a rapidly expanding manufacturing business, for Washington Duke and his sons James Buchanan and Benjamin N. would become leading figures in the manufacture and sale of tobacco products.

Cigarettes were perhaps first used in Spanish America. They may even have antedated the arrival of Europeans. In the late eighteenth century they were to be seen in Europe and the Near East. In North America, traders going to Santa Fe saw men and women smoking *cigaritos.* Sometime around the mid-nineteenth century they were introduced to the eastern seaboard. So far as southern manufacturers were concerned, the production of cigarettes was not begun until 1875. Allen and Ginter of Richmond displayed cigarettes made of Havana tobacco at the Philadelphia Centennial Exposition in 1876. By 1880 several manufacturers, among them Washington Duke and Sons, were ready to begin production in commercial quantities. The Dukes had the foresight to buy the right to use the Bonsack cigarette machine, but not until they had a rather trying experience with 125 cigarette workers brought from Poland to roll cigarettes by hand.

Introduction of cigarettes gave a new commercial impetus to the tobacco industry. Companies were merged, absorbing most of the small operators. Advertising and salesmanship became a major part of the industry. James B. Duke was the major force in the formation of the great American Tobacco Company or trust, which was dissolved by court order on May 11, 1911. He was also a pioneer in developing large-scale national advertising and distribution. Competition after 1911 was considerably heightened, with four major companies competing for customers. At the same time the American Tobacco Company released the stock it held in the highly successful plug manufacturing firm of R. J. Reynolds in Winston-Salem, North Carolina.

The southern companies which comprised the American Tobacco Company complex were not to monopolize the cigarette business for long. Before 1913 cigarettes were sold by gimmick advertising. Picture cards of baseball players, actresses, birds, natural scenes and small silk flags were enclosed in the packages. Various brands competed with one another, but there had been relatively little hard-fisted struggle over the market. R. J. Reynolds introduced the Camel brand in 1913, and with it came rugged competition. The newcomer was a blend of bright, flue-cured burley and Turkish, later Maryland, leaf was added. Treatment of the constituent leaf, particularly burley, somewhat in the fashion of chewing tobacco, gave the Reynolds product a distinctive flavor. Concentrating on this one brand in its advertising, the Winston-Salem company quickly pushed its cigarette to the top of the sales list soon after its introduction in 1913. Happily for its manufacturer, Camels gained from the upswing in consumption of cigarettes in World War I.

R. J. Reynolds was not to enjoy the new national and international military market without a contest. George Washington Hill of the

American Tobacco Company introduced an old company brand Lucky Strike with a new and vigorous advertising push. The toasted quality, derived from the application of heat in the manufacturing process, was emphasized, and the suggestion was made to "reach for a Lucky instead of a sweet," a slogan that aroused candy manufacturers. In the war and postwar years, the battle of the brands took place, with four of them out in front: Camels, Lucky Strikes, Chesterfield, and P. Lorillard's Old Golds.

In many respects tobacco manufacturing has been one of the South's most successful commercial enterprises. It has utilized a native staple crop to the fullest extent, and helped greatly to extend the area of tobacco cultivation in at least four regions of the South. No doubt the manufacture of tobacco in one of the major growing belts demonstrated to the fullest the truth of the contention that manufacturing of farm products within the region of their growth would cut the cost of shipping and reshipping raw and finished materials. It was equally important that the rising tobacco industry in Virginia and North Carolina tapped the vast reservoir of unskilled southern labor. Women and children of both races were employed in large numbers, with no appreciable discrimination involved. As machines were added, this country labor had an opportunity to train itself for the next step in the burgeoning tobacco manufacturing industry. Over the years, automation brought marked changes in the use of labor, as well as in the output of cigarette plants. By the end of World War I machinery was performing most of the work previously done by hand, but a phenomenal increase in tobacco consumption went far toward stabilizing the industry as a big business.

Tobacco manufacturing paralleled the rise of the New South. Although it affected directly only a small portion of the region, it was nevertheless a forceful reminder that southerners did have the capacity to organize and operate a major industry. Success in the manufacture of tobacco led people to advocate the same methods for expanding the textile industry. It was pointed out that the southern cotton belt was far more expensive than the tobacco belts. It was argued processing cotton in the belt where it was grown would greatly reduce costs because of savings on the freight and labor bills; this was not really so, however. Much cotton was grown near the sites of the location of the new mills, but not in sufficient quantity to supply the mills. The bulk of raw cotton to be processed by piedmont mills was produced almost as far from them as from those of the New England area.

Saving on freight rates was perhaps the least significant reason why mills were located in the piedmont sections of the Carolinas, Georgia, and Alabama. The availability of a large reservoir of cheap and unskilled rural labor was an important enticement. There were sources of both cheap water and steam power. Railroads in this section offered transportation to the eastern market at reasonable rates. Finally, promoters in this part of the New South sought the location of cotton mills in their communities with a remarkable single-mindedness and evangelical zeal. They had to overcome less prejudice in their own minds, and in those of neighbors in the promotion of mills, than would have been the case in almost any other form of manufacture. Emotionally southerners had an affinity for cotton production at every stage.

There were cotton mills in the ante-bellum South. In fact it seemed that cotton manufacture would be the region's most successful commercial venture. The period between 1860 and 1880 was to see the loss of a generation of industrial development, and New England came to enjoy a virtual monopoly in the manufacture of textiles. In 1880, however, the South experienced a reawakening. By this date the region had somewhat escaped the enormous social pressures of reconstruction politics, even though it did suffer a severe shock from the defeat of Hancock and the Democrats at the hands of James A. Garfield. The industry which promised the quickest and broadest returns was that which would process raw cotton near the fields where it was grown.

Behind the great crusade for the establishment of cotton mills were expositions at Atlanta in 1881, Baltimore in 1882, Raleigh in 1883, and New Orleans in 1885. As important as these expositions were in exhibiting cotton mill machinery, demonstrating the process of manufacturing, and unifying southern thought on the subject of cotton mills, it was the personal leadership of such men as Captain F. W. Dawson, editor of the Charleston *News and Courier;* H. P. Hammett, mayor and railroad president of Greenville, South Carolina; D. A. Tompkins, a professional engineer; Henry W. Grady of the Atlanta *Constitution;* G. A. Gray; and Daniel Rhyne, which made a thriving textile industry possible. From outside the South, Edward

Atkinson, a New England textile economist, was to have an important personal impact on the region. In 1880 he delivered an address in Atlanta which stimulated the organization of the pioneer Cotton Exposition of the next year. He served in effect as technical consultant on the development of the exposition, in the sense that his suggestions on the cotton industry were followed.

H. P. Hammett was born on a cotton farm near Greenville, South Carolina, and as a young man was intimately associated with cotton marketing and manufacturing. In the postwar period he became actively associated with the development of transportation, water power, and cotton milling. He organized and kept in operation a cotton mill in Greenville during the trying years of reconstruction. By the time of his death in 1891 he had established three mills and became a leader in the founding of the southern textile industry. Broadus Mitchell has said, "Hammett probably inspired more confidence in the practicability of manufacturing of cotton in the South than any other one person."

After 1880 the founding of cotton mills took on the fervor of an evangelical movement. It was the promise of economic salvation for thousands of southerners. People in towns and communities in the piedmont areas of Virginia, the Carolinas, Georgia, and Alabama felt that if they could but secure the location of cotton mills many of their economic woes would be ended. Mills were often projected with the most meager financial backing. Stock was subscribed almost in the sense that it was a subscription to a public charity. Companies were formed with officers who were entirely ignorant of management problems associated with a cotton mill. Men bought machinery and made decisions regarding policies of manufacture almost entirely on faith. Mills were small at first; some of them actually began operation with only a few hundred spindles.

Second-hand, out-of-date machinery was purchased. Only the least complex machines were used at first, and they produced a coarse and cheap material. The argument that a marked saving could be effected by locating the mills in the heart of the raw cotton supply area broke down when it became necessary to send the raw products of the southern mills to the East to be finished.

Availability of cheap fuel and power was of enormous importance to the success of the southern cotton-mill industry. The piedmont provided two sources. River falls offered a generous amount of water power. The cotton mills after 1875 became the pioneer users of water power for industrial purposes. Sites such as the falls of the Catawba at Great Falls, South Carolina, and Lockhart at the falls of the Broad, and power sites along the Haw River, the Yadkin, and Upper Cape Fear in North Carolina were developed to supply power to cotton mills.

By 1890 it was clearly evident that more power was needed to turn the mills, and more flexibility in locating the plants. Water-power sites were too limited in number, and sometimes were too isolated, to permit the best use of transportation facilities. Steam plants were developed. A railroad was built across the Appalachian Highlands to tap the inexhaustible supply of bituminous coal. With the advent of steam power, the textile industry not only enjoyed a free choice of sites but had available the necessary power to operate its heavy machines more efficiently, and to escape the seasonal power failures.

In the field of labor the textile industry no doubt involved a broader segment of southern humanity than any other single regional industry. Like management, laborers were inexperienced. Their biggest asset was a willingness and eagerness to work. When mills began operation there flocked out of the hinterland hundreds of families who were desperate for employment at almost any wages, hours, or conditions of work.

Like the tobacco industry, the cotton mills were able to employ a high percentage of women and children. Sometimes the rate of women employees ran as high as one-half, and of women and children in some mills comprised two-thirds of the labor force. Large families migrated from farms to mill villages so that all members of the family, with the exception of the older men, could find employment. Often heads of families were forced into unemployment and became financially dependent on their families, because they lacked the dexterity and skill to enable them to operate spinning machines and looms.

Wages were low. In many mills they were little if at all above the most meager subsistence level. As the Langley, South Carolina, mill superintendent said, "Labor was very plentiful and they could get 20 per cent more than was required to run the mill. The . . . operatives were made up entirely of the people born and raised in the vicinity." Such willingness to work at low wages pointed to an intense competition for jobs. There developed around country mills villages with all the social mores of the southern rural community. Most families were not prepared for this type of community life. Housing was crude, sanitary facilities lacking, law enforcement defective, and schools and churches frequently inadequate. Once a family entered a mill village to work, it not only separated itself from its rural-farm background but also faced social barriers between itself and much of the society in older towns where mills were located.

Financing the southern textile industry would prove to be an enormous undertaking. In 1870 capital investment amounted to $11,088,315. A decade later it had grown to $17,375,897, and by 1900 it was $124,596,879. Much of this capital was raised from the little southern investor, and some of it from the communities where mills were located. Manufacturers who held mortgages on machinery or stock certificates, or suppliers and commission men who made advances in equipment and accepted stock, were able to acquire considerable stake in southern mills after 1880. The firm of Woodward, Baldwin, and Company of Baltimore was almost the first port of call for southern mill promoters who needed machinery and credit.

Southern promoters made tremendous headway between 1870 and 1900 in developing cotton mills. There were 6526 looms and 548,048 spindles by 1900, a phenomenal increase. By 1883 the South had invested, in three years, over $12 million in cotton mill machinery.

Marketing these southern textile products presented serious problems to the cotton industry. Textiles were bought and sold at New York and Philadelphia market prices. Southern products were seriously handicapped, by their lack of top quality and finish. Northern manufacturers still controlled the bleaching, dyeing, and sizing processes. Southern promoters found themselves overextended after purchasing spindles and looms and so were not able to purchase immediately the specialized machinery needed to produce a high quality product or to train the specialized personnel that could produce premium quality goods.

Generally the southern textile industry enjoyed a phenomenal growth between 1880 and the outbreak of World War I. The industry that was revived after reconstruction was organized, promoted, operated, and managed by people who were almost totally without industrial experience. About 20 per cent of the investment of $100 million was lost because of bad choice of used machinery, poor management, and lack of sufficient capital to make extensions of operations necessary to promote efficiency and economy.

The textile industry began its post-Civil-War years under adverse conditions. New England millmasters had an established industry, the capital, skilled management and labor, and the market. The great majority of southern mills, on the other hand, were organized as community enterprises rather than as privately capitalized businesses, largely by men with very little managerial experience, many of them ex-Confederate officers. And, as has already been mentioned, labor for those mills came from the economically straitened yeoman farmer class. When these factors are added to the lack of capital and the need to establish a dependable market, it is no wonder that southern mill operators saw their industry live through an unreasonably long adolescence. By the end of the 1920's the southern textile industry had reached parity with New England. In 1928 the South had in place 16,074,000 spindles, as compared to 18,856,000 in New England. But earlier in that decade, 1921, a southern textile worker earned only $659.35 a year as against the New England worker's $945.83. The equality, however, was more apparent than real, as Rupert B. Vance indicated in 1927 in a comment on the national position of the southern textile industry:

> One is forced to the conclusion that the basic resource of the southern cotton textiles is not management, nor nearness to raw materials, not necessarily improved technology, but labor that works long hours for low wages. The differential between New England and the Southeast is then the labor differential between a highly industrial area and an area of decadent agriculture.

Meanwhile in the South a crusade was mounted against the child labor that was largely responsible for this cost differential. After a long and bitter fight in several southern state legislatures, child-labor laws were passed. This did not take place, however, until the textile industry had become branded as one which abused women and children. A similar crusade was necessary to protect female laborers from unduly long hours of work, unhealthy conditions inside the mills, and, in far too many cases, unreasonably low wages. Efforts to organize the textile laborers of the South resulted in bitter strikes, violent outbreaks in many of the mill centers, and pressure by millowners to influence state legislatures to take action against the strikers.

World War II saw a rapid recovery of the textile industry. By 1940 the southern mills had become highly competitive with those of New England. They were spinning a high quality of thread to the very finest strand possible. Cloth was of high to fine quality, and there were finishing plants capable of processing completely even the choicest fabrics. Those who argued that the mills should be brought to the cotton fields would have found some satisfaction in the fact that in 1955 there were active in the South 19,027,000 spindles as compared with 3,059,000 in New England. Southern mills consumed annually 8,731,000 bales of cotton to 601,000 in New England, and produced more cloth and other fabrics.

Two-thirds of the tonnage of cotton production in the South was in the form of seeds. Prior to 1870 cotton seeds were regarded largely as waste. Most of them were dumped in some out-of-the-way place where animals could not get at them. If hogs ate them, they soon smothered to death because of the accumulation of lint in their respiratory systems. Cattle sometimes were poisoned by eating raw seeds. After 1880 cotton mills grew in number, and the manufacture of oil, cottonseed meal, and hulls became a fairly profitable business. Cottonseed oil had numerous uses. It could be consumed in the form of shortening by human beings; it was also a base for soaps, and for numerous other products. The meal was valuable as fertilizer and cattle feed. Hulls were fed to cattle as a roughage.

A cotton-oil trust was formed in 1886, and it controlled nearly the entire industry of the South. It had a capital investment of $20 million. Each succeeding decade down to 1920 saw the production plants expanded in size and number. By 1900 by-products of cotton seed brought an income of $58 million, and four years later this had climbed to $96 million. In 1957 the South produced over 4 billion pounds of cotton seed, all of which was converted into oil, meal, and hulls; and oil now had many highly diversified uses.

Not all of the post-Civil-War southern industries were associated with agriculture. For instance, there were coal and iron. The southern coal beds were first discovered by pioneers in the seventeenth century as they moved up the Virginia rivers toward the Appalachian Highlands. Frontier traders and land scouts crossing the mountains reported coal out-croppings in several places. By 1850 some of the southern resources were being exploited. Among these were beds in western Virginia, eastern Tennessee, and the western coalfields of Kentucky. After 1865 the Alabama, West Virginia, east Tennessee, and eastern Kentucky fields were opened to extensive exploitation. Development of coal mining was seriously hindered by lack of cheap transportation. Unfortunately, most of the southern mines were too far removed from navigable rivers to make the use of barges financially feasible. It was necessary to construct railroads up the larger river valleys into the mountain coves to reach the mines. The building of the Chesapeake and Ohio across West Virginia, and the construction of the Clinchfield, Virginia, and Norfolk and Western railroads on the east, and the Louisville and Nashville, and the Cincinnati Southern through the central Appalachian South, opened the mines to cheap transportation. One of the first major fields was that of the New River or Pocahontas region of Virginia and West Virginia. By 1883 coal mining in this area was in an advanced stage of development, and by 1907 was producing 17 million tons of coal. In the meantime the Alabama mines were being exploited at an equal rate, yielding over 14 million tons. As railway lines were extended up the Big Sandy River in Kentucky, and east from Lexington up the Kentucky River, the eastern fields yielded 6 million tons a year.

Though much of the southern coal was burned within the region itself, a good portion was shipped elsewhere. Coal from the West Virginia and eastern Kentucky fields was shipped to the upper Great Lakes industrial crescent; to Cleveland, Detroit, Akron, Columbus, Gary, and Chicago. Southern mines were from the outset operated commercially as captive mines. Industrial management in many instances purchased large areas of coal-bearing lands in Kentucky, West Virginia, eastern Tennessee, and Alabama and exploited their resources as fuel supplies for a primary industry. In 1900 the southern mines produced 22,822,807 tons of coal, in 1920 152,535,715 tons, while in 1945, at the end of World War II coal production had dropped to 109,929,000 tons.

Coal mining actually stimulated some industrial expansion near heavily productive mines. In many places timber resources were harvested at a ruinous rate to supply mine timbers of all sorts; but, like the mining operations, the lumbering activities were of the most impermanent type. The value of manufactured products in the South upped the capital return from a ton of coal to the phenomenal figures of $12 to $60 in manufacturing income from finished products, yet the region took too little advantage of this potential profit.

No other southern industry, except textiles, involved its human labor so deeply in social complexities. Mining in the Appalachian Highlands often took place well away from old settled communities. Mining villages sprang up after 1885 at the heads of hollows and along narrow shoulders of hillsides throughout the fields. Old farm laborers and log men turned miners, and they were joined by large numbers of middle and eastern European immigrants. Old isolated rural and agrarian customs were quickly modified if not ignored, and the miner became dependent upon the operators for everything he ate and wore, and for the shack in which he lived. In a majority of the communities few miners ever saw much cash money from one year's end to the next. These were the people John Fox, Jr., wrote about in his Appalachian novels. They were the same people who had fought in famous blood feuds like the one between the Hatfields and McCoys. Malcom Ross in *Machine Age in the Hills* wrote:

> The first railroad followed the same river valleys and sent spurs up the tributary creeks. Wherever this steel centipede lay across the land the character of hill life changed. The operator built a row of board shacks close to the tipple. The mine village had to be self-contained, so the company-owned store made its appearance.
>
> The new miners liked this arrangement. Three-room houses with many windows were a step up in the scale from one-room cabins lit by a single opening. Neighbors were close at hand. Food required only a short walk to the company store instead of months of labor on sour soil. It was easier to buy ready-made clothes than to weave them by hand. Hard cash was a miracle to the people who had never handled it from one year to the next.

Unhappily for man and country the bare bones of the new industrial life began to show through in the form of social and labor unrest. As attempts were made during World War I to organize the coal miners, violence occurred between the "gun thugs" of the operators and the "agitators" of labor unions. By 1920 the United Mine Workers under the leadership of John L. Lewis had built up the central West Virginia union to a strength of forty-two thousand men. In that year there occurred the extended labor war of attrition known as "Bloody

Mingo," a struggle which was to extend into eastern Kentucky and to make the coal towns of Lynch and Harlan synonymous with bloodshed and confusion. In 1932 the eastern Kentucky coal field was torn by labor strife and the blighting effects of depression. Violence about the Harlan, Lynch, and Pineville mines attracted national attention. Theodore Dreiser and the twelve members of the National Committee for the Defense of Political Prisoners came to Harlan and sent to the outside highly unfavorable reports of conditions. In *Harlan Miners Speaks, Terrorism in the Kentucky Coalfields, Report of the Dreiser Committee,* this group painted a grim picture of the abuse of human rights and resources. That same year student groups from Columbia University and Commonwealth College in Mena, Arkansas, were escorted out of Pineville as undesirable visitors. Coupled with the economic woes of the region were the unsavory political activities of the partisan groups in Kentucky. This was especially true of the election in 1937 in which Governor A. B. Chandler and Senator Alben Barkley were opponents for the United States Senate. Charges were made that supporters of Senator Barkley made political use of the WPA and other New Deal emergency agencies.

In time, machines were to force hundreds of thousands of miners out of the pit, and the conversion of railroad locomotives to use of diesel fuels and electricity caused drastic reductions of demands for coal and threw thousands in the southern Appalachians out of work. Men unfitted for any other labor were now permanently unemployed. There was a heavy migration away from all the southern mining villages. In eastern Kentucky, for instance, mechanization enabled 200,000 miners in 1957 to produce more coal than 700,000 miners had produced in 1920.

Iron mining and smelting is an old industry in the South. Iron was produced in the colonial South, and at one time in the earlier years of the nineteenth century as much as a quarter of the nation's supply came from the region. By 1860, only 11.7 per cent of the nation's output of iron was of southern origin. Principal ore beds were found in Virginia, Kentucky, Tennessee, and Alabama.

During the Civil War tremendous effort was made to bring the central Alabama beds into production. Here coal, limestone, and iron ore could be produced in close proximity, and it was here that the Confederacy hoped to fill its desperate need for iron. At the same time the Alabama iron works became prime targets for union raiders. Major James H. Wilson commanded 14,000 cavalry men of the Division of the Mississippi in this area. Opposed to him was General Nathan Bedford Forrest's command, which suffered defeat at Selma and opened the way to destruction of the Alabama furnaces by Wilson's troops.

Slowly the furnaces were brought back into production after 1865. The story of their restoration was characteristic of most postwar southern industry. A handful of perservering individuals with too little capital and technical knowledge and skill pioneered in the organization of companies. Workings at Shade Valley, Shelby, Briefield, Rand Mountain, and Oxmoor were begun. Perhaps the most important individual involved was "Boss" W. S. McElwain, who set out to reconstruct the Cahaba Furnace. He secured funds in Cincinnati to enable him to restore the furnace, and to expand the local iron business. McElwain overcame all sorts of hardships to carry on his business. Ill health, however, kept him from succeeding.

Before anyone could succeed in the Alabama ore field, a railroad had to be built to give the mills dependable transportation to market. Reconstruction legislators in Montgomery in 1868 threatened to balk adequate north and south connections for the Birmingham area. The legislature was under the domination of John C. Stanton of Boston, who could wield enormous influence over the location of railway extensions in the state. This meant Stanton favored the building of a road directly north from Montgomery to connect with Decatur and Chattanooga. The day was saved by Frank Gilmer, a pioneer promoter of the site of present-day Birmingham, but even so, there still remained a fight to protect it against the "Stanton-Chattanooga crowd."

Just after 1870 five aggressive businessmen arrived on the Alabama industrial scene: Daniel Pratt, Henry DeBardeleben, Enoch Ensley, Albert Fink, and J. W. Sloss. In 1872 Pratt and DeBardeleben acquired a controlling interest in the Red Mountain Iron and Coal Company. Albert Fink was chief engineer of the Louisville and Nashville Railroad Company and early saw the importance of the Alabama mineral belt to that road. Colonel James Withers Sloss, a native of Alabama, was both a railroad builder and an organizer of the Pratt Coal and Coke Company, the first large company formed in Birmingham.

One of the most colorful personalities of the postwar years of the Birmingham iron industry was Henry Fairchild DeBardeleben. A native of South Carolina, DeBardeleben migrated across Georgia to Alabama, where between 1872 and 1894 he was the most active figure in developing the Red Mountain ore workings. Ill health early interfered with his activities, and several times he withdrew temporarily from business to recuperate. He was colorful of speech, often using striking figures—one of which was, "life is a glorified crap game." For him it was. In 1894 he lost all of his immense personal fortune but a forgotten bank deposit of $75,000. Nevertheless he had established himself as "king of the southern iron world."

The Birmingham red ores contained from 37 to 55 per cent metal, and a high percentage of silica and lime. The red hematite was exposed for a distance of approximately 150 miles, and covered an area of 12,000 square miles. It was known to have a depth of 5000 feet, and there were, in 1906, by estimate, more than 2 billion tons of available ore. Surrounding the ore field were rich deposits of dolomite, limestone, and coal. Water, however, was in fairly short supply for heavy smelting until a dam was built across Village Creek; it permitted the impoundment of 2½ billion gallons of water.

Out of the growth of the postwar iron industry came developments at Rockdale, Tennessee, and in Ensley, Bessemer, Birmingham, and Elyton, Alabama. Major trunk railroads were built across the ore fields, and coal and cement workings were developed. Subsidiary industries produced pipe, nails, staples, wire, stoves, wagon parts, and farm implements. Southern pig iron, however, was in a competitive squeeze in the open market. Sometimes it actually failed to find a market. The price was nearly always low, and not until a more efficient process was discovered for producing basic pig iron in 1891 was it possible to begin producing steel on any appreciable scale. From 1872, when Daniel Pratt and DeBardeleben re-established the Oxmoor Furnace, to 1893 and the great depression, the history of the coal and iron business in the South was an account of the struggle to find capital, a market for pig iron, adequate technical and mechanical skill, and a stable corporate organization. In these years there was a constant coming and going of managerial personnel. Companies were organized, went bankrupt, were merged, and expanded so that few had time to establish reputations of any durability. Again it was the usual postwar southern story of too little capital, too limited markets, and the necessity of having to send raw materials out of the region to be processed, thereby losing the profits from finished products.

The Tennessee Coal, Iron and Railroad Company was reorganized in 1886 with A. S. Colyar as president. In 1881 control of the company passed to J. H. Inman, an act which brought the organization under the control of Wall Street. A series of mergers, down to 1907, made this the central industrial organization in Alabama and Tennessee.

When the Tennessee Coal, Iron, and Railroad Company was merged with the DeBardeleben Coal and Iron Company in 1886, J. H. Inman arbitrarily set its capital stock at $20 million. This however, was not substantial enough to save the company from a serious threat of bankruptcy in the great panic of 1893.

The dramatic moment in the history of iron and steel making in the South came when the United States Steel Corporation acquired control of the Tennessee Coal, Iron, and Railroad Company. In 1907 E. H. Harriman placed an order with the Ensley plant for steel rails for all the Harriman roads. Having $7 million in modernizing its facilities, and having outstanding debts approximating $16 millon, the company nevertheless was faced with disaster in the panic of 1907 because the stability of its credit had suddenly vanished. The syndicate controlling the company appealed to J. P. Morgan on November 2, 1907, for the United States Steel Corporation to purchase the Tennessee company. There was also danger that the Moore and Schley Steel Company of Birmingham would fail. If Moore and Schley failed, associated businesses would also fail, thus starting a panic on Wall Street which could not be halted. At the same time there was fear that a Roosevelt Administration in Washington bent on trust-busting would not favor the merger of the Tennessee Coal, Iron, and Railroad Company with United States Steel. Judge Elbridge H. Geary and Henry Clay Frick were sent to Washington to consult with President Theodore Roosevelt. On November 4, 1907, Roosevelt wrote Attorney General Charles F. Bonaparte about plans to merge the two companies, and strongly implied that he had no objection. The burden of President Roosevelt's letter was to the effect that United States Steel did not wish to invest in the Tennessee Coal, Iron, and Railroad Company, but it would do so in order to avoid further economic panic.

Acquisition of the southern smelting properties by United States Steel gave solid financial and managerial support to an industry which have never really known financial security. At the same time, however, it helped further to place a southern industry under eastern control. Imposed upon the southern operation was the onerous "Pittsburgh plus" base for pricing. Under it iron and steel bought in Birmingham bore a price of the local market plus the addition of freight costs from Birmingham to Pittsburgh, thus protecting United States Steel in Pittsburgh from competition. This also gave United States Steel a bonus profit of the added freight cost. The merger with United States Steel made southern iron and steel operations lose most of their regional characteristics and become a part of the great national interests controlled from the board room of J. P. Morgan and Company in New York.

At the time promoters were rebuilding and expanding the iron and coal operations in Tennessee and Alabama, several small and highly localized industries were increasing southern production of manufactured goods. The wagon and carriage business was fairly large in the aggregate, but individual companies were relatively small. Some of them were little more than glorified wood and blacksmith shops. Towns like Louisville, Lynchburg, Chattanooga, and Durant, Mississippi, became famous for their buggies and wagons. By 1890 southern mails were filled with colorful folders and catalogues advertising southern-made vehicles.

Farm-implement manufacturers operated in many southern cities, but the more important plow works were located in Chattanooga, Lynchburg, and Louisville and Maysville, Kentucky. Manufacturers in these towns, such as B. F. Avery and Sons of Louisville, produced plows and other implements especially adapted to the basic one-horse type of southern farming. The Avery Company manufactured a small hillside turning plow which was a miniature model of the heavier plows used on the western plains. The simplified Georgia plowstock, with its detachable shares, was one of the commonest implements in use. These plows were manufactured in many places, some of the "factories" were little more than local blacksmith shops. As years passed, the line of implements came to include improved planters, cultivators, and harvesting machines. The disc harrow was introduced to pulverize southern bottom soils as were heavier harrows.

There were also small plants which produced the meager harness used by southern farmers and teamsters to go along with these farm implements. This consisted of crude horsecollars, made of everything from corn shucks to leather, bridle bits, backbands, trace chains, singletrees, bridles, and hames. Every crossroads store was piled high with these pieces of harness. Walls grew long tails of trace chains, and horsecollars suspended from ceilings became emblems of the country trade.

The presence of oil and gas had been known from the time of the first settlements in the South. Iridescent splotches appeared on stream surfaces and occasionally gas could be smelled. A tar seepage might occur in springs or about salt licks, thus giving rise to such common local names as "stinking" or "greasy" creek or "tar" springs. Wherever men drilled salt wells in western Virginia or Kentucky, they stood a chance of striking a trace of oil and gas, and sometimes they opened small gushers.

At the turn of the century, oil and gas were discovered in Louisiana and Texas. Anthony Lucas drilled the famous Spindletop well near Beaumont in 1900, after he had found traces of oil in salt drillings on Avery Island in Louisiana. By 1908 the southern states had produced more than 350 million barrels of oil, an amount which was increased to 5 billion by 1922. David F. Day, petroleum expert of mining and mineral resources of the United States Geological Survey, wrote, "The future of petroleum production in the South must see many other large pools developed in Louisiana and Texas. Further supplies are probable in Mississippi and in Northern Alabama and with each will come the development of local manufacturing beyond what could be achieved by any other industrial impulse."

Day was correct in most of his predictions. As the Texas and Louisiana oil fields were developed to maximum production, Dallas, Houston, Galveston, Amarillo, Shreveport, and Baton Rouge grew into major industrial centers. Such famous fields as Spindletop, Sour Lake, Damon Mound, Goose Creek, Evangeline, and New Iberia were developed. In time Natchez and Jackson in Mississippi were to feel the impact of oil in their economy. To the north, smaller fields were brought into production in Kentucky and West Virginia.

Between 1930 and 1960 a tremendous complex of pipe lines to carry both oil and gas was laid across the South. Fleets of seagoing tankers, inland river towboats and railroads hauled millions of barrels of crude oil. The Standard Oil Company early introduced oil barges on the Mississippi, Arkansas, and Red rivers. Using such famous old towboats as the *Sprague,* the *Oscar,* and the *Slack Barrett,* it hauled downstream the output of many of the wells in Texas, Arkansas, and Oklahoma. Later the Ashland Oil and Refining Company in Kentucky operated a new type of towboat to transport crude oil upstream to its refineries. Southern cities and towns were connected by natural gas pipelines, and all across the region there appeared pumping and booster stations. Oil refineries were in operation not only near the oilfields but along the Atlantic Coast and on the inland rivers. In 1960 there were nearly one-quarter of a million operating wells producing almost one and a half million barrels of oil. Because of the offshore strikes in the Gulf of Mexico, there was no certain basis for estimating the amount of oil still available in the region. At the same time southern wells produced over 9 billion cubic feet of natural gas, out of a national output of 12.7 billion feet. An adjunct of the petroleum industry was the mining of salt, sulphur, and rock asphalt in Louisiana, Texas, and Kentucky.

Another major southern industry was patent medicines. Nashville, Chattanooga, Asheville, Louisville, New Orleans, and many other southern towns and cities had their proprietary medicine factories. From these came chill tonics, blood tonics, female remedies, purgatives, restoratives, and nerve and muscular specifics. The Chattanooga Medicine Company became one of the most famous of the medicine manufacturers, producing Wine of Cardui, "a female remedy," and Black Draught, a laxative. This company built an important business with a highly profitable national trade, and in time became involved as plaintiff in a million-dollar libel suit against the powerful American Medical Association.

An industry closely related to the conditions of the southern climate was that of producing bottled soft drinks. In 1886 John S. Pemberton, a manufacturing pharmacist, produced a flavor blend from cocoa leaves and cola nuts. This mixture combined with syrup comprised the base for a palatable soft drink. He named his new product Coca-Cola for the two flavoring constituents. Various partnerships undertook to manufacture the basic flavoring and syrup for a growing southern fountain trade. In 1888 Asa G. Candler joined the partnership, and in 1891 he gained sole possession of the product. Candler, perhaps, had a conception of doing no more than manufacturing the flavoring for a limited regional trade.

The real impulse for the sale of Coca-Cola came from Ben F. Thomas, a Spanish-American War veteran. Thomas, a lawyer, sought a product to promote which could be sold cheaply yet yield a profit. He conceived the idea of bottling Coca-Cola, which was being sold by soda fountains in Chattanooga to mix with other drinks. He enlisted the aid of a partner, Joseph B. Whitehead, and the two called on Candler in Atlanta to present their proposition to bottle this soft drink. Candler looked upon the proposition as too visionary and gave the Chattanooga promoters no immediate encouragement. In 1899, however, Thomas and Whitehead were able to negotiate a contract which permitted them to form a corporation to promote their ideas. The new corporation was called the Coca-Cola Bottling Company of Tennessee, and J. T. Lupton was added as a stockholder and officer. Like cigarette manufacturers in North Carolina and Virginia, the soft-drink company had to contend legally with infringers and imitators on the one hand, and moral crusaders against the drink on the other. They conducted a major advertising campaign through the press, by sign board, the bottles and cases of their product, and through generous store displays. In time they were to make their fluted bottle a symbol throughout the world. By 1960, 1065 bottling plants produced and dispensed Ben F. Thomas's "5 cent" drink. For the South Coca-Cola and other soft-drink bottling firms had become parts of a major industry.

Scores of small industries were started after 1880 in the South, but most of these produced goods which were sold in very limited areas. By 1930, and the advent of the Great Depression, it was clear that the South, though it had made fair progress in industrialization, had hardly dented the surface of the urgent need for economic diversification. If the region were to compete with the rest of the nation, industrial expansion was a necessity. This became even clearer with the declining importance of agriculture as a source of livelihood for great masses of southerners.

❧ VII ❧

Education: The Central Challenge

Speaking before the Conference for Education in the South at Athens, Georgia, in 1902, Edward A. Alderman said he believed the South had reached four conclusions: that no civilization could grow in poverty, that public education had come to be an investment, that the state had become the collective will of the people, and that the people would regard taxation as an involuntary tribute paid by civilized man. The turn of the twentieth century completed thirty-five dreary years of the history of education in the region. No southern institution had been more thoroughly disrupted by war or more stigmatized by reconstruction.

This was indeed the era of the "forgotten man" which Walter Hines Page described so graphically to a group of North Carolina teachers in 1897:

> In 1890, twenty-six per cent of the white persons in the state were unable even to read and write. One in every four was wholly forgotten. But illiteracy was not the worst of it; the worst of it was that the stationary social condition indicated by generations of illiteracy had long been the general condition. The forgotten man was content to be forgotten. He became not only a dead weight, but definitely an opponent of social progress. . . .

Page expressed faith in the capabilities of his fellow southerners but said both the aristocratic and ecclesiastical systems of society had failed to develop them. He believed the South's salvation would be in "a public school system generously supported by public sentiment, and generously maintained by both state and local taxation. [It] is the only effective means to develop the forgotten man, and even more surely the only means to develop the forgotten woman."

A historical debate has gone on since 1876 over the origin of the public schools in the South. This debate has at times been strictly a matter of semantics. Public school systems were provided for by the states in their constitutions, and they were in the process of being established at the outbreak of the Civil War. In fact, public schools were in operation well before 1850. All the states had long considered the idea of public control and support of schools, and all but South Carolina had made constitutional provisions for schools. The history of education in each of the southern states followed a practically parallel course. There was a stirring of an idea for public education, but there was an almost total indifference on the part of masses of the people and legislators about giving the idea public financial support. A few leaders accepted the challenge and undertook to arouse the public, but their campaigns had just begun to yield results when the war intervened.

It is unquestionably true that the vast gulf between the public school effort before 1860 and that after 1865 was largely reflected in social and economic attitudes and in differing views as to who should be educated and for what purposes. Prior to 1860, education was mainly shaped by religious groups and the liberal views of figures like Thomas Jefferson. Education was directed to an understanding of the word of God, and sometimes to the vague objectives of serving civilization and free men. There was, of course, an implication of democracy in the early plea for public education, but there was also a confused sense of class patronage and privilege on the one hand, and a strong suggestion of pauperism or public charity on the other. How the original southern concepts of public education might have matured in American social history, had they not been blighted by the Civil War, can now be no more than idle speculation.

In 1865 public education in the South assumed three distinctly new responsibilities. First, the Negro slave had become a free man, and could theoretically compete in a free society, but actually he had to be educated to do so. To the ex-slave himself, education became a symbol of his freedom, and large numbers of freedmen sought this confirmation of freedom with some diligence. Thus postwar southern education became more deeply involved in the question of race than had any other southern cultural institution, even the churches and the electorate. Second, there was put forth not only the concept of public education but of universal public education which involved every southern child of school age. Third, the support of schools was made direct responsibilities of the states and property holders by both constitutional and statutory provisions.

The issue of the sources of public support had been the rock on which public education had been jolted if not wrecked since the 1830's. Reconstruction legislators may have been entirely sincere in their attempts to create public school systems by committing state taxation to it. They were, nevertheless, shortsighted in their failure to enact necessary revenue laws to guarantee financial support for schools. If there had been better planning and a wiser and more tactful approach to the education of the ex-slave, even to the point of involving large amounts of federal aid to special schools designed to orient him properly, it might have been possible to accomplish more successfully the central purpose of conditioning the newly freed Negro and his child for the future. Adopting some of the earlier educational provisions, as defective as some of them were, would have made legislation more palatable to white southerners. But no campaign of any sort was conducted to sell the concept of universal education on its proper merits of enabling southerners to become more efficient individuals. This was especially true where state appropriations and taxes were concerned. It was on this subject of universality of educational opportunities in the South that all questions of publicly supported education hinged. Although this fact was dramatized by the education of the Negro, it had even more fundamental meaning in the education of whites.

The two main sources of resistance shown by southern reclaimers in the years 1870 to 1876 were biracial education and taxes for education. After that date taxation and capital support became the education issues both in the states at large and in the localities. In many respects the Negroes were better off than their white neighbors. There was the oft-repeated story of the stimulus for establishment of the first graded school in Fayetteville, North Carolina. Two white citizens got into a fight which was witnessed by six young Negroes and five white youths. In the trial the Negroes were able to sign their names to the testimony while the white lads had to make their marks. It was said the Negro boys had attended better schools maintained by northern missionaries. Educational activities of the Freedman's Bureau, the missionary activities of private organizations, and support by private individuals had made it possible for the Negro to make considerable headway in his education. But groups aiding Negro education often created ill-feeling and jealousy in southern communities. Writing in 1930, M. S. C. Noble, dean of the College of Education in the University of North Carolina, said, "If the people of the state [North Carolina] had been left to work out the problem of Negro education by themselves, it would have been solved slowly, but when solved, it would have been solved within rather than from without in a clumsy harmful manner by strangers who knew nothing of the proper method of achieving the best permanent results in a southern state." The fact that the educational needs of the Negro would have been supplied slowly was the key to the whole issue.

Some plan of universal education was included in all the reconstruction constitutions, and a considerable body of statutory law was passed between 1865 and 1876. Viewed in a calmer moment and from the perspective of a considerable scope of southern educational experience since the Civil War, a historian could hardly reach any other objective conclusion than that, of all the legislation adopted by reconstruction legislatures of varying maturity and honesty of purposes, that which pertained to education was the most promising.

The vast majority of white southerners were neither prepared nor ready to accept the biracial aspects of reconstruction legislation; they were unprepared to accept the philosophy of the universality of elementary education. The informed were proud and, perhaps, selfish and snobbish in their opposition. Ignorant whites were incapable of grasping more of the idea than the costs. Nowhere in the South were the two points of view more clearly defined than in the debate between the Reverend Robert Lewis Dabney and William H. Ruffner, Virginia state superintendent of schools. Dabney had been chief of staff of Stonewall Jackson's command and was a self-proclaimed aristocrat. Ruffner, the son of a president of Washington College, trained for the ministry in Union Theological Seminary, but became a farmer and a self-taught geologist. After the war he became associated with General Robert E. Lee, and was active in promoting public schools in Virginia. In 1870 he was elected state superintendent without having had any appreciable experience in the management of public schools. Together with John B. Minor, he wrote Virginia's first postwar law pertaining to public schools.

Dr. Dabney opened the debate in an article published in the *Southern Planter and Farmer* in April 1876. Free public schools in his opinion were devices for leveling and destroying the last vestiges of the old southern civilization. The family was the independent unit of society and so it would remain without interference from the state. God intended parents to be a child's educators. He argued that the property of parents should be treated with special consideration. And he objected to public schools because they would prove great social levelers; private and church schools would not do this social injury.

Ruffner's answers to Dr. Dabney were direct. Children could be given moral and religious training without narrow sectarianism. The Negroes as human beings had moral claims against southern society. There would be fostered among them a pride of race, and there need be no fear of amalgamation. Then, in answer to Dabney's contention that Virginia was too poor to support public schools, Ruffner contended the state could ill afford not to make such an investment to improve the minds and earning powers of her citizens.

Although all the southern states, except South Carolina, had made constitutional provisions for public schools prior to 1860, none had devised a tax plan by which the schools could be dependably financed. It was in this area, and not that of actual organization of public schools, where the South had failed. When southerners resumed control of their state governments after 1876, one of their biggest challenges was to find solutions to meet the fiscal needs for school support. Southerners who regained control of public affairs were frugal indeed, and the financial resources they had at hand were extremely limited. The states themselves were deeply in debt, and state credit had been dangerously weakened. Balanced against this was the fact that there was no tax base to be applied to education nor any policy to create such a base. In addition, assessments were ridiculously low, and most haphazardly made. No branch of government could predict from one year's end to the next what the public income was likely to be. With the exception of the poll tax, the burden of public costs were placed almost entirely upon the land.

These financial obstacles to the development of an educational system were severe enough. Equally significant, however, was the attitude of the people themselves toward the whole problem. Southerners, whether private citizens or public officials, tended to regard education either as an unnecessary luxury or, if they were more sympathetic, as something which could only be attended to when economic conditions in the region improved. In addition, many people considered education as a matter of personal responsibility or something to be provided by sectarian institutions. And, most important of all, there was the baffling and irritating problem of educating the Negro, which by itself alone was a burden which could have taxed the ingenuity of educational leaders and public officials.

Education of the Negro involved enormous public costs to which the Negro was unable to make a direct contribution. There were grave questions: should the Negro be educated at all, and, if so, what kind of an education should he have? Behind the questions was of course the fear of integrated classrooms. On the other hand, more thoughtful southerners viewed the issue of Negro education as involving questions of economic productivity and civil behavior. Whatever the attitude, however, the development of public education in the South had this added anxiety which did not vex other parts of the country.

The basic history of educational accomplishments in the southern states, 1876-1910, can be written in a few terse statements. The tax income from low millage returns on even lower assessments of property rates and the indifferent collection of the poll tax made it very difficult to establish and maintain schools. There were numerous courageous and progressive efforts made in the various state departments of education, but long-range plans and clearly defined objectives for a system of public schools were lacking. Oratory and platitudes about the great virtues of education poured forth. There was a dearth of clearly defined answers as to what even the most elementary goals should be, or of awareness of the capacities of the states and communities financially to support universal education. Actually the southern educational leadership proceeded in this period of confusion with little more than the highly limited objective of stamping out illiteracy, and it failed to see that functional illiteracy was even more costly to southern progress.

Even if clear objectives could have been established and adequate financial support made available, there still remained the disheartening lack of capable teachers. There was little recognition in the South that teaching at the elementary public school level was a dignified and promising profession. Tenure was as uncertain as the weather, depending almost always upon the whims of ignorant local political trustees. Salary scales were absurd. No elementary teacher in the entire rural South in 1876 could have lived on his salary even at the most frugal imaginable level. Nor could teachers afford to invest in relatively expensive training dependent upon satisfactory future employment. Conditions of school teaching in the average rural school in the South prior to 1910 can scarcely be described in any other terms than austere and discouraging. Schools were drab and uncomfortable. They lacked satisfactory heating or proper seats. Teaching equipment and supplies had to be furnished by the teacher, and he had to carry them back and forth on his person because of the constant threat of vandalism. Disciplinary problems were often of such an exasperating nature that, no matter how well trained or ambitious a teacher was, he was defeated before he reached the schoolhouse door. In fact it was the problem of discipline which to some extent created prejudice against women teachers, and in the beginning limited the tapping of this source for instructors.

One major effort was made to counteract this shocking situation, and it was to prove a highly effective catalyst. It was the establishment of the Peabody Fund. George Peabody was a Massachusetts Yankee who was highly successful as merchant and banker in Philadelphia, New York, and London. He viewed the Civil War as a mad act on the part of Americans on both sides, but nevertheless he assisted the Union with its fiscal problems in England. As a young man he traveled through the South as a salesman, and immediately before the war he again visited the region and was disturbed by what he saw and heard. There were many problems confronting the South, but none seemed more important to Peabody than the education of its youth. In 1865 he was even more certain of it. Two years later he established the George Peabody Educational Fund with a gift of a million dollars. The original board of trustees was an illustrious one, which included Hamilton Fish, William Cabell Rives, William M. Evarts, Ulysses S. Grant, Governor William Aiken of South Carolina, and Admiral David Glasgow Farragut. In all Peabody gave the Fund three and a half million dollars, but a million and a half dollars in Mississippi and Florida state bonds were repudiated by those states.

In 1867 Dr. Barnas Sears, president of Brown University, was appointed agent of the fund. He had graduated from Brown University, had made a special study of the educational system of Germany, and was a successor to Horace Mann on the board of education in Massachusetts. As a result of his survey of southern needs, Sears proposed a ten-point plan which would emphasize that funds, which were limited, were to be used where the greatest number of people could be assembled; teachers, especially women, were to be trained; attempts were to be made to try to improve state systems of education; and special attention was to be given to the education of Negroes.

Unhappily there were no institutions where teachers could be trained. The colleges and universities were not so organized or motivated that they could care for this problem. Dr. Sears recommended the establishment of state normal schools instead of education departments in universities or the temporary short-term normal institutes that already existed. But there were no resources available to establish such state normal schools. Instead there had to be reliance on the short-term normal institutes. They were the only means by which large numbers of prospective teachers could be given a smattering of rudimentary training. As a result of the advice of Dr. Sears and the Peabody Board, summer normal schools and institutes were organized all over the South. Sometimes they were operated in conjunction with state universities and colleges, or as independent ventures. Local county normals were held whenever a staff and a minimum of teaching candidates could be brought together.

One of the best examples of an early public summer normal school was that operated in conjunction with the University of North Carolina in the summer of 1877. The North Carolina legislature appropriated $2000 and the Peabody Fund $500. An extensive series of lectures pertaining to educational procedures and content was given. Students were charged $10 per month, and less if they supplied their board and lodging. Only men students were given public assistance, but women were permitted to attend. The school opened with 128 men and 107 women the first of their sex to attend the University of North Carolina. The school was so successful that the idea spread across the South. At Nashville, Tennessee, the University of Nashville became the State Normal School in 1875 and then changed its name in 1887 to the Peabody Normal College in Tennessee.

Peabody Normal College, however, could do little more than foster the idea of teacher training and develop some guidelines for the future. Other southern colleges and universities meanwhile were making surprisingly little contribution to public education in this vital area. If every graduate of a southern college had gone into the region's schoolrooms, there still would have been a woeful lack of teachers. Even so, too few southern college graduates were qualified to perform instructional duties. To remedy this situation, a major effort was made in 1902 to serve the whole South with a summer school for teachers. The Southern Education Board, the Peabody Board, Robert C. Ogden, George Foster Peabody, Albert Shaw, Charles W. Dabney, and the University of Tennessee co-operated. The school was organized in the University of Tennessee, which offered the use of its facilities but assumed no responsibility for its operation. The sessions were held six days a week during a six-week term. Its curriculum was virtually all-inclusive, ranging from conduct of one-room schools to the holding of college classes. Teachers or lecturers came from all over the South and much of the nation. The first session registered 2019 students—697 men and 1332 women. Of these, 1500 were teachers in common schools. In 1903, 2150 students were registered, and there were 662 men and 1488 women.

The Knoxville summer school brought southern teachers into communication with each other. Many of the public lecturers dealt with southern educational problems and progress—or lack of progress. Publishers and merchandisers of school supplies exhibited their wares, and for the first time hundreds of teachers got glimpses of what a well-equipped schoolroom looked like, and of the literature available to teachers and pupils. The famous Alabama minister, historian, and social reformer, Edgar Gardner Murphy, was secretary of the school, and he wrote of the experiment:

Here were throngs of men and women giving their precious vacation weeks to better preparation for the services of their profession. Many of them had never known salaries larger than thirty-five dollars per month, many of them were expending practically the whole of their slender savings in meeting the expense for railway travel, for board, for the few necessary books [there were no charges for tuition save the registration fee of five dollars], and yet every sacrifice was made, and the serious work of the school was continued until the end—all in an atmosphere of pervasive cheerfulness and amid every evidence of buoyant and hopeful courage.

In 1909 the George Peabody College for Teachers was created from the old Peabody Normal College with an endowment of $1,000,000, largely for the purpose of continuing the idea of the summer school on a more extensive and permanently organized basis. Too, other southern colleges and universities organized summer schools as they instituted programs of teacher education.

As agent for the Peabody Fund, Barnas Sears had an enormous personal impact on southern universal education, although there is no way to state in a precise way what he accomplished. He did give patient, informed, and aggressive leadership to the public school movement when such foresight and planning were most needed. Nor did this influence stand by itself. In 1881 he was succeeded in office by Jabez Lamar Monroe Curry. A native of Alabama, educated at the Waddell Academy in South Carolina, the University of Georgia, and the Harvard Law School, Curry had a varied career; in the Texas Rangers in the Mexican War, the Alabama legislature, the Confederate Congress and Army, later a college professor and president, and finally as United States ambassador to Spain.

While a law student at Harvard, Curry heard Horace Mann speak on the subject of universal education, and he was stirred by its promises. As agent for the Peabody Fund he had an opportunity to apply some of the suggestions of the great apostle of public education to his native South. Scarcely a major educational advance was to be made in the South between 1881 and 1902 that was not influenced in some way by J. L. M. Curry; in fact, his name became synonymous with public education. He was credited with influencing the establishment of state normal schools for both races in twelve states, helping to organize graded schools in the main cities, and in many smaller places causing legislators to assume responsibility for better rural schools. In addition, his reports and published addresses formed a significant body of educational literature.

It is difficult historically to assess the full impact of the George Peabody Fund on educational development in the South. Nevertheless, it seems evident that, had this support not been available, efforts to organize and maintain public schools would have been seriously handicapped. The region-wide distribution of funds and the support it gave to such vigorous leaders as Sears and Curry, lent tremendous impetus to universal education. No one can really know how effective the fund-implanted ideas of education really were. On the other hand modern critics have regarded some of the later Peabody teacher-training programs as over-emphasizing methodology and techniques of professional teaching at the sacrifice of the actual intellectual content of the subjects involved.

In his report on Virginia schools for 1871, Dr. Ruffner might well have been writing the outline history of southern public education for the next thirty-five years. His report called attention to the obstacles to developing a proper school system: prejudice against public schools, a feeling of poverty among the people, aversion to educating the Negro, lack of schoolhouses and appliances, teachers without professional training, a heavy state debt, and inability to supply schools in every neighborhood. All of these factors were to be present in the following years. Something of the extent of Virginia's public educational problem can be gained from the fact that in 1871 there were 441,021 children of school age (up to twenty-one) of which only 131,088 were enrolled in school, and only 75,722, or 57.7 per cent, maintained an average daily attendance. There were 3014 teachers who received average monthly salaries of $32.36 for three- to four-month school terms. At the turn of the century conditions showed remarkably little change, even though there was a significant increase in the number of children of school age.[1]

Despite all the efforts of reformers like Sears, Curry, and Ruffner, conditions in the South had not changed radically, as a brochure prepared by Charles L. Coons for the campaign committee of the Southern Education Board in 1905 demonstrated. Teachers, for instance, taught an approximate average of 110 days for annual salaries which ranged from $123.46 in North Carolina to $189.00 in Florida. In New York the dog catcher received $1500 a year, and the average southern county jailer received $150 a year per head for care of prisoners. Rural county

(1) There were 691,312 children, of whom 370,595 were enrolled and 58.4 per cent, or 216,464, maintained an average daily attendance. There were 8954 teachers who received average monthly salaries of $32.47.

superintendents fared little better than teachers; their yearly salaries ranged from $250 in Arkansas to $760.95 in Florida.[2]

Coon's brochure also pointed out that eighty out of every hundred elementary school pupils in the South were still rural dwellers. Thus it was evident that the educational problems of the region were over-whelmingly rural in nature. Because of this the educational objective was largely set by the meager debt-ridden system of one-crop agriculture. It was hard for the average southern marginal farmer, caught in the deep depression of the early 1890's, to see where education was either necessary for or helpful to his children. He may have been right, for large numbers of children who had attended three- to four-month term country schools had scarcely been touched by education.

The Coon publication was only one of many such indices in Southern educational history. The South has ever struggled with the handicaps of illiteracy at both levels, actual and functional. In 1900 school-age white illiteracy ranged from 26 per cent in Virginia to 32 per cent for Louisiana and Alabama. Negro illiteracy was only 27 per cent of the total population, but there were 2,519,289 total illiterates above ten years of age as compared with 1,070,245 whites. Almost a sixth of the southern males of voting age in 1900 were total illiterates. Some examples by states were 127,396 white male voters in South Carolina, and 15,711 illiterates.[3] There was no doubt a close correlation of the illiteracy and the fact that only 21.6 of the southern population in 1900 resided in incorporated towns. For whatever glory it may have been for the South, with the exception of New Mexico, the southern states showed the largest decrease in illiteracy in the Union by 1900.[4]

(2) In 1902–3, Mississippi had 7052 schoolhouses worth in the aggregate $920,000, or $130 apiece. Virginia's 8965 buildings were worth $1,953,532, or $218 apiece. North Carolina spent $2.82 per child, Mississippi $3.48, Virginia $3.09, and Texas $7.49. Approximately 69 per cent of the southern rural white children were en-rolled in school in 1902, but only 43 per cent maintained a daily average attend-ance. Negro children were enrolled in about the same percentage as whites, but their average daily attendance was approximately 31 per cent.

(3) Mississippi had 145,815 white voters, of whom 11,846 were unable to read and write, and North Carolina had 286,812 voters of whom 54,334 were illiterates. White illiteracy had decreased in Virginia, between 1880 and 1900 by 7.4 per cent, in South Carolina by 12.2 per cent, and in Arkansas by 13.9 per cent.

(4) Between 1860 and 1870 property values decreased markedly. Real estate assess-ments decreased $401,809,941 and personal property $1,912,333,149, or a total of $2,314,143,000. Per capita wealth averaged approximately $500 in 1860, $285 in 1870, and $600 in 1900. A comparison between estimated value in Ohio and Virginia

There was one remedy for much of the South's inequality of educational opportunity. The federal government might have been allowed to absorb a part of the cost. When the Negro slave was freed, there was a consciousness on the part of some members of the Congress that his education was a national rather than a regional responsibility. Senator George Frisbie Hoar of Massachusetts introduced a public assistance bill to aid all the states, but especially those of the South. Congress would levy a direct tax, and then appropriate $50 million annually to subsidize education. The bill provided for a strong federal stimulus for establishing schools and for supervising them, and was defeated for that reason. In opposing such direct aid and federal supervision, many Congressmen proposed instead that Congress set aside funds from public land sales to be given directly to the states for support of elementary public education.

The subject of federal aid to education was again introduced in 1883 by Senator Henry W. Blair of New Hampshire. The Blair bill, like the defeated Hoar bill, proposed a large appropriation of $77 million to be distributed to the states on the basis of proportionate illiteracy. It did, however, eliminate the element of strong federal control. Between 1883 and 1888 this bill was a subject of much debate in and out of Congress. The rural southern press favored the bill at first, but later, when Senators M. C. Butler of South Carolina, John Tyler Morgan of Alabama, and Robert Love of Tennessee vengefully dragged the red herrings of Negro equality, Yankee interference, and the high tariff across its path, it retreated and bitterly attacked the bill. Earlier Professor John B. Minor of the University of Virginia Law School, and W. L. Wilson, president of Washington and Lee University, were forceful in opposing federal legislation. In the furor

---

will reflect the national differentials. In 1860, Virginia's property evaluation was $793,249,681; in 1870 it was $403,588,133; and in 1900 it was $707,000,000, For the same periods property values in Ohio were $1,193,898,422; $2,233,430,000; and $3,238,000,000. Per capita wealth for each child of school age in Virginia in 1902 was $2099; in Ohio it was $6407. An even greater contrast was shown between South Carolina's per capita property value of $434 and Massachusetts' $1449. Something of the school-age responsibilities of northern and southern states was illustrated in the comparative numbers in North Carolina and Massachusetts. North Carolina had, out of a total population of 1,893,810 in 1902, 650,700 children, while Massachusetts had a population of 2,805,346, and 634,510 children. In 1900 the southern states had 25 per cent of the nation's school children, owned 4 per cent of the school property, and spent 6.5 per cent of the school money.

over the Blair bill the statement was made repeatedly that the South alone could solve its educational problems.

As poor as the South was, it had never actually over-reached its potential tax-raising ability to maintain better schools or to make more vigorous efforts to reach the national level. But such a drive to accomplish this objective would have to capture the imagination of the people, and this would require a crusade that would need all the religious fervor of evangelism. Dr. Edward Abbott of Cambridge, Massachusetts, in visiting the South in 1897, came on the Sale Hotel at Capon Springs, West Virginia. The hotel was operated by Captain William H. Sale, an ex-Confederate soldier. Dr. Abbott persuaded him to invite interested persons to attend an educational conference there in 1898. A special committee was formed, made up of Dr. Thomas U. Dudley of Lexington, Kentucky; Dr. Hollis B. Frissell of the Hampton Institute; A. B. Hunter of Raleigh, North Carolina; Dr. Julius D. Dreher of Roanoke College; and George Benedict of Cedartown, Georgia. Largely a committee of ministers, its members had been primarily concerned with the education of the Negro. Among the persons attending the meeting, however, were Dr. Amory D. Mayo, southern agent of the National Bureau of Education, and General John B. Eaton, United States Commissioner of Education. The meeting could do little more than stimulate interest in the subject of education.

A year later, seventy-five delegates accepted Captain Sale's invitation to attend a second conference. This time the original committee was joined by such highly influential figures as J. L. M. Curry, Robert C. Ogden, Walter Hines Page, and George Foster Peabody. The Second Capon Springs Conference resolved that the education of the white race in the South was pressing and imperative. Some delegates believed that before the Negro could be trained, his white neighbors had to be educated to the point of tolerance. But the conference did recognize that the problems of educating two races should be treated as one.

The West Virginia conferences brought forward a new personal force in Robert Curtiss Ogden. He succeeded the aged and ailing Curry as spiritual leader. Partner and head of the Wanamaker store in New York, Ogden was in large measure a Horatio Alger hero in American business during the last half of the nineteenth century. As a young man he had traveled in the South just prior to the Civil

War trying to collect bad debts for his employer. After the war he was active in all sorts of public crusades, including the chairmanship of rescue work for the Johnstown flood sufferers. He became interested in southern education through his friend General Samuel Chapman Armstrong, and not only helped raise funds for Hampton Institute but also served on its board of trustees. Stressing the business practicality of education, Ogden challenged southern businessmen to insure the future prosperity of their region by promoting universal education. In his view, every human being was a potential producer.

A gregarious man himself, Ogden believed the way to get men to act together was to bring them into warm personal association. He would organize a party of easterners each year and take them in his private railway car to visit Hampton Institute. In New York he gave numerous dinners and luncheons for all sorts of causes, and with all sorts of people present. Just prior to the meeting of the Southern Educational Conference in Winston-Salem, North Carolina, in April 1901, he gathered a hundred guests, one of whom was John D. Rockefeller, Jr., for an excursion to study southern education.

The Winston-Salem conference established the philosophy that the South needed universal education and that it could be brought about through greater public support and more co-operation within the whole region. Again the emphasis was to be on educating whites. J. L. M. Curry was quoted by the *Winston-Salem Daily Sentinel* as saying:

> I hope that out of this meeting will grow unity of effort and cooperation of forces both material and moral, to uplift and educate both black and white. The state schools must do their work. We must proceed first to provide adequate opportunities for the whites. One properly educated white man will help educate a dozen Negroes, while an illiterate white man will hold many more Negroes in the bondage of ignorance and degradation. . . . The education of the white youth of the South is the shortest road to the education of the Negro.

Delegates to the Winston-Salem conference had before them for the first time a considerable body of data. Statistics of a most gloomy nature were presented and discussed. Some of the state superintendents and other politically sensitive delegates took offense at having the failures of their states so cogently revealed. Governor Allan D. Candler of Georgia was reported to have said the South could attend to the education of the Negro without Yankee meddling. Much of the southern press jumped to the conclusion that the conference existed for the benefit of the Negro. Among the most outspoken opposition papers were the Charleston *News and Courier* and Columbia (South Carolina) *State*.

As president of the Southern Educational Conference, Ogden set about creating a functional board that would be able to tackle the southern educational problems in practical ways. This resulted in the organization of the Southern Education Board on November 4, 1901, in New York City, with twelve members on its board. Its primary objective was the creation of a public opinion favorable to universal education in the South. This Board was to administer funds contributed to the movement. At the concluding session Ogden gave one of his famous dinners at the Waldorf-Astoria Hotel, at which Charles W. Dabney, president of the University of Tennessee, suggested the reasons for neglect of southern education were "poverty of population, poverty of the people, and the baneful influence of politicians who control school affairs."

The stated objectives of the Southern Education Board as subscribed to by the fourth conference in Winston-Salem in 1905 outlined the basic educational procedures of the South for the next fifty years. These included increases in local taxation, compulsory education, lengthening of school terms, consolidation of one-room schools into larger units, better preparation of teachers, introduction of vocational education, organization of state conferences of superintendents, and development of some kind of communication between the secondary schools and the colleges.

The fabric of southern educational history, however, was made much more complex and colorful by the philanthropic activities of the many outside agencies that labored diligently in the region to bring about better educational and health conditions. The Peabody Fund, for instance not only supported teachers and teaching institutions. It was the only agency to address itself to the broad problems of educational needs and the establishment of proper schools. In the years after the Civil War the Fund and its agents were the major force in promoting the discussion of public education problems in the South. The Fund was able to exert pressure against ignorance and indifference way out of proportion to the money it spent.

The Negro's educational plight especially interested missionary and philanthropic endeavors. In 1882 John F. Slater of Connecticut created a trust and turned over to its board a million dollars to be used for the advancement of southern public education, or as Slater called it, "the blessings of Christian education." This fund was spent largely in the area of Negro education with special emphasis on the training of teachers. One of the institutions given special assistance was the Alabama State Normal School for Negroes. This school was founded in Marion, Alabama, by William Burns Patterson, a Scotsman, who taught his poverty-stricken pupils the value of self-help and work. The local normals and private and church schools were the leading benefactors of the Slater Fund down to 1920. After that date the fund was used to supplement the income of state schools.

In 1905 Anna T. Jeannes, a Quakeress of Philadelphia, gave the General Education Board $200,000 for the assistance of rural Negro schools of the South. She made gifts to Hampton Institute and Tuskegee, and in 1907 established a trust of $1,000,000, the returns from which were to be used in supporting other educational foundations. Coincidentally, Jackson Davis, superintendent of schools in Hernrico County, Virginia, discovered that Virginia Randolph, a Negro teacher, was doing an extraordinary job with her pupils. Not only was she performing excellently as a classroom teacher, but she had developed a social consciousness among her pupils which showed up in the life of her community and on her school grounds. Through Superintendent Jackson's intercession with Dr. James Hardy Dillard, some of the Jeannes income was given to support Virginia Randolph and a program of supervisory and demonstration teaching. In time the program was extended into Negro schools across the South.

Another northern woman, Caroline Phelps-Stokes, willed the sum of $1,000,000 to the improvement of Negro education. In 1911 her trust began to distribute the first income from the bequest. The Phelps-Stokes Fund was used largely to supplement the Slater and Jeannes funds, and to help improve the teaching standards in southern Negro schools.

The Negro was aided by Julius Rosenwald of Chicago, president of Sears, Roebuck. In 1911 he attended a meeting of the board of trustees of Tuskegee Institute. While in Alabama he visited some of the rural Negro schools in Macon County which had been built by the Institute. On August 12, 1912, on his birthday, Rosenwald set aside $25,000 to be used in supplementing funds raised in Negro communities for the construction of better school buildings. Negroes, their white friends, and the counties were called upon under the terms of the Rosenwald gift to make a supreme effort to finance the construction of satisfactory buildings on grounds ample enough for play and work space. The fund would help finance in a modest way the construction of a building, the employment of teachers, and the purchase of equipment for industrial training. The building, however, must be completed within twelve months.

By 1916, 184 schools had received supplementary Rosenwald assistance, and a year later the foundation was incorporated. Its purpose was to distribute funds through the state educational agencies on a set formula of amounts of each type of schoolhouse built, ranging from less than $500 for one-room schools to $1600 for six-teacher, and $2100 for ten-teacher schools. By 1930 there had been spent in the southern states $20 million to finance the building of Rosenwald schools, and of this amount Julius Rosenwald had contributed $4 million. The five-hundredth Rosenwald school was dedicated on November 21, 1930, at Greenbrier, Elizabeth City County, Virginia, and within fifty miles of where the English settlements were begun and the first Negro slaves arrived in Virginia. The one-story structure contained six classrooms, offices, and industrial arts equipment, and cost $15,997. The Rosenwald Fund, however, was not a foundation in perpetuity. The donor devised in his will that the entire sum of his bequest would be spent within twenty-five years after his death, but before this time the Foundation had received and dispensed $22 million.

All of the above philanthropies were concerned with the educational plight of southerners, especially the Negro. There was, however, a greater problem than mere illiteracy or low-grade training. Education could mean next to nothing for persons so badly beset by health problems that they could hardly function as human beings. Regional diseases such as pellagra, malaria, and hookworm infestation took enormous tolls of persons of school age.

One of the most dramatic campaigns conducted in the South between 1865 and 1920 was that to eradicate hookworm disease. The parasite was especially obnoxious in areas of sandy moist soils, such as those of Mississippi, Alabama, Georgia, and the Carolinas, between the twentieth and thirty-sixth parallels, Hookworm goes through a life cycle from egg to full-grown worm in which it attaches itself to a human host through the soles of the feet. It spends its fecund stage attached to the lining of the host's intestines, and eggs are passed out to the soil with the fecal matter to begin a new life cycle all over again. The parasite was first discovered in 1838 in the intestines of Italian workmen who died while constructing the St. Gothard's Tunnel between Italy and Switzerland. In 1888 Charles Wardell Stiles, an American student in the University of Leipzig, learned of this parasite, and upon his return to the United States he began a search for American victims of the disease. In 1902 he discovered there was widespread infection in some of the southern states. Lieutenant Bailey K. Ashford had found the parasite in Puerto Rico and in 1898 and 1899, and there was fear that American soldiers would bring it home with them. Stiles countered with the fact that the disease was already present, a fact questioned by General Wyman, Surgeon General of the United States.

To prove his contention Dr. Stiles established the first hookworm clinic in America in Columbia, South Carolina. It was, however, the Country Life Commission's visit to the South that stimulated the most excitement about the disease. At Raleigh, North Carolina, Dr. Stiles startled and enraged the governor and some members of the Commission. He was supported, however, by the North Carolina Board of Health, and out of this conference and a meeting of the Southern Education Board in Amenia, New York, in 1909, came the campaign that caused John D. Rockefeller to give $1,000,000 to underwrite a hookworm survey in the South. There was created the Sanitary Commission for the Eradication of the Hookworm Disease. This body was to operate in conjunction with the Southern Education Board and the Peabody Board.

After a considerable amount of nonsensical editorial comment and political breast-pounding about the honor and virility of southern manhood, neither of which the hookworm knew about or respected, the campaign of eradication got underway. Working through the schools, the Sanitary Commission was able effectively not only to publicize the detection and cure of the disease, but to campaign for better sanitation in the southern rural home. In four years, 496,000 school children in 488 southern counties were tested for hookworm infestation, and 40 per cent of them were found to be victims of the disease. Beyond the schools, 892,000 persons were tested in the South, and 34 per cent of them were found to be infested.

Before any marked improvement in southern education could take place, certain changes had to occur: better roads had to be built; local politicians and boards of trustees had to be convinced or replaced; parents had to believe that their children would be better served in larger school units; and an enormous amount of consolidation of thousands of deficient one-teacher schools had to take place. The consolidation movement began in Virginia and North Carolina just before the outbreak of World War I, and reached a state of major application in Mississippi in 1928. But equally important to educational development was the institution of compulsory attendance laws. This was not an especially new idea, since some of the superintendents like Z. F. Smith of Kentucky advocated compulsory attendance as early as 1867. In the 1840's the Arkansas legislature had adopted a compulsory attendance law as the most certain means of attacking illiteracy in districts where parents failed to see that their children attended school. By 1920 compulsory school attendance was required by law in all of the southern states. This did not mean, however, that the objectives of the laws were fully accomplished. Enforcement was lax, and in many cases where states distributed their educational funds on the basis of the count of children of school age it was to the advantage of school districts not to have all eligible children enrolled in schools. After 1954 some of the states recognized that the compulsory attendance laws were an important factor in enforcing desegregation of public schools. In brief the compulsory laws have achieved their purposes only in proportion to local efforts to enforce them.

The biggest educational advance in the first half of the twentieth century in the South occurred in the organization and expansion of high schools. The history of this second phase of free-school development is most erratic. Down to 1910 the high school was regarded as largely an institution of the larger cities and towns, and thus as not accessible to the mass of southern youths. From Robert C. Ogden and John D. Rockefeller, Jr. down to the weakest country school teacher in the most isolated backwoods community, the great drive was directed toward improving the rural school. But changing times and the growing demands at local levels for better educational training made organization of high schools a necessity. Perhaps the heaviest initial pressures came from the colleges and universities that wished to give up their preparatory departments in order to devote all their resources and instructional energies to improving their college-level offerings. These college-related preparatory schools were, with few exceptions, basically the first high schools in the South. Charles W. Dabney said in his book *Universal Education in the South*, "Apparently the people of the South [in 1902] did not know what a real high school was. It was difficult to tell from statistics what the facts really were because a great majority of schools claimed high school status when they only gave a limited number of courses in the high school area." There were high schools in cities like Mobile, Birmingham, Atlanta, Louisville, Richmond, Nashville, and New Orleans, but outside of these, said Dr. Dabney, "The high school of this period was nothing more than an addition of a few miscellaneous courses to the common school." In 1904-5 only 215 boys in Georgia graduated from three- and four-year high schools, while in 1918, a major world war year, the number had only increased to 1500.

In 1905 the General Educational Board offered assistance to the southern states to promote the organization of high schools. In all the states the high school crusade gained momentum, but in Mississippi, with its small country towns and overwhelming rural population, the organization of high schools followed a rural pattern. In 1908 the first agricultural high school with courses in agriculture and home economics was organized. Dormitories were built to accommodate students, a plan of co-operative management of boarding facilities reduced the cost of lodging and meals to a minimum. By 1932 there were 22 of these schools, but in the meantime 427 white high schools and 35 Negro consolidated schools had been organized. Within thirty years Mississippi had gone from the extreme of no high schools to an unreasonably large number of small units.

Within the eleven former Confederate states in 1960 there were 6045 high schools with a total enrollment of 2,273,000 pupils. Mississippi alone enrolled more high school students in 1960 than the entire South in 1900.

By 1945 the southern states were on the threshold of meeting the national educational averages with its white schools, but two hard jolts changed the picture radically. One of these was the rising demand for marked improvement in Negro education, the other the scientific and industrial revolution which challenged education at all levels. In the rising new industrial age in the South there was a clear revelation of how inadequate the education effort really was. Southern youth had made a poor showing in tests and measurements used by the armed forces in World War II. The rate of rejections per thousand for military service in the South was almost ten times that of the Far West, seven times that of the Midwest, and four times that of the national average. The North Carolina Advisory Committee for Equal Protection of the Law in Education concluded among several things that, "The Southeast is the most uneducated part of the United States."

Educational demands had become something altogether different from the philosophical concepts which had spurred on the nineteenth-century crusaders. Now even the most illiterate man appreciated the fact that his children must be educated if they were to compete successfully for livelihoods in the modern South. Recognition of this fact placed him in a terrible quandary, for he was brought face to face with the question of integrated education. In the spring of 1965 the Federal Commissioner of Education ruled, in accordance with the recent Civil Rights Act, that southern school districts must integrate their schools or face the loss of federal funds to support them. Southerners were faced with the dilemma of accepting desegregation or paying much higher taxes to support their schools. Both ideas were abhorrent. As distasteful as desegregation was, illiteracy was a permanent and economically injurious fact. Some individuals turned wistfully to the idea of establishing and maintaining private schools, but continuing costs made such an alternative self-defeating in the end.

But there were some encouraging signs. By 1965 the South had realized the objectives of the crusaders. There were 3,155 school districts in twelve states, and 11,844,239 pupils were enrolled in longer school sessions. The more than 500,000 teachers were the best prepared in the history of southern education, even though they still did not meet fully the challenges of the modern world. There was no doubt about the permanency of universal education; it had now become a central fact in southern life, and so it would remain. Ignorance was far too costly an evil for even the most prejudiced parent to tolerate. Closing the gap with national average achievements was still a spur to the South to make even greater efforts to improve educational standards.

Relman Morin wrote in the introduction of *Southern Schools: Progress and Problems* (1959):

> In other words, the South has not only to make one "great leap forward" but several such leaps in order to catch up with the rest of the nation. Much of what has been done in the past five years comes under the heading of "closing the gap" between conditions in Southern schools and those elsewhere.
>
> The South simply does not have the total wealth or personal income of other regions. It is less than thirty years since President Roosevelt called the South "the nation's Number One economic problem." The money available for schools, therefore, is harder to come by than in the North or West. In 1956, for example, the South had only 22.6 per cent of the total manufacturing employment of the United States, and 18.9 per cent of the total manufacturing payroll.

Though conditions in the South were still improving, it was the improvement itself which made universal education more than ever a basic necessity.

≋ VIII ≋

An Ever-Broadening Educational Challenge

After the Civil War southerners faced serious challenge in regard to Negro education and to higher education. If the white southerner was severely handicapped by lack of educational background, the Negro was by contrast hopelessly ignorant, and had been kept that way by statute law prior to 1865 which forbade his education. In his new-found freedom the Negro was entrusted with social, economic, and political responsibilities of which he could not conceive. There was nothing surprising or mysterious that he failed all three challenges, or that his failures reflected on the entire South. On the other hand, the predicament of the Negro was to have a curiously fermentative effect upon efforts to organize and sustain public education. The plight of the Negro furnished an open sesame to the highly motivated missionary-minded Americans who sought outlets for their zeal. Dozens of organizations were interested in helping to improve the Negro's capabilities to become a responsible American citizen.

Whites no less than blacks suffered from inabilities to apply greater knowledge to their callings, especially in areas of farming and public health. Land-grant colleges in the latter part of the nineteenth century in the South were hardly more than splendid ideas in the statute books and plans. It was not until the turn of this century that they began to achieve most of their stated objectives. Without agricultural demonstration work or applied engineering it was impossible to use even the meager knowledge gained by research and experimentation. From the foundations of the agricultural and mechanical colleges the common man in the South was encouraged to accept higher education as having practical meaning in his monotonous life. Through advanced educational opportunity offered by these colleges it was believed that ultimately southerners would come to live the idyllic lives so gloriously described by orators and editors.

Prior to 1914, achieving better quality higher education was never quite the same challenge in the South that it was in much of the rest of the country. First, not nearly so many southerners were intellectually prepared to enter college as in New England and the old Northwest. Technical demands made upon southerners for earning a livelihood were relatively light, and this was even true in some of the professions. Lawyers, doctors, ministers, and teachers often entered upon the practice of their professions without having finished college. This condition, however, was changed by the end of World War I when the demand for more highly trained people was to have a telling impact upon the South. It was in this period that publicly supported institutions began to make headway in relation to those maintained by religious groups and private endowments. Thus the heart of southern higher education history belongs largely to the advancing decades of the twentieth century.

Significantly the South was to make some of its most important social and cultural advances in education. But even though there was an overwhelming demand for large numbers of technically trained personnel in key areas of regional activities—far beyond the capacity of starved southern colleges and universities to answer—the South continued to insist on maintaining separate education programs for the two races, not only in higher education but in all other education as well. Die-hard advocates of this system held on, even though it had become increasingly clear after 1930 that this practice would ultimately have to be abandoned because of the administrative and financial burdens it would create. By 1945 southern educators faced not only hordes of returning World War II veterans, but also a stiffening demand to admit Negroes without discrimination to all colleges and universities. As protest cases reached the courts, racial barriers in colleges were breached. Too, the federal government itself became more deeply involved in the support of southern higher education, with its defense grants, subsidies to students, and in specialized contracts of all sorts. No longer could public institutions control their entire policies and at the same time accept badly needed federal funds to finance their maintenance and expansion. In this rapidly changing situation, southerners confronted one of the region's most serious cultural lags. Now with students being admitted to colleges and universities without regard to race, the region had to face squarely the inadequacy of Negro education. The quality of Negro education at all levels became more than an academic question to be deplored by statisticians and forgotten by southerners in general. Negro educational history down to 1950 must be considered as a separate strand from the educational history of the region in general.

Ideologically the development of common schools in the South made little distinction between the basic needs of white and Negro. This, however, was not actually true, as was reflected by the intensive discussion of Negro educational needs in the various southern educational conferences. Newly freed Negroes looked upon education as symbolizing both their physical and intellectual freedom. For many ex-slaves it had the deep spiritual meaning of enabling them to read the scriptures. For the Negro as well, one of the key ways in which he could enjoy the democratic way of life and participate in it was through education. And after the Civil War the American people made a commitment to the Negro to provide him with an education. It is significant that, though Negro schools founded during reconstruction were exceedingly poor in quality, and though a deep animosity existed in many places against educating the Negro at all, no southern state repudiated its commitments to support such schools.

The creation of Hampton Normal and Agricultural Institute in Virginia represented a major advance in Negro education. It was founded in 1861 by Mary S. Peake as a school for Negroes. Five years later General Samuel C. Armstrong was placed in charge of Negro contrabands, and in 1870 he became principal of the school. General Armstrong, a native of the island of Maui, Hawaii, born of New England missionary parents, was graduated from Williams College. But before he returned to the East from Hawaii to finish his education, he had been given excellent vocational training in one of his father's mission shops. At the outbreak of the Civil War he became an officer in the Union Army. He was captured by Stonewall Jackson in northern Virginia, fought at Gettysburg, and was given command of the 9th Regiment of Negro troops as a lieutenant colonel. His regiment, without him, fought before Petersburg. At the end of the war he was made a brigadier general and saw service on the Mexican border. In 1866 he took charge of the Negro encampment at Hampton for the Freedman's Bureau. He came to believe that selected Negroes could be trained to be teachers, and that vocational work comparable to that offered in the mission field would answer many of the Negro's educational problems. Between 1868 and 1893 General Armstrong converted the struggling little Hampton Institute into an effective southern educational institution. In 1893 Hollis Burke Frissell became principal and continued the work of General Armstrong. He was well acquainted with Negro problems, having worked with ex-slaves on Saint Helena Island in South Carolina, and having traveled widely in the South. Until his death in 1917 he was a constructive force in southern education.

Hampton Institute was only one attempt at improving the southern Negro's lot by education. The founding of Tuskegee Institute in Macon County, Alabama, in 1881 resulted from General Armstrong's training program. Tuskegee was located in the heart of the Alabama black belt where the Negroes made up 50 to 75 per cent of the population, but where they had made little progress toward improving their condition. There was great need for a school where the simplest rudiments of knowledge could be taught, and where free Negroes could gain practical training for simple work tasks.

This was the situation in which Booker Talliaferro Washington found himself in 1881. The request for a teacher had gone to General Armstrong from George W. Campbell, a former white slaveholder, and Louis Adams, a former slave. Washington had a Negro mother and possibly a white father, and had gone to Hampton Institute from the coal mines of West Virginia. At Hampton he proved diligent both in his labors and his studies. There is grave doubt that he received anything approaching a classical education, but there was never any doubt about his understanding the Negro's educational plight and the attitude of his white neighbors. When Booker T. Washington arrived, Tuskegee had made only the barest beginnings as a primitive elementary school. The Alabama legislature appropriated only $2000. Washington operated Tuskegee by the doctrine that the Negro must first develop the talents and opportunities he had. He preached the dignity of labor and counseled him to exercise patience until he had disciplined himself to assume responsibilities in a more advanced society. The central task of Tuskegee Institute was the conditioning of ignorant country Negroes to accept organized institutional training so they could perform ordinary tasks efficiently, develop the skills in several crafts, and produce enough teachers to begin to meet the southern Negro's educational needs. In emphasizing these themes, Booker T. Washington, more than anyone else of his race, helped to keep alive the hopes of his people at a time when they dropped almost to the vanishing point.

Negro education was not to be accomplished without Negroes' differing among themselves as to how it was to be done. As Gunnar Myrdal observed in *An American Dilemma:*

> The struggle between the conservative and radical groups of Negro leaders became focused on the issue: "individual" versus "classical" education for Negroes. Washington became the champion for the former position, and he was backed by the white South and the bulk of northern philanthropy. W. E. B. DuBois headed the group of Negro intellectuals who feared that most often the intention, and in many cases the results, would be to keep Negroes out of the higher and more general culture of America. This dispute was important in the development of Negro ideologies. It scarcely meant much for the actual development of Negro education in the South, which was dominated by the whites. If Negro education in the South did not become turned entirely into industrial education on the elementary level, the main explanation was, as we shall see, the growing expense of such training after the Industrial Revolution and the competitive interests of white workers to keep the Negro out of the crafts and industry. On the higher level, a non-vocational Negro education had, as DuBois always emphasized, its chief strength in the fact that Tuskegee Institute and other similar schools raised a demand for teachers with broad educational background.

While large numbers of Negroes who attended Tuskegee Institute became teachers, many more became skilled craftsmen and laborers. No matter how well trained or skilled, they still were barred from the craft unions, which meant they could not find labor in keeping with their capabilities.

Booker T. Washington always gave the appearance of being a modest man, but at the same time he was skillful at public relations. He made large numbers of influential friends, ranging from Theodore Roosevelt and Andrew Carnegie down to his poor rural Alabama white neighbors. Perhaps no single act of his ever did more to create good will between him and the white South than his famous speech at the Atlanta Cotton Exposition on September 19, 1895. He reviewed Negro-white relationships in the traditional southern setting, explained briefly his philosophy of Negro education, and anticipated the outcome of the famous Supreme Court decision, *Plessy* vs. *Ferguson*, in emphasizing "separate but equal" relationships. Southerners, captivated by the eloquence of the Negro educator, however, failed to take seriously his statement that the Negro could not be held down in a ditch without the white man's getting down there with him.

The Atlanta speech received wide national publicity, and it helped shape a fresh image both for Booker T. Washington and for Tuskegee. This image was quickly marred by Senator Ben Tillman and James K. Vardaman and the southern rural press. They raised a furor over the fact that Booker T. Washington had dined with President Roosevelt at the White House. Actually nothing of the sort occurred. President Roosevelt was served lunch at his desk while he conferred with the Negro educator, and out of good manners offered a part of it to his visitor. But the demagogues used the alleged gathering to denounce Washington and the government.

In 1915 Booker T. Washington died and was succeeded by Robert Russa Moton. Under his leadership Tuskegee went through the transitional years of World War I and entered the 1920's in a position to help its students to take larger economic and social responsibility in the South. It was during his administration that the famous chemist George Washington Carver was to gain a national reputation through his work with the peanut, sweet potato, clay, and other commonplace southern products.

In Kentucky, Berea College had offered co-racial education down to 1904, when the general assembly of that state enacted the famous Day law forbidding it. Berea, like Hampton and Tuskegee, provided student labor opportunities in lieu of money payments. It placed almost as much emphasis on vocational as upon literary training, and its work with Negroes was largely at the elementary level. Elsewhere after the closing of the Freedman's Bureau, the major effort to support Negro education was made by various private and missionary groups. By 1869, there were 178 private schools with enrollments of 40,000 students, 1600 teachers, and owning $7,500,000 worth of property.

Between 1869 and 1926 the Negro colleges made remarkable progress. By 1926 there were twenty-one publicly owned Negro colleges in the United States, most of which were in the South, and enrollment had risen to 35,662 students. Since 1945 Negro enrollment in formerly all-white colleges and universities has increased with each new annual registration. As Negro high school graduates have received training comparable to that given to whites, the South has begun to get its first practical answer as to what effect education will have upon the Negro's way of life.

Negro schools in rural areas were still vastly inferior to those of whites in 1940. The Great Depression had stunned the southern agrarian system, if it did not destroy it as a central way of life for Negroes. At the same time a rising birth rate among both white and Negro placed an enormous burden on the states to maintain rural schools on a par with town schools and Negro and white schools on an equal basis.

In the larger area of public education in the South after 1865, it was evident that the vast majority of southerners were faced with stiff challenges of economic survival. The overwhelming mass of people lived on farms, and were farmers by vocation. But farming faced serious problems of production and marketing. Schools were needed to train farmers to meet the agricultural challenges that were forthcoming. Although all southern states had made arrangements to establish land-grant colleges in which the agricultural and mechanical arts were to be taught in the generation after the Civil War, these schools were slow in defining the subjects which would be taught and in securing staffs well enough trained to do effective teaching and research. Down to 1900 the average southern college of agriculture was little more than a vocational school located on a public farm, trying to find its mission in southern agricultural life. In Georgia, for instance, the legislature investigated the teaching of agriculture at the University of Georgia and found there was little relationship between what was being taught there and practical farming in the state. In 1906 the Georgia State College of Agriculture was organized in Athens. However, branch agricultural and mechanical colleges were located in each Congressional district, twenty-four branches in all.

The mission of scientific agriculture was more clearly defined in 1887 when Congress enacted legislation creating experiment stations and the agricultural extension service. Basically this dual approach to scientific agriculture was planned to create a reservoir of expert knowledge through experimentation. The extension service was the means by which this new knowledge could be conveyed to farmers in a simplified, personally communicated interpretation and application. With the introduction of these services the teaching of agriculture at the elementary and college level took a much more meaningful direction in the South.

No matter how much knowledge the agricultural scientists gained, it was well-nigh useless unless applied by farmers. The average southern farmer of the era, however, was made up of equal parts of conservatism, ignorance, traditionalism, and stubbornness. It is doubtful that any person or group of persons in the South could convince masses of farmers to do anything outside of their traditional, poverty-engendering routines. To the suggestions of entomologists and extension service personnel that a 200-mile sterile belt be established before the advance of the boll weevil, so that its spread could be checked until more could be learned of its habits and means to combat it, one southern legislature reacted by saying that the weevil was only a "sap sucker" and had always been in the cotton fields; thus nothing could be done about it. In this case the "sap suckers" were in the Texas legislature. No better documentation of the resistance to scientific knowledge and change can be cited than the way in which farmers allowed their soils to erode because they refused to follow scientific advice to terrace their lands and plow rows in contour patterns.

The only effective way of transmitting scientific agricultural knowledge to southern farmers was through their children and by demonstrating better methods in the farmers' own fields. Fortunately, Dr. Seaman Ashbel Knapp had moved to the South in 1886. Dr. Knapp was a native New Yorker, a graduate of Union College, and a practical farmer. Ill-health had forced him to move to Iowa in 1867, where he engaged in livestock-raising. Five years later he became professor of agriculture in Iowa State College, and in 1884 he was made president of that institution.

Ill-health again beset Dr. Knapp, and he was forced to leave the rugged winter climate of Iowa. In 1866 he moved to Lake Charles, Louisiana. Here he tackled the problem of improving local farming conditions, but he found the Louisiana farmers not only indifferent to suggestions but actively resistant. Dr. Knapp enjoyed a close friendship with "Tama" Jim Wilson, who served as United States Secretary of Agriculture for sixteen years. In 1902 he was able to persuade selected farmers in Louisiana, Mississippi, Alabama, and Texas to permit him to help develop demonstration farms. One of these, Walter C. Porter of Terrell, Texas, practiced diversification, used adequate fertilization, and new methods of cultivation. The results were highly gratifying. The Bureau of Plant Industry gave $40,000 for further experimentation. Almost immediately after it was shown what could be done, the number of farm demonstration agents increased sharply. In 1907 there were forty-nine, but just three years later 464 existed in Texas, Louisiana, Arkansas, Mississippi, and Alabama.

Out of the pioneer demonstration projects came the boys and girls' agricultural clubs. These were intimately associated with the schools, and for the first time gave an economic point to much of the rural school program. The first boy's club was organized in Holmes County, Mississippi, and it proved successful from the start. The movement spread rapidly across the South. It was given material encouragement by the General Educational Board, which associated the movement directly with its support of southern schools.

All across the South adolescents engaged in various agricultural activities, all of which were designed to show their elders the virtues of scientific farming. So active a force were these clubs that Congress responded by establishing a plan through the Smith-Lever Act of 1914 which extended special services for the organization and supervision of schoolboy farmers and schoolgirl homemakers. This work was broadened in 1917 by passage of the Smith-Hughes Act. The new legislation established for consolidated rural schools vocation programs fitted to local needs. Each state was given a cash allotment based on the proportion of the rural population to the total population, on a dollar-matching basis by states, and special school districts. By 1934 the federal government, the states, and special school districts had spent over $5,000,000 on Smith-Hughes training.

Many of these features were applied as well in the field of higher education. From 1870 on, the land-grant college became a central institution in southern higher education. It made important contributions in two areas. First, it established firmly the idea that a college education could be placed in the reach of almost every white southerner who was willing to work. Second, it made available in the South a combined vocational-scientific type of training which produced chemists, physicists, engineers, pathologists, and agriculturalists. The curriculums may have been narrow and confined largely to vocational fields, but the liberal arts were not entirely ignored, and in time they were to flourish. When the agricultural and mechanical colleges sought university status, they capitalized on their slender liberal arts foundations to justify their ambitions.

In the field of orthodox or traditional higher education there was less actual break between the ante-bellum years and the postwar world than was true of the public schools. Too, these institutions had a distinct quality that resulted from the cultural influences that governed their development. Private schools were largely church-related, and these, with their emphasis upon the classic and liberal arts, left the social and physical sciences badly neglected.

State-supported universities and colleges tended either to be stifled by privileged and aristocratic exclusiveness or to be handicapped by the ill-defined concept and practices of the land-grant colleges. The history of the various state universities are remarkably similar. All of them had meager beginnings and severely limited financial support. They were confronted with similar attempts to limit their intellectual activities by political, specific economic, and religious interests. Enrollments were low, staff members were too few, for the most part insufficiently trained and ill-paid. The average bachelor's degree from some southern colleges and universities was worth little more than a good academy high school diploma. All of the southern colleges and universities have experienced periods of unrest, invasion of academic freedom, and political tampering.

In the 1920's the blight of fundamentalism challenged the freedom of speech and intellectual inquiry in the classrooms of at least five southern states. Only in North Carolina and Kentucky did anything approaching a determined fight against the fundamentalists take place, which resulted in the maintenance of academic freedom. In Kentucky bigoted ministers undertook to bridle professors in that state's university. They failed because President Frank L. McVey and liberal ministers of Kentucky stood literally at the door of the legislature and fought off the enemies of freedom. The members of the legislature on their own perhaps lacked the courage to resist this inroad. The situation in North Carolina involved a professor in Wake Forest College, a school maintained by Southern Baptists. Professor William L. Poteat resisted the bigots on their home ground and won. This same courage, however, was not to be exhibited in Tennessee, Mississippi, and Arkansas. Anti-evolution laws were enacted in each of these states, and they are still on the statute books; and it is almost a certainty that they could not yet be removed. Despite the fact that there are large numbers of southerners who abhor such curbs on freedom, they are unable to prevail upon legislatures to remove the curbs. Of great importance is the fact that the presence of these ridiculous laws tends to reflect upon the intellectual integrity of the whole region.

Since 1930 southern colleges have matured rapidly. Duke University made the transition from Trinity College under the conservative leadership of William Preston Few, but it held up high standards and kept firmly in view its determination to become a major institution of American higher education. In Nashville, Vanderbilt University under the patriarchial leadership of Chancellor J. H. Kirkland outgrew the restrictive influences of its earlier denominational associations. Tulane University in New Orleans, Emory in Atlanta, and Washington and Lee in Lexington, Virginia, caught new visions of educational possibilities. Under the leadership of Harry Chase and Frank Kidder Graham, the University of North Carolina established new and liberal standards for state university growth. After 1920, research scholars in this institution set a fast intellectual pace for other southern universities. This was especially true in the fields of social studies and physical sciences. Never before in southern history had so many worthy and scholarly books come from professorial studies and laboratories as came from the University of North Carolina.

Edward A. Alderman, the old crusader for public schools, moved from North Carolina to Tulane, and then to the University of Virginia. At Virginia he was able to build on the Jeffersonian traditions of the university. Elsewhere land-grant colleges and their staffs brightened the southern educational horizon—not in a wide fanning glow of intellectual ferment, but in the achievement of brilliant individual faculty and research staffs, often under enormously difficult conditions. Professors like George Petrie of Alabama Polytechnic Institute, Howard Odum and Rupert B. Vance of the University of North Carolina,

Charles S. Sydnor, Jay B. Hubbell, and E. M. Carroll of Duke University, E. M. Coulter of the University of Georgia, John Crowe Ransom, Herman C. Nixon, and Walter Lynwood Fleming of Vanderbilt University, Frank L. Owsley of Vanderbilt and the University of Alabama, George Washington Carver of Tuskegee, Charles S. Johnson of Fisk University, W. D. Valleau, James W. Martin, and Amry Vandenbosch of the University of Kentucky, Walter Prescott Webb and J. Frank Dobie of the University of Texas, and scores of others gave depth and stamina to southern scholarship. Scientists in southern universities not only advanced study and research in their respective fields, many of them contributed materially to significant changes in southern life.

In 1920 there was not a single southern university which could be said to have a library of true scholarly depth and breadth. Harvard University's Widener Library contained more books than the libraries of all the major universities and colleges south of the Potomac. In this year there were 2,678,456 volumes in southern universities and colleges as compared with 24,181,204 in the nation as a whole. Mere numbers, however, actually gave little insight into the quality of individual college collections. Several of the southern states had fewer than 100,000 books in their college libraries, and some colleges had almost as many students as books in their libraries. In the early 1960s, however, five southern universities had exceeded the million mark, and two were well on the way to holdings of a second million volumes. This improvement in library collections also reflected the importance of manuscript holdings of basic research materials. Likewise scientific laboratory facilities have been greatly expanded and improved, especially in physics and chemistry.

Statistically the southern colleges and universities in 1960 presented a strong contrast to New England, the middle Atlantic, and east-north central regions as outlined by the Census Bureau. In the northern tier of fourteen states there were 843 colleges and universities as compared with 622 in twelve southern states. There were enrolled 910,099 full-time students in northern institutions and 876,000 in the South, and the northern institutions granted 180,059 degrees compared to 88,446 in the South. The South in 1960 was still a land of small colleges with relatively limited enrollments.[1]

(1) Plants of the northern institutions were valued at $11,477,034,000 while those in the South were valued at $3,135,036,000.

Today the southern states are faced with the fact that half their high school graduates are entering college. In order to meet this phenomenal expansion of enrollment, established colleges and universities have been forced to expand greatly their physical plants and faculties. Too, the educational effort of the South, especially at the level of college training, has become intimately associated with attracting new industries to the region and supplying personnel to them. The junior or community college has had a leading role in this development. All the states except South Carolina have expanded their two-year college programs, and these institutions are dispersed over a wide geographical area in the individual states. By the 1960's some of the states were in the process of organizing new four-year colleges, and some of the older state colleges and teachers' colleges were being turned into universities. In the six years 1960-66, college enrollment in the South increased from 876,000 to 1,350,000.

The South stood seriously challenged in providing sufficient professionally trained graduates, especially in the fields of chemistry, engineering, physics, business administration, medicine, and nursing. Too, greater emphasis was being placed upon graduate instruction. Only 6.8 per cent of the region's college graduates entered graduate schools as compared with 10.6 per cent nationally. Even so, the South had experienced a 40 per cent advance in graduate enrollment. Besides the efforts of the states, for their individual development several joined in organizing the Southern Regional Education Board, which was designed to support highly specialized types of professional training. For instance, veterinary science students were sent to the College of Veterinary Medicine in the Alabama Polytechnic Institute. There was a co-operative agreement among the universities of Alabama, Tennessee, and Kentucky in the field of public administration. This particular field was given some support from the Tennessee Valley Authority. Universities within themselves developed special areas, such as the institutes in Latin American studies at Tulane, Vanderbilt, and the University of Florida.

Though emotions ran high in parts of the South after the Supreme Court's school decision in 1954, there was a remarkable degree of academic freedom in most colleges and universities. Even in Mississippi two professors wrote books discussing in forthright terms the failures of political and academic leadership to support the admission of James H. Meredith to that institution in 1962 (an incident discussed in Chapter XVI). In the University of Alabama a group of scholars held a symposium in 1964, as part of dedicatory exercises of the Marten Ten Hoor Social Sciences Building, in which several participants were forthright in discussing conditions in the South.

But southern universities are still not free in every respect. The political hand often is fastened about the throats of public universities and colleges as tightly as it draws on the purse strings. It does not take an open and overt act to reveal political controls. Most often politicians have preferred to conceal their acts as much as possible by holding over the institutions the constant threat of reducing financial support. There has ever been much political pulling and hauling in state-supported colleges and universities of the South, and as time has passed there have grown up among institutions in the same state rivalries in which one administration has set the political dogs against another in the struggle to secure support. Too, administrations of some institutions have sought funds not necessarily to raise academic standards but to make impressive physical displays of buildings and stadia to increase enrollments in order to secure more funds. They have not, however, often supported efforts to create a genuine intellectual atmosphere in their colleges where teaching and research are the central facts.

The most disturbing curbs on academic freedom were those of Mississippi and North Carolina. In Mississippi the Board of Higher Education adopted a speaker rule which would prevent the appearance of lecturers on the campuses of state schools who might discuss subjects inimical to the Mississippi way of life, which meant integration specifically. In North Carolina the state legislature enacted a speaker law in 1964 which proposed to curb Communists, speakers who had taken advantage of the protection of the Fifth Amendment. In the summer of 1965, hearings were held in which people of widely differing views of academic freedom appeared before a special legislative committee either to oppose or to sustain the speaker ban law. In November of that year the legislature modified but did not repeal the law; instead, it placed responsibility for speakers and their utterances upon university and college administrations. This was a radical departure from the great days when Harry Chase and Frank Graham had made that university a place where even the most controversial subjects could be discussed. Fortunately, the Southern Association of Schools and

Colleges has exerted an influence in keeping colleges and schools reasonably free. This organization, however, has shown timidity at times in dealing with boards, administrations, and state officials who were clearly in violation of academic freedom.

While attacks have been made upon the expression of professorial and administrative points of view in colleges and universities, there is one area which has largely escaped harassment. There have been at least a half a dozen southern university presses which have greatly encouraged research and writing. Prior to 1920 southern scholars had few if any publication outlets. Again the University of North Carolina was a leader in developing a press. It published the books of many important southern scholars. In time, presses at Duke, Louisiana State, Texas, Kentucky, and Georgia also established distinguished publishing programs.

Southern universities have been handicapped by the inequities existing between their salary scales and working conditions in comparison with other parts of the country. Other sections have constantly been able to outbid southern universities and colleges for personnel and to woo away many of the best southern scholars. Although the region has still not completely put a stop to this situation, progress is being made. Indeed, good scholars are now increasingly coming from other regions to take up positions in the South. A big factor in making this possible was an assurance of maximum academic freedom, and a minimum amount of disruption at many southern institutions.

≫ IX ≪

The Mightier Sword

Culturally the South suffered a great intellectual shock as a result of the Civil War. The Old South had cherished, through patronage at least, a deep interest in the creative arts. Some southerners had collected significant private libraries, while others had subscribed to southern literary periodicals and supported regional writers. Yet for author and bookseller alike the region was largely barren ground, since large segments of the population were either illiterate or not interested too deeply in supporting a more cultivated society. In much of the region there prevailed a frontier influence which shaped cultural attitudes, in which circumstances literary activities appeared impractical and effeminate.

The one broad exception to this was the important position held by the regional newspaper. Newspapers were organized and flourished in fairly large numbers. Few if any of the ante-bellum papers were oblivious to the fundamental importance of partisan politics, and almost all bore party labels. Every southern editor was a militant crusader for his party's nominees for office.

One of the marvels of the South in the Civil War was the fact that so many newspapers continued publication in the face of a severe scarcity of printers and materials. In Louisville, on the northern border, three daily papers endured the war, but they warred among themselves and survived to harmonize their political views and to protest jointly about radical excesses. George Dennison Prentice and his *Louisville Daily Journal* had struggled mightily to preserve the Union, and to oppose many of the policies of the Lincoln administration. His com-

patriot John Hopkins Harney of the *Louisville Democrat,* and William
N. Haldeman of the fugitive *Courier* both faced bankruptcy in 1865.
Prentice, who had combated secessionists and abolitionists was, in
1865, suffering from palsey. Early in 1868 Walter N. Haldeman
and Henry Watterson consolidated the *Journal, Democrat* and *Courier.*
Young Henry Watterson was brought from Nashville in 1868 to take
Prentice's place on the faltering *Journal.* In his new editorial post
the youthful Watterson quickly protested in the columns of the combined *Courier-Journal* the political mismanagement of southern affairs.
From the border land, he was perhaps best situated of any southern
editor to upbraid radicals for their reconstruction blunders.

Throughout the South in 1865 scarcely a score of daily papers had
outlasted poverty and wartime strangulation to continue publication. The years 1865-1920 saw the rise of new and vigorous journals,
and older ones were merged to form stronger publishing unions. In
no area of social and cultural reconstruction did native southerners
make so many positive gains as in the editorial field. As a result, in
the latter half of the nineteenth century the South produced many
highly capable newspapermen.

One of the strongest editorial voices in this era was that of Henry
Watterson. Born in Washington, D.C., in 1840, the son of a Tennessee
Congressman, he had by 1860 more than ordinary apprentice newspaper experience. On the eve of secession he returned to Tennessee
and joined the Confederate Army. He saw active service at Columbus,
Kentucky, Shiloh, and at Chattanooga in 1862. He edited the peripete-
tic *Rebel,* a lively field newspaper which expressed brisk opinions
concerning events in the western theater of the war. Quickly Watterson became one of the most influential political editors in the
country.

Elsewhere in the South newspapermen with fresh vision and grim
determinations sought to direct the South toward a more productive
future. Captain Francis Warrington Dawson, a native Englishman,
and veteran of both the Confederate navy and army, went to Richmond in 1865 to begin his career as editor. He wrote for both the
Examiner and *Dispatch,* but it was in Charleston, South Carolina, as
editor, first of the *News,* and then of the *News and Courier,* that
he made his reputation. Spared the emotions that sometimes blinded
native sons, Captain Dawson was a moderate in politics, even advocat-

ing the vote for freedmen. He saw beyond the mere commercial and
agricultural significance of his region to realize that without a manufacturing industry, recovery of the South would be slow and limited.
He was one of the first editorial crusaders to help bring cotton mills
nearer to the southern fields. He also urged South Carolina farmers
to supply their needs from their own soil, and to stop the drainage
of capital to purchase elsewhere meats, grains, and other commodities
which the South could grow for itself. Unhappily, Captain Dawson's
life was cut short by the murderous hand of Dr. T. B. McDow in
a dispute involving the Dawson family's Swiss governess.

The southern editor's chair was an island in a troubled sea where
a young man could exert an important influence on the recovery of
his region. Not only were there the age-old political challenges, but
also new ones—encouraging the proper utilization of resources, developing industry, organizing schools, fostering new racial relationships,
encouraging new directions for agriculture, and helping the culture
of the New South to mature. In addition, southern politics had to
be reordered.

Chattanooga, a city which was besieged and pounded in war,
gave bright promise of industrial growth, even before the federal
troops had marched away to Georgia. In 1869, Kirby, Gamble, and
Company began publication of a starveling paper, the *Times*. Major
Thomas B. Kirby, a Yale graduate and fledgling businessman, was
an erudite enough editor, but the people of Chattanooga were both
poor and indifferent to his paper. Within five years it was under
the sheriff's hammer in a forced sale. On June 28, 1878, it was again
sold, this time to an eager Jewish lad, Adolph Ochs, who had worked
on newspapers in both Knoxville and Chattanooga, but at twenty years
of age could scarcely claim to have mature editorial experience. From
the outset the *Chattanooga Times* under his management was an opti-
mistic apostle of a new and promising South. Working under conditions of financial stringency, the young editor demonstrated the possibilities of hard work and personal courage in a community where
calamity howlers were plentiful. Without political favor or strong
partisan leanings, Ochs's *Times* quickly became a significant influence
in the Tennessee Valley. It crusaded for the building of railroads,
highways, factories, a university, utilization of the river, improvement

of the Negro's lot, and for the general welfare of Chattanooga. Almost as effectively as the more widely read southern editors, Adolph Ochs and his co-editor John E. McGowan helped to build a New South, and their paper has long survived them as a force in an ever-changing Tennessee Valley civilization.

Many young editors and promoters of the South looked to the future in helping to develop a new regional civilization. From the ashes of Atlanta, sprang the *Constitution*, founded in 1868. This paper spent little time bemoaning the wreckage left by Sherman's army. On the other hand it neither ignored the heavy losses in wealth in the war nor the political issues created by reconstruction. Georgia faced a multiplicity of problems arising from the war and the opening phases of reconstruction. In 1869 the political cauldron in Georgia boiled over. There was a fight to the death between Rufus B. Bulloch and his radical cohorts and the white conservatives. Into this conflict stepped Henry Woodfin Grady, who more than any other individual associated his name with the term "New South."

Henry W. Grady was born in the university town of Athens, in the year of the great Compromise of 1850. His first political memories were the discussions of the issues which had led to secession in 1861. Grady was descended from old native stock which had migrated down the great valley from Virginia to the northeastern Georgia hill country. He received a somewhat disrupted early education, first from his mother's teaching, and then in a private school. He entered the University of Georgia at the end of the war, graduating in 1868. His college experience was colored by the upheavals of reconstruction and the extremities of local politics. Removing himself temporarily from troubled Georgia, Grady studied law in the University of Virginia, but he became interested in journalism even before he left Charlottesville.

Grady's first newspaper assignment on the newly organized *Constitution* was to report a press excursion into north Georgia in 1869. Southern journalism of this period was a lack-luster affair. Many editors of the ante-bellum period were either distraught by the war or found it difficult to adjust to the new era. Even so vigorous a personality as George D. Prentice of the Louisville *Journal* could not recover his old enthusiasm for producing a lively paper. Thus many postwar journals reflected nostalgia, frustration, and despair. This embodied physically the shabbiest aspects of the rising standardization of newspaper production by use of much "ready print" material.

Newspaper plants in the South were victimized by the attritions of war. Machinery was antiquated and worn out. Type metal was scarce, and printing paper was difficult to procure. The number of subscribers was limited, for financial reasons and because of educational handicaps. As a result the average southern paper lacked originality, spontaneity, graphic attractiveness, and readers in profitable numbers.

In Louisville, Watterson caught the torch from Prentice's enfeebled hand, Captain Dawson brought dignity to the Charleston *News and Courier*, but Adolph Ochs and Henry W. Grady were essentially pioneers. Grady's stories on the political mess in northern Georgia in 1869 quickly marked him as a man of force and verve. His reports were highly critical of Bulloch's manipulations—even to the point of charging bargain and bribery. In Rome, Grady accepted employment on the weekly *Courier*, owned and published by Melville Dwinnell.

As editor of the *Courier*, and later of his own paper, the Rome *Commercial*, the twenty-two-year-old newspaperman spoke his mind about politics in Georgia, the Ku Klux Klan, Governor Bulloch, the radicals, and a host of local politicians and editors. In the track of Sherman's drive southward from Chattanooga, Grady had a first-hand opportunity to see his poverty-stricken region rebuilding. As editor he was more master of the quick and sharp editorial jab than of the incisive analytical essay. His earlier writings failed to set a course for his readers. Persistent financial worries were a factor in preventing him from writing more mature editorials. But his career with the two weekly papers in Rome was of short duration.

On his return to Atlanta, Grady was unable to purchase an interest in the *Constitution*, but in 1872 he became a part-owner of the Atlanta *Herald* with Alston and Alexander St. Clair-Abrams. Four years of rivalry between the *Herald* and *Constitution* involved rowdy in-fighting that was reminiscent of ante-bellum political days. Grady, however, wrote almost nothing to arouse the imagination of southerners as editor of the *Herald*, despite the sprightliness of his jabbing paragraphs. In 1880 he purchased an interest in the *Constitution*, and from that time until his death he wrote with a much more far-ranging editorial pen. Grady covered both political news of Georgia and its economic struggles perceptively. He favored building railroads, stimulating economic recovery, and regulating public-service facilities. The *Constitution* was willing to take an active, and, sometimes, decisive hand in state politics. It maintained constant pressure for the creation of a vigorous new South whose politics would be realigned, its people alert, and its physical resources properly employed. With vigorous editorials, the *Constitution* kept up a running commentary of a wide range of public issues.

In late summer 1886, Grady proved his genius as a newspaperman by his melodramatic trip to disaster-torn Charleston, South Carolina, to report the damages of the great earthquake and tidal wave. His stories of this disaster were circulated to a national audience. He had attracted fairly wide attention through his fiery editorials and speeches about the postwar South, but his Charleston stories fixed his name before a national public. Because of the Charleston stories, and those of regional needs, Grady had impressed the southern-born industrialist John H. Inman of New York. In November 1886 he was invited to address the New England Society in New York on the occasion of its 266th anniversary. On December 2, gathered in Delmonico's, was an overflow audience which included General W. T. Sherman, J. Pierpont Morgan, Lyman Abbott, H. M. Flagler, Jr., Russell Sage, and many others of national prominence. Grady spoke without recourse to his manuscript; his effect followed largely from inspiration and from the degree of audience intoxication he produced. When he had finished, he had firmly established the term "New South," and had made his own name synonymous with it.

Actually the "New South" speech in New York was more famous for its flashes of wit, flights of oratory, and pathos than for its incisive concepts and definitions of the South in reality. In a far more substantial speech, Grady defined for an audience at the Texas State Fair in Dallas in 1887 the problems and possibilities of the region. In numerous other speeches and editorials the Georgian urged southerners to revise their economic pattern, and to make the South more self-sufficient. To illustrate his point he used the dramatic example of the Pickens County corpse who took to his clay-bank grave little more that was of Georgia origin than the chilled blood in his veins.

Of equal importance with Henry W. Grady's phenomenal rise as national spokesman for the New South was the success of the *Constitution* itself. Associated with the production of this paper were Joel

Chandler Harris and Evan and Clark Howell. Harris gained international fame both as an editorial writer and as the creator of Uncle Remus.

By 1890 several other daily papers exerted major influences on large numbers of southern readers. Among the older ones were the New Orleans *Times-Democrat*, the Montgomery *Advertiser*, the Savannah *News*, the Richmond *Times-Dispatch*, the Nashville *Banner*, and the New Orleans *Picayune*. These papers had relatively long histories, and gave considerable continuity to the story of the southern press.

As significant as the older papers were, it was the newly organized dailies which discussed southern problems with a freshness and vigor unshackled by the past. Among these were the Columbia, South Carolina, *State*, the Atlanta *Journal*, the Birmingham *News*, the Raleigh *Chronicle*, and the *News and Observer*, the Houston *Chronicle*, the New Orleans *States*, and the Charlotte *Observer*. The last-named paper originated in the crusade to bring about greater industrialization of the South. With D. A. Tompkins, a cotton mill operator, and D. J. Caldwell as editors, the *Observer* quickly established a clearly defined editorial policy of liberal breadth and viewpoint. At Raleigh, Walter Hines Page stirred a provincial and highly defensive society to a rage with his *State Chronicle*. This short-lived paper proved under his editorship to be an idol-breaker which did little to stabilize either its editor's fortune or mental comfort, but no doubt it prepared the way for an even more forthright paper in Raleigh. Page looked upon his fellow North Carolinians as being both mummified and enslaved to the past. Despite the unpopularity of this vigorous young editor and his gadfly paper, progressive ideas were implanted which bore creditable fruits in later years. A fitting successor to the weekly *State Chronicle*, edited in its latter years by Josephus Daniels, was the *Daily News and Observer*. This paper was organized in 1880, and was purchased by Daniels in 1894. From the outset the *News and Observer* was an important political journal emanating from the North Carolina capital. It crusaded from the advancement of education, regulation of trusts, modernization of agricultural methods, and the promotion of the Democratic party.

All across the South small city dailies reflected a certain amount of editorial militancy. The Greensboro, North Carolina, *News*, the

Knoxville *Journal*, the Richmond *News-Leader*, the Memphis *Commercial-Appeal*, the Jackson *Daily News*, and the Louisville *Herald* were all involved in the great crusade for advancing the South. C. P. J. Mooney, a Chicago Irishman, early in this century stood on a bridge in the southern part of that city and saw a long freight train loaded with meat, lard, and grain headed South. This inspired him to go South himself to persuade southerners through the columns of the *Commercial-Appeal* to use their land more intelligently to produce at home their own supplies. In time Mooney became a veritable Joshua, coaxing and leading his people toward the building of a brighter future for the mid-South. He was able by force of personality and hard common-sense to communicate his vision to the sprawling cotton empire of his paper's territory. He made southerners in three states conscious of the importance of crop rotation, soil conservation, and modernization of agricultural practices.

Elsewhere in the South editors conducted courageous forays against stultifying political and social forces. Joel Chandler Harris's son Julian and his imaginative and talented wife Julia Collier bought the Columbus, Georgia, *Enquirer-Sun* and almost immediately assailed the Ku Klux Klan in its heartland. The Harris editorials did little to make the *Enquirer-Sun* a financial success, but they won for the editor a Pulitzer Prize, and helped to unmask the Klan in Georgia and Alabama. Nearby the Macon *Telegraph*, under the direction of W. T. Anderson and Mark Etheridge, battled the Klan and other obstructionist forces. Across the border in Alabama, Grover Hall of the Montgomery *Advertiser* carried on into the twentieth century the forthright policies of Major W. W. Screws, founder of the paper. Together with the Birmingham *News* and the *Age-Herald*, the Alabama journal brought woe to the hooded and sheeted bigots of the Klan. A curious mixed policy of crusading for economic and cultural betterment of a state, and at the same time enunciating a fierce reactionary policy of social relationships, was pursued by Frederick Sullens of the Jackson, Mississippi, *Daily News*. Few southern editors in the twentieth century treated so many subjects with so much vitriol as did Major Sullens. He wrote with the vehemence of the brawling nineteenth-century editors who enlivened American journalism. He no doubt did much to stimulate in Mississippi a resistance to racial adjustment, and to warp opinions on almost every other social issue.

None of the southern papers failed to appreciate the fact that the South faced many challenges. Editors did not always comprehend the extent of southern needs or find solutions to problems. They pleaded for schools, enriched regional life for vastly improved means of transportation, and for improved conditions of public health. Most of them condemned lynching and all other inhuman excesses; they often opposed blatant political mountebanks and other exploiters who sapped man and land of their substance. No editor failed to appreciate the significance of the forces attempting to move the South away from the nation as a whole. At the same time the newspapers sought for the South an important role in the making of national decisions, their editors realized the people would have to be much better prepared for such responsibilities.

Much of the southern cultural dream, however, was to be realized through the influence of the more aggressive editors and journals in the mid-twentieth century. The Atlanta *Constitution* and *Journal* exerted an enormously important bearing on southern opinion. So did the Louisville *Courier-Journal*, the Richmond *Times-Dispatch*, the Miami *Herald*, the Houston *Chronical*, the New Orleans *Times-Picayune*, the Nashville *Banner*, and the Nashville *Tennesseean*. In Atlanta, Ralph McGill combined the virtues of Henry W. Grady with the deep practicality of the Howellses. An able editorial staff in Louisville under the leadership of Barry Bingham and Mark Etheridge made the Watterson paper a liberal journal, speaking in the same fearless voice which "Marse Henry" had used in adjudging the process of reconstruction. The erudite Douglas Southall Freeman gave tremendous literary depth and political insight to the Richmond *News-Leader*, while Virginius Dabney did the same thing for the Richmond *Times-Dispatch*. Jonathan and Josephus Daniels continued the liberal tradition in Raleigh initiated by their father. Mergers and local monopolies between 1920 and 1930 no doubt softened the competitive tone of southern papers, and many even have helped lessen their leadership effectiveness in many areas, but it still did continue to exist.

The city dailies presented their news and editorial viewpoints on a broader canvas than did their neighbors, the country weeklies. In 1865, 182 weeklies survived in the South; and a decade and a half later there were 1827. This statistical note reflects much of the nature of the quick recovery of the southern local press. The journals themselves reflected the basic rural attitudes. Some country editors became almost as famous as those of popular city dailies. Like the dailies, the weeklies depended on politics to furnish much of their news. These papers were often militantly partisan; they had to be to survive. Editing a country newspaper became a prestigious profession in the New South. Where once law, medicine, and the ministry appealed to young men, many now turned instead to become editors. A youth with limited education could almost begin publication of a country paper if he were able to identify one type character from another. He needed little capital, no typographical experience, a rundown building, and a chance at the county's printing business to succeed. Thus it was that local editors became active in politics, supported hand-picked candidates, boomed combined slates, and even ran for office themselves. Because of year-round political involvements their papers intimately reflected grass-roots southern politics.

In a broader area the weekly newspapers portrayed a rural South struggling without capital, suffering the handicaps of staple crop agriculture, poor roads, poor health, a ruinous credit system, and illiteracy. Though local stories of social conditions were seldom analytical, they were sufficiently descriptive to give an intimate sense of the times and of the nature of rural society. Much of the original matter appearing in the weeklies was little more than an indiscriminate recording of local notes. Occasionally an editor was imaginative enough to give verve to his stories, or daring enough to use broad humor. This made country journalism sufficiently hazardous to satisfy even the most foolhardy.

The local editors lashed out constantly at illiteracy, and in their limited ways supported movements for public schools, better-trained teachers, and opportunities for youth. Few southern counties could have organized public schools successfully without the leadership of country editors.

Rural editors reported the sensational local news bluntly. Much of this consisted of murders, lynchings, public hangings, gruesome accidents, and social conflict. In the slow transition from raw frontier to more mature communities, much of the South during the reconstruction period was involved in crime that was often more sensational than that occurring in the Far West. Racial friction gave rise to innumerable incidents. This was especially true of lynchings, which were more often perpetrated against Negroes than whites. Many an indignant country editor wrote in anguish against these murderous orgies. They were less angry, however, about gross racial discriminations which led to lynchings. A majority of them were anti-Negro. Seldom did one express a constructive opinion as to how the newly made freedman—now become Negro tenant farmer—might improve his social and economic position.

One thing was certain: the Negro had a place low on the social ladder, and the editor was certain he should remain there. He had no business voting until he had greatly improved his economic and intellectual condition. He was most appreciated by the editors when he exhibited a sycophantic humility and kept his "place." Country editors could become furious when a Negro postmistress was appointed in Indianola, Mississippi, or a Negro collector of customs was named for the Port of Charleston, or could wax indignant over the greatly exaggerated story of President Theodore Roosevelt's having Booker T. Washington as a dinner guest at the White House. Such incidents provoked the editors into the same kind of demagoguery indulged in by southern politicians.

Out of the country newspaper offices came some of the more compassionate and perceptive southern writers: Joel Chandler Harris, Bill Arp, Yuba Dam Johnson, to name a few. The weekly office was an excellent training ground for youths who wished to advance either as editors or authors. Several popular metropolitan columnists had their first experience on a country newspaper, and they gathered materials which they later used to enliven daily columns. Almost as many successful politicians started their careers as local editors, for the weekly papers provided a good springboard from which to launch a political career.

In their hope for more readers, editors looked to the past with greater nostalgia than could southern authors. Ante-bellum southerners were parsimonious in their support of their writers. Southern books sold poorly, and regional periodicals scarcely got beyond the fledgling stage. This fact was documented by the limited sales of books by Edgar Allan Poe, William Gilmore Simms, Paul Hamilton Hayne, Henry Timrod, John Pendleton Kennedy, and John Esten Cooke. All of them had established reputations, but not one enjoyed an extensive southern readership. In another area, the southern humorist and genre writer had portrayed backwoods southern regional types and conditions of life. Among these were Johnson J. Hooper, George W. Harris, A. B. Longstreet, and James G. Baldwin. But the tensions and emotions of the immediate ante-bellum years had served to destroy much of the southern sense of humor, and had also frustrated the folk-writer. Rapid expansion of the Trans-Mississippi West attracted much attention away from the southern backwoods, and concern with slavery and cotton further obscured the backwoodsman's existence. Much southern talent that might have been developed in the production of creative works was absorbed in the writing of political diatribes in defense of slavery.

An examination of *DeBow's Review* and the *Southern Literary Messenger* will reveal the drift of southern literary production. The Civil War years were most productive of a voluminous body of writing, but remarkably little of this could be called creative. Both American and foreign visitors viewed the southern scene during the war and produced large bodies of published material. Reporters and editors wrote scores of volumes of descriptive books. Semi-official observers of all nationalities and motivations further documented the domestic and political life of the South at war. The great fountain of observer material, however, came from soldiers, North and South, who viewed life from the limited perspectives of authors restricted to the narrow field of military duties.

In the wreckage of war in 1865 no segment of southern life had suffered more than the creative arts. Not only was the continuity of southern writing broken, but many potentially able southern authors undoubtedly lay in soldiers' graves. In was impossible to know to what extent heartbreak and frustration, to say nothing of biting poverty, had stifled southern writing in the immediate postwar years.

Four southern literary men might be considered to have bridged the great gap of war: Paul Hamilton Hayne, Sidney Lanier, John Esten Cooke, and R. Malcolm Johnston. Actually A. B. Longstreet, John Pendleton Kennedy, and William Gilmore Simms lived until 1870, but it can hardly be said they lived long enough to pass a torch of creativeness to a future generation of southern writers. Hayne, the poet, found the confusion of the postwar years extremely vexatious. Even under the most favorable conditions a poet has to struggle to survive, yet he produced at least four extensive works, the *The Moun-*

tain of the Lovers, Legends and Lyrics, the *Broken Battalions,* and *Lives of Robert Young Hayne and Hugh Swinton Legaré.* He wrote extensively for periodicals, but little if any of this material added luster to his name.

Sidney Lanier came out of the war seriously devitalized. Broken in health and spirit, he nevertheless produced a creditable body of poetry, criticism, boys' books, and popular travel literature. He was one of the first postwar southerners to find outlets for his writings in the national magazines. Much of his more enduring poetry was inspired by his native Georgia. Lanier had a broader experience than Hayne. He had served in the Confederate Army as a private and an officer, and was a prisoner of war. He never realized either of his burning ambitions to study in Germany or to become a good musician. An even greater tragedy than his poverty-stricken life and ill-health was the fact that he dissipated his literary energies writing descriptions of health resorts and vacation spots about the South. Despite a sizable body of poetry and ephemera published under his name, Lanier was too involved in metaphysics in his more serious poems to appreciate the great importance of the new age into which he and his region had been catapulted. Nevertheless he will live on in the "Hills of Haugh," "The Song of the Chattahoochee," and "An Evening Song."

Hurt by the war, largely because it disrupted his career as a university professor, R. Malcolm Johnston suffered less emotional shock than his contemporaries Hayne and Lanier. A Georgian by birth, and the product of plantation life, he became a lawyer after graduating from Mercer University. From 1862 on, he ran boys' schools in Sparta, Georgia, and in Baltimore. In 1871 he published his first fictional work in the *Dukesboro Tales,* and by 1900 had published seventeen book-length works. Most of these were character descriptions rather than stories with plots and literary form. Perhaps he more than any other southerner carried over from the Old South an appreciation for the folk quality of the southern scene.

No southern writer in the generation between 1865 and 1900 grasped fully the fundamental implications of the revolution which was occurring in this time. Southerners either took a defensive attitude toward the war and reconstruction, or many of them tried to rationalize and justify the decisions of the past. To them regional failures

Fontana Dam's 408-foot high mass in North Carolina holds back the Little Tennessee. The power plant can generate 202,500 kilowatt hours.

Coker Pedigreed Seed Company

Opposite page, top: Grass is no longer an enemy to southern farmers, nor is grain-growing uncommon.

Opposite page, bottom: No revolution in the cotton-field is greater than that brought about by the plant breeder. This is a modern cotton plant of a superior strain.

This page: A mechanical revolution in the cotton patch. More and more cotton is being harvested by machine pickers.

This page: Cattle on a Thousand Hills. An old southern industry turned into a profitable new one for the modern South.

Opposite page, top: A symbol of the future, this machine harvests pulpwood and thus saves millions of man hours of backbreaking labor.

Opposite page, bottom: An old crop under new management. Plant selection and breeding have resulted in superior trees.

Opposite page, top: Paradise Island Steam Plant, Green River, Kentucky, will have an ultimate generating capacity of 2,430,000 kilowatt hours.

Opposite page, bottom: The Kentucky Dam near Paducah on the Tennessee governs the flood level of the rivers at Cairo, Illinois, as much as four feet. Its power installation can generate 160,000 kilowatt hours.

This page: President's Island Interchange, Memphis, where railway and highway meet the river.

At this paper mill, in Natchez, Mississippi, are manufactured yellow pine pulp products, ranging from rayon tire cord to photographic film.

Widow's Creek Steam Plant of the TVA, which is capable of generating 1,750,000 kilowatt hours, uses 1.5 billion gallons of cooling water each twenty-four hours.

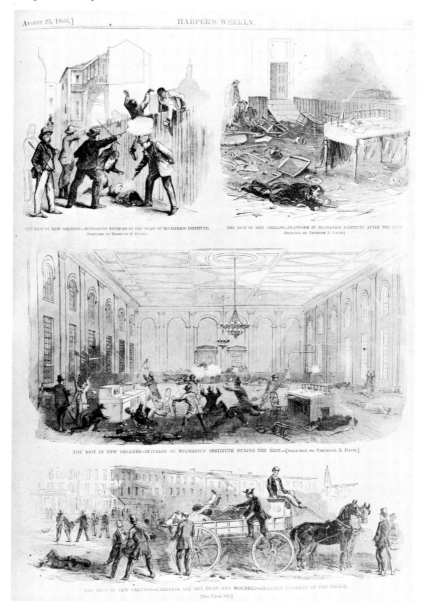

Scene at Mechanics' Institute in New Orleans during the race riot in the summer of 1866.

MISSISSIPPI KU-KLUX IN THE DISGUISES IN WHICH THEY WERE CAPTURED
[FROM A PHOTOGRAPH.]

Top: Ruins of Columbia, South Carolina, after its capture by General W. T. Sherman in February 1865.

Bottom: Ku Klux Klansmen.

Negro demonstrators cross Alabama River bridge on outskirts of Selma enroute to Montgomery, March 1965.

Police Chief Eugene (Bull) Conner's dogs attack Birmingham civil-rights demonstrators, May 1963.

Opposite page, top: Alabama Governor George Wallace (left) confronts deputy Attorney-General Nicholas Katzenbach at Tuscaloosa in June 1963, in a vain attempt to prevent the enrollment of two Negroes in the University of Alabama.

Opposite page, bottom: Under cover of darkness and guarded by federal marshals, James Meredith arrives at the University of Mississippi campus on the night of September 30, 1962.

This page: Dallas (Alabama) County Sheriff Jim Clark prods voting applicant Negro with nightstick.

Martin Luther King leads marchers on Montgomery trek. Dr. King is fourth from right and Dr. Ralph Bunche, Undersecretary of the United Nations, is third from right.

fell little short of being personal failures. No American authors had available to them so stirring a challenge to point new directions, or to exploit so rich a vein of literary themes, as did those writing in the latter decades of the nineteenth century. It was a great tragedy that none fully accepted the challenge. Poverty, frustration, political provincialism, and the social and cultural drives to point new directions bound the literary mind too long to permit the creation of a single broadly interpretative biography or objective historical study, with the exception of William Trent's biography of William Gilmore Simms.

Sentimentalists and apologists were active in creating and praising southern heroes, or in rationalizing the tragedy of the war. Dean of this group was Thomas Nelson Page, scion of a proud Virginia family. To him the stark years from 1865 to 1912 were too harsh for romantic treatment. He escaped into the past and into a civilization which would support a patrician. Like so many of the authors of the New South, Thomas Nelson Page was first initiated into the publication of his works through the columns of the *Century Magazine*. A dozen books and numerous short stories portrayed a time and a people living in a feudal twilight of romance and unreality. His Virginia was a dreamy idyll of Negro slaves, benevolent masters, and sparkling ladies. The harshly realistic life so vividly portrayed by numerous contemporary travelers was missing in *Ole Virginia, The Old Dominion,* and *Social Life in Old Virginia,* and in *Two Little Confederates* and *Robert E. Lee, Man and Soldier.* Page helped open a transitional era in southern literature. His books were given a warm reception by nostalgic Americans, and they helped to create an image of American feudalism which lingered on in various forms, even into mid-twentieth-century America.

This was the age of the local-colorists who portrayed southern life in its many segments and moods. Carrying on the tradition of Baldwin and Longstreet, Samuel L. Clemens of Missouri represented a universality of human nature and human foibles in the humor of at least four books which had distinct southern settings. *Huckleberry Finn* and *Tom Sawyer* portrayed a South caught between the crush of institutions and a rapidly changing frontier condition. *Life on the Mississippi* tapped a central vein of river lore and revealed a rising commerce which contained the germ for uniting the sections. Drawing heavily upon travelers' accounts, Mark Twain, in his bifurcated book on the river, documented the fact of change almost as much as he did life on the river. There was a vast gap between what Mark Twain, Captain Basil Hall, and Captain Marryatt saw in the early years and what Ernst Von Hesse-Wartegg described in the postwar years. Mark Twain drew heavily from the latter. In the *American Claimant*, the author wrote of an age of plungers in which Colonel Sellers, incurable speculator and optimist, expected big returns from his ventures. This book had its background in the sterile ridges of the Cumberlands in Kentucky and Tennessee, where Mark Twain's grandfather had hoped to achieve great wealth.

With less robust humor than that of *Tom Sawyer* and *Huckleberry Finn*, Harry Stillwell Edwards of Sparta, Georgia, in later years portrayed Negro loyalty in *Æneas Africanus*. Partly in rich satire and partly from nostalgia, he described a people in transition and struggling to preserve many of the old customs and loyalties, yet striving to accept new ways. "Æneas," however, was never to attract the wide attention of readers Uncle Remus did. Joel Chandler Harris, creator of the gentle but knowledgable Uncle Remus and his allegorical tales, was an exceedingly timid man. He was almost as much a spirit behind the Atlanta *Constitution* as was Henry W. Grady. But his chief fame was as a southern folklorist of major importance, and the author of more than a score of books. In the Uncle Remus stories, *Free Joe*, and *Mingo and Other Sketches in Black and White*, he dredged a deep vein of African and southern folklore. With a background in rural Georgia on Turnwold Plantation near Eatonton in Middle Georgia, he came to understand the nuances of southern folkways. He absorbed the rich culture of two continents without trying to separate the two streams. With gentle humanity, but with deep humility, Harris portrayed a wisdom and humor of the Negro in a rich drama. Uncle Remus comprised the wisdom of both white and black men plus the shrewdness of members of the animal kingdom, while the fate of free Joe was in fact the great tragedy of the South, which sought to find its bearings in a badly troubled era of change. This change baffled the shy editor and author as much as Uncle Remus and his trickster animal characters baffled their victims and adversaries.

Local-colorists of an entirely different temperament and approach from that of Edwards and Harris revealed a New South in a nostalgic,

but highly localized perspective. Dean of this group was James Lane
Allen of Kentucky. He was born in 1849, and at a time when the
bluegrass region was in its hey-day of ante-bellum prosperity. Around
the Allen farm outside Lexington spread thousands of fertile acres
which produced almost unlimited tons of hemp, tobacco, as well as
pastured cattle and sheep in vast numbers. Like Joel Chandler Harris,
James Lane Allen lived more than half in the age in which he
was born, and the rest in a confused and changing postwar era. The
new age was for him one of conflicting emotions, and a struggle to
reconcile life with the realities of time which forsook many of the
old values. In 1895 he visited Henry Mills Alden, editor of *Harper's
Magazine*, who encouraged him to write of Kentucky. The result
of this encouragement was a series of short stories later to be published
under the collective title, *The Bluegrass Region of Kentucky*. Two
of these stories related to Gethsemane, and a convent in central Kentucky. The "Gray Cowl" dealt with the silent and emotional lives
of the Trappist monks, and "Sister Dolorosa" with the conflict of
the love of a nun for a man of the world. These stories stirred Catholic
anger, and confronted the author with his first experience with public
indignation.

James Lane Allen's first novel was the *Flute and Violin* (1891),
a story of the Reverend James Moore and his struggles in Transylvania
Seminary, and within the Presbyterian Church. There followed in
quick succession, *The Choir Invisible*, *The Reign of Law*, *A Kentucky
Cardinal*, *Aftermath*, and others. Writing in a vein of Thomas Hardy,
Allen revealed an enormous affinity for the land and for nature; but
buried deep in his nature was resentment for the bigotry of his Kentucky neighbors. Allen ushered out the South's age of gentility.

Less probing, and less concerned with the deeper vein of human
emotions, was Mary Noailles Murfree (Charles Egbert Craddock) of
Murfreesboro and Nashville, Tennessee, and later of St. Louis. She
too was of the genteel age and wrote of a land and its characters
from which she was physically and socially detached. Her stories unlike those of her southern contemporaries, were among the first to
be written in something approaching a story formula. She projected
the Appalachian highlanders into fiction, and helped to make them
popular characters in the latter part of the nineteenth century. Miss
Murfree's mountaineers were characters. however, rather than sweaty,

tobacco-stained, isolated superstitious and ignorant flesh and blood beings. Her people lived beyond the pale of sophisticated civilization. She portrayed, for the 1890s, a kind of vicarious realism as experienced by a cloistered patrician who drew more heavily on imagination than first-hand knowledge. She began her career by contributing to *Lippincott's Magazine,* and the *Atlantic Monthly.* In time Miss Murfree wrote of isolated mountaineers with social and literary detachment, while John Fox, Jr., portrayed them in the certain light of an author who lived and worked with his characters. He knew intimately their angers, hates, fears, suspicion, and ignorance. Whatever his writings may have lacked in literary artistry they more than compensated for in the fundamental sociological questions they raised. Constantly Fox sought answers to, "Whence came the mountaineers?" and "How might the isolative barrier between them and the outside world be breached?" These were the basic themes in the *Trail of the Lonesome Pine, Knight of the Cumberland, Little Shepherd of Kingdom Come,* and *Bluegrass and Rhododendron.*

Earlier George Washington Cable of New Orleans wrote of another isolated segment of southern society. The French Cajuns of Louisiana like the mountaineers of Tennessee and Kentucky, were also "contemporary ancestors." In *Old Creole Days, The Grandissimes, Dr. Sevier,* and *Bonaventure,* Cable revealed to America this pocket of civilization which had adjusted itself to the humid swamplands at the foot of the continent. In the *Silent South* (1885) he came nearer dealing with a universal theme of southern life than had any of the local-colorists. His discussion of discriminations against the Negro aroused southerners to such an extent that Cable moved away to Northampton, Massachusetts, and a far less exciting literary career than he had enjoyed in Louisiana.

The local-colorists viewed the South between 1875 and 1920 and asked questions in regard to the fundamental facts of life in the region. Not one of them, with the exception of Cable, treated more than a tiny part of the region and its civilization, and none really was able to project the South or the people into a rapidly changing twentieth century. Bound to the traditional past, or to a narrowing and constrictive present, these local-colorists were unable to accept the new age as a fact in southern history.

Two major southern authors wrote and published through the

transitional age when romance and tradition gave way to realism. These were Ellen Glasgow and James Branch Cabell. Miss Glasgow, the daughter of the president of the Tredegar Iron Works, came from a sheltered background. She had little opportunity to know first-hand the life of the New South outside Richmond. Unlike local-colorists Allen and Murfree, she wrote in the vein of realism. Between her first major novel with a Virginian background, *The Voice of the People* (1900), and *Vein of Iron* (1935), Ellen Glasgow produced seven novels of varying qualities and applications of a formula of sheltered realism. In *Barren Ground* and *Vein of Iron* she treated the passivity of the lives of her Virginia characters. She revealed much about the sense of failure of the southern social system to provide enrichment for human life. Though humor and lightness of touch characterized some of Miss Glasgow's novels, her writings, however, are more specifically characterized by the barrenness and dullness of the lives of her characters. In most of her books there are descriptions of the class struggle which involved Virginia in an age of agrarian revolution and the rise of commerce and industry. She perhaps never fully comprehended the full implications of these facts, or the reasons why the old families disintegrated with the passage of time. Yet she went on searching for meaning from one novel to the next.

Miss Glasgow's neighbor James Branch Cabell seems never to have concerned himself deeply with either realism or current meaning. To the contrary he sought escape from the world into which he was born and had to live. Almost like James Lane Allen in some of his attempts to undate an age, Cabell slipped back into an imaginary world of neo-medievalism, which, in the 1920's helped his readers, if not himself, to escape frank appraisal of their uncertain times. Louis D. Rubin, Jr., compared the struggle of Cabell's characters in the legends in *Silver Stallion* (1928) with the South and the growing myth of the Confederacy. To a considerable degree, perhaps, it was a critique of Cabell's South which had the durability to survive. Its romantic approach obscured the harsh realities of modern southern life.

Ellen Glasgow and James Branch Cabell, writing with severely limited geographical and conceptual perspectives, comprehended little of the greater South into which their contemporary Virginia fitted. They nevertheless were the connectives between the two literary ages. Except for them the whole South might truly have been the "Desert of Bozarth" described by H. L. Mencken. Virginius Dabney wrote in *Liberalism in the South* that "Mr. Cabell and Miss Glasgow were the only southerner writers of fiction who made significant contributions to liberalism from the death of Joel Chandler Harris in 1908 until the 1920's if we except Miss Mary Johnston, whose *Hagar* is a ringing appeal for women's rights, and Mrs. Cora Harris, some of whose work is in the realistic and iconoclastic tradition."

Mencken shocked and shamed the South in the 1920's by labeling it a sterile literary desert. He, however, looked too much at the surface, and failed to perceive that there was a stirring which in time would result in a full-blown southern literary renascence.

In the years immediately before this renascence three authors were of central importance: Elizabeth Madox Roberts, Stark Young, and Thomas S. Stribling. Miss Roberts, a Kentuckian from the border area between the bluegrass and the rocky sterile knobs, wrote of poor yeoman farmers struggling with the problems of the land of their heritage and with their own psyches. Few southern authors got so close to nature as did Miss Roberts in *The Time of Man* (1926), *The Great Meadow* (1930), and *Black Is My Truelove's Hair* (1938). Her people and her writing were caught up in a maze of symbolism which all but obscured their real place as poor and pioneer whites grubbing a livelihood from their fields and making an adjustment to their fate.

Stark Young writing nostalgically about the South from New York, interspersed a web of romance between Roberts and Stribling. In *River House* (1929) and *So Red the Rose* (1934) he took his readers as far back into the Mississippi "poictesme" or "Lichfield" as Cabell and Page did in Virginia. With deep irony he wrote of the period in the past when the cataclysmic present overwhelmed the region. This was a fact readily perceived by T. S. Stribling in *Birthright* (1922), and his southern trilogy, *The Forge* (1931), *The Store* (1932), and *The Unfinished Cathedral* (1934). Few southern authors prior to these years had plumbed so deeply into the mainstream of southern institutions and patterns of frustrations. In many respects the "cathedrals" of Stribling were indeed crumbling affairs. He caught the region in an economic and social motion in which the old mores were being destroyed without new ones replacing them. Yet Stribling's novels were definitely of the New South of the 1920's.

On the extreme fringes, Erskine Caldwell in *Tobacco Road* (1932) and *God's Little Acre* (1933) portrayed the poor white southerner in the very lowest denominator of human animality. Jeeter Lester, Ty-Ty, and Darling Jill represented a primordial stratum of southern humanity caught in the ceaseless wash of regional failures. They came to symbolize the economic and social failures of a society viewing itself largely through the myopia of one-crop tenant-farming, political demagoguery, laziness, and illiteracy. Caldwell's early writings did about as much to call attention to the deep erosion of southern society as did the statisticians and sociologists of the New Deal era.

In *Lamb in His Bosom* (1934) Caroline Miller translated the conditions of life in the lower Georgia South into terms of the lingering southern frontier. She told a story of the stringent naturalism of human beings struggling with the land and of the ebb and flow of life in a primitiveness that was devoid of sophistication in any form, but not without human hopes and emotions.

The southern renascence had many roots. Julia Peterkin of South Carolina gave literary permanence to the gullah Negro of the low country in *Scarlet Sister Mary* (1929), a Pulitzer Prize novel, and *Black April* (1927). DuBose Heyward's *Porgy* (1929), and Roark Bradford's *Gretny People* (1927), *Red Bean Row* (1929), and numerous short stories in *Collier's Magazine* helped to reintroduce the Negro as a theme in southern literature. This time he had escaped the bonds of slavery and existed now in a thralldom of half-freedom and half-bondage to economic stagnation. These books were to release a mainspring of literature that treated Negro life in the region. They were highly transitional in that they helped change views and attitudes toward Negroes from the extremities of reconstruction and the gentler Uncle Remus era.

The renascence began in several places, and largely in the same manner in each place. Tiny islands of creativity were formed in Charleston, New Orleans, Nashville, and Richmond, as well as other towns. The sudden appearance of such little magazines as *Double Dealer* in New Orleans. *The Reviewer* in Richmond, *The Fugitive* in Nashville, plus other short-lived fiction and poetry magazines, documented the burgeoning of significant literary talent. Several of the organized groups were concerned with the writing and the criticism of poetry. A number of novelists, however, also emerged from these various literary groups. In Nashville the Fugitives of Vanderbilt University had in its membership John Crowe Ransom, the dean of the group, Robert Penn Warren, Allen Tate, Donald Davidson, Andrew Lytle, Cleanth Brooks, Jesse Stuart, Merrill Moore, and Randall Jarrell. In Charleston, Josephine Pinckney, Julia Peterkin, Herbert Ravenal Sass, and DuBose Heyward formed a significant cluster of writers who contributed heavily to the southern rebirth.

As important as were the associations of writers in several southern communities, and as important as were their contributions, it was the individual authors who gave the renascence a deeper significance.

Thomas Wolfe, a native of Asheville, North Carolina, was a giant in both physical and literary dimensions. His novels, *Look Homeward, Angel* (1929), *Of Time and the River* (1935), *The Web and the Rock* (1939), and *You Can't Go Home Again* (1940), represented a massive outpouring of a man who experienced life in a voracious way. With the highly creative aid of his editor Maxwell Perkins of the firm of Charles Scribner's Sons, he produced from great sheaves of raw manuscripts four enormous books of great sensitivity. Wolfe felt deeply about the South's past. To him the South had gone off the track somewhere around the Civil War, which represented to him a vast regional symbol of guilt. He also felt that the South could fulfill its economic and social missions almost entirely within the framework of the agrarian tradition.

Of even greater literary importance were the novels of William Faulkner of Oxford, Mississippi. In his formative writing years he was a contributor to the *Double Dealer* of New Orleans. Unlike Wolfe, his earliest novels hardly set the measure of the major books to come. After *Sartoris* (1929), there followed in rapid succession *The Sound and the Fury* (1929), *As I Lay Dying* (1930), *Sanctuary* (1931), and *Light in August* (1932). In these novels Faulkner began a search for fundamental human emotions and reactions against the background of his native region. In the Yoknapatawpha novels, beginning with *Sartoris* and ending with *The Mansion* (1959), he dealt with the passions, frustrations, and quirks of human nature, ranging from burning hatred to spiritual frustration, and with a deep sense of social guilt. In the Compsons, Snopses, Stevens, and McCaslins he revealed an appreciation not only that the present is enchained to the past, but that there is a historical determination in human behavior. Human beings act out the roles already set for them by time itself. There is both a broad universality to Faulkner's novels, and a readily discernible provincialism. The author gathered characters and scenes from the world of central and northern Mississippi. His work showed a great awareness of folk culture, a deeply engrained sense of humor, and an instinctive feeling for violence and human frustration and what results they produced. He wrote with the dark broodings of an ancient dramatist, and the exaggerations of a backwoods humorist. Economic, social, and racial confusion in a South caught in the crises of wasted lands, crop failures, and the dissipation of human bodies and spirits, gave broad dimensions to the Faulkner novels.

Writing during the late 1920's with the fierce passion of some of his characters, that complex human being, William Faulkner, was to bring home many significant literary honors to the South, crowned by the Nobel Prize for Literature in 1950. In the process of his writing he was to create enough symbolism in his novels to keep critics occupied for the next half-century. Already books and articles of criticism exceed the number of Faulkner novels themselves. Increasingly as time went by, Faulkner became a spokesman on issues affecting the South. After the Supreme Court decision of 1954 ordering desegration of public schools, the novelist became involved in the bitter cross-currents of emotion which followed. Not always did he appear as consistent in his views of the changes gnawing away at the structure of tradition as did some of his more symbolical characters who were caught and fixed in the web of history itself. By the time of his death the world of William Faulkner was caught in such violent change, that, despite their high literary worth, the basic values of most of his novels lay within the context of the past.

Robert Penn Warren of Kentucky, a member of the Nashville Fugitives, has written in a far more diversified manner than did Wolfe and Faulkner. In *Night Rider* (1939), *All the King's Men* (1946), and *World Enough and Time* (1950), he examined the structure of southern character and the nature of crisis in two different ages of the South. Writing of the tobacco or "black patch" war of western Kentucky, he portrayed a background for revolt which he knew about first-hand from infancy. The central theme is of politics and the slyness and brutality of a demagogue smashing one power structure and building another while holding to a highly ambivalent set of morals. Some of the sense of regional quality appears even in the face of a raw bare-knuckled struggle for power in a Kentucky society which functioned at a level somewhere between a high degree of sophistication and an unleashed frontier ferocity. In *Segregation* and *Legacy of the Civil War*, the novelist penetrated far below the surface in rendering a profound literary judgment on two basic themes of the southern advance toward the future.

On the bank of the Ohio where the shoulder of the Cumberland Plateau nudges the great river off its direct course, Jesse Stuart has revealed the deep emotional attachment of man for the soil, and revealed the basic struggle of the individual to subdue the forces of nature long enough to extract some of the meager satisfactions from life itself. With less harshness, but no less humorous vigor, Stuart's *Man with a Bull-Tongue Plow* (1934), *Beyond Dark Hills* (1938), and *Taps for Private Tussie* (1944) reflect a rural pattern closely akin in sentimentality, if not in fact, to that of the agrarianism of the Fugitives of Nashville.

Most of the authors of the renascence years in the South were writing when the region was in the first phases of revolutionary change. Just as H. L. Mencken mistook a momentary halt on the dead center of intellectual advancement for complete literary sterility, the Nashville agrarians failed to sense the throb of change which shattered their age. At the very moment the manuscript for *I'll Take My Stand* was speeding north to a publisher, the old agrarian South was expiring. This will possibly remain the South's most highly literate and unintended monument to the end of an age in southern history.

The list of authors of the New South is lengthy. In a region long burdened by social and economic crises, these authors made a determined if not frantic search, for the meaning of regional life and also attempted to universalize southern experience. The renascence of this century was less indicative of a search for new methods to meet the challenges of a new age than an attempt to recapture the strongly humanistic factors in the South's past.

Novelists, poets, and editors were by no means the only interpreters of the postwar South. The historian was to make his contribution. By the very force of circumstances southerners coming out of the Civil War were conscious of the history of their region. This was not always true of those in the ante-bellum period. Their sense of history was more attuned to that of classic times, and of modern Europe. The war, however, had engendered an entirely new sense of the past, and had given history a new implication. Only one southerner prior to 1865 had distinguished himself as a historian, and few had achieved distinction in the field of biography. Following the war Edward A. Pollard, Virginia journalist, published an astonishing number of books, best known of which were *The Last Year of the War* (1866); *Southern History of the War* (1866), and *Life of Jefferson Davis; with a Secret History of the Southern Confederacy* (1869). Daniel Harvey Hill undertook to reveal southern history from a purely regional perspective in his periodical, *The Land We Love*, and subsequently in special articles in *Battles and Leaders of the Civil War*. Jefferson Davis turned historian in his account, *The Rise and Fall of the Confederacy* (1881), and Alexander H. Stephens interpreted American history with a decided southern slant in *A Constitutional View of the War Between the States, A Compendium of the History of the United States* (1872) and *Popular History of the United States* (1882).

In a sense every southern soldier who either wrote of the war as a phenomenon in American history or prepared his memoirs for publication became a historian. The period from 1875 to 1915 saw a considerable volume of rationalization of the causes, conduct, and results of sectional issues and conflict which appeared under the guise of history.

In the field of academic historical writing there was no one before 1890 who achieved any reputation as an objective scholar. A pioneer was William P. Trent, who prepared biographies of William Gilmore Simms and Robert E. Lee. As editor of the *Sewanee Review* (1892) he encouraged the publication of a number of historical essays, and he himself searched for the dominant forces in southern life. Contemporaries of Trent were Stephen B. Weeks, Edgar Gardner Murphy, and William G. Brown. Weeks, a professor at the struggling Trinity College, in Durham, North Carolina, was a highly productive scholar who added to his literary accomplishments the collecting and using of basic source materials. Perhaps the preservation of these materials in the Trinity College Library was of more lasting importance. Weeks was one of the first scientifically trained scholars who helped to introduce into the South the new approaches to the writing and teaching of history from the Herbert Baxter Adams Seminar in the Johns Hopkins University at Baltimore. Bassett, like Weeks, was a product of the Adams Seminar. He succeeded Weeks at Trinity College in 1892 and continued the work of his predecessor. By 1906 he had produced more than half a dozen books, and he had helped establish the *South Atlantic Quarterly*. In an editorial discussing racial antipathy in the South, Bassett compared Booker T. Washington to Robert E. Lee and stirred bitter press reaction in North Carolina. Later he left the South to join the staff of Smith College, and there he continued to write prolifically.

By 1920 a number of southern historians had established solid scholarly reputations. Among these were Woodrow Wilson, William E. Dodd, Ulrich B. Phillips, Walter Lynwood Fleming, Wiliam K. Boyd, James De Roughlac Hamilton, and Eugene C. Barker. Wilson was a native Virginian who spent his productive years outside the South. William E. Dodd, a North Carolinian, was graduated from the Virginia Polytechnic Institute, and then went to Germany to do graduate work. He brought home with him an interest in social history, and a basic knowledge of German research methods. As a professor in the University of Chicago he was to have greater impact on southern historical scholarship through the students he trained than with his books.

A Georgian by birth, Ulrich B. Phillips did most of his advanced graduate work outside the South. Early in his scholarly career he discovered the reward of exploiting the primary sources of southern history. Dealing with slavery and life in general in the ante-bellum South, he was able to introduce both fresh materials and broader interpretations in his numerous essays and books. His last study, *Life and Labor in the Old South* (1930), was to become a landmark in the reconsideration of domestic slavery. His essay, "The Central Theme of Southern History," which appeared in the *American Historical Review*, October 1928, emphasized the importance of the institution of slavery in the making of regional economic and social decisions and in affecting the course of life.

Other southern historians examined the reconstruction period under the tutelage of Professor William A. Dunning in Columbia University. These were the earliest scientific investigations of this highly complex subject. In 1905 Walter Lynwood Fleming published *Civil War and Reconstruction in Alabama*, followed by a publication of a documentary history of general reconstruction. By 1930 a study of this period in all of the southern states, including Kentucky, was in print, and already revisionists were projecting fresher and broader points of view.

An extensive multivolume study of the South was published in 1909. This work, *The South in the Building of the Nation* (13 vols.), was comprised of a series of state histories, and an even more extensive collection of topographical sections discussing the growth of the region. J. A. C. Chandler of Richmond, Virginia, was general editor, but the essays were written by historians located in the southern colleges and universities, and represented almost the sum total of historical scholarship in the region. The thirteenth volume of this series was an attempt to promote popular home study of southern history, and to serve the academic historian in organizing special courses.

A revision of curriculums in southern colleges and universities in the 1920's gave new emphasis to the study of regional history, and graduate schools began training research scholars. Like Weeks, Bassett, and Phillips, these scholars exploited the great masses of source materials to produce an impressive number of books. In 1934 the Southern Historical Association was organized, and began publication of the *Journal of Southern History*. Within three decades, 1930 to 1960, southerners not only rewrote much of their history; they probed deeper and with more objectivity than did the older generation of scholars. Much of this historical literature still lacks depth and interpretative qualities which would make it as impressive in a literary sense as it is in volume.

Historians have by no means been alone in writing about the South and its conditions. It is a far cry from Fitzhugh's *Sociology for the South* to Howard Odum, whose books had such impact on our knowledge of the South. Rupert Vance, working with Odom in earlier years as a colleague, considered the region in terms of the physiological and sociological forces which shaped its economy and society. Both disciplines of sociology and political science reached a state of initial maturity in the years of the Great Depression and the age of the new industrialism. A revolution in the old agrarian society and a phenomenal expansion of higher educational efforts gave social scientists, historians, and novelists new insight and motives for viewing the South and its immediate past.

After World War II the South underwent such rapid changes that there arose a question whether its literary figures would continue to speak with a strong and distinct regional voice. Regional conditions and emotions which had stimulated such a high degree of creativeness no longer prevailed. It was impossible for modern southern writers to "go home again." By 1950, nevertheless, new voices were emerging in the South which were aware of the social and economic revolt occurring in the region and prepared to describe it.

X

Depression and the New Deal

The breaking of the Solid South in 1928 raised hopes in many quarters that a true two-party system was imminent. But the time for such a development had not arrived. The parochial southern white man was still obsessed with the all-pervading fear of the Negro and could not be brought to tolerate a rival to the Democratic party on the state and local level. No matter that southerners might cast their votes for a Republican President to preside over a national government in far away Washington. Only Democrats who understood and sympathized with the "southern way of life" must govern in southern capitals and in any local communities where the Negro constituted a significant fraction of the population. Besides, the hope of a two-party South was dealt a devastating blow by the great depression. During the 1930's the Republican vote in the South declined to its lowest level in history. This was due not so much to a conservative reaction as to the political and social reforms of the New Deal, motivated by economic distress.

The depression of the 1930's struck in the agrarian South with the same fury as in the industrial North. In 1929 the southern cotton crop of 15 million bales had brought an average of twenty cents a pound, but the following year the price dropped precipitously to eight cents. Declining prices spurred increased production, while the world depression sharply reduced consumption. By 1932 there was stored in the warehouses of the world 39 million bales, and annual consumption had dropped to 23 million. The effect on the South was catastrophic; between 1929 and 1932 cotton income declined by two-thirds.

In 1933 the New York Cotton Exchange quoted a price of five cents, and the southern grower received even less. Forced farm sales mounted, and the economic structure of the region crumbled. As declining cotton production forced tenants from their farms they wandered into towns seeking employment of any kind. During the decade of the 1930's the percentage of Negroes in the total labor force of the South declined from more than a third to little more than a fifth.

Part of this decline was due to an outmigration of Negroes from the section, but much of it was due to chronic unemployment. For despite discrimination against them in relief programs, more than two million southern Negroes were on relief in 1933, twice as many as their percentage of the population would warrant. But Negro migration was not all to the North; much of it was an internal movement from southern farms to southern cities. And the overall effect of the migration from farm to city so far as employment of the total population was concerned was, therefore, negative. A few whites might be rewarded with low-paying menial jobs but only at the expense of Negro workers, who were now displaced as porters and handymen, as whites competed for these positions formerly reserved for the Negro. As basic industries like textile mills, lumbering, iron manufacturing, and furniture manufacturing curtailed production, workers were laid off; and wages were driven to subsistence levels and even lower, as both whites and Negroes sought ever-shrinking employment opportunities.

Actually, however, the Great Depression only aggravated conditions long prevalent in southern industry. The textile industry, particularly, had been in a chronic depression for most of the preceding decade. As early as 1921, millowners, to reduce operating costs, began to cut wages, extend the work day, and institute the stretch-out, a program whereby a spinner or weaver tended more machines—often twice as many as formerly—and sometimes even with reduced wages. The stretch-out resulted in the laying off of many workers. As we have seen, the seventy-two-hour week was gone, but the sixty-two- and sixty-three-hour week remained, even for women and sometimes for children. Many southern mills operated regularly at night, when from a fourth to a third of their output was produced. As depression became more acute in the industry, hours and night work were extended still further in a frantic effort to decrease operating costs. Thus, overproduction stimulated more overproduction, and workers were forced to accept conditions which had existed at the turn of the century. Marginal factories were forced out of production entirely, and hundreds of thousands of spindles were being shut down annually during the 1920's, throwing additional workers out of employment. From 1923 to 1931, more than 10 million spindles, or approximately 30 per cent of those in the South, became inoperative.

Many southern textile manufacturers made honest efforts at reform, but these were blocked by a recalcitrant minority. In Alabama, for instance, liberal manufacturers supported a bill in the 1931 legislature fixing a ten-hour work day and a fifty-five-hour week, but the bill was killed in committee. In 1930 the Cotton Textile Institute, a regional manufacturers' association, proposed voluntary reduction of the work week to fifty-five hours for day shifts and fifty hours for night shifts, with complete elimination of women and children under eighteen from all night work. Eighty-five per cent of the industry accepted the proposal, but their reforms were frustrated by the minority who refused to comply and whose wage structure forced the majority to return to the old schedule. As a result, North Carolina mills were operating an average of 66½ hours a week in 1931, Georgia ran shifts of longer than 12 hours, and schedules in other states were as bad.

Aggravating these conditions were the low wages paid southern textile workers, barely three-fourths of that paid their counterparts in New England. And since textiles was the leading southern manufacturing industry it set the standards of employment practices throughout the region—for laundries, merchandising, hotels, restaurants, lumbering. Southern lumber manufacturers, for instance, paid wages barely half what lumber workers were paid on the Pacific coast and only two-thirds those of the national average. But this was not all. In addition to geographical differences, wage scales also had sex and race differentials, with the Negro female being lowest on the scale and Negro males and white females next. In general, the Negro suffered a differential of from 20 to 30 per cent, and the white woman slightly less. This latter was one of the factors leading to widespread female employment in southern textile and tobacco industries.

If reform was to come, therefore, it must be by action of the national government. For in the final analysis, the South was saddled with a surplus of labor which threatened both regional and national standards; her semi-colonial economy was unable to cope with the more powerful and more mature industrial and financial organizations of other regions. The products of southern manufacture were typically standardized, industrial goods. The producers were numerous and small, and not subject to industry-wide collective bargaining on the part of labor even if there had been a disposition on the part of southern workers toward unionism, which there was not, as we have already seen. In 1928 the four leading manufacturing industries of the region—textiles, furniture, steel, and lumber—were almost completely unorganized. The road of the labor organizer was a rocky one in southern communities, where the people were unfamiliar with unions and where the workers lived in mill towns that were citadels of paternalistic capitalism.

Despite this milieu of social conservatism, a wave of unrest, provoked by pay cuts or the stretch-out, swept the textile industry of the South in the spring of 1929. Strikes of a somewhat spontaneous nature erupted in eastern Tennessee and in the piedmont regions of the Carolinas. Organized labor was in difficulty throughout the country at the time, but these strikes were the signal for organizers from the United Textile Workers of the American Federation of Labor to enter the controversy in an effort to furnish leadership to the workers. At Marion, North Carolina, a strike occurred when management began laying off workers who had joined the UTW. When picket lines were set around the mills, management called on the governor for troops. These were sent and soon brought the strikers to accept a settlement. A month later when management, in violation of the settlement, again began discharging union members, the workers struck again. Tension mounted, and when sheriff's deputies used tear gas in breaking up a picket line, firing started. When the smoke cleared, not a deputy had been shot, but thirty-six strikers lay wounded, six of them mortally. The deputies who did the shooting were identified and indicted, but all were acquitted. Meanwhile, four strikers were tried for "rioting," convicted, and given jail sentences.

At Elizabethton, Tennessee, at about the same time, 5000 workers struck two German-owned rayon plants. Grievances were the same as elsewhere: long hours, low wages, and the stretch-out. Although rayon was a new textile industry, much more profitable than cotton or wool, wages paid were no higher than in the more depressed branches of the industry. In the department where the walk-out started, 550 girls were employed fifty-six hours a week at an average weekly wage of $8.96, or sixteen cents an hour. In another department, a man with wife and children earned $12 a week from which he paid monthly rent of $25 plus an additional $1.50 for water and $2.25 for light. Fuel and food had to be purchased independently, and there was no company store in Elizabethton to extend credit.

Within six days the strike had closed both plants completely. Court orders were obtained, enjoining strikers from picketing, and the governor of Tennessee sent eight hundred federally armed state militia to enforce the orders. Streets bristled with soldiers, and machine guns were installed on the roofs of buildings. As at Marion, a settlement was reached and later violated by the companies. When the workers walked out a second time, pickets were arrested and two of the leaders who had been sent in by the UTW were kidnapped and carried out of the state. Soon strikers' families were going hungry, for the AFL, which had discouraged the strike, gave little help to the strikers other than moral support. Morale crumbled, and after ten weeks a settlement was reached on company terms. No provision was made for union recognition, and 1000 union members were blacklisted.

The most serious disturbances of the period occurred at Gastonia, North Carolina, where the strikers were led by Fred Beal and George Pershing, organizers sent in by the National Textile Workers Union, a Communist-controlled rival of the UTW. Although the struck mills were owned by Rhode Island industrialists, community sentiment, through the media of press and pulpit, openly supported them and condemned the strikers. Regional patriotism, religion, loyalty to the Lost Cause, the idea of white supremacy, all joined with the native fear of the Red menace to brand the strikers as subversives. Civil liberties were violated as police authorities and strikebreakers united to harass the strikers and their leaders. Finally violence broke out when a mob of masked men destroyed the strike headquarters.

Liberal editors and educators, including President William Louis Poteat of Wake Forest College and President Harry Woodburn Chase of the University of North Carolina, protested against violation of the civil rights of the strikers, but the effect of their protest was lost when Gastonia Police Chief O. F. Aderholt was killed while attempting to break up a strikers' meeting. At almost the same time, a woman striker named Ella Mae Wiggins was killed when armed men fired from an automobile into the truck in which she was riding to a strikers' meeting. Fred Beal was not even present at the scene of Aderholt's killing, but he and six other strike leaders were indicted for "conspiracy to murder." No credible evidence was presented at the trial to substantiate the charges, but the defendants were convicted and sentenced to prison terms of from five to twenty years. The identity of the man who actually did kill Ella Mae Wiggins was clearly established, but he was acquitted.

The strike was doomed from the outset. Gastonia, like most southern communities, regarded the principle of unionism as a move against progress and against the inalienable right of an employer to fix the conditions of employment. Perhaps the greatest of the forces working against the strikers' success was the lack of unity that existed within the labor movement in the South. At Gastonia, the greatest textile-manufacturing center in the country, only a handful of mills were involved, and the workers of the fifty or more unaffected mills could not be persuaded to join in the movement, even though the same conditions against which the strikers were protesting prevailed in their own plants. Indeed, even in the mills that were struck, many workers refused to walk out and instead acted as strike breakers.

Although the strikes of 1929 failed, they marked a milestone for southern labor. The unions collapsed for the time, but out of the disturbances there grew a class consciousness among southern mill workers; and unionism, which had appeared unthinkable shortly before, just as the idea of a break in the political solidarity of the Democratic South had been unthinkable a year before, was now a reality. Henceforth southern labor unions would be more than a figment of the imagination.

Gastonia revealed, too, that a small segment of southern workers, like some in other sections, were prepared if necessary to follow Communist leadership for truly radical solutions to their problems. For it was apparent that the small core of strikers who remained militant after the first few weeks were well aware of the revolutionary aims of Beal and Pershing. Even to countless conservative southerners who were not members of the working class it was apparent, more so than in Populist or reconstruction times, that the South's economic life was controlled by financiers from Wall Street or industrialists from Pawtucket. Rightly or wrongly, they blamed the Yankee for the depressed condition of their own section. And as the depression deepened about them and more disorder threatened, many began to despair of recovery under the old order. Whatever chance there may have been of a real revolutionary movement developing, however, was forestalled by the coming of the New Deal.

The upper South had opposed the northern, Catholic, urbanite Al Smith in 1928, even though he had as his running-mate the rural, dry, southern Protestant, Joseph T. Robinson of Arkansas. In 1932 many southern Democrats led by Pat Harrison of Mississippi opposed Franklin Roosevelt's nomination. Largely through the efforts of Huey Long, however, other southerners came into line and Roosevelt was nominated and elected. After all, Roosevelt had a rural, patrician, background which somewhat obscured to most southerners the remarkable similarity between his program and Smith's.

At first Roosevelt and the New Deal were welcomed with all but universal enthusiasm in the South, although it should have been obvious that his latitudinarian social and constitutional beliefs regarding the need for government planning and regulation in the industrial world of the twentieth century would run counter to fundamental southern attitudes of state-rights. But both on the farm and in the cities, workers' conditions had deteriorated so badly during the early years of the depression that anything that promised relief in the dramatic terms of the New Deal was grasped eagerly. By 1932 the average gross income of cotton farm families had declined to $216, a drop of almost 400 per cent in four years. In the same period the value of all southern farm products decreased by more than a third, and that of manufactured products by 40 per cent. The number of workers employed in manufacturing in the region was lower by a fifth, wages were down by a half, and the number of destitute southerners on relief rolls was three times the rate for the country as a whole.

The New Deal program addressed itself to both national and regional problems. The basic commodity of the South, cotton, was dealt with through the Agricultural Adjustment Act. To strengthen the credit structure of the region, cotton production was cut so that the surplus noted above would be used up and prices would rise. The 1933 crop was already in the ground when the act was passed, and it promised to be a bumper one. To prevent an addition to the surplus, growers were paid to plow under every third row. As a result the price rose to ten cents, practically double that of the previous year. In 1934, production was reduced by almost a third through contracts whereby growers withdrew acreage from production in return for government payments in the form of cash rentals for the acreage withdrawn. More than $400 million was paid out under the original cotton program through 1935. In addition, the Bankhead Act of 1934 placed a federal tax on all cotton ginned in excess of quotas allotted. Through all these measures cotton income more than doubled.

Close study revealed, however, that the lion's share of the benefit payments went to the landowner, who received rental for acreage taken out of production at his tenant's expense; while the tenant was forced off the land, to become a casual day-laborer or else to go on relief rolls. One study showed that the average payment to the landlord was $822 per plantation, while the aggregate received by all tenants per plantation was only $108. The program was thus a subsidy to planters, and was a reflection of the planter influence in its administration. For Oscar Johnston, operator of the largest plantation in the United States at Scott, Mississippi, was manager of the Federal Cotton Pool and special assistant to the Secretary of the Treasury on matters of farm finance.

Neglect of the tenant and cropper in the first AAA, however, was due less to design than to ignorance of the deplorable conditions under which they lived. As news of their plight became known, the Roosevelt Administration was preparing amendments to the act to give them a larger share in adjustment payments, when the whole program was nullified by the Supreme Court in 1935. Meantime, the act had won for the time being the warm support of the influential planter class for the New Deal.

An entirely different reaction was achieved by the National Industrial Recovery Act. The purpose of this law was to spread work and create new jobs by having federally enforced forty- or forty-four-hour weeks replace the traditional fifty-five- and sixty-hour work weeks. At the same time floors placed under wages by the law maintained the southern differential, even the regional differential between white and Negro, and were consequently very low in most industries. Even so, the minimum of twelve dollars a week in cotton textiles was better than most southern workers in the industry had ever known.

Codes drawn up under the act for different industries also banned labor in factories for children under sixteen. This had a salutary effect, even though much child labor in the South was in occupations unaffected by the codes. The right of workers to bargain collectively was protected by Section 7A of the act, and this was perhaps the part of greatest controversy in the South. Even though employers generally disregarded it, and although this act, too, was shortly nullified by the Supreme Court, Section 7A proved valuable in the end to the cause of labor. For it stimulated the movement of southern workers into labor unions, and the right to collective bargaining guaranteed for the first time under the NIRA was later protected by the National Labor Relations Act, which survived constitutional challenge before the Court. As a consequence of Section 7A and other features limiting employers' control over the codes, most big business opposed the NIRA, even though they liked the feature of the act which freed them from anti-trust laws. Soon they began to clamor for its repeal, and they rejoiced when the Supreme Court declared the act unconstitutional in 1935.

Underpinning the entire New Deal program was relief of the unemployed, first under the Federal Emergency Relief Administration (FERA), and later under the Works Progress Administration (WPA). So acute was industrial unemployment and farm tenant displacement in the South that without this program human suffering would have been overwhelming. Southern state and local governments of the period were not keyed to massive programs of poverty relief, even if governmental funds or credits had been available, which they were not. Consequently, wage rates would have been driven even lower than they were. When the Roosevelt administration was installed, the federal relief program was already under way, and southern wage differentials provided in the NIRA codes were reflected in the FERA payments; generally the southern family received about half the amount paid families in other sections. Southern employers, opposed even to the relief principle itself, insisted on the differential enforced against the section. Their primary concern seemed to be the preservation of a cheap labor supply in the South. This must not be permitted to disappear through relief payments which might be on a par with wages. Accordingly, the average monthly payment per family in the South in 1933 ranged from a low of $3.96 in Mississippi to $13.89 in Louisiana.

The regional average for the eleven states was less than $7.00, while the national average was $15.07. Three years later the regional average had increased to more than $13.00, but by that time the national average payment had grown to $30.43. A differential between white and Negro benefits was also preserved. In Mississippi, where about half the population was colored, the Negro family, in June 1935, averaged $7.09, while the white family averaged $11.13.

The Social Security Act of 1935 also brought assistance to states for old-age pensions and for dependent children and the blind. By 1938 all southern states except Virginia had plans for old-age assistance approved by the Social Security Board, eight states had programs approved for dependent children, and nine had plans approved for aid to the blind. The portions of the act pertaining to unemployment insurance provided for no contributions by the federal government; they merely brought federal pressure on states to enact unemployment insurance laws. Under all features of the Social Security Act, benefit payments were very low, but these were raised as time went on. The importance of the act was that federally supervised basic human welfare programs were initiated.

Another measure of great significance to the South was the Bankhead-Jones Farm Tenant Act of 1937, which grew out of recommendations of the President's Committee on Farm Tenancy. The act provided loans for tenants, sharecroppers, and farm laborers to purchase farms. The sum appropriated was hopelessly inadequate, and in the early years the Farm Security Administration had to be highly selective in making loans. Even so, almost 2000 loans for the purchase and improvement of farms were made in the first year of the act.

To replace the provisions of Section 7A of the Supreme Court-voided NIRA, the Roosevelt Administration secured passage of the Fair Labor Standards Act in 1938. It provided both minimum wages and guarantees for the right of collective bargaining by workers. The wage levels were set far too low, beginning at twenty-five cents an hour, and had features which made possible preservation of the southern differential. Still, opposition of southerners to this measure was so great that it had to be brought before the House of Representatives over the opposition of the southern-dominated Rules Committee.

To replace the Agricultural Adjustment Act, which had also been nullified by the Supreme Court, Congress passed the new Agricultural

Adjustment Act of 1938. This provided for crop limitation in cotton, corn, tobacco, and peanuts, all southern crops of importance, through benefit payments for "soil conservation," and through marketing loans. The fixing of marketing quotas was contingent on approval in a plebiscite by two-thirds of the farmers raising each crop. Cotton farmers favored the plan overwhelmingly, and others only less so. In return for federal support-prices on cotton or other commodities, farmers agreed to accept the quotas given them and to pay a penalty tax on all they sold above the quota. A limit of $10,000 was placed on benefits to any one person for land taken out of production; a floor was placed under small producers' quotas below which they could not be reduced; and landlords could not secure increased payments to themselves through the displacement of croppers and tenants. This measure, largely because of its voluntary feature, withstood its constitutional test. Despite its salutary features, an unprecedented drop in cotton exports in 1938–39 to the lowest figure in half a century produced an alarming situation. Had not the government been able to hold the surplus off the market, a collapse in the cotton economy would have followed.

Thus, the New Deal, by crop restriction on one hand and price supports on the other, managed to halt declining prices of staples, such as cotton, rice, tobacco, and peanuts. Cotton acreage was reduced by almost one-third, to 28 million acres. The price of cotton rose, but the reduced acreage created unemployment among tenants and sharecroppers. Meantime, too, the currency had been devalued, so that the increased price was somewhat illusory. Also, world production outside the United States was increasing greatly, much faster than consumption, so that exports of American cotton dropped steadily throughout the decade.

Nevertheless, the immediate effect of New Deal programs was pleasing in the South. Besides, the prominent part southerners were once more playing in national affairs restored the section's influence, which had been blighted by the 1928 split. As the New Deal program went into high gear, however, it frightened southern conservatives. For it threatened the political control which they had held since the end of the progressive period that followed Populism. The increasing liberalism of the New Deal, its appeal to the sharecropper and textile worker, people heretofore unmoved by traditional southern politics, was alarming to dominant groups dedicated to state-rights principles. Worst of all, the interest of the New Deal in the welfare of the Negro was a threat to economic interests as well as to social mores. For it was clear by this time that the New Deal planned to disregard state-rights in the South through a combination of national programs including the highly imaginative Tennessee Valley Authority, bounties on southern staples to farm tenants, rural rehabilitation, rural electrification, agricultural resettlement, domestic allotments, farm mortgages, and crop loans. All these were supported by southern Congressmen, until the social implications that went with them were more clearly outlined. Enthusiasm for them flagged, too, as overproduction of cotton after 1936 brought a drop in the price of that staple from fourteen cents to eight. As a consequence, banks refused to finance the least productive farms. These fell into hands of financiers, who for a time were able to collect benefits by taking these lands out of production.

Resentment against the New Deal by farmers also was directed at the WPA programs, which they said raised their labor costs. Opposition to the New Deal developed, therefore, among southern Congressmen who wished to have the best of both worlds: federal price supports and subsidies on the one hand, state-rights on wage rates and on the race question on the other. In general, most southerners in Congress supported the New Deal on farm measures, but a large number of them joined the anti-New Deal bloc on such issues as labor legislation, farm tenancy, social security, and the WPA.

Meantime, as Democrats once more had become the majority party in Congress, southerners had moved into chairmanships of committees. This enhanced the influence of southern Congressmen in the Democratic party. At the same time it widened the gulf between them and the President who, forced to depend on cities for his electoral vote, had to shape a program that appealed to labor and the Negro and which would consequently be hostile to the peculiar needs of the conservative southerners. For a time, the great popularity of Roosevelt with the masses forced the conservatives to retreat before him. The result was compromise, but compromise that worked to the southern Negro's advantage. For the New Deal program was aimed at improving the lot of all poor people white and black alike, and the issue was not just one of white against black. By educating southern people through agencies like the Farm Security Administration and the insuring of Negro voting in the AAA crop-control elections, the New Deal brought tenants and sharecroppers, both white and black, into participation in decisions affecting their community.

The wrecking of much of Roosevelt's program by the Supreme Court, together with his overwhelming re-election in 1936, led him to undertake the reform of the Court. The proposal rocked the country and the party, and brought the struggle between President and southern Congressmen to a climax. But the death of Senator Robinson of Arkansas foredoomed the defeat of the Court-packing bill. Robinson had pledged enough southern votes to insure the passage of the bill, but his death released these pledges and the Senators deserted en masse.

This setback came shortly after the President's own overwhelming victory at the polls in 1936, and he now decided on a further step, the defeat of incumbent Democratic Congressmen who had thwarted him—the purge of 1938. Leaders of his southern opposition had been Vice President John Nance Garner, Senators Carter Glass and Harry Byrd of Virginia, Richard Russell of Georgia, Ellison D. "Cotton Ed" Smith of South Carolina, Pat Harrison of Mississippi, Josiah Bailey and Robert Reynolds of North Carolina, and Congressman Howard W. Smith of Virginia.

The personification of opposition to the New Deal, as Professor Jasper Shannon has shown, was Senator Walter George of Georgia. George had opposed the holding company bill in 1935, the government reorganization bill of 1937, the wages and hours bill of 1938, as well as the Court-packing bill. In a speech at Barnesville, Georgia, in August 1938, the President gave an unqualified endorsement to George's opponent, a young attorney named Lawrence Camp. He said that although George was his personal friend, on most public questions "he and I do not speak the same language."[1] But even Roosevelt's Georgia friends resented his interference in the state primary. They gave their support to George, and the press of the state was all but unanimous for him. The result was a setback for the President, for not only did George win, but the President's candidate ran third behind Gene Talmadge. Even so, George got only 141,000 votes in the

(1) Jasper B. Shannon, "Presidential Politics in the South, Part II," *Journal of Politics,* I (Aug. 1939), 278–300.

primary out of a total of 1,500,000 Georgians of voting age. Roosevelt had already lost campaigns against Cotton Ed Smith in South Carolina and Millard Tydings in Maryland.

Then suddenly, the President began getting favorable decisions from the Court which he had been prevented from packing: on the Wagner Act, a new AAA, and a wages and hours law. Instrumental in changing the Court's philosophy toward the New Deal was the militant Alabama New Dealer Hugo Black, whose appointment to the Court by the President in 1937 had further antagonized southern conservatives. To add to the discomfiture of the southerners, a presidential commission labeled the South the country's number one economic problem. Furthermore, the tremendous growth of the Democratic party nationally under Roosevelt—a growth partly accounted for by the great migration of southern Negroes to northern cities in the period following the First World War—had again lessened the influence of the South in party affairs. For so long as the Democratic party was a minority nationally the South could exercise a veto at national conventions. The two-thirds required for nomination of candidates, adopted under Jackson a century before, insured this. But northern confidence, bolstered by the popularity of Roosevelt in 1936, changed this rule at the Philadelphia convention. Henceforth, a bare majority of delegates might nominate, and the power of the South was thus diminished. Four years later at Chicago, the platform of the party was written by Senator Wagner of New York. It was a clarion call for repudiation of state rights and for advocacy of all-out nationalism. Roosevelt was nominated, and he pledged equal protection of the laws for minorities.

But the fact that it was now possible to nominate and elect a Democratic President without southern votes did not erase the dependence of the President upon southern committee chairmen in Congress, chairmanships it has been noted, derived from the seniority that came as a result of the one-party system. For the chairmen had the power to strangle in committee all legislation which they disliked. They were "conservative foxes in charge of liberal coops." For the remainder of the New Deal, therefore, a skillful behind-the-scenes struggle went on between southern Congressmen and New Deal administrators, neither being able to get along without the other. Roosevelt was aided by southern liberals like William B. Bankhead, Lister Hill, Sam Rayburn, Claude Pepper, Maury Maverick, Lyndon Johnson—and even by racists like Theodore Bilbo. But conservatives like Carter Glass and Walter George opposed all measures which might cause the South to lose the great industrial advantage of cheap labor.

The program of the New Deal would have a lasting influence on the South. Coming into power at a time of acute economic and social crisis, the Roosevelt Administration had the courage to force through a program of reform over the opposition of the centers of political power in the region. And while the program fell short in many ways of what the southern situation called for, yet it manifested a profound concern for the needs of the mass of the underprivileged, white and Negro alike. The New Deal program reached a peak in 1938 and then seemed to slacken its efforts. Perhaps it was merely pausing to regroup for a final push. Had it made the drive, it might have accomplished much more than it did to equalize the economic and cultural opportunities of southerners with those in other sections. But the Second World War came, and the efforts of the administration were turned to the survival, first of Great Britain, and then of the nation itself. But the reforms of the New Deal left a heritage that the nation would not forget, and which progressives would not let southerners forget.

⚹ XI ⚹

The South in the Electrical Age

Basic to the growth of the New South has been the generous use of the region's various sources of power. Since 1920 the South has seen its demands for industrial and domestic energy grow beyond anything that could have been imagined at the beginning of the period. Not only has marked industrial expansion created demands for development of cheap power sources; universal domestic use has also done so. There can be little doubt that production of plentiful electrical energy ushered in a new age of southern growth, and led to new approaches in all sorts of southern problems.

Use of water power to develop industrial energy dates from the beginning of English civilization in the South. By 1634 two water mills were operating in Virginia. Soon after, other mill wheels appeared, powered by the currents of the rivers James, Cape Fear, Savannah, and along the myriad creeks and smaller rivers of the tidwater. Almost the first structure built after the cabins themselves was the community mill. The farther settlers penetrated into the lower piedmont, the more power sites they developed along the headstreams of the eastern rivers.

Beyond the Appalachians, water mills, utilizing strong stream currents, ground rich harvests of grain, sawed lumber, turned lathes, and textile machines. In Kentucky, and especially in the rich central Bluegrass, water mills converted mountains of grain into meal and flour for the rich New Orleans trade.

The streams of the South have been almost as important historically for creating power as they have been as internal channels of transportation. Pioneers moving westward quickly adopted the crude flatboat to transport families and goods, and then to haul bulky produce to market. After 1811 the steamboat not only increased the volume of river-borne freight but made the rivers much more efficient channels for two-way trade.

Six years after the Civil War the South produced 185,188 units as horsepower by water, and this figure was rapidly expanded, especially in the piedmont of the Carolinas and Virginia where the textile industry was being organized. Every decade afterwards was to see marked growth. But down to 1920 electricity was little more than a novelty for much of the South; it was mainly used for illumination. Steam dominated power in these years, and the Appalachian mines provided cheap coal for this power.

The first steam-generating plant was built in the United States by the Edison Company in 1882. That same year a hydroelectric plant was placed in operation at Appleton, Wisconsin. Five years later electrically driven streetcars were operating in Binghamton, New York; New York City; and Richmond, Virginia. It was not until 1904, however, that a significant amount of electricity was generated in the South. Interestingly, it was James B. Duke of the great American Tobacco Trust who was to become the pioneer entrepreneur of the electrical generating industry. In 1896, M. C. Whitener had attempted to generate and distribute electricity from a small plant on the Catawba River in South Carolina. This stream, with its rocky rapids and heavy volume flow, challenged the pioneers of hydroelectricity. There are at present ten major power sites within the 220-mile stretch of this piedmont stream. From Lake James near East Marion, North Carolina, to the Wateree Basin near Camden, South Carolina, there is a drop of 1056 feet. Along this heartland river were located many of the major cotton mills of the New South. Within its basin are also the towns of Marion, Hickory, Newton, Gastonia, and Charlotte in North Carolina, and Rock Hill, Fort Mill, Lancaster, Chester, Great Falls, and Camden in South Carolina.

In 1904 Duke had just seen his vast tobacco empire dismembered by Supreme Court decree. He seemed bored and perhaps disenchanted with the highly competitive tobacco industry he had helped create. That year he suffered from a mild case of erysipelas and was kept at home nursing a painful foot. His physician, Dr. W. Gill Wylie,

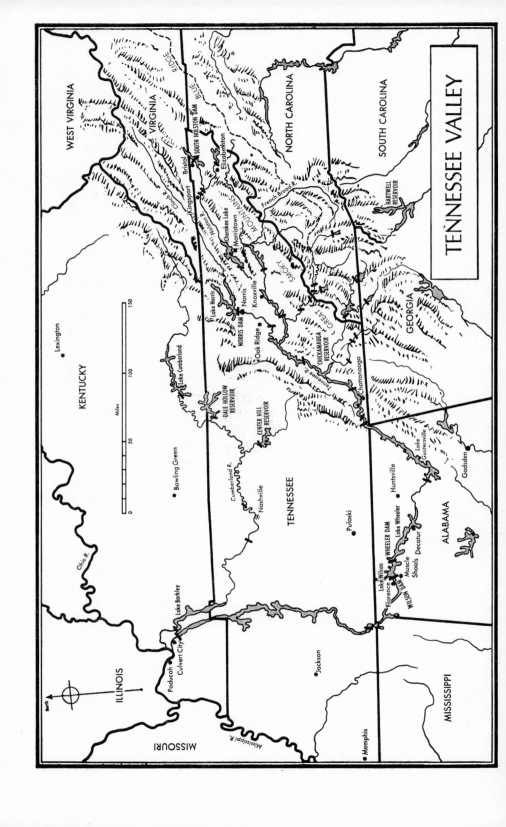

TENNESSEE VALLEY

seemed as much interested in the generation of electricity as in the practice of medicine. He had invested in a small generating plant on the Wateree River at the Great Falls in South Carolina, and was enthusiastic about the promise of this new southern industry. Duke himself had made a small investment in a plant in South Carolina with most unsatisfactory results, but Dr. Wylie's enthusiasm stirred his interest anew. He knew a young engineer, W. S. Lee, who had shown promise in the field of hydroelectrical engineering. Lee was invited to New Jersey to discuss the possibilities of the Wateree-Catawba Basin with Duke. The ailing industrialist questioned young Lee at length and was impressed with his knowledge and zeal. Lee was told to make a preliminary survey of the Catawba and to estimate what it would cost to develop a hydroelectric industry. Offhand, Lee estimated it would cost $8 million, and he was sent home with $100,000 to finance his initial survey.

In June 1905 the Southern Power and Light Company was organized. It absorbed the Catawba Power Company and its 10,000-horsepower generating plant at Indian Head Shoals. A dam and a generating plant were begun immediately at Great Falls, where the Wateree was blocked just below the confluence of that stream and the Catawba. Between 1905 and 1925 a series of dams and generating plants were constructed along the Catawba between the Great Falls and the Bridgewater empoundment. By 1927 the Southern Power Company was generating approximately 900,000 horsepower, and had 3500 miles of transmission and distribution lines. This was the beginning of large-scale generation and transmission of electricity in the South.

Following the initial development of the Duke and Southern Power interests in the Catawba-Wateree Basin, electrical utility companies were formed in all of the other southern states. These ranged from systems like that in Georgia, which covered the whole state, to smaller plants such as the Memphis Power and Light and Louisville Gas and Electric, which distributed current within highly restricted areas. Up until 1920, however, the industry was far more impressive in its corporate structure than in actual generation and distribution of electricity. The companies were still pioneering. All of these state corporations made some effort to develop local waterpower potentials. In Kentucky the Kentucky Utilities Company, a subsidiary of the Insull empire, constructed a dam across the turbulent limestone-entrapped Dix River and began the first hydroelectric generation in that state. At the Falls of the Ohio the Louisville Gas and Electric Company constructed a plant to exploit the unharnessed power of that site. In South Carolina the South Carolina Gas and Electric Company dammed the blood-red Broad River at Par Shoals, and the Saluda just above Columbia to form Lake Murray, one of the first of the big artificial lakes in the South. Along the Tugaloo, Tallulah, Coosa, Tallassee, and Chattahoochee in Alabama and Georgia, dams fed power to power systems. The development of these latter sites brought about the organization of the piedmont transmission complex, which facilitated broad-scale distribution of electricity all the way from southern Alabama to North Carolina. By 1930 the southern power companies were playing an important role in developing southern industry and were becoming a force to be reckoned with in southern politics. They virtually held within their grasps the economic future of the South.

There grew out of World War I a practical and philosophical conflict over whether government should enter the electrical power production field. Actually, arguments had arisen the moment the first individual had suggested use of public funds for internal improvements. Framers of the Constitution had reckoned with government responsibility for rivers, harbors, and post roads, but in practice the involvement of the Federal Government in these areas depended largely upon the personal attitudes of Presidents, and of forces within the Congress.

The history of internal improvements in the Tennessee Valley was almost as long as was that of the United States as a whole. The navigation of Muscle Shoals by commercial craft was a subject of endless discussion almost from the date of the famous Donelson expedition, even after the construction in later years of a railroad. With the advent of the age of electricity, the Muscle Shoals site took on new importance. In 1916 Congress took the first step toward the development of the public generation of electricity in the Tennessee Valley. This was not, however, the first time Congress had noticed the potential of the Tennessee River. In 1899 a franchise was granted the Muscle Shoals Corporation, but the company allowed its franchise to lapse without constructing a generating facility. In 1903 Congress again attempted to grant a private company a franchise, but President Theodore Roosevelt vetoed the bill. In 1906, however, he approved a blanket bill proposing the construction of a dam cross the Tennessee for the generation of electric power. Again the franchise was allowed to lapse. Three facts no doubt accounted for these early failures. First, Muscle Shoals was a most difficult place for a private company with limited engineering skill and capital resources to operate; second, the seasonal flooding of the area threatened a power installation with destruction; and finally, there was the problem of managing transportation through any barrier constructed on the river.

Congressional action in 1916 was stimulated not so much by the demand for electrical power as by the pressing need for nitrogen for munitions and agriculture. By the end of the war in 1918 the United States government had spent $17 million in the construction of the still-unfinished Wilson Dam near Sheffield-Tuscumbia in Alabama. Some $90 million had been invested in the construction of two nitrate plants, two steam plants, a quarry, a large block of land, a workers' village, a stock of platinum, and other properties. With the stimulus of war removed, there was no pressure to complete the facilities either of the dam or the nitrate plants. There were also grave doubts whether the equipment in the first nitrate plant was safe or practical to operate. Thus the government had on its hands a very expensive piece of property with no plans for its future development and use.

Between 1918 and 1933, Wilson Dam and its associated properties about Muscle Shoals became the source of great public discussion and concern. In this period 138 pieces of legislation were proposed dealing with the disposition of the expensive government properties in the Tennessee Valley. In 1921 Henry Ford offered $5 million for the $107 million worth of public properties. He would purchase these in fee simple. Ford would complete Wilson Dam, but at public expense, and then lease it for a hundred years for an annual payment, the total of which would be less than the initial expenditure of $17 million for Wilson Dam alone. Under Ford's management there would be almost no guarantee that the Muscle Shoals site would yield the public any distinct benefit despite its enormous public investment. Congress failed to accept the Ford offer, even though there was strong support for it.

In 1922 the Alabama Power Company bid $5 million for the Muscle Shoals properties, and offered to complete Wilson Dam. It would not, however, undertake to manufacture fertilizer. Congress also rejected this offer. Then a combination of the Alabama Power Company, the Tennessee Electric Power Company, and the Memphis Power and Light Company offered to purchase most of the properties, and to build Wheeler Dam higher up the river at public expense, or the companies would build the dam and charge a third of its cost to transportation. A special arrangement was proposed by which chemical fertilizer would be produced. Again in 1926 the companies renewed their offer with some revision of agreements, largely concerning the manufacture of fertilizer.

A commercial fertilizer manufacturer came forward with an offer to lease the Shoals property for fifty years. The offer provided for no risk and for acquisition at the end of the period of $125 million worth of public property. Again the offer was refused by Congress. Yet there still prevailed strong sentiment among the public and in Congress to sell Muscle Shoals and Wilson Dam to Ford. In the meantime Senator George Norris of Nebraska undertook to get legislation passed that would not only retain the properties in public hands but extend the development of other sites to the whole Tennessee River Valley. The government would produce low-cost chemical fertilizers, and the Army Engineers would complete Wilson Dam.

Three factions arose in Congress, and conflict among them prevented legislative action that would have settled the issue in the public interest. There were those who wished to sell outright Wilson Dam and the fertilizer projects to Henry Ford at only a token amount of their cost and value. There were some who were swayed by the power lobby and who wished to gain possession of these valuable properties for them. There was a small group which favored continuing public control and extension of development within the Valley. As early as 1921 a bill named after Secretary of War Newton D. Baker, who recommended it, was drafted, providing for government operation of the Muscle Shoals installations. Senator Norris introduced his first bill in 1922. Passed by Congress, it was vetoed by President Calvin Coolidge for no stated reason. Subsequently Norris introduced other bills in 1924, 1926, 1927, and 1928. President Herbert Hoover vetoed the last bill with a decisive statement of opposition to government participation in industry. Central purposes of the Norris bills were completion of Wilson Dam, operation of the nitrate plants by the Department of Agriculture, and the creation of a public power corporation to dispose of electrical current. The Norris bill of 1928 proposed a far more extensive development of the Tennessee River system than had the earlier ones.

Between 1918 and 1930 the South experienced several economic and social shocks which placed an altogether different emphasis on the future public control of the Tennessee River and its 80,000-mile watershed. There were recurring floods, especially the devastating one of 1927 which did heavy damage in both the Tennessee and lower Mississippi valleys. In addition, the entire central South had suffered a serious economic setback because of the post-World War I recession and the cessation of work on Wilson Dam.

In the broader area of southern economy, farm tenantry ran a wild course after 1918. By no means was this a new southern problem, but it became more acute in the 1920's. Inseparably linked to tenantry and general economic failure were soil abuse and exhaustion. For almost a century these problems had been discussed both by farmers and their critics. Statisticians had on many occasions published estimates of soil losses from water erosion. In 1909 W. W. Ashe said in an article in the *Review of Reviews* that "there are in the dissected upland areas of the South more than 500 million cultivated acres now all idle." Soil exhaustion, which came from leaching of the elements and erosion, was to blame. It was said 50 million tons of earth a year were borne away from upland southern farms, and that the Tennessee River alone carried away 11 million tons. The geographer J. Russell Smith estimated that between 1880 and 1929 the southern cotton belt lost by erosion an area as large as Belgium.

No area of the South was more exposed to potential loss of its soils than the Tennessee Valley. Slopes about its headwaters were excessively steep, rainfall was heavy, torrential waters tore away the soil, and farmers and lumbermen continued to clear away the soil-protecting forests. Cultivated fields were left exposed without soil-retaining cover crops. During the crusading years of Gifford Pinchot and Theodore Roosevelt in the first decade of the century, there were indications of a desire for positive public action in the region.

In 1933 Congress finally passed the Tennessee Valley Authority Act, the purposes which were the full development and conservation of the resources of the Valley. The basic aim of the Authority was the development of power sites along the Tennessee and its tributaries.

The act, however, set forth specific objectives: improve the navigation channel, control floods, promote reforestation, reclaim and redirect use of marginal lands, further the agricultural and industrial development of the Valley, provide for the national defense by the operation of properties at and near Muscle Shoals, and generate electrical power.[1]

The T.V.A. reflected both the new social-welfare of the times and traditional institutional approaches and social attitudes. Fertilizer was to be manufactured largely for the use of the people and agricultural institutions of the Valley. Power was to be generated primarily "for the benefit of the people of the section as a whole and particularly the domestic and rural customers to whom the power can be made available, and accordingly that sale to and use by industry shall be a secondary purpose, to be used principally to secure sufficiently high load factors and revenue returns which will permit domestic and rural use at the lowest possible rates and in such manner as to encourage increased domestic and rural use of electricity."

Executive powers of the Tennessee Valley Authority were concentrated in a corporate board to be comprised of members "who profess a belief in the feasibility and wisdom of this act." This meant in practice a directorate of three members with one acting as chairman of the board. The act contained a broad ultimatum to the board of directors to approach the problems of the Tennessee Valley and its people with a broad unity of purpose, and they were granted a wide range of power to accomplish its objectives. The Tennessee Valley Authority was by no means the first government agency to be created with a unity of purpose or with so clear-cut authority to act, but it was the first public agency ever created to operate so clearly and extensively in the social lives of a people and in their economic institutions.

The T.V.A. was in large measure the realization of past efforts to secure substantial government support for internal improvements. Certainly no governmental agency in history had been given so com-

---

(1) The purposes of the Act were summarized in Section 213. "for the especial purpose of bringing about in said Tennessee drainage basin and adjoining territory . . . (1) maximum amount of flood control; (2) the maximum development . . . for navigation purposes; (3) the maximum generation of electric power consistent with flood control and navigation; (4) the proper use of marginal lands; (5) the proper method of reforestation . . . and (6) the economic and social well-being of the people living in said river basin." To this was added a seventh purpose. Defense.

plete a mandate to serve so broad a purpose in so precisely defined a region. The people of the Tennessee Valley were in need of strong central leadership and expert planning. Large areas of the great valley were caught in the pinions of economic and social depression if not abject poverty. At the same time the more promising industrial areas were unable to develop properly. Fortunately, no insuperable physical barriers lay across the Tennessee River, nor had any of its headstreams been blocked so as to complicate the drafting of a unified plan of area development all the way from the crest of the Great Smokies to the Ohio River at Paducah, Kentucky.

The central force in the Valley was the main stream of the Tennessee itself, which extended around a vast 650-mile elbow from just above Knoxville to the Ohio by way of Chattanooga, northern Alabama, western Tennessee, and across the western end of Kentucky. There were five major headstream tributaries—the French Broad, Holston, Hiawassee, Little Tennessee, and Clinch. These drained parts of Virginia, North Carolina, Georgia, Alabama, Mississippi, Kentucky, and almost all of Tennessee. In 1933 there were approximately three million people in the specific Valley area, and approximately four and one-half million in the larger territory affected by its development. The drainage system encompassed about 41,000 square miles, an area approximately equivalent in size to Kentucky. In the area were 255 million acres of land, more than half of it under forest cover. There was a tremendous yearly rainfall over the whole valley, but it fell in an erratic pattern. It ranged from ninety-three inches near Highlands, North Carolina, to thirty-seven inches near Asheville. On the average fifty-two inches fell annually in the area, with the heaviest downpours coming between December and May. The Tennessee River has the fifth highest waterflow volume of the rivers of the United States, being outranked only by the Mississippi, Ohio, Columbia, and Missouri.

Historically the Valley was directly in the path of the early western frontier expansion. Such historic places as the Watauga Settlements, Sycamore Shoals (where Richard Henderson and the members of the Transylvania Land Company negotiated the treaty of cession with the Cherokee Indians), Bean's Station, Fort Loudon, and Brainerd's Mission. The river itself was on the route of pioneers moving from eastern to middle Tennessee and the Cumberland Valley, and down to the rich cotton lands of northern Alabama. During the past century and a half there had developed along the headstreams an isolated Appalachian society of Americans whom some sociologists called contemporary ancestors. There survived among these people many folk customs, manners, economic practices, and attitudes which were more attuned to the seventeenth and eighteenth centuries than to the harsh twentieth in which they lived. Culture patterns such as those described by Mary Noailles Murfree, Horace Kephart, John C. Campbell, and scores of casual travelers who visited the region still prevailed in places in 1933.

Agriculture was the dominant economic interest. The farming pattern ranged from the barest mountain patch subsistence cultivation to the huge cotton plantations of northern Alabama and western Tennessee. The general social and economic patterns, however, were influenced largely by yeoman farmers who dredged the land for a living and who supplemented farm incomes with small-scale lumbering. Throughout the valley "peckerwood" sawmills had for generations gnawed away at the virgin forests until most of the virgin timber of top quality had been squandered. But in many isolated and land-locked parts of the steeper mountainous areas, stands of virgin timber could still be found. Poplars reached upwards a hundred feet or more to get above cliff tops to find sunlight. Walnut, oak, maple, buckeye, and chestnut filled the isolated coves, and stood guardian over the flat shoulders of the cliff breaks. Conversely the rock-ladened domes rolled out in fixed waves of scrawny growth which could never do more than survive and hold back the torrents of rain which swept them. Man still had the frontiersman's attitude toward woods; they were there to be cut down and gnawed to pieces with little or no thought of the future. Almost no reforestation had been done before 1933, and forest management in the South was still something only rich men like George Vanderbilt practiced.

The Tennessee Valley was dotted with dust-ladened and tobacco-stained villages which grouped themselves about dreary courthouses in hill counties, or mud-splattered palaces of justice in the lowlands. The most significant urban centers were Knoxville and Chattanooga. About the headwaters of the Holston, Clinch, and French Broad were Kingsport, Elizabethton, Bristol, Johnson City, and Asheville, Downstream were the old cotton towns of Huntsville, Decatur, Tuscumbia,

Florence, and Savannah, and in Kentucky the old river town of Paducah. These places were caught in economic crisis with the failures of the old cotton and tobacco systems, and, in the case of Decatur, the reorganization of the mechanical division of the Louisville and Nashville Railroad. Paducah was largely a sleepy Ohio River town which served a fairly large agricultural back country of the Purchase region of Kentucky.

Perhaps no other part of the United States had a more homogenous population. The people of the Valley were descended largely from the old population stock which first crossed the mountains. Remarkably little immigration had penetrated the region in the latter part of the nineteenth century. The region had common mores, and attachment to the land ran deep. Although a rather heavy migration of common laborers had drifted away to the rising industrial centers to the north of the Ohio in the 1920's, there was a general return home of the unemployed after 1929. In the Valley they felt that in times of panic they could at least dredge a bare subsistence from the soil. Like the Cherokees before them they buried their ancestors in the Valley, and they had built their churches and their poor little schools there. They had sprinkled their towns and crossroads villages, had raised court-houses to symbolize the law, and jails to lock up the incorrigibles in the Valley.

In one act Congress affected more deeply than ever before the grass-roots feelings, the spiritual ties with the land, and the prejudices and anger of the region's people. For thousands it meant complete dislocation from their historic place on the land.

Passage of the T.V.A. Act also brought the United States government squarely into conflict with the private power companies, who were little more than pioneers themselves, feeling their way timidly within municipal limits, and thickly settled suburban areas. They still had not supplied a Valley industry with a satisfactory quantity of power, and the promise of the future was a cautious one at best. Chief of the private interests were the Commonwealth and Southern, the Georgia, Alabama, and Tennessee power companies, the Kentucky Utilities Company, and the Memphis Power and Light Company. The projected Tennessee Valley Authority was to operate in the heartland of most of these organizations, and resistance was strong. Supporters of the program had to carry on a vigorous publicity campaign to secure favor for the government project and to let the public know how much was involved in the enormous undertaking. In Chattanooga, for instance, the *News* was militantly in favor of the government's entering the field of generating electrical power and carrying on the other functions outlined in the Norris Act, while the *Times* was cautious almost to the point of opposition, and the *Free Press* was actively opposed. In Kentucky the *Courier-Journal* supported the project, while the Knoxville papers had mixed emotions.

The bitterest critics branded the Tennessee Valley Authority a long step toward total socialism. Washington would become master of affairs in the Valley, and orders and directives from that source would direct the course of the lives of the people. Private industry would be driven out of existence, and investments would be nullified. Localities would be robbed of taxes, and institutions such as schools and hospitals would be starved for lack of support, or they would be so regimented that there would be little freedom left. Because the legislation of 1933 virtually made the Tennessee Valley Authority a monopoly in the field of generation and sale of hydroelectric power, resistance to it naturally revolved around the subject of power development. This had the effect of obscuring the importance of other aspects of the Authority's responsibilities. Controversy centered on the application of the "yardstick" gauge to ascertain what it actually cost to produce and distribute electric current. In its public relations, in its press releases, in official speeches, and in private conservations with people in and out of the Tennessee Valley, the Authority seemed to place its greatest emphasis upon the benefits of cheap power distributed over a widely dispersed transmission system. This concept naturally all but blinded the great masses of people to the larger purposes of the project. Even those who were immediately endangered by recurring floods thought largely in terms of the availability of electric current. In the final analysis this probably was the least significant aspect of the huge project.

Before the act creating the Tennessee Valley Authority was three months old, it was challenged in the courts. A case was brought in the federal district court which sought to restrict the sale of power generated at Wilson Dam. An attempt was made to forbid the Authority from generating more current than was needed by the fertilizer plants. The navigational and defense provisions of the act were challenged as being designed to divert the Authority from its central purpose of generating competitive hydroelectric power. The district court held for the plaintiffs, but on appeal the Tennessee Valley Authority won in both the circuit court and Supreme Court. The Supreme Court upheld the constitutionality of the Tennessee Valley Authority Act in the Aswander case, which in the more important sense saved the Authority from going the way of other New Deal agencies buried by the Court. In upholding the constitutionality of the Authority the Court validated the whole range of the Authority's activities, even though the complaints and decisions were confined narrowly to the issue of surplus power generation at Wilson Dam

Following the adverse decision in the Aswander case, eighteen power companies brought suit charging that under guise of flood control, navigation, and national defense the United States government was creating a vast power conspiracy. This time Newton D. Baker was chief counsel for the companies, with Wendell Willkie as a spearhead. The circuit court in this case, *The Tennessee Electric Power Company* vs. *The Tennessee Valley Authority*, upheld the Authority on every point. It decided that the Authority was carrying out the flood control, navigation, and power production mandates in good faith. The case was later dismissed by the Supreme Court on the ground that the utility companies had suffered no legal injury and therefore lacked a common basis for suit. The actual constitutionality of the Tennessee Valley Authority Act was conclusively established in 1940 in the Appalachian Power Company case, which did not specifically involve a complaint against the Authority.

Because of the wide implications of the Tennessee Valley Authority Act, the development of the great Valley became a huge task of public relations, research, planning, relocation, and construction. Fortunately the Authority possessed the strength of the government combined with the flexibility of a private corporation. Congress gave the Authority a status distinctly different from that of any other governmental agency. It was responsible to no cabinet officer or agency. It reported directly to the President and Congress, received direct appropriations, had its new projects and extensions of old ones reviewed and approved by Congress. The Authority was allowed to enter directly into contracts, negotiate purchases and settlements for property and damages, sell and buy property, and perform its own construction tasks without being required (as other government projects were) to take competitive bids or employ private contractors. It was authorized to manage its huge personnel problems under its own rules, free of the restrictions of the civil service. Its accounts were subject to audit by the General Accounting Office, but that agency had no control over the Authority decisions. But in time the activities of the Tennessee Valley Authority were to be under almost nonstop scrutiny by Congress.

Though the courts had cleared away legal barriers to the operation of the Authority, many details remained to be negotiated before full development of the Valley could get underway. Municipal power distributive agencies had to be setup to insure an outlet for current generated at the dams. State legislation was needed to authorize Tennessee municipalities to form utility corporations, and then to allow referenda in cities prepared to undertake such a venture. In 1935 the citizens of Chattanooga voted, 19,056 to 8096, to organize the Electric Power Board of Chattanooga, and funds were secured from the Public Works Administration to finance the construction of a distributive system of transmission lines.

The biggest issue facing the Authority at the outset was the acquisition of private utility properties. After extensive negotiations the Authority, through negotiations between David Lilienthal and Wendell Willkie, was able to purchase the holdings of the Tennessee Electric Power Company.[2] In accepting the transfer, Lilienthal made the whimsical observation, "This is sure a lot of money for a couple of Indiana farmers to be kicking about." Willkie in reply made an impassioned plea for private enterprise, and condemned the Tennessee Valley Authority as a threat to private utility ownership.

Now that the judicial, legislative, and private barriers were removed, the Authority faced the task of organizing a construction force, completing its detailed surveys, and of building dams. Lilienthal called this task a "seamless web." The authority was fortunate in its first board of directors. Lilienthal, an imaginative lawyer and member of the Wisconsin Public Service Commission, was named chairman. Ar-

(2) On August 15, 1939, formal transfer of the holdings was made in New York City, and the Tennessee Valley Authority and thirty-two municipalities and local co-operatives agreed to pay $78,425,095 to the Tennessee Company, a subsidiary of the Commonwealth and Southern holding company.

thur E. Morgan, an engineer and president of Antioch College, was selected because of his wide experience in hydraulic engineering and flood control. Harcourt A. Morgan, president of the University of Tennessee, was an agricultural specialist with extensive experience in this field within the Valley itself. All three men were tough-minded and aggressive. Supporting these specialists was a small army of geologists, hydrologists, engineers, foresters, agriculturalists, economists, public health experts, cartographers, archaeologists, social workers, and lawyers. The vital facts, human and physical, about the Valley had to be ascertained. Archaeologists were called upon to locate the prehistoric and Indian remains in the region. Crews removed bodies and remains from low-lying cemeteries. Land specialists faced the massive task of relocating families. Public health experts were called upon to determine many facts, the most important of which was the breeding habits of the mosquito *Anopheles quadrimaculates,* so that malarial fever could be wiped out. Resource specialists had to take a comprehensive look at the region as a whole. It was one thing to speak of these matters in more or less sweeping generalities in a Congressional act, and quite another to determine the facts on the ground. Perhaps no problem was greater than the psychological and emotional one of removing people from the land. At times it was difficult to reconcile the great humanitarian objectives of the Authority with the uprooting of people. The people in the Tennessee Valley were removed from their homesteads where they and their forebears had lived for generations. Homes, barns, schools and churches, had to be given up, thousands of sentimental landmarks erased. Most important of all, perhaps, hundreds of farm families looked out over fertile stretches of bottom lands which had supported them over the years and felt that the removal was a sin against nature. Roads, railroads, telegraph and telephone lines had to be relocated. Bridges had to be abandoned or elevated above flood level.

In larger measure the main challenge was to co-ordinate the Tennessee River and its tributaries into a unified and responsive operating system. This problem was made more complex by the need for navigational management, flood control, and the efficient generation of electricity. In 1933 Wilson Dam was in existence but incomplete, and Wheeler Dam had been located a short distance upstream. Fortunately no other barriers had been constructed in the region. On October

1, 1933, construction of Norris Dam on the Clinch River was begun. A labor force of 11,000 men had been assembled. Most of them came from the Valley and most were unskilled in the tasks they were undertaking. A system of screening, testing, and registering potential workers was set up to choose the labor force without the political interference and red tape that is all too often associated with civil service. In time this labor force, which ultimately numbered over 200,000, was to build eight major dams on the main stem of the Tennessee and sixteen on the head or lateral streams. In all there are now thirty-two major dams on the waters of the Tennessee, six of which are the properties of private companies.

In the construction of the dams, Authority engineers undertook the largest single construction project in the history of civilization. Into the first twenty dams went 113 million cubic yards of concrete, rock, and earth, or twelve times the volume of materials used in the Egyptian pyramids. The rest of the statistics are equally staggering.[3]

Carrying out flood control and transportation mandates the Authority estimated that as of 1962 its system averted cumulative damages from flooding in the lower Ohio and Mississippi valleys of over $31 million and that the flood crest of the Mississippi and Ohio at Cairo has been lowered by two to four feet. Flood protection at Chattanooga alone, based on the damages of four earlier floods, saved the city $295 million in damages. In 1933 the river carried 32 million ton-miles of gross freight, much of it sand and gravel, and in 1960 it carried 12 million ton-miles of freight of a much higher classification. Since 1933 the river has floated two and one-third billion ton-miles of cargo. In 1961 about a quarter of a million acres of water was used in marine lockage, none of which passed through the power turbines.

Present-day forest resources return half a billion dollars, with prospects for a billion-dollar return by 1975. In the area of Valley agriculture phenomenal changes have occurred. Some of these are reflected in more intelligent land usage, the availability of higher grade

(3) The reservoirs created by the dams cover 604,460,000 full pool acres, and there is a 10,492-mile shoreline. The shoreline of Kentucky Lake alone would extend from Chicago to Los Angeles. At full-gate stage of elevation the surface of the watered areas amounts to 22,413,260 acres, and at normal operational stage, 14,622,120 acres. By 1965-66 the board of directors estimates there will be a generating capacity of 15,367,860 kilowatts. To date the Tennessee Valley project has cost approximately one and a quarter billion dollars.

chemical fertilizers, the improved knowledge on the part of experiment and extension staffs, the activities of the plant genetics, and a high degree of mechanization on the farm. The Authority has had enormous influence in developing a more productive type of agriculture, and bringing in new approaches to agriculture. Since 1933 the pattern of farming and rural life in the Valley has been greatly altered. Agricultural specialists employed the old scheme of Seaman A. Knapp in reaching the farmers. By use of demonstration farms and plots they were able not only to attract the attention of neighboring farmers, but to exercise considerable control over such experiments as land conservation, revision of land usages from row to cover crops, and the conversion from staple crops to hay and livestock and from open fields to forest lands. More than forty-five thousand farmers participated in the demonstration program. As a result, three million acres were removed from traditional forms of cultivation, and a million acres converted to hay production and pasturage by 1960. Income from livestock in the Valley, meager in 1933, was up to $325 million by 1960.

The old southern cotton belt had been victimized by high-priced but low-analysis fertilizer since 1870. Cost of freight alone on this product would have yielded a respectable profit on annual cotton crops. At the same time it is most doubtful that the quality of fertilizers available, or the practice of application, contributed much in the way of increased production. Neither experiment station nor practical farmer had made sufficient progress in fertilizer research. Both agricultural specialist and farmer did know, however, that soils of the South desperately needed nitrogen and phosphorous. Since the creation of the chemical project as Muscle Shoals, the manufacture of adequate fertilizers for the farms of the region had been a matter of prime consideration. In fact, it had been a central fact in much of the proposed legislation between 1920 and 1933. By use of the plot or demonstration farm method, both chemists and soils experts were able to produce adequate chemical contents and formulas to promote maximum production. Between 1933 and 1955 Authority chemical plants produced three and a half million tons of fertilizer, two million tons of phosphates, and one and a half million tons of nitrates.

After thirty years the argument still continues, sometimes with considerable fury, for and against the Tennessee Valley Authority.

The great Valley sprawls out with its blue lakes fingering their way into hundreds of coves. Sand-covered shoulders swarm with fishermen and bathers, and the lakes are criss-crossed by motorboats. Tugboats labor away at shoving long tows up and down the vast reservoirs, and high-tension pylons stake out paths off into the blue haze over half the ridges of the Valley.

The answer to how well the yardstick theory has worked may be irretrievably buried in the mass of electronic economic details and the thousands of pages written for and against it. Domestic rates have been materially reduced in this area, even to as low as a third of the rate in 1933. Before the T.V.A., the domestic consumer was predominantly an urban dweller. It was too expensive to construct transmission lines to the remote farmhouses, and too, there was uncertainty about either the capacity or willingness of this customer to pay his bills. Thus in 1933, in the nation as a whole, there were only 166,000 rural consumers of electricity, and no doubt this number was greatly swelled by New England farmers who lived only short distances away from the sources of current generation in fairly concentrated population areas. Two years after the passage of the Tennessee Valley Authority Act, Congress authorized establishment of the Rural Electrical Authority to serve rural consumers. This authority grew out of an initial attempt to organize a rural co-operative plan for the purchase of T.V.A. current. A meeting was held in the backroom of a furniture store in Corinth, Mississippi, in 1934 to draw up plans for a rural co-operative. In 1935 Congress created the Rural Electrification Authority, largely as a lending agency which would facilitate the organization of co-operatives and the building of transmission lines, private laterals, and the organization of business facilities for the efficient conduct of a utility business. Patrons of this new agency would almost all be small domestic rural consumers. This was the dawning of a new day in the South. In 1930 there was electricity on one farm out of a hundred in Mississippi, one out of thirty-six in Georgia, and one out of twenty-six in Alabama and Tennessee. The situation was much the same in other southern states. In 1936 Howard Odum wrote in *Southern Regions*:

> A greater flow of electricity in the Southeast is, therefore, one way of expansion which can scarcely be questioned. In addition to the rapidly increasing cultural aspects of a developing region in which "electric light

and power has come to be almost as essential as the bread we eat and the water we drink," in the Southeast it is a measuring rod of immediate resources for the increase in industry, large and small, and for *bringing the region up to standards already obtaining* in some other regions. The Southeast, for instance, has less than 5 per cent of its farms electrified as compared with the whole of the Northeast and the Far West with from 30 to 60 per cent.

Several facts account for lack of electrification on Southern farms prior to 1935. Distances from sources of generation to rural consumers were often great, and the supply of electricity generated was limited. There was no credit structure by which construction of either trunk lines or individual farm laterals could be financed on a long-term plan. Farm consumption unfortunately was regarded almost altogether in terms of illumination instead of a rather heavy use of domestic power. Finally, the private utilities focused their attention upon the urban customer and skimmed off the cream of a readily accessible high-revenue market.

Both the preamble and section 10 of the Tennessee Valley Act emphasized the importance of the distribution of electrical current to farmers, and they no doubt anticipated the organization of many electrical co-operatives; as a matter of fact there were several co-operatives involved in the purchase of the Tennessee Power and Light Company. By 1934, 85,000 farms in the seven-state Tennessee Valley area had been electrified.

Elsewhere in the South the Rural Electrification Authority was able to purchase current in wholesale lots from private companies. Every year since 1935 the rural electric lines have continued to be extended until today only the most remote farmhouses are not connected with transmission lines, and only the most poverty-stricken rural family has not produced enough money to purchase current for radio, television, and washing machine. Indeed, the census showed in 1958 that approximately 90 per cent of the farms in the region reporting were supplied with electricity.

The Rural Electrification Authority has raised many issues. One of them is that of competition with private companies. The problem has been intensified by the expansion of suburban communities and a reluctance by co-operatives to relinquish their territory and customers. In some areas they generate their own power and become formidable competitors because they are able to secure financing at a low rate of interest and to produce current at a cheaper rate. A thorny issue is that of taxation. In 1963 the South Carolina Tax Study Commission considered the unfair competitive position of the co-operatives held against the private utilities in the tax field. No doubt the rapid expansion of the suburban population, the unusually successful experience of the co-operatives with rural customers, and the rapidly expanding use of electrically propelled domestic and farm equipment have made this market far more attractive than it was in the one light bulb days of the 1920's.

The availability of relatively cheap electricity has had deep meaning for the modern South. It has had an enormous impact in urban expansion and the standard of living. It has had an equally strong impact on industry. Indeed, the modern industrial South could not exist without this power resource.

Nowhere is the power revolution in the South more clearly reflected than in rural areas. Since 1935, motors have come to do the milking, pump the water, wash the clothes, turn the hay, run the mills of all sorts, irrigate fields, turn woodworking lathes and other machines, and even power "peckerwood" sawmills. This saves human labor and greatly expands the productive and efficiency capacity of the farm and home. But the availability of cheap electricity has also had a real but incalculable psychological and sociological influence on the southern countryman. He has come to view his home in a new perspective. His diet has been vastly improved, his sanitary facilities radically altered, even to the point of virtually eradicating the hookworm and mosquito, and the great barrier of silence between him and the world at large has been breached. Farm homes and countryside have changed greatly in appearance. This has been especially true where community improvement associations have been active.

In the broad field of national security the Tennessee Valley Authority has made vital contributions in supplying electrical energy and transportation facilities to numerous industries. Its most dramatic contribution, however, was the Manhattan Project at Oak Ridge, Tennessee, where research had a large role in the creation of the atom bomb in the closing year of World War II. Later the Redstone Arsenal near Huntsville, Alabama, utilized a large volume of electrical energy in rocket research and the exploration of outer space.

In the enduring conflict between the economic philosophy of the T.V.A. and private utilities there arises the perennial charge of "socialism," or as President Eisenhower phrased it, "creeping socialism." Critics of the Authority cast observations in several forms: the Tennessee Valley Authority is not a tax-paying utility. This criticism has been made despite the return to the states and local governments of payments in lieu of taxes. Conflicts also developed with the individual states over local and corporate taxation. Section 13 of the 1933 T.V.A. act provided for repayments to states and localities of money in lieu of taxes where revenue-bearing property was absorbed into the corporations. A formula was established by which the Authority would make payments against power operations. This principle was in direct contradiction to the traditional exemptions of federal property from local and state taxation in so far as actual payments were concerned. The amount of payments in lieu of taxation was determined, after extended discussion with tax consultants and state officials, and after local values were set. By 1943 the Authority had paid $5,320,000 in tax replacements. In a single year payments approximated $2 million.

There may never be agreement between advocates of public and private control on the meaning of the yardstick or the methods of its application. The T.V.A. can point to the remarkable lowering of rates, especially to rural and big corporate customers, as evidence of the vast extension of the use of electrical power in the region. At the same time fundamental questions were raised about the figures used by the Authority's accountants. By 1948 the federal government had invested $807 million in the Authority in direct appropriations and property transferals. Annual Congressional appropriations for 1949, 1950, and 1951 were estimated at $27 million, $52 million, and $96 million, respectively. Income and net income from power were allocated on the basis of the development of the Tennessee Valley, a fact which took into consideration three or four of the projects that shared in operation and income costs besides power production. Critics of the Authority have said that these rates are based on a tax payment basis of 4.25 per cent, whereas private industry pays 18.7 per cent, and if the federal income tax of 38 per cent were added, the income of the Authority would be drastically reduced.

There can never be agreement as to cost and yield of transportation, flood control, the manufacture of chemical fertilizers, relief from erosion damage, and improved agricultural practices. Private power operations, with emphasis upon profits, never could, nor should, have gone so far as to develop and conserve all the resources of eighty thousand square miles of Valley land, nor could they deal with the "seamless web" of the region. But it is in this sprawling area of social and economic development that critics find their strongest arguments for their charges of socialism.

Proponents of T.V.A. say that the unending needs of the region can only be met by an overall authority with the force of government behind it. Return on the vast federal investment cannot be determined only by dollars; it must also be reckoned in terms of homes and lands saved from floods, of human lives spared the grief of tragedies, of thousands of acres of flourishing new growth of timber and a rising income from proper forest management, improvement of agricultural practices and income, and the increase in industrial income and employment since 1933.

Two southern scholars, Calvin B. Hoover and Benjamin U. Ratchford, expressed the opinion in their study, *Economic Resources and Policies of the South*, that the T.V.A. "has been of real significance and value to the area affected, and to a lesser extent, to other areas." After raising many questions about the Authority's fiscal system they concluded that, "It has promoted industry where it was needed most, and it has raised incomes where they were lowest. It has facilitated a balanced economic development of the area. It has put natural resources to work and helped to conserve and improve soil and forest resources. In all of these respects, it has been a successful experiment."

No doubt it has been all of this. Private industry has increased to a phenomenal degree in the Valley, even in the Appalachians about the headstreams. Almost every town has its new industry. A corporation like the Great Bowater Paper Company located near Calhoun, Tennessee, the Chemstrand plant at Decatur, Alabama, the big chemical plants at Calvert City near Paducah, and the atomic installations at Oak Ridge and Paducah are of enormous importance.

The general Tennessee Valley complex had 150 electric distributors comprised of 97 municipal systems, 51 co-operatives, and 2 private utilities by 1956. Four years earlier its generators had produced 21 billion kilowatt hours. Its productive capacity was 4.5 millon kilowatts, and power was still in short supply. Industry bought approximately

5 billion kilowatt hours in 1945, and approximately 6.5 billion seven
years later. In the gross use of electric power the region used 1.5
billion kilowatt hours in 1933; 11.5 billion in 1945; and 23 billion
in 1952. In 1963 the Tennessee Valley system had an expectancy capacity of over 3 billion kilowatts.

One of the sharpest issues between public and private power generation and sale arose in November 1954 when the Atomic Energy
Commission signed a contract with two private utility companies to
construct a generating plant at West Memphis, Arkansas. This plant
was to cost $107 million and would feed electrical energy into the
Tennessee Valley lines for use of the atomic energy program. This
so-called Dixon-Yates contract stirred a sharp controversy in and out
of Congress. Opponents argued the new facility was not needed since
the steam plants of the T.V.A. were being placed in operation. In
the meantime, the Memphis city commission voted to build its own
generating plant and withdraw from the T.V.A. system, a decision
that weakened both the T.V.A. and the proposed project at West
Memphis. In the meantime the Senate Antimonopoly Committee un-
covered "evidence of fraud" in which vital information had been with-
held from the public, and a conflict of interest issue was raised. Finally
the contract was voided in November 1956. Seven years later the
Memphis city commission voted to rejoin the Tennessee Valley system.

In the South as a whole, by 1963, private utilities had an installed
generating capacity of over 30 billion kilowatts, municipal plants accounted for more than 14.5 billion and public installations for 13 billion.
In 1960 it was estimated that the region still had an underdeveloped
water-power potential of 13.5 billion kilowatts, but this gap was rapidly
being closed by the construction of such dams and reservoirs as those
on the Santee-Cooper rivers, the Barkley Dam on the Cumberland,
and the Clark Hill Dam on the Savannah. The South Carolina Gas
and Electric Company, the Duke Power Company, the Georgia Power
Company, the Mississippi Power Company, and the Kentucky Utilities
Company had greatly expanded their facilities. At the end of World
War II both the private and public companies were making heavy
use of steam generating plants to produce the great bulk of the power
for industry. By the early 1960's the T.V.A. had steam plants in operation throughout its area. The South's first atomic installation is being
jointly planned and operated by the Virginia Power and Light Com-

pany, the Duke Power Company, and the South Carolina Electric and Gas Company at Parr Shoals near Jenkinsville, South Carolina.

Widespread generation and use of electric power has set the modern South apart from its economic past. These forces have wiped out old social and economic barriers and given new perspectives to the people. To a large extent the wide distribution and use of electricity have accounted for many of the modern refinements of southern life.

⨯ XII ⨯

The Tide of Industrial Progress

Just as 1920 marked the end of an agricultural era in the South, 1930 marked the beginning of a new industrial age. Earlier industrial development had been closely synchronized with the region's agriculture and basic resource development, but after 1930 this was not especially true. Manufacturers and capitalists began to expand beyond the traditional lines of industrial growth. Before any economic growth of importance could occur, however, elementary problems of transportation had to be solved.

The South's postwar economic growth was hampered greatly by the condition of its railroads, which had been badly damaged in the Civil War. Unhappily, 1860 was the year when many southern railroads were on the verge of completing construction of their main systems. Approximately ten thousand miles of lines were either seriously disrupted or totally destroyed during the war; those of Georgia, the most highly coordinated of any in the region, were probably the hardest hit. It was not until 1880 that the South again gathered the financial and management momentum to restore and extend its railroads to the point of promise reached in 1860. In this latter year there were 19,051 miles of track in operation, and this was extended annually until 1910, when the total reached 69,718 miles.

Industrial change has been most clearly reflected in the fields of transportation. Population and freight concentrations were widely dispersed, thus involving the building of long stretches of railroads and highways to produce even a minimum amount of freight revenue. Raw materials such as lumber, coal, iron ore, petroleum products, and cotton and tobacco were in the heavy category, but had to be hauled long distances for processing. There was historically a lack of capital with which to finance the building of rail and highways. In the case of railroads both capital and management control came largely from without the region. Finally, there was sore lack of productive and diversified industry to create finished products.

Between 1870 and 1910 the southern railway systems were organized and consolidated. Among the larger ones were the Louisville and Nashville, the Illinois Central, Southern, Chesapeake and Ohio, Atlantic Coastline, Seaboard Airline, Norfolk and Western, Nashville, Chattanooga, and St. Louis, Southern Pacific, Mobile and Ohio, Gulf, Mobile, and Northern, and the Central of Georgia. Unlike the railways of other sections, none of these had serious competition from lines serving the same route. All were built to serve one of two main purposes: connect the Atlantic seaboard with the inland river system, or the Gulf of Mexico with the Ohio and upper Mississippi valleys and the Great Lakes. The reason these roads were extended was to haul heavy goods long distances, and away from the South; they were not thought of as adjuncts to a rising manufacturing industry in the region. Because of the intense rural nature of the South, sparsity of freight concentration, and lack of regional capital stake in the roads the South perhaps suffered some discrimination in the formulation of policies and rates. After 1920 economists and historians attached what now appears to have been undue importance to this issue. Differentials in freight rates may have been important enough to have narrowed the profit margin on raw materials shipped out or brought into the region between the two World Wars. A series of complex rulings by the Interstate Commerce Commission has allowed southern shippers to enjoy equality with those elsewhere in the country, if in fact they were discriminated against. In 1949 Benjamin U. Ratchford and Calvin B. Hoover wrote in their report on the economy of the South for the Joint Committee studying the impact of federal policies on the South:

> First it may be well to discuss one elementary misconception. Some arguments have implied that it was generally cheaper to ship a carload of freight from, say, New York to Atlanta than to ship the same carload from Atlanta to New York, and that this difference existed because of the caprice of evil design of the railroads. In general this is simply not

true. As a general principal freight rates to and from points in the South and elsewhere will be the same. The Interstate Commerce Commission requires that when differences do exist in the rates for movements in different directions these differences must be justified by differences in costs.

The difference in rates has not been presented in its true perspective and its importance has been greatly exaggerated. Most attention has been concentrated on class rates, which have ranged some 28 to 30 per cent higher in the South than in the Northeast. But very little traffic, comparatively, moves on class rates.

Later, in 1951, in their book, *Economic Resources and Policies of the South*, they discussed this subject further, saying:

Thus, while differences in freight rates existed, their importance was greatly exaggerated. Most of the "horrible examples" which had been cited have been rates for commodities of minor importance. Such rates may be obsolete and of no appreciable importance to anybody. If there were any considerable amount of traffic to move on such rates, the roads might well revise them or make new ones; the railroads are interested in developing new business along their lines and are willing to consider new rates when it appears profitable to do so.

By 1910, when railroad building reached its peak in the South, there were approximately seventy thousand miles of trackage in operation; by 1962, however, approximately ten thousand miles had been taken out of operation, half of it abandoned since 1940. A mere statistical analysis gives little idea of the situation as a whole. It is nearly impossible to make a meaningful statement about the precise number of passengers carried by rail, or the total amount of freight hauled annually. It is safe, nevertheless, to say that in this age of automobiles, buses, and airplanes both rail passenger trains and the number of passengers carried have dropped phenomenally.

Southern railroads in 1945 were geared closely to rising industry. Not only did they speed up their trains, but in many instances,—for example, servicing special industries in Atlanta and other key cities which had assembly plants—they synchronized operational schedules with those of industry. In an even more important aspect of operations, old-fashioned freight cars were replaced by cars designed for highly specialized uses to facilitate the movement of both raw materials and finished products. Despite the expansion of highway, river, and air traffic, southern railroads were more important after 1945 than at any time in the past century. Every year saw the development of new points of freight concentration, which went far toward overcoming old obstacles to economic expansion of the earlier agricultural South. In many instances these points of concentration were expanded by co-ordinating highway and rail traffic with "piggy-back" trailer vans, which became increasingly popular.

Though the South was reasonably well served by railroads prior to 1920, the region still had further, urgent need for improved transportation facilities. The southern rivers went largely unused by industry in the years between the end of the old-style packet boats in the 1880's and the introduction of modern, shallow-draft, powerful towboats in the 1920's. It was true that rather large tonnages of coal, iron and aluminum ore, steel, and grain were moved on the rivers, but tonnage was indeed light as compared with what it became after 1940. Development of the long narrow freight-bearing barge and the shallow draft diesel-powered towboat revolutionized river-borne traffic. The Mississippi system carried 88,980 traffic short tons of freight in 1940, 223,950,000 tons in 1959, and 257,962,000 tons in 1962. The Ohio River alone carried nearly 30 million tons in 1940, over 85 million in 1963, and approximately 95 million in 1964. The Tennessee and Cumberland carried approximately 17 million tons in 1962 over the slack water channels created by the hydroelectric dams. There was little romance and no dazzle about the boats of the 1960's as compared with those of a century ago, but they carried more freight than at any time in the history of the rivers. They carried not only coal, aluminum ore, and grain but also automobiles, heavy and bulky construction materials, crude oil, and gasoline. New Orleans, Memphis, Louisville, Nashville, Chattanooga, Mobile, Tuscaloosa, Huntsville, and Ashland, Kentucky, were principal river ports. At Memphis the large President's Island complex alone was constructed as an important adjunct to use of the Mississippi River system.

The mainstay of internal southern transportation, historically and as a future potential, were the highways. No other fact in southern history has been of greater importance than the effort to span distance with the network of roads which would be passable throughout the year. Southern highway history was written largely in mud, dust, and flood waters. In 1900 a traveler crossing most parts of the South underwent an ordeal of physical endurance as taxing as that of making a safari in India or Africa. In 1918 the region had an astonishingly large mileage of roads, but only 13 per cent of these miles were surface, which meant they had been given a coat of sand and gravel. The rest of the roads were deep in mud and dust, were crooked and uncoordinated, and led nowhere. Because of the South's extensive area it was necessary to build long stretches of roads as interstate connectives, and to maintain a staggering mileage of local roads to serve community needs. By 1959 there were 575,761 miles of improved roads in the South, and this meant a vastly increased amount of hard-surfaced all-weather roads; there were 78,628 miles of primary routes. In 1964 Congress made provisions for an additional system of interconnecting roads to be constructed throughout the Appalachian region. Never before had the South been so tightly laced together by efficient overland transportation facilities.

Behind the twentieth-century advances in highway construction was a long and frustrating history of trying to improve overland travel and transportation. One simple statement will summarize the problem: the South was caught in a primitive age in which neither talent nor capital was available to build roads. Between 1865 and 1900 little was actually accomplished by the states and local communities in the building and maintenance of highways. Attempts were made to provide roads by two relatively painless but wholly impracticable and inefficient methods. State legislators attempted to avoid the wrath of tax-shy constituents by creating a system of public roads without a heavy financial burden. Laws provided that all able-bodied men between twenty and sixty years would be "warned out" either to work on the roads or supply an equivalent amount of materials and the use of teams and implements. Under this system laborers employed the same primitive implements to gut and destroy the roads that they used in their eroded cotton fields.

Some parts of the South attempted to avoid the financial burden of maintaining roads by turning their management over to toll companies. These companies were required to build roads and bridges to prescribed, but wholly inadequate, specifications, and to maintain them at certain standards. There was a considerable difference, however, between standards prescribed in instructions and the way they worked out in practice, and both the "warning" and toll practices were failures. Only in counties where demands for roads were pressing were local officials conscientious enough to try to maintain passable roads. Viewed as an entire region, the South in 1890 had made almost no progress in public road administration. Nationally it was not until 1893 that the United States Office of Public Roads was established as a subsidiary of the Department of Agriculture. Following this date, good-roads conventions were held in Richmond, Virginia, and Houston, Texas, and the National Road Parliament in Atlanta.

The first major step in southern highway improvement came when state aid began to be appropriated and highway commissions created. This was done between 1900 and 1917. Public aid was administered by the newly created agencies, but most of them were so severely limited in construction experience that at first they did little more than distribute such literature as they could find on the subject of building and maintaining highways. They resorted largely to demonstration projects in the hope that local highway officials would respond by building better roads. Some of the states made convicts available for road building, a practice still followed in several southern states. Pioneers in this area were Virginia, North Carolina, and Georgia.

Prior to 1920, highway financing faced great difficulties in the South. Actually there were only three sources for taxes available: toll collections, contracting of bonded indebtedness, and direct taxes on property. The sale of highway bonds secured by a collection of special taxes provided revenue in several states and counties. This practice, however, depended upon favorable reactions from voters in several contiguous counties, a condition which was most difficult to achieve. Without the co-operation of several counties, improved roads promised to be nothing more than disconnected links.

While all types of economic pressure ultimately brought about the building of better roads in the South, it was the country editors who first promoted the idea. From 1880 on, they hammered away at the conditions of southern roads. Some of their editorials made local roads appear to be nothing more than muddy trails. At no season of the year could roads be used with any comfort or efficiency, and local editors argued that in this fact lay much of the reason for the South's backwardness. So long as roads were poor it was impossible to organize and operate industrial plants, or to improve towns, farms, or the countryside in general. If the South remained mud-splattered in winter and dust-laden in summer, they said it could expect to be

a poor out-of-the-way section of the nation. Regional highway conferences supplied much of the impetus necessary to stimulate a more
vigorous editorial crusade, and this crusade was maintained even into
the era of the multilane interstate system, which eventually by-passed
the editors and their communities and left them with only broken
town streets to fuss about.

Introduction of the automobile to the South at the turn of this
century placed heavy pressures on states to organize and administer
state highway departments. By 1910 it was clear that more than mere
laws and revenue support were needed to plan and build highways.
At that date there was not a single highway engineer in the South
who had had enough experience to design a modern interconnecting
state or county road, or enough knowledge of even primitive road
machinery or draining and surfacing of roads to construct one. The
only subject in which there was an accumulation of background
knowledge and experience was bridge construction. This had been
gained largely from the building and maintaining of railway bridges.
To a certain extent highway engineers also learned something of the
difference between grading and filling in making a railway grade and
doing the same for a highway.

North Carolina was a pioneer in the enactment of state aid of
highway legislation in 1901, but it was not until 1914 that the state
made a direct appropriation for this purpose, and then only $5000.
In 1918 that state appropriated $20,000, and the following year it took
a long step and appropriated $1,010,443.[1]

Following World War I, the rising use of the automobile and
truck made clear the need for improved highways. No longer was
highway construction associated with pleasure travel and local transportation needs; it had now become clear that good highways were
fundamental to the promotion of industrial and economic expansion.
What the country editors had said for so long in their columns was
now being demonstrated as a fact. Again North Carolina was a pioneer.
In 1921 it issued $50 million in highway bonds to finance the prompt
construction of an inland system of modern roads. This bold step

(1) Funds from all sources in the latter year amounted to $6,717,345. In contrast,
South Carolina appropriated $27,161 from state funds, and it was not until 1917
that a department of highways was organized. By 1919 South Carolina increased
its appropriation to $2,434,774 from all sources, and only Alabama with an
expenditure of $1,812,413 was lower in the South.

was a national sensation and stimulated similar action by other states. Tennessee followed North Carolina's lead and went heavily into debt to build roads, while Virginia adopted a "pay as you go" policy under which it built roads as funds became available, with the result that its highway system was both slow in developing and much less efficient compared to other states. During the 1920's and 1930's state delegations visited Tennessee and North Carolina to see what those states had accomplished. There were prophets of doom who predicted that both states would be sold in bankruptcy at their statehouse doors because no state could contract so large a bonded indebtedness and survive. The prophets proved wrong. In 1956, for example, North Carolina incurred a second obligation of $76 million to finance the construction of 1771 miles of new roads in addition to federal and local funds made available under the Federal Highway Act of 1956.

A boon to southern highway construction was the enactment by Congress on November 9, 1921, of the initial Federal Highway Act, which in time gave both material assistance and encouragement to southern highway construction. The Act made the arterial roads of the South a part of the numbered federal system, and so gave them more than a local or state significance. A heavy increase in both domestic and industrial traffic forced radical changes. In 1914 there were 170,487 motor vehicles of local registry in operation on southern roads; five years later, this number had leaped to 1,130,348; while in 1963 there were 22,044,000, of which 3,813,000 were trucks and buses. By 1919 Texas, with 331,310 motor vehicles, had almost twice as many as the twelve southern states had five years earlier. By 1960 there was great need for multi-lane roads with limited access points, urban by-passes, and the relocation and regrading of many of the older routes. Like the rest of the nation, the South had become a land of highly mobile people dependent upon a flexible system of transportation.

It is impossible for a historian to more than hint at the great changes the motor vehicle has brought to the South. Clearly the old bonds of isolation were destroyed, urbanization and industrialization hastened, and southern labor enabled to live well without having to live right next to factories and mines. The improvement of education was spurred. Even the drive for civil rights was facilitated by access to modern highways. A frightening negative fact, however, was the maiming and killing of people on the roads. In 1919 seven southern cities with populations of 100,000 had 174 fatalities, while in 1962, 12,938 persons were killed on southern highways in twelve states, a figure that represented slightly more than a third of the fatalities in the United States as a whole. In six selected years, 1950 to 1962, 13,375 persons were killed on Georgia and Florida roads alone.

One major benefit of this modern system of highways was the ability of people in the South and from outside the region to move about. Thus the tourist business became one of the South's richest assets. No doubt the South's most enduring and most profitable sources of income were its tourist attractions. These ranged from highly variable natural scenery to old homes, ancient cities, great natural and man-made bodies of water, atomic energy installations such as those at Oak Ridge, Tennessee, and Paducah, Kentucky, and the missile and space flight activities at Redstone Arsenal in northern Alabama and at Cape Kennedy in Florida. Most of the region has a beneficial climate the year round a major attraction for tourists. The Gulf and lower Atlantic coasts draw visitors during the winter, and the upper Atlantic coasts and bay coasts during the summer. The sprawling Appalachians and their valleys and national parks and forests give a taste at least of the American wilderness. Because of early spring seasons in the lower South, gardens from Mobile to the James River attract vast numbers of visitors.

It is difficult if not impossible to separate the casual tourist driving through the South on a sightseeing trip from those seeking the more active forms of recreation offered by gulf, lake, and mountains. Creation of large artificial lakes in the South since 1930 added immeasurably to southern outlets for recreation. Income from both tourists and sportsmen increase phenomenally. It is safe to guess that today the income from these sources brings the South at least two and a half billion dollars. In some states the tourist income has equaled or exceeded that from major crops and livestock sales. It is impossible to gauge the actual income from tourism, since state promotional agencies inflate reports on the amount of money coming in. Tourist expenditures involve far more than the purchase of lodging, meals, gasoline, and services. Manufacturers, farmers, merchants, and scores of service, professional and business people also profit from the trade.

By mid-twentieth century tourism and recreation had become a central business activity in many parts of the South. Everywhere people were engaged in organizing and directing folk and historical pageants, developing natural spectacles, digging up relics of all sorts with which to stock local museums; they even organized western types of gunfights and gold-rush villages. It was somewhat incongruous to drive through western North Carolina, for instance, and see huge bill-boards advertising daily gun fights, and picturing western type gun-men "shooting it out." Yankees coming South could not say positively that they had been around the region until their automobile bumpers were plastered with stickers proclaiming the wonders of Rock City, The Old Jail, Maggie Valley, Silver Springs, Natural Bridge, and the Tweetsie Railroad.

Lakes created by power dams were quickly rimmed with cottages and boat docks. Chambers of commerce in towns about the lakes posted signs along main roads indicating access side roads. Boat and sporting goods merchants hailed the opening of lake recreational areas with more enthusiasm perhaps than they would have greeted the building of a new city. Restaurants peddling their peculiar brands of southern cooking and motels all but obscured the scenery which they so often advertised as their main attractions. Added to this was the fact that by now the South had recovered if not more than recovered, the cost of the Civil War from tourist visits to the battlefields. It was fortunate, in a grim sort of way, that since the Civil War had to be fought, its battles occurred mostly in the South. Battlefields have proved durable attractions; many are maintained as historic sites by the Department of the Interior.

Since 1930 recreational income has rapidly become a vital factor in the southern economy. One indication of this is the expensive pro-motion campaigns carried on by special divisions within state govern-ments. In 1955 the Florida budget for promoting the state's tourist attractions was $450,000 alone, and it was predicted that each dollar spent would return $125 within a year. Tons of expensive colored leaflets, booklets, guides, and glossy photographs were distributed to periodicals and visitors with the expectation of rich returns. Modern southerners hoped to seduce tourists where as their forebears in the late 1860's and 1870's had spent their capital on the printing of volumes of statistics, booklets, and leaflets to attract immigrants to their region.

The South's involvement in recreation goes far beyond mere tour-ism and individual recreation. School and "professional" college ath-

letics became big business as early as 1925. The annual income from
spectator sports ran into hundreds of millions of dollars. The development of a successful football team in a southern university city was
worth nearly as much to local businesses as a good tobacco crop or
a successful livestock industry. Again no one could be specific about
the amounts of income derived from this source, but the amount was
high, even judged in terms of that received and expended by college
athletic departments alone. A star quarterback and a good end were
worth almost as much in income to a southern community as a small
shoe factory, or a chemical plant. Thus it was that businessmen were
quick to patronize local athletic teams, for it has proved to be good
business for them.

Improved transportation facilities and the campaign to bring tourists South are only two parts of the rapidly changing twentieth-century
South. No doubt a more lasting and fundamental change has resulted
from the location of new industrial plants in the region. Since 1920
southerners have carried on campaigns to modernize economic procedures. Inducements of all sorts have been offered to management to
bring new plants to the South, including abundant resources and a
large body of unorganized, compliant labor. This drive actually involved more than merely tempting management to bring plants and
working capital into the South; it meant a complete reversal of economic direction. The region faced a major challenge in its attempt to
bring its average income level up to that of the rest of the nation. In
1930 individual incomes would have needed to be advanced 100 per cent
to accomplish this objective, in 1950 it required a 50 per cent adjustment, and in 1964 approximately 29 per cent. The southern per capita
average in 1964 was $1179 as compared with a national average of $2366.
even with that much improvement, nine southern states still ranked at
the bottom of the fifty states in average personal income. The average
could only be raised to the national level by increasing the industrialization of the region. No longer could the great mass of southern people
look to agriculture for employment; mechanization of farming was
driving hundreds of thousands of people away from the land and
into towns to seek other forms of employment.

There remained the question of what type of new industries would
be brought into the region. Would they be the kind that would create
slums and sweatshops or the type that would require heavy expendi-

tures in plants, machinery installation, and materials? The South had already invested heavily in the textile and extractive industries, and both of these had spawned neighborhoods of sub-standard quality where social and cultural attainments were extremely low as compared with industrial communities elsewhere. To profit from the addition of new industries, the South would have to raise not only the average personal income but also the quality of life industry would produce. Strikes and other forms of labor unrest in the coal and textile industries during the late 1920's and 1930's were convincing proof that poor communities could be festering sores of revolt and violence.

In the South depression and agricultural revolution occurred almost simultaneously. There was no question as to whether or not the South would choose between agriculture or industry; that choice was made for it at a national level. After 1933, with the development of the Tennessee Valley Authority and the expansion of private utilities, a sufficient amount of relatively cheap electrical current was made available, and the conservation of water provided an ample supply of that most precious of all southern resources.

A major southern asset was the region's people. There was growing awareness of the need to train workers for the new industries. Chemists, physicists, engineers of all kinds, and well-trained graduates of schools of business administration were in brisk demand. No longer were major industries in the United States willing, like the old coal mining and textile ones, to undertake the production of materials and services with illiterate and inefficient labor. As more sophisticated machinery was introduced into the manufacturing process, there was greater demand for operators with training and good educational background. But the quality of southern labor left much to be desired, as indicated by the region's high rate of draft rejections for reasons of educational deficiency. Every attempt of southerners to call attention to these deficiencies in order to bring about improvement of the schools worked against its campaign to attract new industries by emphasizing even more strongly the region's shortcomings.

No one in the South, unless he were completely oblivious to changing conditions about him, could have been unaware that the region's unsettled race problem was a distinct economic liability, especially after 1940. Gunnar Myrdal's *An American Dilemma* was eloquent on this subject, as were *What the Negro Wants* (edited by Rayford W. Logan), L. H. Foster's *Race Relations Report*, W. J.

Cash's *Mind of the South*, and numerous other books and special reports. It was what the Durham Manifesto and Principle of 1942 tried to say. Finally *Brown vs. Topeka School Board* and subsequent Court decisions pertaining to Negro education made clear that in the new industrial South a part of the population could not be left untrained and unprepared and still expect it to be productive in modern America. In August 1965, the Columbia (South Carolina) *Record* quoted that state's attorney general, Daniel McCleod, as saying to the Rotary Club of Manning: "Before the court in 1954, the state of South Carolina was forced to admit that Negro school facilities, although indeed separate, had not been kept equal and were in fact inferior to those enjoyed by white students." Governor James Byrnes of that state said in his inaugural address on January 16, 1951, that, "To meet this situation we are forced to do now what we should have been doing for the past fifty years. It is our duty to provide for the races substantial equality in school facilities. We should do it because it is right. For me that is sufficient reason." Governor Byrnes knew that such a policy was basic to industrial expansion. Stories of lynching, of Ku Klux Klan activities, and of other regional and racial disturbances all made it more difficult to bring new industry into the South. Upheavals in Little Rock, Birmingham, Montgomery, Tuscaloosa, Oxford, and New Orleans had an adverse effect on industrial expansion in those areas. Chambers of commerce in Birmingham, Little Rock, and Jackson made their attitudes clear on this point. These disturbances were of sufficient economic importance to receive generous coverage in the *Wall Street Journal* and other financial and industrial publications.

Even more important, these conditions meant that virtually a third of the southern population was denied an opportunity to prepare itself fully to function productively in a new industrial society. Emotions were so badly stirred after 1954 in parts of the South that large segments of the population either did not calm down long enough to reckon the damages wrought by extremists or they simply did not want to consider the high cost to the South of illiberal racial attitudes.

Almost as costly as racial unrest was faulty political organization and administrative leadership. In some states industrial management felt reassured that it would not be subjected to difficulties in its relations with government. It was not always so; every southern state constitution contained much red tape and legal difficulties for new industries. The dead hand of Populism still rested upon the region in these outmoded constitutions. Southern political leadership itself was subjected to enormous local pressures, and there could be little assurances that it would not in turn put pressures on industries. As McLaughlin and Robock (1949) said, "Among the concerns covered all were interested in costs and efficiency of local government." Often there was a vast gulf between what departments of economic development and state chambers of commerce said about industrial possibilities in a state and what industrial firms discovered when it came time to deal with local and state officials. The political slush fund and campaign solicitations, so much a part of the old agrarian-oriented political system, contained a decided element of hazard for an industrial one. Management could easily find itself in the middle of contending political forces and suffer from both of them. In addition, it was virtually impossible at times to persuade rural voters and legislators to enact laws favorable to modern industry in the fields of taxation, highway use, lowered trade barriers, ownership of large blocks of real property, and sound public financing. It was difficult to make political projections which would parallel financial and management ones.

By 1933 it was clear that the old southern agrarian states had to supplement a shrinking agricultural economy with income from industry or face bankruptcy. Both Mississippi and Louisiana, for instance, had instituted active programs to attract industry from other sections of the country. Mississippi was in the hardest pinch of any southern state. Its per capita income was in the lowest bracket; the old lumbering industry had cut-out virgin stands of pine and hardwood and had only limited resources with which to continue operation. Small farms were rapidly failing and were being consolidated into larger holdings. The state was losing population, but under the existing economic conditions, perhaps not fast enough. Some means had to be found to reverse the disastrous trend. In 1936 the general assembly enacted legislation permitting the offering of generous concessions to industries if they would come to the state. The program, designed to span the past to reach the future, was to "Balance Agriculture with Industry." An agricultural and industrial board was created, and this body went in search of industries that could be moved. Public billboards were placed alongside railways and highways, advertisements appeared in national periodicals, and bales of promotional literature went out from the offices of the board. Everything in the state, from beauty queens to historic homes in Natchez, was presented as an attraction. Inquiries were given thorough attention, often involving expensive surveys and research. Under the new law communities and counties could go hunting for industries on their own, and could offer concessions, in the forms of tax waivers and plant facilities. These, however, had to be approved by the central agricultural and industrial board.

Georgia, Alabama, Kentucky, South Carolina, and Tennessee made tax concessions to prospective industries. Other advantages were granted in the form of buildings, special highway spurs and street connections, improvement of local services such as fire-fighting equipment, and added police protection where needed. Tax concessions, however, have in some cases proved costly to both local communities and industries, largely because they have come at the expense of community services at a time when these services should have been expanded rather than cut. In their excellent study, *Why Industry Moves South*, McLaughlin and Robock raised grave doubts about many of the southern techniques of attracting industry. It was their opinion that specific and expert knowledge of an industry under consideration was far more impressive and useful to management than concessions, and certainly the availability of trained people and the existence of stable political and educational conditions were far more persuasive than fancy advertising and promises of special treatment.

Between 1936 and 1955, 138 industries located in Mississippi under the terms of the Balance Agriculture Law. Local bond issues ranged from $10,000 to $4,750,000. In addition the state promised a sizable reservoir of willing laborers who desperately needed jobs. A survey revealed that 72.1 per cent of the people were rural; the median age was 24.6 years. These were people displaced for the most part by the technological revolution on the cotton farms. There were such large numbers from which prospective employers could draw that, in some instances, there were eight hundred to a thousand applicants for every two hundred available jobs.

There were other problems, in Mississippi and elsewhere. States had to be certain that northern industries with labor troubles at home did not come South to repeat their unhappy histories. There was also the problem of hit-and-run moves: the generous concessions offered by the states were certain to attract fugitive industries which would move in and take full advantage of concessions and then move out at the end of the grace period. Astute planning was necessary to prevent this kind of brigandage—and in general this planning was successful. There was trouble with employers in declining lumbering and farming industries, who saw the new competitors offer higher wages, better working conditions, and more continuous employment to their employees.

The drive to secure location of new industries in the southern states reached the proportions of a frantic pursuit. State legislatures appropriated large sums of money to organize and sustain research bodies, with their specialists and expensive advertising campaigns. North Carolina organized the research facility known as the Golden Triangle, which drew on the specialized talents of scholars at North Carolina State University, the University of North Carolina, and Duke University. Kentucky organized the Spindletop Research Center, patterned after that of North Carolina. Functioning partly in conjunction with the University of Kentucky, the center offered the extensive research services of industries already in the state to those considering moving there. Kentucky also financed the extensive Fantus Report, which presented a detailed analysis of eastern Kentucky as a potential base for a successful industrial development. By 1955 southerners were fully convinced that the industries which could best exploit southern resources were among the most sophisticated and technically minded of any in the country.

The chemical industry developed many plants across the South, which were engaged in the production of synthetic rubber, cellulose products, synthetic fabrics, raw chemicals of many varieties, explosives, commercial fertilizers, and many other products. Commercial or chemical fertilizer manufacturing had a long history which extended back into ante-bellum years, but since 1933 and the renewal of public interest in the Tennessee Valley development, fertilizers of much greater nutrient values have been offered for sale. Cellulose consumption has greatly increased in such plants as that of the Eastman Kodak Company at Kingsport, Tennessee, the Celanese Corporation of America plants in Virginia and South Carolina, the Chemstrand plant in Alabama, the DuPont plants in Virginia, South Carolina, and Kentucky, and the various chemical complexes in Louisiana, Florida, and Texas. One of the most dramatic developments in this field was the rise of Calvert City just below the Kentucky Dam on the Tennessee River near Paducah.

Southern industrial expansion has varied markedly since 1930. Unlike earlier efforts to industrialize the South, no attempt was made to develop industries which confined their interests to the processing of southern materials alone. A large number of the newer industries were small and manufactured products which had little or no relationships to the historical economy of the South. Among these were plants producing electric light bulbs, small tools, drugs, plumbing and light fixtures, spring hinges, automobile and electric motor parts, baby foods, electric typewriters and computors, shoes, sporting goods, and automobiles. Many of the modern factories have been located away from crowded urban centers, and often away from railway connections. They have no workers' villages about them, and laborers often travel long distances to work. From the standpoint of external appearances, many of the modern southern industrial plants were carefully designed and landscaped, often looking not unlike schools and small cottages.

The basic question continued to arise, even after the data of the 1960 census were available, as to how well the South had succeeded in its economic development. This question cannot be answered with any degree of certainty because of the large number of variable and complex factors involved. In 1962 the region spent over $2 billion on the construction of new manufacturing plants of varying sizes and importance which employed more than one and a quarter million laborers. By 1958 there were 56,366 plants employing approximately three and one-half million workers, and in 1964 this number was over five million. Value added in the region by manufacturing was more than $31 billion, as compared with a national value of nearly $180 billion. The statistics for the South showed a phenomenal increase, but were still slightly more than a sixth of the national income as a whole.

After 1945 there remained no old agrarian South to which most southerners could return if economic necessity forced them to do so. By the end of World War II the region had set itself up on a course in which it had to develop an industrial system that would more than balance itself with agriculture. Never before in its history, despite its continuing inequality in many areas with national achievements, has the South come nearer exploiting more intelligently and profitably most of its resources. It has definitely become a region dependent upon an ever-increasing industrialization for large capital returns.

⚜ XIII ⚜

The Great Crusade and After

The coming of the Second World War ended for a time the liberal-conservative cleavages in the South over the New Deal. No other section gave the President more united support in his efforts to aid Britain in the 1940-41 period of neutrality. The America First Committee, an organization whose aim was to keep the United States out of war, scored no gains in the South. Draft extension and the revised neutrality act would have been defeated without the all-but-unanimous support of southern Representatives and Senators. The internationalist sentiment of the South during the period was a reflection of the peculiar social and economic conditions prevailing there. The ruin of cotton export trade was balanced by the $10 billion which the federal government poured into the section for defense plants, although the presence of these same plants would promote an isolationist sentiment in the postwar years. In October 1941, however, 88 per cent of southerners polled thought it was more important that Germany be defeated than that the United States stay out of the European war. This in contrast to the approximately 63 per cent of Americans in other regions who favored intervention.

But the New Deal and the Great Depression combined with World War II wrought profound changes in southern society. The nation rediscovered how backward the region was and undertook to remake it, a move that provoked resentment among southerners. Such phrases as "economic problem number one" and "reactionary southerners" caused bitterness in the South against northerners, as also did controversies over segregation in the armed forces. Then, too, anti-racial propaganda during the war with Hitler made white supremacists uneasy. As Jasper B. Shannon has pointed out, the Negro with a job and with a wartime FEPC to protect it, was unwilling to accept his former position in southern society. Besides, millions of southern whites and Negroes during the war had served in other sections of the country and even in foreign lands, where southern traditions were not a way of life. This experience doubtless changed the attitude of many of them toward southern racial mores.

Until Roosevelt's capture of the northern Negro vote in 1933, the South had felt secure on the race issue. But when the northern Negro shifted to the Democratic party both national parties sought his vote, offering platform inducements that would not be tolerated in the South. By the mid-1930's it was clear that the votes of northern and eastern states were vital to Democratic success nationally, while southern votes no longer were. Realization of this in the post-World War II era eroded southern loyalty to the party and renewed the former controversy between conservatives and liberals in the South.

Meanwhile, rules barring Negroes from Democratic primaries had come under attack. At first the state governments took no part in barring the Negro from membership in the Democratic party and participation in its primary: that was done by party rule. Soon, however, statutes regularized the nominating process; and since these made the primary part of the election, an entirely different situation was created. Most statutes left to the state party organization the right to fix rules of eligibility beyond those prescribed by the primary law, and party rules everywhere excluded Negroes. But the Texas legislature went one step further. In 1923 it incorporated a white restriction in its compulsory primary law: "in no event shall a negro be eligible to participate in a Democratic party primary . . . in the State of Texas." This led to a successful attack on the law, the Supreme Court holding the section in conflict with the Fifteenth Amendment.

Texas promptly repealed the law and substituted a provision which gave the state Democratic committee power to prescribe qualifications for membership, whereupon the committee passed a resolution barring Negroes. But the Supreme Court invalidated this. It reasoned that since the executive committee acted under authority granted by the legislature it was equivalent to the state's barring Negroes. Texas then repealed the provision which gave the party power to set qualifications; thereupon, the state party convention assumed authority to fix membership rules for the party. The convention promptly ruled that only white Texans were eligible for membership in the party and thus to vote in the primary. This action was sustained by the Supreme Court in the Grovey case in 1935, the Court holding that the party in Texas was a "voluntary" association, and that no state action was involved. By 1944, however, seven of the nine judges of 1935 were gone, and the Classic case in New Orleans had been decided. In that case the Court ruled that the primary was "an integral part" of the election process. This laid the ground for reconsideration of the rule in the Grovey Case, and in *Smith vs. Allwright*, the Court declared unconstitutional the Democratic party rule in Texas which excluded Negroes from the primary.

Reaction to the Allwright decision was varied. Louisiana did nothing, relying on her constitutional requirements of literacy and "good character." How effective these were may be judged from the fact that fifteen years later there were still many Louisiana parishes with Negro majorities where not a single Negro was registered. States of the upper South also did nothing, but for a different reason. Having fewer Negroes, they were more tolerant and accepted Negro voting as inevitable. South Carolina, on the other hand, unable to find a better solution for her problem, repealed all laws making the primary "an integral part" of the election machinery. In their place, the Democratic executive committee set up regulations for Democratic "clubs" whose members must be white. In a suit testing the law, Federal Judge J. Waties Waring, a native of Charleston, ruled the new procedures unconstitutional, pointing out that private clubs "do not . . . elect a President of the United States, and the Senators and members of the House of Representatives." It was time, he added, for the state to fall in step with the rest of the nation and adopt "the American way of conducting elections." Waring's decision stood when the Supreme Court refused to review it. Thereafter, South Carolina Democrats permitted Negroes to vote, but only if they would take an oath professing support for "social and educational separation of races," and opposition to any FEPC law; but Judge Waring nullified these requirements also.[1]

In Arkansas the Allwright decision was soon accepted. At first

(1) Quoted in Key, *Southern Politics*, 628.

Democrats there toyed with the idea of separate primaries for state and national elections under the theory that the federal Constitution protected rights of voters only in the latter. In the 1946 elections, however, Negroes voted freely for both state and Congressional candidates, except in the Mississippi River counties, where most of them did not vote at all. The following year the legislature repealed the double-primary law and adopted one permitting the state parties to fix qualifications for membership. The party thereupon prepared a statement of principles which voters must subscribe to: support of segregation of races in schools and public places and opposition to intermarriage. In practice, however, except in the river counties, Negroes have not been prevented from voting in Arkansas, and the statement of principle is rarely, if ever, invoked.

In Georgia, the usual requirements of literacy, good character, and an ability to explain the requirements of good citizenship were not often resorted to so long as the white primary prevailed. After the Allwright decision intimidation became the most effective device to prevent Negro voting. As late as 1960 there were some Georgia counties where not a single Negro was registered; in two of them, Negroes constituted 80 per cent of the population. Negroes feared both economic and physical retaliation and despaired of ever voting, regardless of federal protection. Meantime, Negroes voted freely in large cities like Atlanta. Even there, however, the county unit system already described, where in state-wide elections the winner took all, tended to nullify the large Negro vote.

Mississippi experimented with a requirement that voters must pledge to support principles of the party as stated by the executive committee. The commitment demanded by the committee included an anti-FEPC pledge and opposition to federal anti-poll-tax and anti-lynching laws. But the tests were superfluous in succeeding elections, for very few Negroes even attempted to register. As a matter of fact, until recently, never in the twentieth century have as many as 10 per cent of the Negro voting-age population of Mississippi been registered, and normally not more than 5 per cent. This contrasted with 63 per cent of whites in 1954 and 67 per cent in 1960. After 1954 the Mississippi law required applicants to read, write, and interpret the state constitution, and after 1960 they had to be of "good moral character" and have their names and addresses published in a local paper for two weeks. Reprisals, both economic and physical, that might have followed for any Negro bold enough to publicize his determination to register and vote under these conditions, together with the apathy for politics which had been bred in the Mississippi Negro by decades of intimidation and suppression, were sufficient to keep new registrants under this law to a minimum. For those daring few who attempted to comply with all specific requirements, there was still one formidable hurdle. Any qualified elector might challenge the "good moral character" or the literacy of any applicant, and the registrar had unlimited discretionary power both in regard to the applicant's character and his ability to "interpret." Poll-tax receipts were still being called for in local elections in 1964, even though the Twenty-fourth Amendment had outlawed the poll tax in federal elections.

In an effort to neutralize the Allwright decision, Alabama adopted the Boswell Amendment to the state constitution. This added to existing qualifications others requiring that the voter "understand and explain" the state constitution, that he have "good character" and that he understand "the duties and obligations of good citizenship under a republican form of government." For a time the Boswell Amendment would meet Alabama racist expectations, but only for a time. By 1960 authorities were resorting to extreme measures to prevent Negro voting. In Macon County, where Negroes outnumbered whites more than three to one and where a large proportion of the Negroes were literate, registration places were located at great distances from Negro communities, and Tuskegee, with a large Negro population, was outrageously gerrymandered so as to put the Negro majority outside its borders. Literacy tests for Negroes were so interminably slow that most Negro applicants gave up in despair. First the applicant had to fill out a form with forty-eight blanks. Even the personal-history statement demanded of the applicant could be difficult. He might be asked his old military serial number, his social security number, or the exact street numbers of two persons who could vouch for his having lived in his neighborhood long enough to establish eligibility. An error in any of these details could disqualify him. Succeeding in this, he would be asked to write from dictation lengthy quotations from the United States Constitution. Following this he would be given four questions from a set of a hundred on government. Many of these were quite straightforward—"Name the president of the United States"—but a few were quite ambiguous. "Congressional districting is required to be done by: legislature, state courts, Congress, United States Supreme Court." After this, the applicant would be asked to read four excerpts from the Constitution and answer questions concerning them. Next, he had to sign a statement that he had received no help on the test, that he had been given all the time he needed, and waiving any right to a copy of the test. Finally, he had to sign an oath that his answers were true, that he supported the constitutions of the United States and of Alabama, and that he did not believe in nor was he affiliated with any group which advocated overthrow of the state or federal government by force. Those who did not give up before the end were rejected for trivial errors on tests, while, in violation of the law, whites either were not tested or were given assistance. The result was that almost all white applicants were registered, while only about 10 per cent of the Negroes were.

United States Attorney-General Robert F. Kennedy exhibited to the Senate Judiciary Committee in July 1963 copies of Negro registration applications from Birmingham which, although legible and responsive, had been rejected as illiterate. Asked to name some of the duties and obligations of citizenship, a white applicant replied: "Support the Law." He was accepted, but a Negro soldier who answered: "To vote, to obey the laws of Alabama, to obey the laws of the United States, to bear arms against any enemy, to support the Constitution of Alabama and the United States," was rejected. Justice Black, in nullifying a similar voter test law in Louisiana in March 1965, declared:

> Colored people, even some with the most advanced education and scholarship, were declared by voting registrars with less education to have an unsatisfactory understanding of the Constitution of Louisiana or of the United States. This is not a test but a trap sufficient to stop even the most brilliant man on the way to the voting booth.

Evidence was convincing, he added, that registrars used their unlimited discretion to purge from the voting rolls "thousands of Negroes, but virtually no whites."

Despite all the new obstacles, however, it was generally agreed that the Allwright case marked the beginning of the end for Negro disfranchisement. Improved Negro education made literacy tests, if fairly administered, ineffective, and Negroes were growing militant in their demands for fair administration. Disfranchisement depended more and more on violations of the southerner's own laws. Liberal forces in the North were joining in the attack, and the Supreme Court was making things increasingly difficult for segregationists. Registration of Negroes increased dramatically, although the increase was uneven throughout the section, varying from less than one per cent in Mississippi to more than 25 per cent in Tennessee within two years. By 1950 there were about 900,000 Negro registrants in the region, and by 1958, 1,250,000. By 1960 about 26 per cent of the adult Negro population of the South was registered, as compared to 60 per cent of white adults. This varied again from 5 per cent in Mississippi to 48 per cent in Tennessee. The chief impediment to the drive outside the deep South was Negro apathy, but Mississippi, Louisiana, Alabama, and Georgia still resorted to violence, threats of violence, or arbitrary refusal by registrars. This was true more in the rural than urban areas of those states, although it was practiced to a degree in many cities.

In 1948, President Harry Truman made civil liberties the central point of his program, and southern conservatives went into open revolt against him. In contrast to 1928 when the hard core of Democratic loyalty was in the rural, black-county regions, the center of the opposition to Truman was in the black belt. The revolt had its beginning in 1944 when the Mississippi Democratic convention placed uninstructed electors on the party ballot. The hope then had been that other states would follow the example and that a large bloc of uninstructed southern electors might in a close election seize the balance of power. The Mississippi plot had been defeated, however, when the legislature, under Bilbo's influence, nominated another slate of electors pledged to Roosevelt. These had soundly defeated the anti-Roosevelt group. It would have been madness for Mississippians to have bolted after this, for Roosevelt was sure to win without them. Only Texas conservatives adopted the Mississippi plan, and there also the regulars won.

By 1948, Roosevelt was dead, and the Congressional elections of 1946 had given encouragement to Republicans and southern conservatives alike. In his inaugural message in January 1948, Mississippi Governor Fielding Wright denounced the proposals of the President's Committee on Civil Rights, which called for an end to segregation, poll taxes, enactment of a permanent Fair Employment Practices Act, and an anti-lynching bill. Wright called on southern Democrats to break with the national party, whose program, he said, was aimed at destruction of southern mores. In mid-March a special meeting of the Southern Governors' Conference advocated that all southern state Democratic conventions pledge their electors to vote in the coming election against any candidate favoring civil rights legislation, and that they send delegates to the Democratic National Convention instructed to vote against Truman's nomination.

Meanwhile, when Truman asked Congress to implement the recommendations of his Committee on Civil Rights, Governor Wright called for a mass meeting of southern Democrats in Jackson in early February. With bands playing *Dixie* and spectators waving the Confederate flag, the meeting of some four thousand resolved that outside interference increased racial tensions and that southerners best knew how to deal with southern Negroes. Significantly, it also resolved that the effort of the federal government to acquire title to tidelands oil was a violation of state-rights. Two weeks later, the Mississippi Democratic executive committee resolved to take all necessary measures to insure that its delegates to the national convention as well as its electors should vote against any nominee who would not openly oppose the recommendations of the President's Civil Rights Committee. They also resolved to instruct Mississippi's delegates to withdraw from the national convention if a civil rights plank was included in the party platform. At a second mass meeting called by the Mississippi Democratic executive committee at Jackson in May, resolutions were passed urging all southern states to choose delegates to the Democratic National Convention pledged to oppose the nomination of anyone who advocated civil rights legislation. The conference agreed to meet again at Birmingham after the national convention.

At Philadelphia, the convention called the bluff, if bluff it was, of the state-righters. Led by Hubert H. Humphrey, at the time mayor of Minneapolis, it rejected a mild civil rights plank reported by the platform committee and adopted instead one commending Truman and urging civil rights legislation that would guarantee nondiscrimination in voting, in employment, and in protection of all civil liberties. Thereupon, the Mississippi and about half of the Alabama delegations walked out. Truman was nominated over the southern candidate, Senator Richard B. Russell of Georgia, by a margin of five to one.

On July 17 the adjourned Jackson Convention reconvened at Birmingham as planned and organized the States Rights, or Dixiecrat party. Senator J. Strom Thurmond of South Carolina was nominated for President and Wright for Vice President. Their expectations rested on the hope that northern Democrats would favor a southern Democrat over a Republican, and that Republicans would favor a southern over a northern Democrat. The Dixiecrats did not expect to win the election. Their strategy was to prevent either Truman or Thomas E. Dewey, the Republican candidate, from getting a majority of the Electoral vote and thus throw the election into the House of Representatives. The prospect was enhanced by Henry Wallace's candidacy on the Progressive ticket.

In the campaign that followed, the liberal-conservative battle in the South was fought to a showdown: the liberal wing supporting Truman, the conservative Thurmond. In Tennessee and North Carolina, where the Republicans were a threat, the Democrats closed ranks and supported the national ticket. In Virginia, the legislature refused to pass a bill sponsored by Senator Harry Byrd and Governor William N. Tuck which would enable the state Democratic convention to instruct the state's electors against Truman; thereupon, the Democratic executive committee announced its own neutrality between Truman and Thurmond. In Tennessee Boss Ed Crump of Memphis announced he would not support Truman, but his candidates for governor and United States Senator went down in the primary before Gordon Browning and Estes Kefauver. Even Crump's henchman, United States Senator Kenneth McKellar, refused to follow Crump and supported Truman.

In Florida, even though there was no local Republican threat and the Democrats could have afforded to throw away their votes on Thurmond, the liberals led by Senator Claude Pepper carried the state for Truman. In Arkansas, the conservatives in the delta counties attempted to seize control of the party convention and instruct electors for Thurmond; but liberals led by Senator William Fulbright, Congressman Brooks Hays, and Sidney McMath won control and defeated the conservative efforts. In Texas, as in Florida and Arkansas, civil rights was less an issue than the economic policies of the New Deal-Fair Deal. The struggle between liberals and conservatives was a draw in the state convention: liberals could not win a delegation to the national convention instructed for Truman, but neither could conservatives win approval of instructions to delegates to bolt if the two-thirds rule was not restored. In the fall election Truman carried the state.

In only four states of the deep South, South Carolina, Alabama, Mississippi, and Louisiana—states where there was a large proportion of Negroes and no real Republican opposition—did the Dixiecrats meet with success. Even there, however, victory was made possible only through clever tactics. Dixiecrats despaired of persuading local leaders to abandon the party that had been all but a religious affiliation for them and their families for generations. But Dixiecrats were able, by appropriating the regular Democratic label on the ballot and thus pledging the Democratic electors to Thurmond, to place loyal Democrats in the paradoxical position of "bolting" their party. Even white supremacists like Senators Olin Johnston and Herman Talmadge, however, refused to join the movement.

The election proved a shock to southern Dixiecrats. Their plan would have succeeded if Texas, Arkansas, Georgia, and Florida had been carried. But Truman's hard campaigning, Dewey's over-confidence, and Wallace's complete ineffectiveness proved their undoing. Also, too many southern Democratic politicians who privately wished the movement well feared retaliation if they joined the Dixiecrats, and the Democrats won. Another factor in Dixiecrat failure was fear of loss of Congressional seniority by southern Congressmen if they should bolt.

The Dixiecrat split brought the influence of southerners in the national Democratic party to ebb tide. Henceforth, the section would have even a smaller voice in national affairs. Too late, conservative southerners realized their mistake in 1936 in permitting elimination of the two-thirds rule in nominating conventions. Thereafter, the section could neither rule nor ruin. Furthermore, it was apparent that a cleavage had come now between the deep South and the upper South. Truman carried the upper South and the election in 1948 while losing four of the deep South states. The South had also moved a great distance from pre-New Deal political patterns. Capture of the cotton textile industry by the South and capture of the northern Negro vote by the Democratic party began the process that was to free southern conservatives from unquestioning loyalty to the national Democratic party. For the textile industry brought to the South inclinations toward a protective tariff not unlike traditional northern Republican tariff concepts. This, together with Roosevelt's and Truman's wooing of the northern Negro vote, weakened the South's historic devotion to the Democratic party.

But textiles were only forerunners of an avalanche of industry migrating to the South, bringing with it a revolution that would urbanize the section, diversify its economy, and produce a large migration both into and out of the region—technicians, managers, businessmen moving in and Negroes moving out. Cotton's relative importance was lessening and industry's growing. By 1940, southern industry was already over twice as valuable as its agriculture. Fierce competition between communities for new factories and more jobs was bringing new interests which dimmed if they did not actually drive out old loyalties.

Under these economic pressures, regional cohesion was pulling apart, so that the Negro question was left as the sole unifying force. This was a powerful force, which a two-party system doubtless would help abate, but the end of which could not yet be seen. Nevertheless, the economic revolution was producing a social revolution, which in turn was eroding many old beliefs and customs that had held back the section. Cultural influences, together with news media, especially radio and television, were nationalizing American society, and this was having political implications. Group and class conflicts crossed sectional lines, and these conflicts were forcing political parties to adopt national programs to deal with them. Rural southern Democrats, even Dixiecrats, were often sectional only on race. On other issues they frequently were allied with rural people in other sections, most of whom were Republicans. This alliance of rural politicians rested largely on the mutual antipathy both groups had toward urban people, but such antipathy was greatly exaggerated.

The so-called coalition in Congress between southern Democrats and northern Republicans was largely a myth; for except on issues dealing directly with race or with extension of federal powers which might lead to tampering with race relations, southern Congressmen from urban districts and Senators with large urban populations such as Tennessee, Florida, and Texas voted almost invariably with northern Democrats on party measures. It was the rural southerner and the rural northern Republican who were responsible for creating the illusion of an alliance. On almost everything but racial issues, southern and northern industrialists found they had more in common than either had with his workers, just as northern and southern doctors, farmers, teachers, workers, businessmen also found much common ground. Furthermore, widespread prosperity which accompanied industrialization and urban growth in the South showed signs of breaking down the apathy of the masses toward politics, education, and labor. The ending of the poll tax in some states, together with the outlawing of the white primary everywhere, was contributing mightily toward increased political activity by these masses.

If the South was more conservative than the rest of the country then, it was because it was more rural. But there was more to it than this. Rural areas in all sections were over-represented in state legislatures, but this was more true of the South than of other regions. And democracy in the South consequently was beset with a conservatism begotten not only of an undemocratic rural control of state legislatures but one in which the ruling rural minority had a historical dedication to the county as a unit of government. The undemocratic nature of Georgia's county unit system in electing state officers has already been noted. Equally inequitable was her legislative apportionment. Fulton County (Atlanta) had about a fifth of the population of the state but elected only 1 of 54 state senators and 3 of more than 200 representatives. Similarly, Jefferson County, Alabama (Birmingham), had more than 20 per cent of the state's population but elected only 1 of 35 senators and 7 of 106 representatives. The southern half of Alabama, dominated by the black belt, had far less than half the state's population and wealth and paid less taxes proportionately on its property. Yet it had a majority in both houses, a majority chosen by a minority, as has been shown, invariably dominated by its own white minority dedicated to the preservation of the status quo. Sometimes this rural minority was joined by urban conservatives, eager to retain the rural majority in the legislature so that white supremacy would be preserved or union labor subdued. This coalition of conservatives from rural and urban areas stubbornly refused to permit reapportionment, despite state laws requiring that it be done every decade.

Meanwhile, Republican strength was growing by leaps and bounds, not only in the upper South but also in the lower. Also, the tradition of the Solid South, already twice broken in 1928 and 1948, was now but a memory. In 1952, Eisenhower broke it a third time, getting 48 per cent of the popular vote of the section as he carried Texas, Florida, Tennessee, and Virginia; four years later he did even better when he carried Louisiana in addition to the other four. This was in marked contrast to the four states of the deep South carried by Thurmond in 1948, and indicated two streams of discontent in the South with the national Democratic party. It was the rural voter who supported Thurmond; the urban voter, Eisenhower. Furthermore, it was the upper-class urban voter who supported Eisenhower, as "prosperous Southern urbanites acted like Yankees." Also, since the urban population was growing and becoming more prosperous, time seemed on the side of the Republicans, at least in Presidential elections.[2] All in all, Eisenhower carried 60 per cent of southern urban districts.

By 1960, a new dimension had moved into southern politics—the Negro vote—and this Negro vote could no longer be ignored by politicians. From the time of the New Deal and even before, Negroes had voted in the cities and their numbers were growing. Furthermore, they had been, since the New Deal, moving into the Democratic party. They were responsible for Adlai Stevenson's narrow victory in Louisiana in 1952 as well as for his defeat there in 1956, when the Negro vote in the South shifted heavily to Eisenhower, possibly as a result of the Supreme Court's school integration decision in 1954. In 1952 Stevenson also carried the Negro districts of Atlanta by two to one; in 1956 he lost the same districts by seven to one. By 1960, there were signs that the southern Negro was switching back to the Democratic party. Also, by 1960 it was no longer unthinkable for southern whites to admit that they were Republicans, although some southerners, not yet ready to make the final break, preferred to call themselves "Democrats for Nixon." Possible recruits for the Republicans were agrarians who had for generations blindly voted Democratic, but whose loyalties had been eroded by racial policies of the Democratic party of Roosevelt, Truman, and Stevenson. Many of these had voted Dixiecrat in 1948, but as the national Democratic party became more committed to liberalism, a conservative Republican party would be a natural refuge for them. Yankee *émigrés* who had moved South as repre-

(2) Donald S. Strong, "Durable Republicanism in the South," in Allan P. Sindler, ed., *Change in the Contemporary South* (Durham, N. C., 1963), 174–94.

sentatives for northern business were also helping build a southern Republican party.

Nor was the Republican trend shown only in Presidential elections, as was true in the 1928 and 1948 revolts. While not one of the 22 Senators, and only 7 of 106 Representatives, from the region was a Republican in 1960, yet Republicans were winning local elections in states of the upper South and in the Southwest. Of 1794 state legislative seats in the South in 1960, Republicans held 61. But a formal realignment of parties in the South still awaited a liberal trend in the nation which would permit southern liberals with national party support to defeat southern conservatives and take control of the Democratic party. One reason the South had not yet united in a determined revolt against the New Deal-Fair Deal Democrats who controlled the national party was that the Republican party offered no refuge for them. The white supremacist's world had turned upside down after 1932. Moving to the Republican party could avail him little in the long run, for the national Republican party, like the Democrats, could no longer ignore the Negro vote and still hope to carry the large industrial states needed for victory. And the succession of Republican candidates: Landon, Dewey, Wilkie, Eisenhower, and Nixon spoke out as militantly on race relations as did Roosevelt, Truman, Stevenson, and Kennedy.

That the section had become a battleground was demonstrated by the avidity with which candidates were campaigning there. In 1960 Nixon appeared in every southern state and Kennedy visited six, making ten speeches in Texas alone. And the Democratic Vice Presidential candidate, Lyndon Johnson, made sixty speeches during a whirlwind tour of eight states. In the end, Nixon carried Florida, Tennessee, and Virginia and got almost 40 per cent of the vote of the eleven southern states. He lost South Carolina by a meager one per cent of the vote cast. He, too, carried sixty-eight southern metropolitan counties. Mississippi chose eight noncommitted electors who cast their votes for Harry Byrd, as also did seven electors from Alabama and Oklahoma.

The Nixon defeat did not discourage southern Republicans. A few weeks later a special election saw a Republican, John Tower, chosen to the Senate seat vacated by Johnson. In 1962, four new Republican representatives, in addition to the seven already there, won seats in Congress, and Republicans were elected to local offices, such as mayor of Mobile and public prosecutor of Lowndes County, Mississippi. That year, also, the Republican gubernatorial candidate in Texas received 45 per cent of the vote, and Republicans there contested eighteen of twenty-three Congressional districts. Besides, there had emerged on the national scene a leader whose public statements made him dear to the hearts of southern conservatives and Dixiecrats—Barry Goldwater. Despite an eleventh hour movement to thwart him, Goldwater was nominated on the first ballot at the Republican convention in San Francisco. A few weeks later the Democratic convention at Atlantic City nominated President Lyndon Johnson by acclamation.

Although his previous record on civil rights had placed him among the moderates, Goldwater voted against the Civil Rights Act of 1964 and against Senate cloture which cleared the way for a vote on the bill. Also, he had become reactionary in his opposition to expanding federal authority. His votes on the Civil Rights Act, together with his general state-rights philosophy, insured the support for him of every southern nullifier. State-rights extremists, losing control of the Democratic party in many southern states, hoped to take over the Republican party in the South and make it dominant there. Their adherence was not an unmixed blessing for the Republican party nationally, however, as events would soon prove. After all, a larger proportion of Republicans in both House and Senate had voted for the Civil Rights Act than had Democrats. It was ironical, too, that the party of Lincoln should become a haven for white supremacists, civil rights violators, and other dissidents. It would also transfer to the national Republican party the internal schisms and frustrations the national Democratic party was freeing itself of.

There was another irony in the deep South's partiality to Goldwater. In any southern state he might win, he would doubtless carry on his coat-tails Republican Congressmen. This would deprive southern states of the one important influence they still exercised in the national government, the chairmanships of the formidable number of Congressional committees earned through seniority. This would accelerate the gradual decline in southern influence dating from the change of the two-thirds rule in the Democratic nominating convention in 1936. In 1964 southern Republicans held 11 of 84 southern House seats. If

Goldwater's expectation should be realized even modestly, the Republicans would gain at least ten or twelve additional seats. The newly elected Republicans would have no seniority and thus no claims on chairmanships, whereas the veteran Democrats they would displace had both. As a result, southern influence in future Congresses would be further weakened. On the other hand, a victory by Goldwater that did not carry local candidates to victory also would leave Democrats in control of Congress and of southern courthouses, and the patronage that went with those offices would be lost to a fledgling southern Republican party.

Despite such a confused set of crosscurrents attached to Goldwaterism, many southern Democrats including Governors George C. Wallace of Alabama and Paul B. Johnson of Mississippi announced for him. Governor Johnson prevailed upon the Mississippi state Democratic convention to refrain from naming a slate of Presidential electors pledged to Goldwater because it would compete with the regular Republican ticket for Goldwater votes and thus might enable the loyal Democrats to carry the state by a plurality over the two Goldwater tickets. This action gave the Mississippi voters a clear-cut choice in the Presidential election without endangering their status in the state Democratic party.

Hopes of Republicans and Goldwater Democrats were high throughout the South, even though Goldwater's opponent, Lyndon Baines Johnson, was born and bred in the South and until recent times was not altogether inimical to segregationist voters. The great number of local and Congressional candidates on the Republican state tickets indicated southerners were prepared to risk all in an effort to build a new conservative party whose national affiliate was conservatively oriented. In Louisiana, where Democrats outnumbered Republicans 100 to 1 on the registration lists, the Republican gubernatorial primary winner in March polled almost 300,000 votes, which was nearly two-thirds as large as that of the Democratic winner, John J. McKeithen. Never since reconstruction had a Republican candidate for state office polled more than 86,000 votes. When the state had gone for Eisenhower in 1956, GOP candidates in state-wide races were defeated three or four to one.

But there were signs sufficient in the upper South to give Republicans misgivings, had they read them right. The so-called backlash,

white reaction to militant Negro civil rights demands, would be important, both North and South. On the other hand, so would be the
Negro vote, which in large northern states had for years been the
balance. And new Negro registrations in the states of the upper South
in 1964 were greater than the margins of victory there four years
before. In Tennessee, for example, many thousands of Negroes had
registered as a result of the new Civil Rights Act, and they were
all aligned with the Democrats who had embarked on a liberal program
embracing the civil rights revolution. "When the polls close on the
night of November 3," said a Memphis Negro leader, "Goldwater
can wait until the Democrats hit 70,000. That's how many votes we're
going to put in the box for Johnson."[3]

Goldwater was overwhelmed in the election, carrying only five
southern states in addition to his home state, Arizona. But even victory
in the five southern states was a Pyrrhic one for the Republican party.
For the forty-seven electoral votes of South Carolina, Georgia, Alabama, Mississippi, and Louisiana, the party paid a fantastic price—the
solid vote of six million registered Negroes, more than two million
of them in the South. This Negro vote was important in the northern
states, where it probably was decisive in the victory of Robert Kennedy over Kenneth Keating in New York, of Otto Kerner over Charles
Percy in Illinois, and of incumbent Senator Stephen Young over Robert
Taft, Jr., in Ohio.

But it was also decisive in throwing Virginia, North Carolina,
Florida, and Tennessee to Johnson, for in each of these states the
Negro vote was greater than Johnson's majority. Johnson got an estimated 95 per cent of the Florida Negro vote, 99 per cent in North
Carolina, 90 per cent in Virginia, and 98 per cent in Tennessee. In
one ballot box in a Negro district in Nashville, the vote was 2152
to 15. The 75,000 Negro Democratic ballots cast in Memphis alone
was greater than the victory margins of the two Democratic senatorial
candidates Ross Bass and Albert Gore; and it elected the first Negro
legislator in Tennessee since Reconstruction.

In Mississippi, the state with the highest proportion of Negroes,
Goldwater polled an astonishing 87 per cent of the vote. But Negro
wards there went overwhelmingly for Johnson. In Mound Bayou the
vote was 270 to 0. In Atlanta, Georgia, the traditional Negro Republi-

(3) Quoted by Richard Harwood, in Louisville *Courier Journal*, Oct. 25, 1964.

can vote turned Democratic, and Johnson carried Fulton County by 24,000 votes. The Negro vote in the county was 49,000, and it went for Johnson by an estimated 99 per cent. It was thought that abolition of the poll tax by the recently ratified Twenty-fourth Amendment had overcome whatever backlash there was in Virginia and threw it back into the Democratic column for the first time since 1948. Ironically, the rock-ribbed Democratic Fourth District of southside Virginia's tobacco belt, which had remained loyal in the four preceding Presidential elections, went Republican. Two Negro precincts in Richmond gave Johnson majorities of 1257 to 4 and 1770 to 6.

The Negro vote in the South thus emerged as a force that must be reckoned with in the future. And since the Negro voter registration drive promised to continue and was not unduly hampered in South Carolina, Georgia, and Louisiana, these states would doubtless become more moderate as the 1964 Civil Rights Act became established. In Mississippi, as in the black belt of Alabama, the Negro vote should be small for some time to come. But the country passed a milestone on the issue of civil rights in 1964. It was now generally acknowledged that Negroes were entitled to the political rights which they demanded.

Republicans scored spectacular Congressional gains in the deep South, electing seven new Congressmen. Five of these were chosen from Alabama, the first in ninety-two years. In Louisiana, however, where Goldwater got the largest vote of any candidate in history— more than 500,000—four Republican candidates who were openly riding his coat-tails failed to unseat their Democratic opponents. House Whip Hale Boggs of New Orleans, who had voted for civil rights, was re-elected. In Mississippi, Goldwater carried into office the only Republican candidate for Congress.

Republicans carried Alabama by two to one. True, the Democrats had no chance to vote for President Johnson, for the Democratic electors were pledged against him. But Republicans saw the election as a turning of the tide in the state. They were well organized, whereas the Democrats had been practically without an organization since the division between state-righters and loyalists in 1948. The Republicans claimed that henceforth they would be a major force in the state, for they elected not only five Congressmen but state and local officials as well: legislators, constables, justices of the peace. This was a blow to the national ambitions of Governor George Wallace, for it completely nullified the good showing he had made in Wisconsin, Indiana, and Maryland primaries in the spring. Being a liberal on most issues other than the Negro, he could not join the reactionary Republican party in his state. At the same time he had contributed greatly to the Goldwater vote which swept so many of his friends out of office. Liberal Alabama Democrats regarded the election as a blessing in disguise in that it removed from office entrenched conservative Congressmen against whom a liberal had no chance in primary elections. These loyalists looked forward optimistically to 1966 when they might run liberal Democrats against the Republicans.

The 1964 election re-emphasized what previous elections had indicated—that there are two Souths. There is the deep South of Mississippi, Alabama, Georgia, Louisiana, and South Carolina, where race is still the all-pervading issue; and there is the upper South, where the race issue in its more impassioned implications is abating. Indeed, the deep South itself can also be subdivided in its devotion to racial dogma, with Alabama occupying first place and Mississippi a close second. It is also apparent that the geographical area of the "deep South" is becoming smaller, while the upper South is growing. Said the editor of the Montgomery (Alabama) *Advertiser*, in 1955 after attending a Citizens' Council rally: "The truth is, we southerners and our latter-day 'peculiar institution' of segregation are compressed into a fortress whose perimeter is shrinking along the border states, with defection in such states as Tennessee. Further, the feeling in North Alabama is mild compared with that in South Alabama."[4]

(4) Thomas D. Clark, *The Emerging South* (New York, 1961), 232.

❧ XIV ❧

The Negro

Emancipation of the Negro had made him no longer a marketable chattel subject to sale, and to this extent it had freed him from the bonds of involuntary servitude. This was, of course, a giant stride forward for the Negro. But for the better part of a century thereafter his progress seemed interminably slow; indeed, at times he seemed to retrogress. For gains won in the aftermath of the Civil War during radical reconstruction were soon lost, and he slid backward into a despised state of neglect and isolation which in some features seemed more degrading even than slavery. Under slavery he had at least been a valuable chattel.

At the end of the Civil War and for many years thereafter the congenital inferiority of the Negro was all but universally agreed on, not only in the South but in the North and among the learned as well as the uneducated. As late as the third decade of the twentieth century the distinguished sociologist, Howard Odum, eager to aid the Negro's aspirations, thought this was true, although Odum would later change his mind. It was thus commonly believed even among his well wishers that the Negro was incapable of reaching a level of intellectual sophistication where he might hope to assume a posture of respectability in a society as advanced as that of nineteenth-century America: only in slavery, or when that was abolished in some controlled inferior caste, could he be made to bear his share of the burden of the society of which he was a part.

With the abandonment of the Negro by his northern protectors after 1877, he was again returned to the mercy of native whites. But there would be a difference now. Under slavery the vast majority of non-slaveowning whites had been largely isolated from the Negro, and there had been only a labor issue between the white man and his slave. Under the new order there would be created a race issue. In a sense and to a degree, all whites had been aristocrats under slavery because they were free. After redemption, white men who had seen Negroes occupy superior positions to their own during radical reconstruction were resolved that it should not happen again. Accordingly, they set about creating a caste system based, not on law as was slavery, but on biological inferiority. In this new order the Negro would be the bottom layer, regardless of wealth or personal merit; even lower than he had been in slavery, for then he had looked down upon the poor white. And it became the principal aim of the new southern society to see that the Negro did not rise above this lowly position.

Under slavery there had been no occasion for social segregation. The Negro's status was so clearly inferior that artificial barriers were unnecessary. There was no need for segregation laws in education; for public schools, except in cities, were almost nonexistent even for white children, and there was no inclination to educate the Negro even if laws had permitted. Nor was there felt to be a need to enforce segregation in other areas. Slaves and masters traveled on the same coaches, ate at the same restaurants, occasionally attended the same theaters. Even after the end of the war, compulsory public segregation was not instituted at once. In Columbia, South Carolina, the freedman was admitted to all public assemblies; in Charleston he was barred from indoor theaters, but he could attend circuses, camp meetings, and "shows under canvas." There were even a few cases of intermarriage between the races, more often between white men and Negro women, although interracial marriages were frowned upon.

In a reaction to what southern whites regarded as the excesses of radical reconstruction, local ordinances in redeemed states began to require racial segregation in public accommodations. Consequently, just before the end of reconstruction, in 1875, Congress passed the Civil Rights Act. This act provided that all persons, regardless of race, were entitled to full and equal enjoyment of accommodations in public conveyances on land or water, at inns, theaters, and other places of public amusement. That the idea of compulsory segregation was still not deeply engrained is witnessed by the fact that the Congressional law was supported by legislation passed in some states with little opposition. As late as 1885 Negroes rode freely in first-class railway coaches in South Carolina and Virginia. They served on juries, attended political conventions as delegates, and their dead were even laid away in common burial grounds. In 1891, the Tillman-controlled South Carolina legislature defeated a Jim Crow railway bill. At the time the Charleston *News and Courier* observed that it was "a great deal pleasanter to travel with respectable and well behaved colored people than with unmannerly and ruffianly white people."[1]

But relations between the races were already deteriorating. In 1883 the Supreme Court had ruled that while states were forbidden to abridge the privileges of citizens, private corporations might do so without violating the Civil Rights Act. Thereafter, as Negroes began moving into industrial towns where they competed with white workers for jobs, the demand for segregation laws grew, and between 1887 and 1891, nine southern states had provided for Jim Crow railway cars. By the turn of the century all southern states had done so. When these laws were tested, the Supreme Court ruled in the case of *Plessy vs. Ferguson* (1896) that segregation was not in itself discrimination so long as the separate accommodations were equally good or bad for both races.

Soon there followed more comprehensive laws: segregation on street cars, in waiting rooms, dining cars, restaurants, and in sleeping accommodations. From these laws the states moved rapidly to segregation in courts, prisons, schools, factories, libraries, parks, playgrounds, theaters, hotels, hospitals, barber shops, cemeteries, and residential districts—anything that might suggest social equality. By the second decade of the twentieth century members of the two races were becoming isolated from one another in all phases of society save that which clearly identified the Negro as an inferior. It was a paradox that passage of these laws coincided with the democratic revolution in the South when the Farmers' Alliance was capturing control of legislatures and while progressive leaders like Vardaman, Aycock, and Hoke Smith were overthrowing regimes of the conservative redeemers.

(1) Quoted in Woodward, *Origins of the New South*, 210–11. The discussion of Jim Crow laws in the succeeding pages is based largely on Woodward's account.

Segregation was maintained throughout the period on the theory laid down in *Plessy vs. Ferguson:* that the separate accommodations must be equal. Almost invariably, however, Negro accommodations were inferior and markedly so. In districts where Negroes did not vote the inequality extended beyond accommodations in public institutions: streets in Negro sections of cities went unpaved, public utility service was more primitive, police and judicial systems were organized to prevent equal protection for Negroes. Negroes were never placed equitably on public payrolls, and higher paid jobs were completely closed to them. These conditions prevailed for more than half a century; indeed, nothing was done to improve them until the New Deal of the 1930's. Then the federal government would make gallant efforts to eliminate the worst of the discriminations, but even then, as we have seen, it was more difficult for Negroes to get on relief rolls than whites in similar circumstances, and when they did get on their grants were smaller. A generation after the New Deal, in 1965, the Secretary of Agriculture admitted that there was still discrimination against Negro farmers in the South in his department's programs. The federal Civil Rights Commission, at the same time, charged that "there are two distinct Southern agricultural economies—one white and the other Negro," and as a result, Negroes were relegated to a separate, inferior, and outdated agricultural economy.

Discrimination was justified by whites on the ground that Negroes paid little taxes and thus received more benefits from government than they were entitled to, but never was this excuse thought to apply to the poor white who also paid little taxes. Nor was the fact that a few wealthy Negroes paid high taxes thought reason enough to secure them greater public benefits than poor Negroes. The determination to "keep the Negro in his place" varied in intensity among upper and lower class whites. The upper classes had no fear that the Negro would challenge their social position or compete with them economically. The lower classes, however, were threatened by the freedman's economic competition and were determined to set up and maintain a social distinction. Political pressure from lower-class whites swung upper-class whites to support of their program. Henry Grady told a southern audience in 1885 that "the supremacy of the white race of the South must be maintained forever, and the domination of the negro race resisted. This . . . truth . . . has abided forever in the marrow of our bones and shall run forever with the blood that feeds Anglo-Saxon hearts."[2]

Education of the southern Negro widened the gulf that developed between the races soon after reconstruction. For it brought to the Negro a keener sensitivity of the humiliation of segregation, and the educated Negro hesitated to intrude where he might suffer insult and humiliation. He resented also, more than in the past, the inferior caste to which the white man had relegated him. The result was that he withdrew from association with whites, so that there was less sympathy between Negroes and whites in twentieth-century America than had existed between their grandparents when one was slave and the other master. Under slavery the Negro rarely was thrown with whites other than his master's family, and often personal attachments existed there. But with emancipation few attachments grew between leaders of the two races, and a lack of concern for and ignorance of the needs of the descendants of their grandfathers' slaves developed in southern whites of succeeding generations. As the Negro read the books and grasped the ideas of the white man, he came to realize how much of an alien he was in his native land, and he resented it. And the grandson of the slave-owner, sure in his own mind that he understood the Negro and knew what was best for him, was deluded into thinking the Negro was contented with his lot. Living in different sections of the same community, worshiping in different churches, segregated in all public gatherings, the Negro and the white man went their separate ways as though they inhabited different worlds, barred by the color line from any act of friendly sympathy that might suggest a breach in the caste system.

Tight segregation of the races was said to be a means of preventing miscegenation. Undoubtedly there were also hidden motives of economic interest on the part of the white man. Southern white men did not want the Negro to be successful as a freedman. The landless white wished to drive him out so that he would not be a competitor in the effort to rent good lands: the landowner wished to keep him impoverished, and thus a source of cheap labor. In the years that followed emancipation a few Negroes became wealthy landowners and businessmen; but generally the price of land was too high for them, and most of them labored for cash wages or else as tenants

(2) *The New South* (New York, 1890), 104.

or sharecroppers. The census of 1880 showed that emancipation had done little to change the economic status of the Negro. Almost 90 per cent of southern Negro workers were either farmers or servants, and not one Negro farmer in five owned the land he worked: in some districts not one in a hundred. In Georgia, where at that time Negroes were almost half the population, they owned less than 2 per cent of the land, 8 per cent of the cattle and farm animals, and 5 per cent of farm tools. It could be truly said that the Negro there "not only worked the white man's land but worked it with a white man's plow drawn by a white man's mule."

In the decades that followed there was some improvement. By 1910 almost 25 per cent of Negro farmers owned the land they worked. By 1930, however, this figure had slipped to 20 per cent. Ten years later the number of Negro farmers in the South had been reduced by migration, but the ratio of owners to tenants and croppers had not changed. By that time, Negroes still constituted more than a fourth of the southern farm population, but owned less than one-twelfth of the southern farm property. But that did not tell the whole story; for Negro farmers, more than white farmers, depended on the cotton crop for their livelihood; and cotton growing was primitive agriculture at its worst, requiring little intelligence or initiative. And as we have noted, the great fluctuation in its price made it a most hazardous crop. Since it was so risky and depended on outside credit, loans were expensive. Consequently, cotton planters and merchants charged their tenants usurious rates for advances on food and other necessities. Since four out of five southern Negro farmers were tenants, croppers, or wage workers; and since nine out of ten of this class were cotton farmers, the annual income of Negro farmers was far below that of white farmers, a large number of whom were landowners.

In the 1880's, when prices were generally high, the Negro wage-earner might receive from $60 to $100 a year and rations worth another $25. In the next decade, when cotton prices fell sharply, he could hardly expect more than $50 in wages. Fifty years later, in the 1930's, the net income of Negro wage hands, croppers, and cash tenants in the eastern cotton belt ranged from about $150 for wage laborers to a high of about $500 for tenants. A large portion of their income, indeed if not all, went to the storekeeper who furnished supplies on credit through the year at a 50 to 100 per cent mark-up. The storekeeper secured his debt as we have seen by a mortgage on the land, if the farmed owned any, and if not, by a mortgage on the growing cotton crop.

In his ignorant condition, the Negro was at the mercy of any unscrupulous landlord or storekeeper. W. E. B. Du Bois at the turn of the century told of the Georgia Negro farmer of his own acquaintance who paid for a farm on the installment plan three separate times, only to have the landlord-vendor pocket the money and deed and leave the Negro landless and a laborer at thirty cents a day on the land stolen from him. He told, also of his personal knowledge, of a storekeeper who stripped a tenant of "every single marketable article—mules, ploughs, stored crops, tools, furniture, bedding, clocks, looking-glass," without benefit of warrant, law officer, or any kind of legal process, in defiance of the law providing homestead exemptions, and without making any accounting to anyone.[3]

The Negro farmer's income reflected his living conditions. Families of eight or ten lived in one- or two-room cabins built of rough boards with neither plaster nor sealing material to keep out the weather. One door and a square hole in the wall with wooden shutters provided the only light. There was no glass, no porch, no outer ornament of any kind. A bed or two, a wooden chest, a table, and a few chairs were the only furniture, and an open fireplace served both for heating and cooking. By all accounts, most dwellings were dirty, dilapidated, poorly ventilated, and smelly.

If he left the farm the Negro's lot was little better. In the antebellum South the Negro had been both a menial worker and a skilled craftsman. White mechanics of that day protested against slave competition which drove earnings down, but politically potent planters were not disposed to restrict their slave mechanics. With emancipation, the Negro lost his white protector, and the result was a steady trend driving the Negro from skilled to unskilled work. Whereas five or six artisans in 1865 were Negroes, by 1900 they were all but eliminated. Booker T. Washington's efforts at Tuskegee to change this were ineffectual, for crafts taught there were largely obsolescent in a rising industrial economy. In the industrial expansion that followed World War I, Negroes found new opportunities, but only in the least desirable and least competitive jobs: in lumber mills, coal mining, railroad main-

(3) *The Souls of Black Folk*, 170–71.

tenance work, and in unskilled work in turpentine, iron, steel, and fertilizer manufacturing. They were excluded from railroad operating jobs, from gas and oil well work, from the paper and pulp industry except as wood cutters, and from the South's chief industry, textiles, except as janitors. In towns and cities they were not employed as bus or street-car operators, as telephone or telegraph operators, nor generally in the furniture industry. In banking, insurance, and in wholesale and retail merchandising, they were employed only in menial capacities: as delivery men, porters, janitors, and charwomen.

During the depression of the 1930's the Negroes' position deteriorated even further, for as we have noted, they were pushed out of jobs by competition from whites who always got preferred treatment. They had held a near monopoly as hotel waiters and bellboys, but they now were largely replaced by white bellboys and white waitresses. Employment declined for them both absolutely and relative to the whites in the more desirable fields of food manufacturing, laundries, cleaning and dyeing, in railroad maintenance, and in iron and steel manufacturing. At the same time, there was little gain for them in less desirable occupations in coal mining, in construction work, in lumber milling, or in domestic service, even though whites in ordinary times did not intrude on these "Negro jobs."

The Negro was, of course, a submerged element in the industry of the country everywhere, but his situation was much worse in the South than elsewhere. Technical improvements had tended to transfer unskilled jobs to skilled, and hence to white workers. The result was that Negroes were found only in retrogressing industries, stagnating occupations which were more strenuous physically, dirtier, and less attractive. The decline in handicraft industries as well as progressive automation accentuated the general trend, as in commercial laundries, where there was a spectacular decline in Negro washerwomen in the 1930's. As machines replaced wheelwrights and coopers, they, although white men as a rule, then took over less skilled jobs of Negroes in the same plants. Increased use of steel in construction displaced carpenters, one of the few skilled crafts still open to Negroes at the time.

During the early years of the twentieth century, Negroes were almost universally barred (locally if not nationally) from labor unions. This was rationalized by southern whites on the assumption that the

Negro could not learn skills or work with machines. Conversely, where Negroes demonstrated great manual dexterity, as in tobacco culture, this was pointed to as proof of their low intelligence; for it was perversely argued that superior races were notoriously unclever with their hands. Northern labor unions, eager to build their membership in the industrially backward South, had catered to these southern prejudices and adopted a "lily-white" program not unlike that of the Republican party. Spurred on by the New Deal in the 1930's, the CIO, the United Mine Workers, and the Farmers' Union set out to organize workers regardless of race. By 1935 there were twelve thousand Negroes in the miners' union, but progress elsewhere was slow. Efforts of agricultural workers, regardless of race, to better working conditions, drew public disapproval of planters and public officials. The Ku Klux Klan was revived to combat the CIO and other race-mixing unions. In 1943 only 12 per cent of southern Negro industrial workers were organized, as compared to 30 per cent of southern whites and 44 per cent of northern Negro workers.

The discriminatory conditions of Negro industrial employment were reflected in his wages. In 1935-36, Negro families in thirty-four, Georgia, Mississippi, North Carolina, and South Carolina towns and villages had annual incomes of less than $330, while white families in the same locations averaged $1220. Seventeen per cent of the Negro families had incomes of less than $250, but were not on relief. Only 4 per cent had incomes as high as $1000. Conditions were somewhat better in the larger cities; yet in Atlanta, half the Negro families had incomes less than $632, and half the "broken" Negro families had incomes of less than $332. At the same time, the Works Progress Administration reported that an income of $900 a year for a family of four could be adequate only on an emergency basis. Five years later, conditions had not improved. A study in 1940 revealed that between a third and a fourth of southern Negro urban and village families had annual incomes between $326 and $357.

With the outbreak of the Second World War, there were few skilled Negro workers in the South and no facilities for training the unskilled. Even the few skilled Negro workers sometimes went unemployed because of race prejudice. As the war boom progressed, however, more jobs became available to southern Negroes, either at home or by migrating North. Training programs for Negro workers also were organized. Even in these, however, the Negro was discriminated against both North and South, but more so in the latter. Although more than 25 per cent of the southern labor force in 1942 was Negro, only 7.5 per cent of those referred to pre-employment or refresher courses were Negroes. The local office of the Portsmouth, Virginia, federal employment service in advertising for workers in 1942, classified jobs by race, with the unskilled and domestic reserved for Negroes. Even the United States armed services, although offering young Negroes economic opportunity, did not eliminate segregation generally until the postwar period. Until April 1942 the Navy and Marine Corps would not accept Negroes, even on a segregated basis. Negro pilots were not accepted in the Air Force until later still.

Notwithstanding handicaps, urban Negro income grew rapidly during the Second World War. Between 1940 and 1944 average family income in two housing projects in Atlanta increased 65 per cent, despite a decrease in the number of family workers. This was due not only to increased pay in some occupations but to changes to better jobs. Negroes who had earned $360 as janitors became machine operators at $1500, and porters who earned $520 became United States mail clerks at $2600. One domestic maid increased her income 800 per cent when she became a drill operator.

With the coming of peace in 1945, Negroes, who lacked seniority in established industries because of their more recent employment and also because of the shutting down of war industries, were laid off in great numbers. The end of the wartime imposed FEPC in 1946 also lost them what protection they had enjoyed against discrimination. At the same time, however, the CIO and AFL launched Operation Dixie to eliminate racial discrimination in labor unions. Success achieved in textile, lumber, and food-processing industries indicated a lessening of racial barriers to union membership. Despite these gains, the median incomes of southern urban Negro families in 1946 was still only $1527 compared to $2709 for whites. Almost 28 per cent of Negro families had incomes under $1000 as compared to less than 8 per cent of whites. Also, "right to work" laws passed by southern legislatures in the postwar period retarded union membership in general. Urban Negroes were living from day to day, and they had scant security for the future. They were always the last to be employed and the first to be laid off. And in periods of business recession, as we have seen, they were even squeezed out of those jobs ordinarily reserved for them. Thus, chronic unemployment often became their fate and government relief their normal way of life. In a year of unusual prosperity, 1965, 50 per cent of the unemployed or out-of-school youths of the country were Negroes, yet they constituted only 15 per cent of that age group.

Whether in large cities or small towns, the urban Negro lived in segregated neighborhoods. The Civil Rights Act of 1866 gave the Negroes the right to hold land just as whites, and in 1917 the Supreme Court nullified a Louisville, Kentucky, ordinance restricting Negroes to one section of the city. Thereafter, practical segregation was effected throughout the South as in much of the North through private restrictive covenants in deeds. These were upheld by the Supreme Court in 1926, but voided after 1948, when the Court reversed itself. Economic conditions, however, as well as social mores, generally proved sufficient to prevent southern Negroes from moving into upper-class white neighborhoods. As a result they generally crowded into tenements or into back alleys in one- or two-room shacks which rented exorbitantly for 15 or 20 per cent of cash value. Often the neighborhoods had no sewers, or if they did the houses had no plumbing, and outdoor toilets served many families.

Under the American political system where public officials are so responsive to voters' sentiments, the disfranchised southern Negro was doubly disadvantaged by segregation in slum areas. Officials did not need to see that streets were paved or lighted, that there were adequate hospitals, schools, sewers, garbage disposal; for it was well known that people living in those neighborhoods did not vote in great numbers. On the other hand, where Negroes were permitted to vote as in the upper South in general and in some large cities in the deep South, neighborhoods were rewarded with improved streets, playgrounds, housing projects. Negroes in Atlanta defeated a bond issue until they were assured of adequate schools, and Negroes in Dallas in 1939 were given a high school and a graded school after they supported a bond issue there. These developments seemed to demonstrate the truth of the contention that all progress for the Negro in the South was dependent upon his securing political power.

But all southern Negroes did not fall into only the two classes of farm and urban labor. Just as segregation caused a breakdown of

communication between the races, it created the necessity for the
black man to design a social order of his own. He did this by copying
the white man's: excluded from participation in the white world, the
Negro built a duplicate. As segregation became established, the Negro
soon developed social and economic classes and the institutions which
accompanied them: churches, schools, banks, theaters, professions, and
other services. In this society, the business and professional man occupied first place, just as he did in the white. Education and lightness
of color also helped determine class. Negro professionals, although
excluded from serving white clients, had almost a monopoly of the
black. They were, therefore, in the paradoxical position of both suffering from segregation and benefiting from it.

But there were additional handicaps suffered by Negro professionals. Negro teachers, whether in the schools or in the colleges,
taught only Negroes. Negro doctors could not as a rule practice in
southern hospitals. They were denied opportunity for internships and
residencies, clinical facilities, and membership in county and state medical societies. This tended to make all of them general practitioners.
Since extension of public health service caused them to lose their patients, they were opposed to all "socialized medicine" schemes. Negro
lawyers were few in number, comprising less than one-half of one
per cent of the bar in most rural southern states. Rarely did they
appear in court to defend Negroes against white litigants, but confined
their efforts to criminal practice and to disputes between Negroes.

Probably because of the great insecurity that surrounded his
everyday life, the southern Negro moved but slowly toward a stable
family life. Marriage among slaves was unknown to the law of the Old
South, and sexual promiscuity was not only practiced by slaves but
often encouraged by masters. Invading Union armies disrupted what
meager family life did exist on the plantations, and the completely
demoralized Negroes who wandered about the country in the wake
of the armies became extremely dissolute. In reconstruction days,
marriage was legalized and gradually accepted, although there continued for decades to be much cohabiting without benefit of clergy,
particularly in the rural South, where conditions of society more nearly
resembled those of slave times. Women were "heads of families" in
more than a fifth of southern Negro households, while fewer than
a twelfth of white households were without a husband and father.

A distinguished Negro scholar in 1949 stated that there was still great uncertainty about the marital status of Negroes.

Courtship began at an early age and often involved sexual relations, frequently resulting in pregnancy. Mores of the community imposed no sense of impropriety in such cases, except that during courtship the girl properly had only one man. Even after marriage, no misbehavior was attached to "outside affairs," although throughout the South among better-class Negroes, morals of the daughters were strictly guarded and constancy in marriage emphasized. Among the poor, however, family life suffered because mothers and wives had to work to supplement meager incomes. Then, too, the unusual mobility of Negro life often broke up families, sending men and women to work in different locales. In many such cases, they simply moved in with another mate, even if legally married, and without bothering to get a divorce. According to a statement issued by the Urban League in 1965, 25 per cent of Negro women were separated or living apart from their husbands, as compared with 8 per cent of white women who were. Sex relations between white men and Negro women, common during slavery, persisted after emancipation, particularly with lower-class white men. It has probably decreased in recent years, but as late as 1951 it was still not uncommon.[4]

In addition to the family, the principal social organizations of the freedman were the church and fraternal orders. Before emancipation, slaves had worshiped in the master's church, but tiring of segregation in the lofts the freedman withdrew and formed his own congregation. The greatest number went into the Baptist Church, probably because of the tendency to emotional stimulation in the services of that sect, and also because education and training were not prerequisites for the ministry to which many Negroes aspired. Negro religious services, particularly in the rural South, were marked by dancing, shouting, groaning, jumping frantically up and down, crying, beating of breasts, frantic embraces, and abject groveling until complete exhaustion. In addition to its ordinary function, the church served the Negro also as a theater and a social forum. Fraternal organizations, frequently open to both sexes and often with a secret ritual, gave the Negro an opportunity to develop leadership as well as community

(4) E. Franklin Frazier, *The Negro in the United States* (New York, 1957), 215, 280–319 *passim*.

and racial consciousness, and were a dominant influence in his social life.

It is almost universally believed that Negroes have been more criminal than whites and statistics seem to bear out this belief. But statistics on crime, unreliable at best, are even less trustworthy in regard to Negroes. The FBI's annual report for 1964, for instance, disclosed that Negroes, who made up only 11 per cent of the country's population, accounted for more than 28 per cent of the crime. But Roy Wilkins of the NAACP pointed out quite properly the misleading implications of this announcement; for dragnet arrests for a crime committed by one or two people frequently resulted in the arrest of dozens of Negroes, most of whom were subsequently dismissed. But their names were in the record books as arrested on criminal charges, and in the public mind Negro arrests were equated with Negro crime.

Most Negro crime had to do with theft, generally petty theft, and mayhem. Much of the theft charged to southern Negroes may have been regarded by them as compensation for starvation wages and for exploitation by dishonest or unscrupulous landlords and storekeepers. Booker T. Washington, relating an incident when his mother stole a chicken from her master's coop and fed it to her hungry children, concluded that "No one could ever make me believe that my mother was guilty of thieving. She was simply a victim of the system of slavery."[5] Rarely were Negroes guilty of "white collar" crimes, violation of anti-trust laws or income-tax evasion. They have also been relatively low in sex offenses.

In the years following emancipation the increase in Negro criminality was at least partly due to the convict-lease system. Another explanation for the unusually high incidence of Negro crime was the tendency on the part of southern police officials to assume the guilt of any Negro charged with crime or apprehended under conditions even faintly suspicious. This same inclination to assume the Negro's guilt existed among whites in general; thus, all-white juries, which prevailed everywhere in southern states, were easily persuaded by zealous prosecutors to convict Negroes on doubtful evidence that would not prevail against a white man. It is quite probable, therefore,

(5) *Up From Slavery* (New York, 1907), 4–5.

that exclusion of Negroes from juries increased significantly Negro convictions for crime in the South.

Police brutality in exacting confessions, often from innocent Negroes, was also a factor in Negro crime statistics. The police, usually coming from classes that were socially insecure, with little education and training for their work, held the Negro in contempt and were notorious for the use of intimidation and violence on Negro suspects. When the violence resulted in the death of the suspect, the dead but unconvicted Negro became merely another criminal statistic. Of 479 Negroes killed by whites in the South in the dozen years between 1920 and 1932, 260, or over half, were killed by police. Nor were such victims always suspected felons. In 1945 a Negro named Hall was beaten to death by Sheriff Claude Screws of Baker County, Georgia. Hall was in jail for protesting the police beating of his aged father. In 1958 James Brazier was beaten to death while in jail at Dawson, Georgia, for participating in a civil rights protest; and a Negro was fatally shot by an Alabama state policeman in March 1965 while engaging in a peaceable demonstration protesting against disfranchisement. In 1954 alone the federal government prosecuted thirty-two police officials for brutality to Negroes, but without obtaining a conviction.

Of course, both police brutality and exclusion of Negroes from juries were manifestations of the total denial of political rights to the Negro in a society that was otherwise ultra-democratic in administering its system of justice. For judges, prosecutors, sheriffs, jailors, constables, and other administrative officials were elective and were thus responsive to the inclinations and prejudices of the voters. And since the Negro had no active part in selecting these officials, and since he had no part in the jury except to appear before it as a potential victim, the whole system—police, prosecutor, jailor, and jury—were arrayed against him. Thus, democracy itself, so long as the Negro had no active part in it, worked to his disadvantage in the quest for justice. It may well be, too, that part of the high Negro crime rate stems from the Negro's belief that he cannot obtain justice in the white man's courts and that he must exact it for himself.

This uneven-handed justice for the Negro resulted not only in an extraordinarily high conviction rate but also in the imposition of harsher penalties than were imposed on whites for the same crime. The complex scheme of Mississippi justice outlined by Professor James W. Silver held true in general for all the South: "One standard of justice prevails when a Negro commits a crime against a Negro, another when a Negro commits a crime against a white, still another when a white commits a crime against a white, and a fourth when a white commits a crime against a Negro."[6] The undue severity and discrimination he suffered under such practice caused the Negro to regard both the police and the courts with distrust and those convicted as martyrs.

Regardless of the injustice he suffered or the reasons for it, there seems convincing evidence that Negro crime increased greatly after emancipation, and the increase was progressive. Between 1904 and 1910, the number of Negro convicts increased five fold, while in the country as a whole homicides committed by Negroes were at a rate seven times that of whites. It is not so clear, on the other hand, that homicides by southern Negroes are out of proportion to homicides by southern whites; for the South was a land of violence long before the Negro obtained his freedom. Through most of the nineteenth century, long after the practice of dueling had ceased elsewhere, southern gentlemen defended their honor with pistols at ten paces, while lesser folk settled their differences with bowie knives, bludgeonings, eye-gougings, or plain fisticuffs.

The tendency to violence which had grown in the southern backwoods and which had been perpetuated in the *code duello* of the planter did not abate with the passing of the old regime. On the contrary, the New South was more given to violence than the Old. A decade and a half after the redemption, the state of South Carolina reported almost three times as many homicides as all of New England put together. At the same time, Virginia and North Carolina each reported four times as many homicides as Massachusetts; Georgia almost six times as many, and Tennessee more than seven times as many. All of these southern states were smaller in population than Massachusetts, all were high in their percentage of rural native-born Americans, and few had slum areas comparable to Massachusetts with her high percentage of immigrants. In the same year, Michigan had only a fourth of the homicides reported in Alabama; Mississippi had five

(6) *Mississippi: The Closed Society* (New York, 1963, 1964), 152.

times as many as Wisconsin; and Louisiana had almost five times as
many as Minnesota. Texas had more than three times as many as
Kansas and Nebraska combined. Much of this killing could be attrib-
uted to the Negro, but not all; for in South Carolina and Texas, at
least, the percentage of homicides by whites was much greater than
their proportion of the population. On the other hand, according to
a report of the FBI issued in 1937, the murder rate in the eleven
Confederate states was 23.23 per 100,000 people living in towns and
cities of 10,000 or more, and most of it occurred in Negro slum areas.
This rate was five times as great as in the north-central and far western
states, six times as great as in the mid-Atlantic area, and eighteen
times as great as in New England.

The reasons for southern violence cannot be known for certain;
they can only be surmised. One theory is that the very nature of
southern society, the simple, direct, and immensely personal world
in which the southerner lived, placed great stress on the inviolability
of what he regarded as his honor, but which in another milieu might
have been regarded as mere ego. Any insult or affront must be redressed by simple, direct means. Partly, perhaps, this was because
the white man during reconstruction felt frustrated at his inability
to obtain justice in the Yankee-controlled courts. The only justice
he thought he could obtain was that which he secured with his own
hands.

Under this theory, not only must private wrong be redressed,
but public offenses as well. The southerner's impatience and impetu-
ousness at the law's slow pace led him to demand instant satisfaction
not only for personal insult but also for what he regarded as violation
of fundamental rules of social order. When confronted by a crime
that aroused his passions he was unwilling to let the law take its course
in some dim future and uncertain way. This tradition antedated reconstruction; for long before hatred of the Negro had begun to affect
its behavior, the South had become a region addicted to lynch law.
In the twenty years before the Civil War more than three hundred
persons, 90 per cent of them white, were said to have been hanged
or burned by mob action in the section. But this tradition of vigilantism, which in other regions passed with the frontier conditions
which inspired it, continued far into the twentieth-century South.
And the Negro, who had been relatively immune from white violence

during slavery except for the whippings his master might administer, became after reconstruction the chief object of the white man's violence.

There are no statistics of lynch law prior to 1882, but it is well known that Negroes became victims of mobs frequently during reconstruction. Curiously, in the early years of statistic-keeping, more whites than Negroes were victims, 595 to 440 between the years 1882 and 1888. The following year the figures changed, when 76 whites and 94 Negroes were lynched. In 1892, the highest recorded year, 69 whites and 162 Negroes were mob victims. In the ten years from 1918 to 1927, there were 455 victims of whom 416 were Negroes, 11 of them Negro women. Between 1889 and 1940 there were 3833 lynchings, 90 per cent of them in the South and with about 80 per cent of the victims Negroes. The number reached a peak in the early 1890's, averaging about 200 annually, then began to diminish with the Negro's general acceptance of inferior status. There were never fewer than 75 in any one year until 1904, but they rose again to 88 in 1908. They dropped to 35 in 1917, rose to 75 in 1919, then dropped to 25 in 1924. During the 1930's the annual average was about 10. There were 6 in 1936.

During the 1940's and early 1950's, the practice all but disappeared, only to be revived in the renewed racial disturbances of the past decade. When Mack Parker of Poplarville, Mississippi, was taken from jail in April 1959, shot and thrown into a nearby stream, he became the 3441st Negro victim since Tuskegee started compiling lynching statistics. Meantime, however, untold numbers of threatened Negroes had avoided lynching by flight or else by conforming their behavior to that demanded by segregationists. The most common offenses charged against the victims were homicide and attempted rape. One authority has estimated that at least a third of the victims were innocent of the offenses for which they suffered. State, but not local authorities, generally attempted to prevent the lynchings, but once the crime was committed little effort was made to bring lynchers to justice. From 1900 to 1929 there were only 8 cases involving 54 persons convicted for lynching, and all got light or suspended sentences. Most lynch mobs were made up of lower-class whites, but occasionally some of the middle and upper classes took part. Few whites ever spoke out against the criminals.

In addition to the planned lynchings, there were riots in which Negroes fought back against whites. The Houston riot during the First World War resulted in the killing of seventeen whites. As a consequence of this riot, thirteen Negroes were hanged and forty-one others were sentenced to life imprisonment. An Atlanta riot in 1906 killed ten Negroes, two whites; a 1919 riot in Phillips County, Arkansas, resulted in the deaths of more than twenty-five of both races. There were also great numbers of killings of Negroes by white men which did not have the semiformal trappings generally associated with mob lynching. After redemption the courts, now in the hands of white men, gave immunity to white killers of Negroes. Rarely did the killing of a Negro by a white man call for legal inquiry, or if it did the verdict of the coroner or jury was invariably "self-defense" or "justified homicide." There was, for instance, the case of Lamar Smith, shot to death at high noon in front of a Mississippi courthouse in August 1955. Three white men were indicted but never brought to trial because, a Mississippi judge explained, no white man in that state could be persuaded to testify against another for killing a Negro. Thus, at least in a passive way, did the southern judicial system encourage violence.

The decline in lynching after 1900 was probably due to the rising standard of living and to improved education. Federal anti-lynching bills, which were kept from passing only by Senate filibusters, also contributed to the decline, as did work by organizations of southern white women who ridiculed claims that the practice was a protector of womanhood. It is worthy of note that men like Vardaman and Tillman, who in political campaigns advocated mob violence, as governors were leaders in the move to curb lynching. Vardaman called out the militia, commandeered a train, and took personal charge of a move to prevent the lynching of two Delta Negroes. Tillman supported a provision in the South Carolina constitution of 1895 which permitted the removal from office of sheriffs who through negligence or connivance permitted a lynching. He also supported a provision making the county where a lynching occurred liable for damages of $2000 or more, the sum to be paid to heirs of the victim.

Another factor in the decline of lynching was the mass exodus of Negroes from the neighborhood of the crime. Planters, faced with a labor problem, demanded that the practice cease. Most important, however, was urbanization; for lynching was almost altogether a rural, agrarian act of violence. After 1914, lynchings in towns of ten thousand or more were practically nonexistent. The feeling prevailed in those communities that no self-respecting white would participate in lynchings. Also, fear and hate of the Negro were diminishing to the vanishing point in such communities.

The most effective means the southern Negro found to fight back against the economic and social injustice which surrounded him was to migrate. Shortly after redemption he began leaving the South in great numbers. More than two hundred left South Carolina in 1878 for settlement in Liberia. The following year a movement to settle in Kansas began which would take to that section within a few years more than 5000 Negroes, mostly from Louisiana and Mississippi. But this was merely a start. By 1910 more than 6000 Negroes were moving out of the South annually, most of them to northern cities. In 1860 only 345,000 southern-born Negroes lived in the North; fifty years later this figure had tripled. The great period of migration, however, took place during and after the First World War, when nearly 2 million moved. Whole communities sometimes picked up their meager possessions and joined the hegira. In 1900 about 90 per cent of all American Negroes still lived in the South; by 1930 only 78 per cent did.

There was a steady relative loss in Negro population in all southern states, but those of the deep South, where conditions were harshest, lost most. The movement was further stimulated by the cotton restriction program of the AAA during the New Deal which pushed many Negroes off the land; but it was spurred as much by increased opportunity in northern war industry as by a change in the southern agricultural economy or by race persecution. In the war industries boom during the Second World War a quarter-million Negroes also moved to the Pacific coast. By 1958 New York had more Negroes than any southern state and Illinois ranked sixth in Negro population. Needless to say, the exodus created problems for southern whites more than had runaway slaves in the ante-bellum South, and strenuous efforts were used to dissuade departing Negroes. When propaganda and bribery of Negro leaders failed, threats and even violence were sometimes resorted to.

Migration from southern farms to southern cities was nearly as great as the migration out of the region. In 1860 only 6.7 per cent of southern Negroes lived in cities, where they constituted less than 20 per cent of the population; but between 1900 and 1930, more than 2 million Negroes moved from rural to southern urban areas. By 1950, more than half of the southern Negro population lived in nonfarm areas, and they counted nearly a third of the urban population in the South. The Negro population of the black belt shrunk accordingly: from 4 million in 1900 to 2.5 million in 1940. Where formerly Negroes had been a majority of the population of that area, by the latter date they constituted only a quarter. Mississippi, however, was an exception to this general trend, for the Negro population of the Delta counties had a relative increase during the period.

This greater diffusion of the Negro population, both throughout the country and within the South, brought limited benefits to the southern Negro. City life, even in slum dwellings, had advantages over rural: less discrimination, less brutality, better economic opportunity, and better cultural advantages. The remarkable change in the racial geography of the South also produced political change. For the exodus of Negroes from the black belt reduced the total population of those regions, with a consequent shrinking in the influence of black-belt whites in shaping the dominant political tone of the state.

It is not to be suggested that those Negroes who left the region reached a land of Gilead where impartial justice awaited them. But that is another story which does not concern us here. Most of those who remained, however, learned to adjust their behavior so as to conform to the ideas of the dominant whites. The Negro studied the white man more than the white man studied him. Artfully and adroitly, he accommodated his manners to the weaknesses and foibles of the whites and used his knowledge to eliminate friction and to further his own interests.

This ingratiating behavior clothed the Negro with certain "racial characteristics" which were not necessarily his true nature, such as improvidence, apathy, and laziness. It also tended to reward servility, obsequiousness, and humility rather than competence, and thus reacted to the white employer's disadvantage. Not only did it cause the white man to put up with careless and shiftless work because no more was expected of Negroes, but he himself became an addict of the same slow inefficiency. George W. Cable noted this at the turn of the century: "The master-caste tolerates, with unsurpassed supineness and unconsciousness, a more indolent, inefficient, slovenly, unclean, untrustworthy, ill-mannered, noisy, disrespectful, disputatious, and yet servile domestic and public menial service than is tolerated by any other enlightened people."[7]

Meanwhile, Negro leadership had experienced considerable transition. If any one person could be considered spokesman for the race in the first decades after emancipation, that man was Frederick Douglass. Born at Tuckahoe, Maryland, the son of a slave woman and an unknown white man, he learned to read and write as a house servant in Baltimore. He escaped in 1838, fled to the North, came under the influence of William Lloyd Garrison, and joined the abolitionist movement. He was a natural orator, and in the reconstruction and post-reconstruction periods he was a militant although ultimately ineffective crusader for suffrage and civil rights for the freedman.

When Douglass died in 1895, his place was taken by Booker T. Washington, whose leadership is discussed in connection with education. Of an entirely different mind from Washington was William E. Burghardt Du Bois, who for a decade before Washington's death challenged his leadership. Unlike both Douglass and Washington, Du Bois had been born of free parents in Massachusetts and was educated at Fisk, Harvard, and Berlin. Joining the faculty of Atlanta University in 1896, Du Bois started at once a systematic and scientific study of the Negro. Seeing the same conditions that Booker T. Washington saw in the plight of the southern Negro, Du Bois had a somewhat different perspective. He charged Washington with surrendering the Negro's political rights to the white man's harsh code of caste, and he issued a clarion call for more aggressive action on the part of the Negro in the overthrow of discrimination.

Du Bois's call resulted in a meeting of two dozen Negro intellectuals at Niagara Falls in the summer of 1905, where an organization was formed to wage an unending war on segregation. Washington and his philosophy of "separate but equal" were denounced, and a bitter enmity developed between the two great Negro leaders. So long as Washington lived, the struggle between them for leadership was an unequal one; for Washington had influence with whites. He advised Presidents on federal patronage for Negroes; by his influence with white advertisers he could make or break Negro newspapers;

(7) *The Negro Question* (New York, 1890), 23.

he virtually directed white philanthropy for Negro education and welfare. But with Washington's death in 1915, no other Negro in the country had the stature or the talent of Du Bois, and he became, in effect, the new Negro spokesman.

Meantime, in a race riot in Lincoln's home town, Springfield, Illinois, in the summer of 1908, more than a dozen Negroes were killed, while mobs controlled the city for two days. This event brought white liberals in the North to the Negro's side. A call for a National Negro Conference went out over the signatures of fifty-three leaders, forty-seven of whom were white. Included in the list were Lincoln Steffens, William Dean Howells, Oswald Garrison Villard, John Dewey, Jane Addams, and Florence Kelley. The leaders of the Niagara Movement joined with this group, and from their union there emerged in 1910 the National Association for the Advancement of Colored People. Du Bois left his professorship in Atlanta, moved to New York, as director of the new organization and editor of its journal, *The Crisis*.

At first the NAACP was largely a white organization, Du Bois being the only Negro official. Within a few years, however, a number of Negroes were placed on the board of directors. In recent years both races have been well represented in its national organization, but local chapters are made up almost altogether of Negroes. But Du Bois during most of his life was its guiding genius and gave it direction, and the conciliatory policy of Washington gave way to militance in the Negro movement. Making shrewd use of publicity to dramatize lynchings and all forms of discrimination, the NAACP kept active lobbies in state and national capitals to get fair play for the Negro. It acted as a sentinel over his rights, and brought legal action to prevent injustice. It paid counsel for Negroes involved in law suits regarding segregation or discrimination. In 1919 it issued a statement of principle calling for abolition of legal injustice for Negroes, an end to discrimination in railroad travel, equal opportunity for Negro children in education, assurance of common rights of citizenship for Negroes, and an end to lynching. Largely through its efforts, the House of Representatives passed the Dyer Anti-Lynching bill in 1921. Similar bills cleared the House on numerous occasions but always were killed in the Senate through the filibuster, which took advantage of the Senate rule of unlimited debate.

and more southern Negroes, and the old program of patient forbearance advocated by Washington was gradually eroded in urban centers. In 1940 the Association issued a new eight-point program which, in addition to repeating the unrealized aims of the 1919 statement, called for an end to share-crop peonage, elimination of suffrage discrimination, and equal educational and employment opportunities.

Because the NAACP had its main strength in the North it was suspect in the South, where segregationists falsely attempted to equate it with Communism. Nevertheless, the organization steadfastly acted as "a watchman on the wall," intervening again and again on the Negro's behalf. Ralph Bunche, who was not entirely sympathetic with its program, credited the NAACP for "setting a new pattern of thought among Negroes." Its vigor in fighting for Negro rights in the courts "opened the eyes of the Negro to an entirely new vista."[8] It also opened the eyes of a new breed of politician in both the great political parties.

Formed in the same year as the NAACP and co-operating with it in many ways was the National Urban League. But the Urban League traditionally concentrated on bread-and-butter problems, working behind the scenes to improve job and living conditions for Negroes, while leaving the work of agitation and political activity to others. Its membership was basically middle-class and the League's executive director, Whitney M. Young, Jr., himself a Negro, took pride in the basic conservativeness and social conformity of middle-class Negroes. At the other end of the spectrum of responsible organizations working for the improvement of the Negro was the Congress of Racial Equality (CORE), with chapters in all parts of the country, and the Student Nonviolent Coordinating Committee (SNCC). These organizations had less patience than did other civil rights groups, and they took the lead in the 1960's in the more militant phases of the picketing and sit-in protest demonstrations of the period.

The New Deal outlawed discrimination in employment in such agencies as WPA, PWA, NYA, and the CCC. All these had to do with public, not private, employment, and most of them died with the end of their work programs. As the nation geared for World War II, the federal government made repeated but generally ineffective efforts to get private industry and labor to remove bars to equal

(8) Quoted in Gunnar Myrdal, *An American Dilemma*, 833n.

employment opportunity. In the program designed to train labor for defense work, only a small fraction were Negroes. In June 1941 President Roosevelt, issued his executive order forbidding discrimination in defense employment, and established an emergency Fair Employment Practices Commission to deal with violations. The chief significance of the wartime FEPC lay not in its accomplishments but in its trail-blazing. It was handicapped by lack of authority in nondefense industry, lack of power to subpoena witnesses or to enforce its findings. It could only report violations and call on the President for punitive action. At the end of the war it expired.

With the end of the wartime FEPC, local volunteer councils began to organize for permanent state and national FEPCs, with groups truly representative of the communities. By mid-1945, fifty such councils, aided by the NAACP and other organizations, were bringing pressures for a permanent FEPC. By 1948 both major parties had nondiscriminatory planks in their platforms and both Presidential candidates pledged support. But Congress adjourned without creating the Commission that year, as it would do repeatedly in years to come. In the House, the Rules Committee, dominated by Virginia's Howard Smith, blocked action: in the Senate, southerners threatened filibuster. But the NAACP and its allies worked on, sounding the alarms that kept Negroes from losing by default what little gains they had made.

By mid-twentieth century the Negro, while striving for improvement, still had a demonstrably inferior position in relation to the white man in the South. Despite remarkable achievements of individuals of his race, the typical southern Negro seemed to regard himself as shiftless and well adapted to his wretched condition. He seemed to confirm the charge of the white southerner that it was he who was responsible for the backwardness of the South. Constituting one-fourth of the population of the region, the Negro would have to have his lot dramatically improved before its agriculture could be reformed, its industry developed, and the national economic standards attained. The South and the Negro seemed to be caught in a vicious circle where each was holding the other back. Only through forceful and sustained action from the federal government would this impasse be broken.

XV

Urbanization of the South

By many standards of measurement the South since 1870 has been a vast rural island of isolated humanity. Even though the region made manful efforts to attract immigrants, little was accomplished. The European immigrant, either because he misunderstood the land and its industrial potential or because he disliked the racial and social conditions existing there, passed up the South for the great eastern and midwestern industrial cities and the agricultural states in the Northwest. As a result the southerners were left to multiply from a basic pioneer stock of British, western European, and African origins. By 1960 this pattern had scarcely been disturbed. Foreign-born in the southern states ranged from 0.1 per cent in South Carolina and Mississippi to 2.8 per cent in Texas.

The resource which did most to shape southern history in the years after 1865 was its people. During the first decade after the war, there were approximately 10,773,000 people, of whom 6,612,182 were white. A century later these numbers had expanded to 36,295,000 whites and 10,068,310 Negroes. These figures symbolize both the human facts and the comparative productive capacities of the two periods. Whether black or white this was an indigenous population which was entrusted with the social and economic fate of the South. Between 1870 and 1965 the population of the South had exhibited considerable vibrancy, often in negative form so far as southern progress was concerned. There was a tremendous amount of movement within the region, and even more away from it. Had the population born in the southern states during the past century remained there, the present number of southerners would be at least quadrupled. During these years a constant stream of immigrants left for other parts of the Union. In the first postwar years white southerners moved to the expanding western frontier to escape the austerity and discouragement of reconstruction in their native states. The Negro was almost as restless.

Howard Odum wrote:

> The story of the Southeast's migration is not only a continued story of the South's economics but also of its agrarian culture, since it is from the rural South that the people have moved most. This is true in three major aspects of movement; namely, from rural to urban within the several states, from rural to urban in inter-southern state migration, and from other regions than the Southeast.

In 1930 of more than 28 million native-born in the South, some 24 million were born in rural districts. The rural South was already overpopulated, and 6.5 million people were forced to move elsewhere, over half out of the South entirely, the rest to southern towns and cities. J. T. Woofter, Jr., has said that the South exported about one-fourth of its natural population increase.

The quality of individuals in this horde migrating from the South was highly variable. Among the migrants were illiterates who were prompted to move away in hope they could both better their economic and social conditions. Among them also, though, went men and women who were well educated and trained and thus urgently needed in the region to assume leadership positions. Thus the South was deprived of talent it needed to improve conditions in the region and to diversify its economy. Migration took away from an already severely limited supply of trained people necessary to make the South competitive with other sections of the country. Conversely, the migration of poor ill-educated, untrained people, unfortunately went far to shape the southern image outside the region.

The heaviest migration has occurred since 1920. In the pre-depression decade, 1920-30, the Southeast lost nearly 3.5 million persons, while in the decade, 1950-60 it lost over 3 million, almost half of them Negroes. States of the old black-belt cotton regions lost Negroes more heavily, while states in the mountainous Appalachian sections lost mainly whites. In the 1940's only Florida, Virginia, and Texas showed an increase in population, and Florida alone had an increase in its Negro population. During the 1940's and 1950's the percentage loss of white population ranged from 0.3 in South Carolina to 19 in Arkansas. Arkansas, Mississippi, Alabama, South Carolina, and Georgia lost the most Negroes.

Large numbers of young people between the ages of twenty and thirty-five took part in this migration. Since 1940 this drainage of human resource occurred among those with the most education—those who had completed at least the ninth grade—most of whom were bound for urban centers. In the 1940's, more than 4 million persons in this age group left the South.

The same pattern occurred within the South itself. There was great movement away from the rural areas into the cities, and here too it was those with educational background and leadership potential who tended to move. Between 1920 and 1948, the urban population of the region increased by over 9 million. In the next decade, 1950-60, nearly 3 million southerners changed counties, which indicates the increased restlessness and mobility of people within the region; this figure, however, fails to take account of the large number of families who moved within the limits of their own counties. These population statistics indicate quite conclusively that southern farm population has been shrinking at a very rapid rate during the past 50 years. Simultaneously, and especially since 1945, industrial communities and urban centers have undergone tremendous growth.

This movement of whites has produced a violent change in the region. Youth have moved from poor rural schools to those presumably of better quality in urban centers, and they have then gone into industrial and commercial services. Farmers became industrial employees, public service workers, and retail store clerks. Likewise, towns have turned into cities, with corresponding changes in their institutions and appearance. A different kind of southern urban life had existed in those small towns, many of them county seats and a few of them state capitals—Raleigh, Columbia, Montgomery, Tallahassee, Frankfort, Jackson, and Austin—and still relatively small cities. Originally the capital cities had substantial historical and economic importance, for their business was almost exclusively that of politics and providing services for state employees and officials.

The county-seat communities have been of major significance to southern life, yet it is to be doubted that many of them have contributed materially to the creation of a southern urban civilization. Almost invariably they have been farmer towns, catering to rural customers and county officials. Primarily they were market centers in which were located gins, warehouses, cotton buyers, tobacco sales floors, livestock pens, and railway depots. It was to these towns that mule and horse drovers from Kentucky, Ohio, Missouri, Iowa, and Kansas brought hundreds of animals early each spring for sale to farmers. Drummers representing big-city wholesale houses came with their wares to canvass both town and country merchants, to corrupt local morals, and to patronize the rambling old-fashioned hotels which were often more famous for the tables they set than for the comfort of their beds.

In some southern states like Virginia, Kentucky, and Tennessee county court day was an important institution, not necessarily because of judicial transactions, but rather as a gathering and market day. Horses, mules, cattle, dogs, poultry, and everything else that a farmer or his wife could think of to sell were brought to town to be peddled on court day. Politicians, noisy evangelizing preachers, peddlers, con men, patent-medicine quacks with their minstrel antics, women's bazaars, and petitioners all found audiences and customers among the throngs gathered for the meeting of the court or board of supervisors. Here news, rumor, and gossip were passed along. Many a crusader working for a cause or exploiting a prejudice was able to mold public opinion at these gatherings, a fact which often accounted for the peculiar political responses of the region.

The county seat was more than this; it was also the place where the weekly newspaper was published, where banks operated, where doctors, lawyers, and dentists had their offices, where one departed from and returned to in traveling beyond county limits. General merchandising houses lined their main streets, and fertilizer warehouses, cotton oil mills, and produce houses, filled their alleys. Lumber and crosstie yards, ice houses, and coal yards were standard establishments, and no southern town could be progressively respectable without them. Most southern town general stores differed little from their rural counterparts. They carried in stock about every item of merchandise offered by wholesale merchants and jobbers. Some town stores offered a somewhat more sophisticated type of goods, especially in men and women's clothing. This was particularly true where Jewish merchants operated stores. In large numbers these merchants had served arduous apprenticeships as pack peddlers through their territories before they accumulated enough capital to open main-street stores.

Southern urbanism was hardly true urbanism in the modern sense. The line between country town and countryside was scarcely perceptible, and only a very small portion of the population of these places fell within the more recent technical classification of rural non-farm. The great majority of people living in southern towns had themselves moved in from the country, and had left behind numerous relatives. Occasionally an enterprising local leader attempted to make the distinction between town and country more precise by organizing booster and culture groups such as men and women's service and social clubs. Attempts were made to improve the quality of town schools over those of surrounding rural neighborhoods. Religious activities were somewhat more dignified and ministers serving town charges often were more inhibited than those for country congregations. Town preachers often were better educated and socially more sophisticated, and congregations themselves tended to be more important as social clubs than as mere religious bodies. Small-country-town society exhibited a tight-knit social and family provincial snobbery which denied progress on the one hand and belied urbanism on the other. It made little difference whether a county-seat town was located in central Kentucky or south Georgia, there was little if any really discernible difference between them.

Unlike the old county-seat towns and villages that revolved about southern farming activity, hundreds of mill villages and towns were organized to serve special industries. After 1870, around the rising cotton mills villages developed with workers who were even more essential to the success of the mills than was the machinery itself. Actually most of these places never became truly urban communities. They were socially and economically suspended between a rural-farming community pattern of life and a specialized industrial one. Their inhabitants seldom broke sharply with their rural backgrounds, and many of them probably returned eventually to farms. Churches and schools were largely of the rural types, and religious manifestations were often of a highly expressive or emotional nature. Schools had the same deficiencies that rural schools in general had. Recreation was severely limited and again was more nearly of the rural type than that of an organized urban community. The earlier mill villages did differ from older farming communities in that people lived in close proximity in overcrowded housing, the company owned and controlled housing; the daily routine was dependent upon the operational schedules of the mills, and goods were sold and credit controlled by company stores. An individual southerner living in a mill village made a tremendous surrender of personal independence of the kind he knew on the farm. No longer could he set the length of his work day, be absent from work without risking loss of his job, or control the conditions under which he worked. Since members of his family usually worked in the mills too, the family's freedom of action was often restricted. The worker also found it difficult to exercise an independent judgment in public matters in many instances.

Early villages were comprised of rural people who had had no previous experience in close communal living. There were problems of breaking old personal habits, especially in areas of sanitation and public health, and of invading the privacy of neighbors, or of having one's own privacy invaded. Public water sources were contaminated at the outset, little or no public provision was made for sewage disposal, and the old shackles of rural illiteracy and ineffective schooling were seldom broken by the move to a mill village. Women and children labored under unhealthy and unsafe conditions, and this constantly threatened life and peace of mind. The outbreaks of epidemic diseases threatened whole villages with disaster. Individual moral stamina was subjected to greater temptations and strains than was the case on mountain and piedmont farms. Thus a new and more relaxed social code frequently grew out of the new patterns of mill village associations. This was sufficiently true in most cases to cause the raising of social barriers between older, smug county-seat type communities and the new communities organized around the mills.

Though the conventional mill villages contributed little to the central urbanization of the South, some important towns and cities did grow up around the mills and were vitally influenced by an expanding textile industry. Among these were Greensboro, Burlington, Durham, Charlotte, and Gastonia in North Carolina; Spartanburg, Greenville, Gaffney, Honeapath, Columbia, and Belton in South Carolina; and, West Point in Georgia. Charlotte, Greenville, and Spartanburg became major administrative headquarter cities for mills that operated in many towns and villages surrounding them.

Opening of coal and iron ore beds along the spine of the Appalachians brought about the organization of hundreds of villages and coal camps. The southern coal camp had all the shortcomings of the textile village, plus some of its own. Physical surroundings, despite the great beauty of the mountains, were about as ugly and repulsive as man could make them. With its eternal sulphurous smoke haze, dust, and nauseous burning slate piles coal mining destroyed every vestige of beauty and local pride. Usually villages were located on the floors of deep coves where flash floods constantly threatened life and health. Because coal seams were highly exhaustible, few mining villages were ever constructed with the thought of permanency, hence the use of the more precise term "camp." Coal-camp houses were small and flimsy, sanitary facilities were either unknown or most primitive, water supplies were constantly contaminated, parasitic infection ran high, and other diseases, especially tuberculosis, spread rapidly.

At periods during and immediately following World War I when national industrial expansion used tremendous tonnages of coal, wages were relatively high and miners lived extravagantly in what was called the silk-shirt era. Crime rates were high, and standards of moral and social behavior fell below those of older and more stable communities. Churches were poor, and were often of the highly emotional pentecostal type. Schools were equally defective, largely because they lacked adequate housing, mature teachers, local tax support, and the deep concern of state departments of education.

As in the textile industry there came into existence some important permanent communities which either grew up about the mines or were deeply influenced by the industry. Among these were Birmingham, Bessemer, and Ensley, in Alabama; Chattanooga, Harriman, La-Follette, Jellico, and Knoxville in Tennessee; Middlesboro, Pineville, Harlan, Pikeville, Madisonville, Hazard, and Greenville in Kentucky; and Huntington and Charleston in West Virginia.

Lumbering created hundreds of villages and camps but few permanent towns as this industry moved across the great timber belt between 1870 and 1920. The southern lumber camp, like lumber camps everywhere in America, was a rowdy amoral place where inhabitants lived by the bare-knuckle code of the wilderness. Seldom did these places have a life expectancy of more than two to four years. To speak of morals or culture in a southern lumbering village, or of local pride, is like discussing social order in bedlam. Some early lumbering communities, however, have survived the passing of the mills which gave them growth. Among these are Georgetown, South Carolina; Brunswick and Waycross, Georgia; Jacksonville, Florida; Selma, Alabama; Meridian, Laurel, and Columbia, Mississippi; Bogalusa and Shreveport, Louisiana; and Crossett, Arkansas.

During the latter half of the nineteenth century and the first two decades of this, the southern industrial village reflected more the conditions of the expanding western frontier than of rising urbanization. It is true that the removal to villages by rural southerners broke old rural ties, and hundreds of thousands of southern rural dwellers were started on the road away from farms and cities both within and without the South. The internal migration and the rise of newer types of industries dependent upon easily renewable supplies of raw material contributed materially to the growth of larger and more stable urban communities after 1940.

After 1900 the rapid growth of towns and cities began to transform the traditional agrarian South. As in every other phase of southern life the towns had widely differing histories. Predominantly the South has been a land of rural traditions stoutly protected by countrymen. A sampling of statistics is sufficient to establish this fact. In 1900 there were only fifteen southern cities with 50,000 or more population, and only three had more than 100,000—Louisville, New Orleans, and Memphis; only Louisville and New Orleans topped 100,000 in 1870. As late as 1920 there were only nine southern cities which had more than 100,000 population, with New Orleans and Louisville still at the head of the list.

The older southern city was founded and flourished for a variety of reasons. New Orleans, Houston, Galveston, Norfolk, Jacksonville, Mobile, Savannah, and Charleston were port cities which depended almost as much upon the sea for trade as upon their hinterlands. New Orleans differed somewhat from the others because it had both sea-going and river trades, which accounted for its accendancy throughout most of the nineteenth century. River trade sustained Louisville and Memphis, enabling both places to establish region-wide supply trades.

Both had excellent railroad connections, and were important agricultural markets. Staple crops such as cotton, tobacco, and cattle contributed materially to the rise and growth of Richmond, Atlanta, Dallas, Fort Worth, Lexington, Durham, and Augusta, Louisville, Richmond, and Durham were early tobacco market and manufacturing centers. Lynchburg, Lexington, Kentucky, Danville, Virginia, and Winston-Salem were marketing and warehousing centers. Railroads contributed heavily to the growth of Nashville, Chattanooga, Atlanta, Louisville, Jacksonville, Dallas, Little Rock, Roanoke, and Miami. The development of mineral and petroleum products helped to expand the populations of Baton Rouge, Birmingham, Chattanooga, Dallas, Fort Worth, Houston, and Knoxville. In later years Jackson, Mississippi, was influenced by an oil strike in its commercial area. Universities contributed materially to the growth of Nashville, New Orleans, Atlanta, Durham, Knoxville, Austin, Lexington, and Baton Rouge.

Up until 1930 these main centers, despite increasing growth pressures, actually represented little if any appreciable break with restrictive southern social and economic traditions. It took a depression, two world wars, the availability of cheap electrical current in large amounts, the mechanization of agriculture, and the "go-getting" boost of state industrial commissions, chambers of commerce, and the Junior Chamber of Commerce in particular, to bring about rapid growth and internal change.[1]

---

(1) The rate of urban expansion of communities in the South was further indicated in the costs of new housekeeping units in a sampling of standard metropolitan statistical areas. In 1960-63, Atlanta householders increased annual expenditures for new housing under contract from $124,068,000 to $200,271,000; Birmingham from $38,551,000 to $43,319,000; Fort Worth, $48,837,000 to $56,665,000; Louisville $45,081,000 to $66,884,000; Memphis, $33,322,000 to $48,540,000; and New Orleans, $61,678,000 to $131,366,000. For the same cities spending figures for 1925-29 were: Atlanta, $10,153,000 and $12,564,000; Birmingham, $16,662,000 and $8,234,000; Fort Worth, $8,434,000 and $11,262,000; Louisville, $29,504,000 and $13,205,000; Memphis, $15,316,000 and $8,062,000; and New Orleans, $16,345,000 and $11,971,000.

In 1960-1963 southern towns and cities had made advanced plans for 6964 public works projects out of 33,236 for the nation which include water systems, sewerage disposal plants, bridges, irrigation ditches, streets, and public housing at costs between $100,000,000 and $500,000,000. Construction expenditures in the South rose from $1,182,000 in 1940 to $9,994,000,000 in 1963, out of a national expenditure of $45,546,000,000. These figures indicated a tremendous gain in 1963 over contractual expenditures in 1940 or 1950, but actually they represented a slight loss in proportionately national expenditures of from slightly more than a fourth to slightly less than a fourth.

By 1960 there were some 14,461,000 housing units in the South as compared with 5,693,867 in 1920, and the quality of the southern home had increased markedly. From a surface view the southern community was vastly improved in appearance. Both country and urban homes had changed for the better, more substantial types of construction were used, and brick and stone had supplanted the cheap types of frame construction of former years. A surface view, however, hardly reflected the actual conditions within the home so far as its efficiency and comfort were concerned. By 1964 almost 98 per cent of southern homes had access to electric current, and had some kind of electrical appliances. Running water, a bathroom, and refrigeration had almost become standard equipment, to say nothing of radio and television.

The rate of urbanization in the South since 1930 is to be measured in several ways; first, by the elementary count of farm, nonfarm, and urban populations which included people engaged in farming and living on the land, persons living on the land but not farming, and those living in towns and cities. In 1950 there were 9,712,000 farmers, 10,276,000 rural nonfarmers, and 18,505,000 urban dwellers. By 1960 the farm population dropped to 5,417,000, nonfarmers had increased to 14,376,000, and urban dwellers to 26,679,000.

A second way of counting the central portion of urban population is by listing cities with 100,000 or more population. In 1960 there were thirty-three such cities in the South. A third gauge used for more comprehensive measurement is that of the standard metropolitan statistical area, and by this system in 1960 there were sixty-four of these either in the South or spreading over into the region. A standard metropolitan statistical area is a fairly new population measurement used by the United States Census Bureau and defines a county or group of contiguous counties having at least one central city of 50,000 population. Obviously the statistics of southern population change annually with both rural nonfarm and urban groups increasing materially, while the rural farm category continues to shrink. With these shifts in population one fact in southern history is largely concluded. No longer will the southern farm serve as the important breeding ground both for a large southern urban population and for a large number of immigrants to other regions, as it has in the past. Furthermore, it seems not unreasonable to speculate that less of the southern popula-

tion will leave the region as more industries are introduced, service
type of employment is made available, and metropolitan areas continue
to grow.

Most interesting of the new major population categories are the
rural nonfarmers. These people now represent the second largest portion of the population of the South. They are largely southerners
who seek nonfarm employment, but cling to a love of the open countryside and refuse to move into crowded cities. Many of them have
in fact moved out of the cities in search of space and quietude. They
farm on the side, and many industrial workers, working shorter industrial days, are able after work in a factory to operate mechanized
farms or cattle ranges with even more success than their fathers did
by full-time farming.

Six urban centers in the South have reached the status of major
metropolitan areas—Atlanta, New Orleans, Memphis, Houston, Dallas,
and Louisville. In October 1959 the Atlanta area proclaimed itself
a metropolis with a million population. More than this, Atlanta has
developed the characteristics of a true metropolitan center. It is the
seat of a Federal Reserve Bank district, a transportation center for
railways, highways, and airlines, and was a major branch office and
branch plant city for large American businesses and industries. The
federal government maintains important district offices here, and so
do many publishing houses. Atlanta, however, is not purely a branch
office and plant city, for several industries of national significance
were founded and developed there.

Atlanta also has a number of important social and cultural manifestations. Two major newspapers with wide regional coverage and national significance are published there; the city is a key convention
and conference center. There are several universities and colleges in
the area, and the city ranks as a major art and music center for the
South. Of as great importance as any, Atlanta made a significant break
in the early 1960's with Georgia's ingrained agrarian political control
of the state. The abolition of the unit system, which gave the rural
counties a predominance of political control, suddenly gave Atlanta
a new political significance.

Many of the same characteristics apply to other metropolitan centers in the South. New Orleans and Dallas have made almost as important social and economic growth. Louisville and Memphis have changed

substantially in response to modern conditions. Louisville, however, has not maintained its historical vibrancy in many areas. For instance, it has not undergone as rapid a population expansion as the other cities. But like the other major cities, it has made a sharp break with the past. As industries have located in these cities, they have attracted other industries and services to locate about them. And in turn industrial employment has created an enormous impetus for expansion of the population and the cities' other facilities.

While southern cities developed many characteristics of American cities everywhere (mercantile establishments and public institutions, for instance), geographical and environmental conditions have often fostered individuality. Miami and adjoining Miami Beach, for instance, have grown within this century into major tourist centers. An extraordinary amount of the commercial activities of these places center on the tourist business. The population of this standard metropolitan area is comprised heavily of transients in search of sunshine and winter warmth, or it is comprised of retired persons escaping the harsher climate of the North. Citrus- and vegetable-growing, lumbering, manufacturing, chemicals, and coastal shipping are important, but all remain secondary in relation to the great service industries which cater to tourists.

No southern city has had more rampant metropolitan expansion than Houston. This Giant of the Gulf has a metropolitan population of 1.25 million people, and in the 1960 census it ranked as the nation's seventh largest city. Outwardly it gives the appearance of a booming shipping, oil, cattle, cotton, manufacturing, and merchandising center. Few if any metropolitan areas give such flamboyant evidence of growth and prosperity. The site of two rich universities, a medical center staffed by doctors of international reputation, and other educational and cultural institutions, Houston represents in many ways the urban maturity of the South. On the other hand it has monstrous problems of law enforcement, crime, health, public welfare, and social order which are more characteristic of a frontier town.

Nearby to Houston are the twin cities which in their combined metropolitan areas have a population of 1.6 million. Dallas and Fort Worth have many characteristics in common with Houston. They have great concentrations of wealth derived from cattle, oil, cotton, land, and manufacturing. They are the commercial and financial nerve centers of the extreme western edge of the South. Though well-integrated transportation systems connect these centers with the rest of the southern region, they remain highly individualistic. They combine a personality of the cotton South with the bolder and more adventurous personality of the cattle and oil-producing West.

Along the upper Atlantic coast, Norfolk, Portsmouth, and Newport News, Virginia, with a population of three-quarters of a million people, constitute a wide-ranging metropolitan area. Norfolk especially is an important port, and both maritime and naval activities are major enterprises. One of the most important defense nerve centers of the Atlantic defense system is the naval and air station in this area. Much of the eastern South's petroleum, fishing, and chemical fertilizer industry is near these cities. Unlike metropolitan centers discussed above, the Virginia urban complex represents modernity as well as a form of early American culture as old as the colonial beginnings in this region.

The southern city's most serious problem remains its Negro population. At the beginning of the reconstruction period Negroes began a rather heavy migration from plantations to some of the towns. This was especially true of such cities as Richmond, Charleston, Augusta, Savannah, Mobile, New Orleans, and Memphis. The horde of travelers and observers who viewed the South prior to 1886 to determine the effects of war and reconstruction noted this fact. It was difficult for the country migrant to find employment or to establish any kind of stable family life, but the excitement of town life drew him to it. From the beginning, segregated quarters were established into which the colored population was crowded. Housing was poor, streets were muddy and dusty paths, sanitary facilities were largely those which nature provided, disease was rampant; and tuberculosis, for instance, took a high toll of life. Crime was widespread, and there was constant friction between Negroes and law enforcement officers. These are the quarters which current civil rights crusaders have labeled ghettos.

Prior to 1950 the urban Negro was dependent upon urban services for employment, and these ranged from draymen and janitor to house maid, Pullman car porter, and waiter. Except for a few islands, like the Negro section of Durham, North Carolina, colored professional and businessmen had difficulty in establishing themselves. Doctors were dependent upon Negroes for patients, and lawyers were virtually barred from the courts, or faced enormous handicaps in the practice of law.

By 1910 the flow of Negroes to southern cities had quickened. A few statistical examples will illustrate this fact. In 1900 Atlanta had a Negro population of 35,782; in 1910, 51,978; and in 1960, 182,820. Comparable figures in other cities for these years were: Birmingham, 16,583; 61,238, and 184,725. New Orleans, 78,158; 89,672; and 234,931. Jacksonville, 16,721; 29,370, and 82,744. Smaller cities and county seat towns also gained rapidly. In the latter years approximately 2.25 million nonwhites lived in thirty-two cities with populations in excess of 100,000. This represented slightly less than a fourth of the entire southern Negro population of 10,178,308 in the South.

As the Negro moved in larger numbers into southern urban centers he brought about a significant change in his traditional relationships with his white neighbors. He now became an active competitor for jobs in the new industries springing up about the cities. He sought membership and equal treatment in labor organizations, and equal pay for his services. He demanded better schooling and special vocational training for his children, a stronger voice in political affairs, and a new deal from police authorities and public officials. He also asked not for separate but full access to public accommodations and facilities—he asked access to all facilities such as stores, restaurants, hotels, and transportation facilities. In the cities the Negro enjoyed a certain amount of anonymity and impersonality which greatly strengthened his courage in voicing protests and making demands. A good example of this was the result of the early sit-ins which opened lunch counters and stores to all customers. The federal courts and the Interstate Commerce Commission helped him on his way with favorable decisions. A special citizens' commission in Charlotte, North Carolina, recommended full access to public accommodations, and thus alleviated much of the tension built up by the more active demands. The bus strike in Montgomery, Alabama, achieved its purpose, as did other types of protests in Atlanta, Louisville, Greensboro, and Columbia. Integration of public schools took place with greater ease in the cities than in rural communities. In Birmingham and New Orleans racial conflict was sharpest. The angriest anti-police protest occurred in Birmingham, where Negroes objected strongly to the racists' expressions and the activities of a chief of police. The Negro vote may have been an important factor in bringing about his defeat when he ran for Congress.

Two of the most serious problems confronting Negroes in the southern urban community were profitable employment and adequate housing. Negroes have faced tremendous competition for jobs from white neighbors, and they have been confined to living in less attractive and crumbling areas of towns and cities. They have found it difficult if not well-nigh impossible to break into the spiraling rings of suburban expansion. Both white dwellers and real estate developers have resisted their moving into new neighborhoods. Many suburban charters contain both anti-Negro and anti-Jewish clauses which though perhaps worth no more before the courts than the ink used in writing them up, nevertheless have reflected an attitude. Public-housing facilities in most cities have improved physical conditions, if not the quality of life, for both poor white and Negro in many areas. Negroes also have been able to purchase homes of good quality which have been left by white families moving into the outer rings of the cities. Between 1948 and 1953, they bought twenty-four thousand such homes in Richmond alone. No doubt this fact was repeated in every other growing southern city. Private capital has found a profitable outlet for investment in Negro urban homes of this quality. But so far there has not been any appreciable move by Negroes from the older areas immediately downtown into the newer suburban communities. Even so there were some racial resentment and incidents over Negroes' moving near the downtown areas of Knoxville, Birmingham, and Dallas.

Since 1930 southern towns and cities have undergone changes if not revolution. No aspect of city administration was adequate to solve problems created by industrial expansion and the influx of rural immigrants. Police departments were still operated largely by town justice-of-the-peace-type mayors and semirural police constables recruiting their forces most often from rural newcomers themselves. Schools were inadequate before the immigration rush began, and by 1945 were almost hopelessly overcrowded and confused. Sanitary facilities, never adequate, were now overloaded, as were welfare and public health agencies. Churches experienced growth but were not prepared to serve the emotionally exuberant newcomers. Housing was not only in short supply, much of it was twenty-five years out of date.

In the South, as in the rest of the nation, cities had begun dying at the heart as early as 1920. Main-street buildings were small, antiquated, and shabby. Homes encircling the center areas were also outmoded and decaying. Streets, once just adequate for horses, buggies, and wagons, were too narrow and winding to accommodate the rising numbers of automobiles. No longer was a public hitching rack good enough to serve the big city trade. Parking places became as much sought after as building sites. Both families and businesses began a flight from the spread of main-street blight.

Rings of new homes encircled every town and city in the modern South. Memphis, for instance, grew into bands of suburban colonies of single and split-level houses pasted on small lots, and lined up in endless rows that resembled the contours and terraces of modern farms. These housing whorls were broken occasionally by shopping centers with their plantation-sized parking lots. Chain grocery stores, variety, discount, and chain clothing and shoe stores pursued customers to their suburban lairs. Churches, schools, post offices, and branch banks did the same thing. Thus southerners' lives were forced into standard patterns that left little if any room for regional individuality.

Critics everywhere were quick to point out that the omnivorous bulldozer, monster that it was, had uprooted thousands of acres of farm and forest without much rhyme or reason. Newspapers were filled with a constant outcry over location of new roads and streets, construction of public housing units, the location and administration of business zones, and the protection of residential areas. Many persons came to regard city and public planners, traffic engineers, and zoning authorities as agents of chaos, corruption, and confusion. Where once editors unloosed their ire on the bedeviled farmer and his shortcomings, they now went after the new city devils with even greater fury.

The Redevelopment Housing Act of 1949 set off a good part of this conflict. Under the Act's provisions, cities could secure substantial loans to cure urban blight. Fifty-one cities in the South made application for such aid by 1952, and twenty-seven of these had populations under fifty thousand. Vance and Demerath in *The Urban South* said in 1954:

In a review of planning and developments in the South, the so-called "model" town should receive mention. There are new towns, built in relatively recent times and developed presumably with benefit of the best technical aid of their time. The number of these communities which has been developed in the South as compared to other regions of the country is impressive. There are several planned towns in the South which reflect the results of planning from the outset.

Among these are Coral Gables, Florida, and Norris City, Oak Ridge, and Kingsport in Tennessee. Otherwise the southern urban centers, though new in matters of expansion and problems, are still reminiscent of the days when they served a backward and restrictive agriculture area.

The modern urban South faces new social problems as a result of its shifting population base. Juvenile delinquency and crime require new and perhaps more imaginative and drastic modes of solution. Youth separated from access to traditional rural recreational areas has to be served by carefully planned and expensive urban recreation, a fact which is still difficult for an older generation of taxpayers and public officials to understand. In 1962 the South had approximately eight murders per 100,000 population as compared with four and a half for the nation. In other categories the southern rate deviated but little from the national average, except for larceny over $50 and automobile theft. The rest of the nation led by a considerable margin in the latter crime.

It seemed clear that in urban expansion, whereby the region had to face problems created by urban living, the South had moved more fully into the mainstream of American life than in almost any other area. But a growing monotony of city life affected the South as it did other parts of the country. A suburban community on the outer fringes of Atlanta looked no different from one near St. Louis, Milwaukee, or Chicago. Downtown sections of all these cities were filled with the same type of smoky antiquated buildings. A housewife had little or no difficulty in adapting herself to life in a new city, whether it be North or South. In the mid-twentieth century it became increasingly difficult to absorb the atmosphere of the South in its city streets, permeated as they were with gasoline and diesel-oil fumes and clogged by the everlasting five o'clock traffic jams.

❧ XVI ❧

Enter the Supreme Court

Negro education has been a vital issue in southern educational history since 1865. It is necessary, however, to consider this subject further within the context of the removal of barriers to racial discrimination itself. Racial discrimination was manifested in lack of economic support for schools, failure of Negro leadership, prejudiced political leadership among whites, and a tradition of ignoring the Negro's education needs. To destroy these barriers has required a long, tedious process of changing laws, of establishing judicial decrees, and of revising the whole structure of southern thinking on the subject of universal education. After 1930 a central educational issue was that of destroying "Jim Crowism" in public schools. A series of revolutionary court decisions dealing with almost every aspect of racial discrimination has given the changes in educational approaches in the racial areas more of a legalistic than a pedagogical flavor. The long, traumatic legal battles in this area constitute some of the most exciting advances in all of American social and cultural history.

The Fourteenth Amendment had been added to the United States Constitution in the post-Civil War years at a time when Congress had a very low regard for the executive and judicial branches of the federal government; the Congress, therefore, made specific provision for the Amendment to be enforced by Congress. It would be the courts, however, that would have the most to do with the enforcement of the Amendment, and for half a century the Supreme Court would by its decisions make the Amendment inoperative. In line with the Amendment, Congress passed in 1875, as has been noted, a Civil

347

Rights Act specifically prohibiting racial segregation in inns, public transportation, or places of amusement; eight years later, the Supreme Court found the statute unconstitutional. The Amendment, said the Court, prohibited only discriminatory acts by state governments: Congress had no power to proscribe discrimination by private persons or corporations. Justice John M. Harlan dissented, arguing that public agents and licensees of the states were bound by the same restrictions as the states; but the general public, tired of efforts to give the Negro special protection and disillusioned with results thus far achieved, was not outraged as it had been by the Dred Scott decision a quarter of a century before. There was a general acceptance of the philosophy of white supremacy, and Congress, glad to surrender its responsibility, breathed a sigh of relief.

Then followed the veritable deluge of state discriminatory legislation already referred to. Before the end of the century the Supreme Court, in the celebrated case of *Plessy vs. Ferguson,* would give further aid and comfort to the cause of segregation. In that case, as we have seen, it laid down the "separate but equal" doctrine: segregation *per se* was not in violation of the Fourteenth Amendment so long as accommodations were equal. Thereafter segregation became a southern way of life. In case after case the Supreme Court upheld the "separate but equal" doctrine, never bothering to ascertain if the separate facilities were equal. By state law throughout the South, and even in the border states, Negroes were prohibited from mingling with whites in schools, hospitals, railroad cars, streetcars, and places of amusement.

In no area of southern society was the race issue a more intimate part of the region's social matrix than in the public schools. In all of the areas of social relationships either covered directly or by implication in both the civil rights legislation and the subsequent *Plessy vs. Ferguson* none involved so much emotionalism as the attempt to establish and maintain integrated public schools. Had universal public education been a well-established fact in southern life in 1869 it might well have been possible that the issue of racial relationships would have been given broader and more immediate attention by both the Congress and the courts. It was not in fact until education became such a necessary preparation for acquiring and keeping jobs that this issue was pushed to the forefront in the courts.

The reconstruction constitutions established free public schools for all, the first time the southern states had really enjoyed anything that might be termed educational systems in the more modern sense. But the whites were divided on the school question: conservatives, who established the black codes and who wished to keep the Negro as a servile worker, were opposed to education for either poor whites or Negroes. Klansmen burned schoolhouses and beat both white and Negro teachers, expelling them from communities as carpetbaggers or scalawags when they could. Moderates, on the other hand, men like Henry Wise and Alexander H. H. Stuart in Virginia and Gustavus Orr in South Carolina, accepted the end of slavery and urged education for the freedmen as not only their right but as indispensable for the ultimate welfare of society in the new South. Yeoman farmers at first co-operated with Negroes in establishing the new system, but they would later become violent opponents of Negro education.

Integrated schools were attempted for a time in Virginia, Mississippi, Texas, Louisiana, and South Carolina, partly at Congressional instance. But a combination of factors—the overthrow of the last of the radical reconstruction governments in the southern states, the compromise arrived at in the Hayes-Tilden election, and a general spirit of weariness with the problems of the freedman—cooled Congressional ardor for integrated schools after 1875; and Negroes were led to accept separation on the promise that their schools would receive a fair division of public funds. This promise was kept for a time; for the conservatives who came to power feared at first both federal intervention and the opposition of the Negro, who was still not entirely and permanently eliminated as a voter. Even so, educational funds for both races were greatly restricted during the period, so much so that by 1880, there were still almost 5 million illiterate adults in the South, almost 90 per cent of them Negroes.

The climax of the agrarian revolt in the 1890's brought a change in the method of distributing school funds. In a move to expand education for the whites at the expense of the Negro, local school boards with connivance of state officials diverted from Negro to white schools state funds appropriated on a per capita basis to their districts. This resulted in some improvement in the education of white children, but not for all white children. For since funds were allocated to districts according to the total school-age population of both races, white schools in districts with a large Negro population benefited over white schools in districts with a small Negro population.

In 1912, for example, the average per capita expenditure for white children in the South was $10.32 as compared to $2.89 for Negro children. But in those counties where Negroes counted less than 10 per cent of the population the figures were nearly equal: $7.96 for whites and $7.23 for Negroes. On the other hand, in black-belt counties where Negroes were more than 75 per cent of the population, the Negro per capita was only $1.78 as compared to $22.22 for whites. The discrepancy was even greater in secondary schools; for economic and other pressures caused a progressive acceleration in the Negro dropout rate, and a much greater proportion of white children attended secondary schools than did Negro children. In 1930, 15 per cent of rural southern Negro adults had no formal schooling whatsoever, and another 40 per cent had not gone beyond the fifth grade. Only 5.5 per cent had any high school training as compared to 28 per cent of rural whites who had. Ten years later, there was but scant improvement. The census of 1940, for instance, revealed that 50 per cent of adult Alabama Negroes and 68 per cent of those in South Carolina had fewer than four years of schooling, and this at a time when a year spent in rural schools in those states constituted very little schooling indeed. The percentage of southern whites who had gone as far as the twelfth grade was tenfold greater than that of Negroes.

From what has been said it must not be supposed that the southern white child was receiving a superior education judged by national norms. On the contrary, even the white schools in rural areas at the turn of the century and later were open only during the few winter months, and per capita expenditures were only about one-third of the national average. It was only in comparison with the Negro that the southern white child received a superior education.

The inequity in educational opportunity extended to all phases of the program, in school facilities as well as in quality of teachers. There were no schools at all for Negroes in some areas; in others, there were too few. There was a lack of necessary equipment, inferior preparation of teachers, a differential in salary between Negro and white teachers, a complete disregard of truancy laws in so far as Negroes were concerned. Although Negroes constituted 34 per cent of the rural school-age population of the region in 1940, only 3 per cent of the school transportation funds were spent for them. No money at all was spent for transportation of Negro children in Mississippi, and in Georgia and South Carolina they received only one-half of one per cent of the total spent on this service. Some Negro children had to travel almost twenty miles to school, and their families had to either pay for private bus service or else board their children in town.

The average pupil load per teacher was almost a third higher in Negro schools, and the average value of school property per child was almost six times as great for whites as for Negroes; in Mississippi it was fourteen times as large. While the average spent per pupil for white teacher salaries was only twice as great in the entire region, in the black-belt districts it was twenty-five times as great. In 1930-31, 23 per cent of Negro as compared to 6 per cent of white elementary teachers had received no education beyond high school. In Mississippi, Georgia, and South Carolina, Negro teacher salaries were only about one-third those of white teachers. In Louisiana and Alabama the differential was not so great; but even in North Carolina, the most fair-minded of the southern states in this regard, the Negro teacher taught more students than her white sister for one-third less salary. In 1940, teacher salary differentials based on race were declared unconstitutional by the Supreme Court, but most localities disregarded the ruling.

Inequality in school buildings was even greater. In 1935, 55 per cent of Negro children were taught in one-room schools, and another 20 per cent were taught in two-room schools. In addition, many schools were housed in nonpublic buildings: in churches, lodges, vacant stores, tenant houses. Gunnar Myrdal visited a rural Negro school about 1940 not far from Atlanta. The teacher was a girl of about twenty who had had only a high school education. In questioning the students, Myrdal found no one who knew who the President of the United States was, or indeed, what the President was. Only one boy thought he knew what the Constitution was, but he confused it with the Atlanta newspaper by that name. One boy who impressed the visitor as unusually bright thought Europe was in England and that Booker T. Washington was a "big white man." None had ever heard of the NAACP. After numerous such visits throughout the region, Myrdal concluded that the typical rural southern Negro school was one where "a poorly trained and poorly paid Negro woman must control and teach a group of children from a poor and uncultured home background, in an over crowded, dilapidated, one-room school house, where she must perform at least some of the janitorial and administrative duties."[1] Myrdal's findings seemed confirmed when nine of ten illiterate World War II draftees were southerners, two-thirds of them Negroes.

Nor were conditions much improved in higher education, even where federal funds were involved. In 1936-37 Negro colleges in the South received only 5 per cent of land grant college funds expended in the section and less than 8 per cent of PWA funds for construction for new schools in the South. An equitable distribution of federal funds would have given Negro colleges $5 million instead of $1.9 million. The difference of more than $3 million was diverted to white colleges. Furthermore, there were no public libraries designated for Negroes, and only 10 per cent of the 774 public libraries of the region served Negroes.

For a long time, Negro intellectuals did not press for an end to school segregation, concentrating their efforts rather on securing a more equitable distribution of funds; for just as segregation had certain advantages for other Negro professionals: doctors, lawyers, undertakers, and bankers, so too did it insure employment for many Negro teachers who would be displaced in a desegregated system. Spurred on by ominous warnings emanating from Supreme Court decisions in the 1930's and 1940's, however, southern whites themselves undertook remedial measures. By 1954, southern Negro pupils, although still segregated, were having about three-fourths as much spent on them as were white pupils; and efforts were going forward in most places to equalize physical facilities, pay of teachers, and the number of pupils taught by each teacher. But Mississippi, as usual, lagged far behind. As late as 1959-60 local expenditures per pupil there still favored the whites by a ratio of almost four to one.

But reform, such as it was, was too late in coming; for an aroused national government had determined that segregated education could no longer be tolerated. Starting with 1937, there came a change: that year Hugo Black, ironically a former member of the Alabama Ku Klux Klan, was appointed to the Supreme Court, and there began emanating from his pen and later from Chief Justice Fred M. Vinson's,

(1) *An American Dilemma*, 903, 947.

a series of opinions upholding rights of individuals under the Fourteenth Amendment, many of them involving Negroes. The segregation walls in education began to tremble in the Gaines Case in 1938, when the Court ruled that Missouri denied a Negro his constitutional right when it refused to admit him to the state university law school, even though it made provision to pay his tuition outside the state. It ordered Missouri to furnish him equal facilities with white students regardless of whether any other Negroes sought the same opportunity.

A similar ruling in 1948 compelled the University of Oklahoma to admit a Negro to its law school rather than furnish him aid to attend an out of state school. Meantime, the state of Texas had set up a separate law school for Negroes. In the case of *Sweatt vs. Painter* in 1950 the Court, although refusing to overturn expressly *Plessy vs. Ferguson*, the foundation of the "separate but equal" doctrine, ruled that a separate law school for Negroes was inferior to the all-white law school at the state university. This was a landmark decision, for in it the Court discovered that segregated education was inherently unequal. Such things as the reputation of faculty, prestige, and position of alumni, although incapable of objective measurement, could not be equal in separate institutions. This was a long step, indeed, on the road to *Brown vs. Board of Education*.

Meantime, as we have seen, the Court had moved with equal deliberation to invalidate the white primary, segregation of Negroes in interstate carriers, segregated juries, discriminatory private property covenants. All greatly undermined segregation doctrine and helped set the stage for the revolution that would shake the country in the decade after 1955.

The Brown Case was not the first public school case to come before the Supreme Court. In 1951 a three-judge federal court by a two to one vote upheld the constitutionality of segregated schools in Clarendon County, South Carolina. The case was appealed to the Supreme Court and in January 1952 was remanded to the lower court for additional consideration of a school board proposal to equalize facilities. When the case was returned to the Supreme Court in the fall of 1952 there were now additional cases from Kansas, Virginia, Delaware, and the District of Columbia. The Kansas case was listed first, and thus the historic decision bore its name: *Oliver Brown et al vs. Board of Education of Topeka, Kansas*.

Oliver Brown, a Negro clergyman in Topeka, Kansas, sued the Board of Education in federal district court because his daughter had to travel twenty blocks to a Negro high school while a white high school was only four blocks from their home. After adverse decisions in the district and circuit courts, he appealed to the Supreme Court. In 1952 the Court placed the case on the fall docket to hear arguments on the intent of the Congress and legislatures which had adopted and ratified the Fourteenth Amendment, on the power of Congress and the courts to interfere with segregation, and the proper nature of any court decree which might outlaw it. The re-argument took place the following year and was docketed for the spring term without any indication as to what turn, if any, a decision would take on the fundamental question of segregation.

Monday, May 17, 1954, began as a quiet day in Washington. The greatest excitement in the capital and in the nation as a whole centered on the feud between Senator Joseph McCarthy and the Army. At noon the Supreme Court began what was expected to be a routine session. Then Chief Justice Warren announced, "I have the Court's opinion and decision in . . . Oliver Brown versus the Board of Education."

Calm turned to excitement, as reporters scribbled notes and then rushed to telephones. Wires hummed, as news of the decision was transmitted throughout the country and beyond. For this time the Court had faced squarely the doctrine enunciated in *Plessy vs. Ferguson* half a century before, and the older decision was flatly reversed. Henceforth, in the field of public education, the doctrine of "separate but equal" had no place. Segregated schools were by their nature, infringements on personal rights, and the Brown girl and persons similarly situated were deprived of the equal protection of the laws guaranteed by the Fourteenth Amendment. It was a day to remember. For the impact of the sweeping affirmation of the inherent illegality of compulsory segregation went beyond the schools: to playgrounds, recreational and health facilities, public accommodations, housing, voting. More than that, it awakened the conscience of America. For Negroes, it was a turning point in their long struggle; for southern segregationists it was Black Monday.

The opinion opened a flood tide of litigation, as efforts were made to translate its verdict into action in neighborhood schools. Many communities outside the South that had professed desegregation since pre-Civil War days, were to be charged with *de facto* segregation. Some northern cities, under pressure, began to transport Negro pupils by bus to white neighborhood schools. In the seventeen southern and border states and in the District of Columbia, all of which required segregated schools by law, there were varied reactions, from willing acceptance of the mandate to hostile defiance. Progress came fast in the border states and in the District of Columbia where, after a plea by President Eisenhower, schools were desegregated in the fall of 1954.

The Court ordered desegregation of schools, not precipitately, but with "deliberate speed," and the deep South took full advantage of the grace period and more. Citizens' Councils, made up of community leaders, sprang up everywhere screaming defiance of the Court. Perhaps if the section's real leaders, men like South Carolina's James F. Byrnes, Virginia's Harry F. Byrd, Georgia's Richard B. Russell, had spoken out in support of obedience to the order, the history of the times might have been different. It may be, however, that such a posture at the time was untenable for a politician from the South and might have resulted only in his repudiation by his constituents. In any event, they chose not to follow such a course. Instead, they went even further than was perhaps necessary in denouncing the decision, and in doing so they greatly tarnished the image they had established over the years as responsible statesmen. For they permitted and even encouraged their people to follow a course that would lead eventually to violence, degradation, shame, and ruin. Two years later, nineteen southern Senators and seventy-seven Congressmen issued a manifesto pledging the use of "all lawful means" to effect a reversal of the decision. Signing the manifesto were such moderates as Senators J. William Fulbright of Arkansas, Lister Hill and John Sparkman of Alabama, and Congressman Hale Boggs of Louisiana. Only Estes Kefauver and Albert Gore of Tennessee abstained. Lyndon Johnson was not asked to sign because of his position as majority leader of the Senate.

Even the southern churches failed to give the decision the support that might have been expected of those professing the common brotherhood of man. The Southern Baptist Convention endorsed the decision as morally right; but most white Baptist congregations, according to the *Baptist Recorder,* fought desegregation, refusing membership to Negroes who applied. Hundreds of white churches of all Protestant denominations turned Negro worshipers from their doors when they presented themselves for Sunday services. It was a disappointing contrast to the Catholic Church, which spoke out forthrightly against racial discrimination as a violation of the Christian ethic.

The argument of the segregationists was that the Court had exceeded its authority, had buttressed its opinion with sociological and psychological theories instead of legal precedents, had misinterpreted the Constitution, and that its edict was therefore null and void and need not be obeyed. The spirit of John C. Calhoun was exhumed, and reactionaries studied and expounded the all-but-forgotten doctrine of state interposition advanced by the South Carolina nullifier more than a century before. The so-called demagogue, who had all but disappeared from the political scene in the South, was given a new lease on life, and men like Orval Faubus, Ross Barnett, and George Wallace, would play the new game to the hilt. "The integration issue has submerged other political questions in the Deep South," wrote an observer in the autumn of 1955, "and in many places election campaigns have been turned into contests among the candidates to surpass each other in promises of maintaining segregation."[2]

In an abortive effort to avoid compliance with the decision, legislatures in Georgia, Mississippi, and South Carolina took initial steps to abolish public schools. Virginia's constitution was changed to permit aid to private segregated schools, the "freedom of choice" plan. Indeed, had it not been for governors of great integrity in those states and also in Florida the legislatures would have destroyed public schools there altogether. Even North Carolina's legislative committee on education debated whether or not to end public education, but this issue did not reach the floor of either house. In Louisiana, only the valiant efforts of the unbalanced governor, Earl Long, prevented his legislature from destroying the educational system there. Some states and local authorities cut off funds from schools attempting to desegregate; others adopted "pupil placement" plans. School districts were gerrymandered outrageously by legislatures, and laws were passed to curb activities of the NAACP. As one by one these laws fell before federal court decisions, enraged southerners resorted to violence. One of the first

(2) *The Nation,* XLXXXI (Oct. 22, 1955), 339-41.

outbreaks was at Clinton, Tennessee, where a school was dynamited in September 1956. There were also acts of violence in Birmingham and Tuskeegee, Alabama, and in Nashville, Tennessee, but these incidents paled into insignificance before that at Little Rock the following September.

The Little Rock school board under the lead of Superintendent Virgil T. Blossom had worked out a plan of gradual desegregation, starting in high school in 1957 and descending through the elementary schools by 1963. Orval Faubus, serving his second term as governor and wanting to run for a third, needed an issue that would counterbalance the traditional two-term limit. Seizing integration as the issue, he predicted trouble if nine Negroes who had registered for the public high school under the plan showed up when classes started. When they did show up he ordered them away. Until this development there had been no indication in Little Rock that there would not be peaceable compliance on the part of school officials, students, and citizens. When the Negroes were finally admitted, escorted by federal marshals with a court order, a howling mob formed. Faubus called out the state militia and forcibly removed the Negroes from the school. President Eisenhower responded by calling the militia into federal service and ordered the Negroes readmitted; then, on the request of Mayor Woodrow Mann, he sent a thousand United States troops to hold back the mob and escort the students to class. Violence was a constant threat throughout that year and part of the next. There were numerous bomb scares, and education had to be forgotten while schools were hastily vacated. But the federal troops stayed on, and eventually five of the nine Negroes were graduated from Central High and enrolled in college.

Apparently unaware that he had done so, Faubus had moved the desegregation issue into a new phase. By resorting to nullification and state interposition, doctrines so antiquated as to be all but forgotten in all sections of the country except the South, he had placed Arkansas in open rebellion against a specific federal court order; he had dismayed southern conservatives; he had discredited to a degree the Citizens' Councils; he had forced the national government to meet the challenge of state rebellion; and he had stiffened the resolve of Americans in general that the Constitution must be obeyed by all.

But the lesson of Little Rock was not heeded everywhere, and

violence resulting from the Court's decision reached a climax at Oxford, Mississippi, on the night of September 30-October 1, 1962. There
a small army of United States marshals attempting to protect Negro
student James H. Meredith, whose admission to the state university
had been ordered by the federal courts, was threatened by a mob
aroused by Governor Ross Barnett's posture of defiance of the federal
authority. While Mississippi state troopers looked on, the marshals
were taunted, then menaced, and finally attacked with a barrage of
missiles. Use of tear gas bombs by the marshals only drove the mob
to new fury. Before the night of terror ended two men were killed,
one a French reporter covering the incident for his newspaper. The
Mississippi legislature, after an investigation, placed the entire responsibility for the riot on the marshals, but a stout-hearted faculty group
at the University of Mississippi denounced the report as entirely false.
Instead, they praised the forbearance of the marshals in the face of
extreme provocation and placed full blame on the state police and
on the mob.

Meantime, in the elementary and secondary schools of the South
desegregation was moving at a snail's pace. Five years after the Brown
decision, only fifteen southern school districts had been desegregated,
none in the deep South. By 1961, large cities like Atlanta and Little
Rock, the latter now restored to peace, had desegregated their high
schools, but only a few Negro children living in white school districts
were affected. Ten years after the Supreme Court's mandate, 90 per
cent of southern Negro children were still attending all-Negro schools.
In the deep South the percentage was much higher.

But if the wheels of justice ground slowly they ground inexorably,
for the courts were striking down every subterfuge that the most
nimble-minded state-rights logicians could construct. In 1962 the Supreme Court, in a case emanating from Jackson, Mississippi, ruled
that segregation of any kind based on race was "frivolous," and it
was useless to attempt justification of any statute attempting it. Meantime, the University of Georgia and the Georgia Institute of Technology had admitted Negroes in January 1961: Georgia Tech without
compulsion and without incident, the University of Georgia only after
a night of rioting. Thereafter, the Georgia legislature repealed its segregation laws. Soon after, Clemson College in South Carolina admitted
a Negro without disturbing South Carolina's calm. The University

of Alabama did so in defiance of Governor Wallace, who was made to appear ridiculous when he dramatically "stood in the door" of the university in an attempt to prevent the admission of two Negro students. The Negroes were quietly registered in spite of him and housed in university dormitories. One of them, Vivian Malone, was graduated two years later. In 1965 she went to work for the Justice Department in Washington.

By September 1964 there were indications that the people of the South, although with great reluctance, were beginning to accept the end of segregation as inevitable. Greenville, South Carolina, that month voluntarily integrated fourteen previously all-white schools. Twelve other counties in the state had also desegregated their high schools without protest or violence. Georgia had more than nine hundred Negroes in twenty-eight integrated schools, most of them in Atlanta it is true, but with token integration in nine other cities. Americus, Georgia, which had been a trouble spot the year before, and would be one again in 1965 over Negro voting, admitted four Negroes to its white high school. Albany, Georgia, where hundreds of Negroes had been jailed two years before for street demonstrations, admitted twenty-one Negroes to five high schools; and Columbus, Georgia, admitted two Negroes to a white high school. Birmingham, Alabama, which had also experienced violence in 1963, expanded integration with nothing worse than peaceful picketing on the part of the segregationists.

Desegregation was also expanded that year at Mobile, Huntsville, Gadsden, and Tuskeegee. Just the year before, state troopers had barred integration at Tuskeegee High School, and the school had been closed for a year. Now there were fourteen Negroes in the mixed student body. Eight Negroes were admitted to two white high schools and an elementary school in Montgomery. In Arkansas, there were twenty-one desegregated districts with almost nine hundred Negroes in previously white schools. Florida had desegregated twenty of sixty-seven counties without trouble, and there were an estimated eight thousand Negroes in that state attending previously white schools. High schools were integrated in Greensburg and Baton Rouge, Louisiana, and New Orleans integration had moved through the fourth grade. Integration was moving at so rapid a pace in Virginia, Tennessee, North Carolina, and Texas that firm figures were unavailable. Even in Mississippi, the last of the hard-core states to desegregate, sixteen Negroes entered four Biloxi elementary schools, and one Negro registered at Carthage, the birthplace of Ross Barnett. But at the same time, fourteen Negroes were turned away when they attempted to enter a white high school at Canton which had not yet been specifically ordered to desegregate. With token integration beginning in Mississippi, all states had at least some.

At this time, too, the Supreme Court struck down one of the great challenges to its decision of ten years before. Rather than comply with the Court's mandate to end segregation, Prince Edward County, Virginia, had closed its public schools in 1959. In an opinion written by Justice Black the Court, in May 1964, unanimously held that the federal Constitution did not permit the abolition of schools in one county of a state while they remained open in other counties. Black indicated, further, that the pace of desegregation must pick up. "The time for 'deliberate' speed has run out, and that phrase can no longer justify denying these . . . children their constitutional rights." Six months later, a federal court of appeals outlawed Virginia's tuition-grant system to private schools, calling it a "transparent evasion" of Negroes' rights.

Despite progress made through 1964 it was clear that in the deep South there was only a token integration. Nevertheless, pressures were growing, and it was becoming apparent to those who had eyes to see that violence and closed schools did not pay: that they brought with them economic and social decay. For four years following the Little Rock disturbance not a single new industry had located there. Race riots, federal troops patrolling streets, disturbances of the peace created unfavorable images that chambers of commerce sought to minimize. Furthermore, federal agencies were adopting policies that would make it impossible for southerners to enjoy the advantages of both worlds: federal aid for education on the one hand and segregated schools on the other. The United States Department of Health, Education, and Welfare, had allocated $372.6 million for schools in the ex-Confederate states for 1965 and a bill before Congress contained $500 million for 1967. Before school districts could qualify for a share of the funds, however, they were required to submit evidence a year in advance that they were complying with the civil rights law of 1964.

This was the most powerful coercive tool the federal government had ever used against segregation. It reacted on recalcitrant state officials in a way that court desegregation orders could not: instead of raising constitutional questions it raised practical questions of state finance and increased taxation that would be required if federal support were curtailed. A chastened Governor Faubus declared that the new federal regulations "must be lived with." He argued that Arkansas not only needed the money but that Negroes badly needed the better training that would be provided by the upgraded, desegregated schools. In Mississippi, the fortress of segregation, cracks were beginning to appear in what had been almost a solid front of resistance. The state stood to lose $22,500,000, and community leaders in such cities as Greenville in the Delta and Tupelo in the Tennessee River hills were urging compliance.

As a result of these pressures, by the end of August 1965 there were reports of desegregation of public schools on a massive scale in the deep South. It was estimated that the number of Negroes attending former all-white schools would pass the 125,000 mark, almost double the number of the preceding year. Even though this would leave 95 per cent of the Negroes in all-Negro schools, the increase represented a significant change in segregation practices. Several school systems, including Atlanta's, decided to open schools to all applicants regardless of race until space was exhausted. Hundreds of Atlanta Negro children, including a son and a daughter of Martin Luther King, joined white pupils without incident. In Philadelphia, Mississippi, where three student civil rights workers were killed only the year before, nine Negroes attended classes at a previously all-white school without any disturbance. In South Carolina, more than six hundred Negroes enrolled in formerly white schools. This was six times the number enrolled the previous year. Alabama expected more than a thousand Negroes in previously white schools.

Certainly this was progress, even though the speed with which the desegregation of schools moved was considerably slower than many civil rights advocates had hoped for. Meanwhile, much of the Negro attack on segregation was being directed against other forms of discrimination.

❧ XVII ❧

Exit Jim Crow

In the preceding chapter we saw the consequences of the school desegregation decision on the southern states and the stimulation it gave Negroes to bring ever-increasing pressure on state and local authorities in a drive to secure for their children complete equality in educational opportunity. But segregated education was just one focus of the Negro's attack on discrimination. The fact was that almost a century after emancipation the nation was engaged in another revolutionary movement, this time a Negro revolution. In this revolt Negroes were demanding not only equal treatment under law but an equal role in a completely desegregated society: in housing, employment, public accommodations, as well as in education.

At the time of the First World War, the Negro had been encouraged to believe that with victory would come a remarkable change in the American social order. The war was being waged to "make the world safe for democracy," and even the militant Du Bois had called on Negroes to close ranks until the Central Powers were defeated. But the Negro's hopes, as we have seen, were not realized. By the time of World War II he was thoroughly disillusioned. In the North as well as in the South he was sullenly skeptical about the future. A Negro editor wrote of "this strange and curious picture, this spectacle of America at war to preserve the ideal of government by free men, yet clinging to the vestiges of the slave system." A young Negro draftee put it even more bluntly: "Just carve on my tombstone, 'Here lies a black man killed fighting a yellow man for the protection of a white man.' "[1]

(1) Quoted in Myrdal, *An American Dilemma*, 1006–8.

362

A decade after the Second World War despite much progress, the Negro's lot everywhere, but especially in the South, was still far below that of the white. About twice as large a percentage of southern Negroes were farmers, they had about half the average income of whites, and more than three times as many were unskilled or service workers. In towns and cities more of them lived in inadequate housing, without running water or private toilets. Their death rate was one-third higher than that of whites. Not only did they attend segregated schools, they lived segregated lives. By 1955 their leaders had resolved that humility, patience, and forbearance had run their course and had failed utterly to improve the lot of their people. They now determined to lead the Negroes into a campaign of civil disobedience: of boycotts, sit-ins, demonstrations in the streets.

The opening battle of the Negro revolution was fought in Montgomery, Alabama. There in the evening of December 1, 1955, Mrs. Rosa Parks boarded a bus and took a seat, not in the front section reserved for whites, but in the first seat toward the front of the unreserved section. Every other seat was taken when a white man boarded the bus. The driver ordered Mrs. Parks to surrender her seat and stand in the rear of the bus. When she refused, police were called and she was arrested.

Bus transport regulations in Montgomery were not peculiar to that southern city, for generally in the deep South Negroes were required to ride in the rear and even stand, though vacant seats might remain in the front section reserved for whites. On the other hand, if seats reserved for whites were all occupied, whites could move into the unreserved section and demand seats of Negroes. In some instances, Negroes were required to board the front of the bus, pay fares there, then dismount to re-enter the bus by the rear door. There were numerous complaints that buses would pull off with a Negro's fare in the box but before he got to the rear door of entry. Bus operators commonly referred to their black passengers as "niggers," "black crows," and "black apes."

Mrs. Parks's trial was set for Monday, December 5, and a quickly planned protest boycott developed for that day. Leaflets calling for the boycott were given wide distribution. On the Sunday before, Negro ministers endorsed the boycott from their pulpits. On December 5 the buses appeared practically empty. Ordinarily, Negroes consti-

tuted about three-fourths of the passengers, and it was estimated that
the boycott was about 99 per cent effective.

Meantime, sensing the need for organization and leadership, Negro
ministers and civic leaders on the afternoon of December 5 formed
the Montgomery Improvement Association. For president of the Association they chose a twenty-seven-year-old Atlanta-born Negro minister who had arrived in Montgomery to assume his first pastorate
shortly before the boycott struck. Martin Luther King had obviously
not been the instigator of the boycott, and much of the subsequent
planning was done by the executive board of the Association. But
it was King's oratory and his leadership that inspired the rank and
file in the months that followed. While studying for his doctor of
philosophy degree at Boston University, King had become impressed
with the philosophy of civil disobedience as expounded by Henry
David Thoreau and Mahatma Gandhi. He planned to forge it into
a weapon with which to fight segregation.

At a mass meeting called by the Association for the night of
December 5, resolutions were carried without dissent calling for con-
tinuation of the boycott until: (1) courteous treatment of Negroes
by bus operators was guaranteed; (2) passengers were seated on a
first-come first-served basis, with Negroes sitting at the rear of the
bus and progressing toward the front and whites seated from the front
toward the rear; and (3) with Negro bus operators employed on predominantly Negro routes.

As a substitute for bus transport, the Association organized car
pools. More than three hundred private automobiles, including twenty
station wagons, traversed the city from early morning until late at
night, picking up and depositing passengers without charge. Cost of
this operation was said to run five thousand dollars a week and was
paid for by private contributions. Even Police Commissioner Clyde
Sellers admitted that the system moved with "military precision."

At first the city government tried to halt the boycott by persuasion. When this failed, rougher tactics were adopted. Arrests for
minor and imaginary traffic violations were made. Hoodlums bombed
the homes of King and other leaders. Finally came mass indictments
based on an anti-labor law of questionable constitutionality. All leaders
of the Montgomery Improvement Association were indicted, and King
and others were convicted and sent to jail. Still the boycott went

on and gathered momentum week by week. Being jailed in the cause became a mark of distinction, and some who were passed over were said to feel slighted.

The basic philosophy of the boycott was that of nonviolent resistance: refusal in a peaceable manner to co-operate with forces of segregation. Accompanying the nonviolent resistance was a determination among the Negro leaders to drill into their followers the conviction that they were, in their peaceable resistance, freeing the white man of a heavy burden. "We are not out to defeat or humiliate the white man," said King, "but to help him as well as ourselves." For, "the festering sore of segregation," was an indignity to all America, not just to Negroes. And victory would be, not victory alone for the Negro, but a victory "for justice, freedom, and democracy."

To white segregationists he said: "We will match your capacity to inflict suffering with our capacity to endure suffering. We will meet your physical force with soul force. We will not hate you, but we cannot in all good conscience obey your unjust laws. . . . But we will soon wear you down by our capacity to suffer. And in winning our freedom we will so appeal to your heart and conscience that we will win you in the process." At the same time King maintained that primary responsibility for obtaining full equality rested with the Negro. For integration when it came would not be "some lavish dish" that the white man would pass out "on a silver platter, while the Negro furnishes merely the appetite." On the contrary, Negroes must be willing to work, sacrifice, and if necessary even die for it. But if physical death were the price that must be paid "to free our children from a life of permanent psychological death," then so be it. No death could be more honorable. And this would be the final test and the true meaning of passive resistance.

As the boycott extended through the winter and spring of 1956, there was talk of economic retaliation against Negroes: of loss of jobs and eviction from rented homes. But these were idle threats, and Negroes were too well aware of their many advantages to take the threats seriously. Long months of operating empty buses was bringing the transit company face to face with bankruptcy. The intertwining of the Negro and white economies was even more clearly revealed by the abortive suggestion that Negroes be discharged from their jobs. For unemployed Negroes meant no rent for white landlords and a wholesale reclamation of merchandise purchased on the installment plan. As one Negro remarked, "Our schools may not be integrated, but our dollars sure are." A second string to the boycotters' bow was the unwillingness of Montgomery housewives to dispense with their house servants. When the mayor urged them not to call for their maids but to discharge them instead, one woman said: "The mayor can do his own cooking if he wants to. I'm going after my cook." The boycott dragged on through the summer and fall, with the community growing desperately weary of the conflict. Mercifully it was brought to an end, just a fortnight more than a year after Mrs. Parks started it all on that fateful winter evening. In mid-December 1956, a federal court ordered all Montgomery buses completely desegregated, and the community breathed a sigh of relief.[2]

Almost overnight Martin Luther King became an international figure. He traveled to India and Africa, where he was welcomed by emerging nations as a fellow soldier in the fight for freedom. Shortly after the boycott, King and his followers organized the Southern Christian Leadership Conference. This was a federation of anti-segregation groups and served as a clearing house for information and planning and as an agent to collect funds. SCLC's first opportunity for leadership in the militant civil-rights movement came with the sit-in demonstration that started when four Negro students were ordered to leave a variety store in Greensboro, North Carolina, and refused to do so. They sent for King, and he rushed to their support. The Student Non-violent Co-ordinating Committee (SNCC) was organized, and this became an arm of the SCLC.

King was jailed in his hometown of Atlanta for participating in a sit-in there. Freed by order of Mayor William B. Hartzfield, he was jailed again by order of a judge who had previously placed him on probation for driving without a license and now revoked the probation because of the sit-in. Indeed, the sit-ins gave King a sterner test than had the boycott, for many moderates who could accept the boycott as a rightful exercise of freedom of choice were disturbed by the implications of trespass in the sit-in. They could not embrace wholeheartedly King's instructions to his followers to obey the law when the law was right and just and in line with the moral law of

(2) Claude Sitton in the New York *Times*, Jan. 22, 1961; *U.S. News and World Report*, XLI (Aug. 1956), 82.

the universe, but to disobey it when conscience told them the law was unjust. To many it seemed that King could not have it both ways: compliance with desegregation laws because they were the law of the land, but disregard of those laws which conflicted with his beliefs. On this dichotomy the moral cause of the Negro lost ground with many who before the sit-ins had sympathized with it. But King and his followers would not be turned from the course they had charted. Sit-ins and freedom rides, organized Negro efforts at massive attacks on Jim Crow laws, took place for the next several years in all parts of the South. And in retaliation, Negroes endured physical beatings and jail terms.

Birmingham was the final and signal victory in this phase of the campaign. There in the fall of 1962 the Reverend Fred Shuttlesworth urged an all-out boycott of Birmingham merchants until lunch counters and other facilities in stores were desegregated. By the spring of 1963, after six months of the boycott, business in the city was badly depressed, but the white merchants were still adamant. Shuttlesworth then led his followers into the streets, calling for mass prayer meetings on the court house steps. When Police Commissioner Eugene (Bull) Connor refused to grant a permit for the demonstrations, the Negroes defied him, and scores were jailed. Martin Luther King again was sent for, and again he responded.

In the great mass demonstrations that followed city officials panicked. They manhandled Negro men and women, turning not only fire hoses but police dogs on them. King was again jailed but released. On the Monday after Easter, Negro children were brought into the demonstrations, pouring into Birmingham churches to sing, pray, and dance. The following Thursday three thousand of them left the schools to demonstrate in the streets, and they too were jailed. Day after day more students demonstrated, and night after night their parents prayed and raised money to bail them out.

Meantime, Birmingham Negroes, refused service at lunch counters in department stores where they were shopping, resorted to sit-ins. This would be the signal for the closing of the counters while police removed the sitters by force, often with more force it seemed than the occasion required. Birmingham officials and other southerners contended that the force was justified because the Negroes were "trespassers," and that if occasionally they were roughed up by police or by white mobs that gathered, this was no more in violation of law than were the trespassers. Civil rights leaders responded that the Negro "trespassers" had been invited into the stores, not only by the management but by national and local advertising media. Furthermore, the merchant had been licensed by city and state to do public business. Could the merchant, they asked, claim the Negroes were trespassers when they refused to be turned away from one counter while at the same time they were being urged to purchase at all others? Could a publicly licensed merchant be a "public" vendor at one counter and a "private" vendor at another? Could a Negro be a welcome customer when he wanted to purchase a toothbrush, but a "trespasser" when he asked to buy a cup of coffee? Could Negroes be legally arrested for advocating a boycott of stores where they were publicly humiliated? Opinion throughout the nation seemed to agree that the South was once more on the wrong side of a great moral issue in a struggle which she was foredoomed to lose.[3]

Pictures of police dogs attacking Negro demonstrators were flashed around the world and were damaging the nation's international image. Burke Marshall, chief civil rights aide in the Justice Department, was dispatched to Birmingham to attempt to secure a truce there between Negroes and businessmen; and at the urging of President Kennedy native southern business leaders living in the North traveled through the South in an attempt to change the attitude on the part of business leaders there. Results were not altogether unpromising. Within a few months two-thirds of Birmingham counters and restaurants were desegregated; and within a year after the Birmingham riots, four-fifths of southern cities of ten thousand and more population had desegregated at least one type of privately owned public facility. The number of southern cities with desegregated theaters increased that same year from 109 to 287, the number with desegregated restaurants from 141 to 298, the number with desegregated hotels and motels from 163 to 267, and the number with desegregated lunch counters from 204 to 355.

These figures suggested that conciliation was not a futile gesture in all parts of the South, particularly in the urban South. They suggested, too, that the urban Negro with money to spend was a threat to segregated merchandising, and more and more white merchants

(3) Ralph McGill, *The South and the Southerner* (Boston, 1963), 224-5.

were subject to persuasion by the Negro's purchasing power. As Martin Luther King had discovered in the Montgomery bus boycott in 1956, the economies of the white and black communities were mutually dependent.

The disturbances of 1963-64 closely followed passage of a moderate Civil Rights bill in 1962. The original bill's stronger features had been watered down in committee, and the final bill was unable to insure liberties demanded by civil rights advocates. The disturbances thus became a prelude to the Civil Rights Act of July 1964. Not since reconstruction had a bill with such sweeping federal authority in this area been debated in Congress. Among its strongest provisions were:

1. A ban on discrimination by establishments offering food, lodging, gasoline, or entertainment to the public.

2. A fair labor standards section which forbade discrimination by employers or unions in hiring, firing, promotion, apprenticeship training, or job referrals.

3. An authorization for federal agencies to withhold grant funds from any program permitting discrimination.

4. Authority for the Attorney General to file suit to compel desegregation of schools, playgrounds, parks, libraries, swimming pools.

5. Tighter provisions to prevent denial of Negro voting rights in federal elections.

6. Establishment of an agency to help local communities voluntarily settle racial disputes.

7. Extension of the life of the federal Civil Rights Commission to 1968 with added powers.

The bill was debated from time to time in both houses of Congress for a year. Its most difficult hurdle was in the Senate where, in an effort to prevent a vote, southerners launched the longest filibuster in American legislative history. The southern bloc was united in opposition to the bill for different reasons and to different degrees. Senators Kefauver and Gore of Tennessee, both of whom had refused to sign the Manifesto of 1956, would not support the filibuster but neither would they vote for cloture. Ralph Yarborough of Texas and Lister Hill and John Sparkman of Alabama were regarded in the North as southern liberals, yet they could not support the bill, for they were prisoners of the political sentiment of their states. Indeed, of the eighteen Senators expected to vote against the bill, at least seven—Yarborough, Sparkman, Hill, J. William Fulbright, George Smathers, Russell Long, and Olin B. Johnston—did not seem to have their hearts in the battle to defeat it. Of the remaining eleven, only James Eastland of Mississippi and Strom Thurmond were regarded by northerners as racists.

For two and a half months through the spring of 1964 southerners held the floor in unlimited debate. The bill was an administration measure, but it could not have been passed without Republican support, particularly that of Senator Everett M. Dirksen, minority leader. All but six Republicans stood with him on June 10 as the filibuster was ended by a vote of 71 to 29. The Senate then quickly passed the bill, and it went to the House where it was rushed through on July 2 by a bi-partisan majority. Just three hours after its House passage it was signed by President Johnson. In signing the bill the President made a conciliatory statement calling for the closing of the "springs of racial poison" and for the laying aside of sectional animosity.

Passage of the bill produced mixed reactions both North and South. Representative John Lesinski of Michigan, the only northern Democratic Representative to vote against the bill, was defeated for renomination in the Democratic primary by Representative John Dingell, who had voted for the bill. Reapportionment had placed them in the same district, and the new district contained much more of Lesinski's than of Dingell's old district. On the other hand, in a plebiscite in neighboring Detroit a segregationist housing ordinance received majority approval. In Tennessee, Representative Ross Bass, who had voted for the civil rights bill, defeated an opponent of the bill for the Democratic nomination to the Senate and then went on to win the Senate seat in the November election. And Representative Charles L. Weltner of Atlanta, Georgia, who had voted against a similar bill when it passed the House in February, switched and voted for the amended bill in July. In doing so, he said: "I would urge that we at home now move on to the unfinished task of building a new South. We must not remain forever bound to another lost cause." But Representative Howard W. Smith, of Virginia, chairman of the Rules Committee, predicted the law would cause violence, bitterness, and would loose on the South "a second invasion of carpetbaggers." Ironically, and with no apparent relationship, passage of the bill coincided with major race riots in Harlem, Brooklyn, Rochester, Jersey City, Elizabeth City, Chicago, and Philadelphia. In these riots there were 5 killed, 750 injured, almost 2000 arrested, and millions of dollars of property damage.

There was violence in the South, too. In all the Mississippi Delta country the division between whites and Negroes had grown deep and wide, and observers wondered if it would ever be bridged again. Communication between the races seemed to have broken down completely, and there appeared to be a determination on the part of both groups to make no concessions. Moderates, fearful of the militantly segregationist Citizens' Councils, remained ominously silent, while racists screamed defiance of the national government. A Negro attempting to register in LeFlore County, Mississippi, was shot and wounded by three white men. In June 1964, Medgar Evers, field secretary of the NAACP, was shot and killed from ambush in Jackson. Byron de la Beckwith, a white segregationist from the Delta, was indicted but discharged after two juries failed to convict him.

A crisis was reached in midsummer when two hundred volunteer college students from other sections of the country, under the sponsorship of the Council of Federated Organizations went to Mississippi to conduct a Negro registration drive. Segregationists met the students with violence. Three of the students, a Negro and two whites, were mysteriously slain shortly after having been released from jail in Philadelphia, Mississippi, where they had been held on a speeding charge. Weeks later their bodies were unearthed from a shallow grave dug at the foot of a recently constructed dam. During the long summer, 4 other students were shot but not killed, 52 suffered beatings, and about 250 were arrested. Thirteen Negro churches were destroyed by fires or bombings, and seventeen other churches were severely damaged. For all this, results, so far as new registrations were concerned, were meager. Only in Panola County in the hills of the northeast was there a significant addition to the voting roster, 350. Elsewhere, applicants were confronted by the traditional barriers, the most difficult in the nation. Nevertheless, the spotlight of publicity focused on the state as a result of the drive and the resultant murders, convinced many that the state would never again be permitted to discriminate cavalierly against Negro voters.

There had been comparative peace in Alabama for a year prior to January 1965. Then Martin Luther King, just returned from Stockholm where he received the Nobel Peace Prize, led a Negro voter registration drive in Selma, county seat of Dallas in the heart of the black belt. At the time only a few hundred Negroes were registered there as compared with twelve thousand whites. King's efforts frustrated by the interminably slow and irritating delay, he took his followers into the streets in mass demonstrations, planning even a fifty-mile march over the highway to Montgomery to dramatize the Negro protest. This was broken up on Sunday, March 7, by mounted police with clubs and tear gas. Aroused white citizens from all over the country rushed to Selma to lend support to the Negroes. There at night on March 10, four northern clergymen were brutally attacked in the street by white hooligans and one of them, James J. Reeb, a white Unitarian minister from Boston, died two days later of a fractured skull.

Spontaneous demonstrations by shocked citizens in communities from Boston to Hawaii demanded federal protection of civil rights crusaders in Alabama. More than two hundred students camped in protest outside Boston's federal building. Students began sit-ins at the Liberty Bell in Independence Hall, Philadelphia; others marched silently down Broadway in Manhattan, carrying a coffin and a sign bearing the names of those who had died for civil rights. Governors in Michigan and Kentucky joined in large protest marches in Detroit and Louisville; and the governor of Hawaii telegraphed Alabama Governor Wallace that the "savage oppression of human rights in Selma is a disgrace to the entire nation."

Two weeks after the first attempted march to Montgomery was broken up, Martin Luther King, this time protected with a federal court order as well as with federal marshals, a federalized national guard, and hundreds of FBI agents, resumed the trek from Selma. Four days later, twenty-five thousand marchers, only a few hundred of whom had been permitted to march the entire journey, followed King up Dexter Street in Montgomery to the state capital. Governor Wallace refused to meet the delegation or receive its petition, but King, standing over the spot where Jefferson Davis had taken the oath as president of the Confederate States more than a century before, saluted his disciples. With the Confederate flag flying from the dome above, he assured them that "We have overcome."

The next day a horrified world learned that a few hours after King spoke, Viola Liuzzo, a white mother of five who had come from Detroit to aid in the demonstration, had been shot to death on a lonely spot on the Selma road. She was driving a car, shuttling demonstrators back to Selma from Montgomery. Sixteen hours later President Johnson, in a cold fury, announced that the FBI had arrested four Ku Klux Klansmen in Birmingham and charged them with the crime.

Meantime, President Johnson, in an unprecedented personal appearance before a joint session of Congress in such a cause, asked for legislation providing for federal registrars in states and counties where as many as 50 per cent of citizens of voting age were either unregistered or had not voted in the preceding election. Virginia, North Carolina, South Carolina, Georgia, Alabama, Mississippi, and Louisiana would be covered automatically by the bill, and individual counties in other states would also be included.

By midsummer the bill had become law, and federal registrars were rushed at once to rural counties in Alabama, Mississippi, and Louisiana, to enroll Negroes who, for one reason or another, had been refused registration by state voting officials. The law closed all visible loopholes left by other voting-rights measures and seemed certain to assure the registration of all Negroes who applied. All the applicant was called on to do was to fill out a simple form (if he was unable to write the registrar would fill it out for him) indicating his name, age, and length of residence, and whether he had been convicted of a felony without subsequent pardon. If he met these nondiscriminatory state qualifications, the registrar placed his name on a list of qualified voters. At the end of each month, registrars were to send their rolls to appropriate state and local election officials who were required to add the list to their own books. A state official might question the qualifications of any such registrant, but the challenge was to be heard by a federal officer and resolved in fifteen days. If an election was held in the interim the registrant could vote. On election day, federal poll-watchers were to observe all aspects of the election, both the casting and the counting of ballots. Stiff criminal penalties awaited any who dared intimidate or coerce voters or tamper with ballots. Under another feature of the law, the Attorney General of the United States filed suits challenging the constitutionality of the poll tax in Virginia, Alabama, Mississippi, and Texas, the four states still requiring the tax in state and local elections. In March 1966, in a sweeping decision, the Supreme Court ruled the tax invalid. Just a fortnight earlier, the Court had sustained the constitutionality of the voting act itself. At about the same time, the United States Court of Appeals for the Fifth Circuit at New Orleans invalidated the 1965 election in Sunflower County, Mississippi, the home of segregationist Senator James O. Eastland, because Negroes had been excluded from the election. The county had 8783 white persons of voting age, of whom 80 per cent were registered. Of its 13,524 Negroes, only 1.1 per cent were registered.

As the period draws to a close, what are the prospects for the future? Indications are that despite the remarkable progress in recent years, the road to political, economic, and social justice for the Negro will still be a long and tortuous one. By individual achievement in almost every phase of American life the Negro has demonstrated the falsity of the charge that members of the race are incapable of intellectual or artistic excellence. Yet, the long period of discrimination he has suffered in all sections of the country and in all phases of life seems to have left the Negro with a feeling of inferiority which he cannot easily shed. Negro apathy toward political participation, even in the North; Negro lack of training for skilled jobs; inferior Negro education in most places—all these will retard economic progress for all but the few indomitables who will not be denied. Roy Wilkins expressed the fear that three hundred years of "first slavery and then segregation may have shredded the Negro's spiritual innards so badly that we will have to wait for another generation to do the intra-group, self-help work that must be done."[4] At the same time and despite the injustice of it, the embarrassingly high Negro crime statistics will tend to hinder social acceptance for the race as a whole.

Much depends on the course now taken by moderate white southern politicians. Most southern Congressmen are too committed publicly to white supremacy to shift to an advocacy of Negro voting. But emancipation of the southern politician could be attained only when Negro voting strength there was such that the office-seeker would have to solicit Negro votes rather than demonstrate that he favored white supremacy more than his opponent. That day has not yet arrived. In the summer of 1965 it was estimated that fewer than half

(4) Louis E. Lomax, in Louisville *Courier Journal*, July 7, 1963.

the eligible 5 million Negroes were registered, although the number had doubled in seven years. If equal percentages of both races were registered, Negro votes would be one-third of the white vote. If the Republican party should become a threat to the Democratic party, both parties would solicit the Negro vote. This would not only solve the Negro's political problem, it would revolutionize his social and economic position as well.

Observers reported in 1964 that younger politicians emerging in the South were circumspectly silent about "keeping the Negro in his place." Perhaps their silence was motivated by the expectation that by the time they were ready to run for office there would be no anti-Negro record to use against them with the expected Negro voter. Furthermore, Supreme Court decisions in 1964 ordering reapportionment in both houses of state legislatures on the principle of "one man one vote" should doom the present unfair disfranchisement of the cities. Changes brought about by more equitable urban representation, together with changes resulting from new civil rights legislation and from the outlawing of the poll tax, may revolutionize the political behavior of the South. Reapportionment in the Georgia legislature in the spring of 1965 as a result of the Supreme Court "one man, one vote" ruling gave Negroes a voice in the state capitol for the first time in half a century. Negroes won eight seats in the reapportioned house and one in the senate. And Republicans gained seventeen of forty-seven contested seats in the spring election, a gain of thirteen seats over 1964's total.

With the poll tax ruled unconstitutional in state elections in Virginia, Alabama, Mississippi, and Texas, even greater changes may be expected. In more than a hundred southern counties, Negroes outnumber whites. In Mississippi, for instance, Negroes could control one-third of the state's legislative seats, for they outnumber whites in twenty-nine counties which have forty seats in the 122-member body. In Georgia, Negroes outnumber whites in thirty counties, in Alabama twelve, in North Carolina ten, in South Carolina nine, and in nine Louisiana parishes. The more likely prospect in the immediate future is the election of more white officials with liberal racial views, as the new Negro vote is aligned with white moderates. This had already occurred in Atlanta where a Negro minority and a white moderate vote together elected a racially liberal mayor.

Even where Negroes gained a voting majority in local communities, there seemed no universal disposition on their part to take complete control of the government. In Alabama's Macon County, a Negro majority of voters chose only two of their race to the five city council seats in Tuskeegee. They elected only one Negro each to the county governing board and to the board of education. Thus, it cannot be assumed that Negroes always vote as a bloc. If they should win full civil and economic rights, there would be little reason for them to do so.

Meantime, despite intermediate periods of violence to prevent desegregation and reluctant but peaceable acceptance by southerners of the inevitable, progress is being made. Justice and democracy make their advances haltingly, with many twists and turns, and not always do they move in unison. And the American dream is more often approached as a result of class and group strife than through periods of undisturbed calm and social contentment. As gains are made on one front, frustration and retreat are often experienced on another. While mass arrests of Negroes attempting to register were being made in Selma, Alabama, in the winter of 1964-65, a grand jury in Philadelphia, Mississippi, was returning indictments against eighteen white men including the sheriff and his deputy for the murder of the three civil rights workers in the summer of 1964. True, the indictments would not result in convictions. But the returning of the indictments was in itself a sign of progress in Mississippi. Furthermore, people of conscience and integrity in that state were beginning to speak out. In McComb, where sixteen Negro establishments had suffered bombings in a period of a few months, six hundred community leaders published an appeal for obedience to the Civil Rights Act. In Pike County, a state judge, in what seemed a return to frontier law, placed all suspects in the bombing cases on probation for a period of five years, threatening that if more bombings occurred the suspects would be summarily jailed. At about the same time, the district attorney of Hinds County, in exposing trumped-up charges against a Methodist minister, said: "If an instance such as this occurred to an American citizen in one of the Iron Curtain Countries, all of us would rise up in righteous indignation. When it occurs right at our front door, we blithely turn our backs because the racial problem is involved."[5]

In February 1965, Mississippi's largest business organization,

(5) Quoted in Silver, *Mississippi: The Closed Society,* 99.

the Economic Council, told Mississippians that "order and respect for the law must be maintained. Lawless activities in the state by individuals and organizations cannot be tolerated. . . . Registration and voting laws should be fairly and impartially administered for all." It called upon Mississippians to take "positive action" to achieve goals of "justice, harmony, and continued development." "We recognize," they said, "that the Civil Rights Act of 1964 has been enacted by Congress as law. It cannot be ignored and should not be unlawfully defied."[6]

This resolution was echoed in advice given by Mississippi's attorney general, Joe T. Ferguson, to the sheriffs of the state. "We must put our heads together and recognize that we are part of the Union," said Patterson. "We are bound by laws of the United States and the decisions of the United States Supreme Court. . . . We must be realistic and recognize that [the 1964 Civil Rights Act] is the law of the land."[7] And Governor Paul Johnson, who only a few months before had acted as spokesman for nullifiers, could only agree with his attorney general. Mississippi, he said in a speech in Jackson, was "part of this Nation and we're going to act as part of this Nation. . . . Law and order will prevail. . . . We're not going to be the pushing-boy for [ultra-segregationists] ever again. . . . We are not only the architects but helped build the doghouse we now find ourselves in," he added.[8]

Equally as sharp had been the break with his past record of racism of another southern politican, Georgia's Senator Herman Talmadge. As governor of Georgia in 1954 when the Brown decision was handed down, Herman Talmadge had preached defiance and nullification. But he told a Negro audience in 1965 that race-baiting was over in Georgia, and that he regarded it as his duty to represent "all the people in Georgia." He also promised to appoint Negroes to policy-making positions if he should become governor once more.[9]

These remarkable changes in attitude were truly revolutionary. They suggest that if the American dream of equal opportunity is not on the threshhold, at least segregation in the heart of the deep South is crumbling before the relentless attack of the conscience of mid-twentieth-century America.

(6) Quoted in Louisville *Courier Journal*, Feb. 2, March 4, 1965.
(7) *Ibid.*, Feb. 28, 1965.
(8) Quoted in Washington *Post*, March 1, 1965.
(9) Louisville *Courier Journal*, January 7, 1966.

⚥ XVIII ⚥

The Evolving South

For a century and a half historians of the South have struggled to distinguish between fact and regional clichés and shibboleths. This is true partly because southern economic and social institutions changed so slowly during much of this period that very few basic issues emerged. By 1945, however, southern historical equilibrium was as severely upset as it had been in 1860. Every phase of regional life involved, in the latter period, fundamental readjustment. The federal courts alone opened the way to deep revision of many old patterns in such far-ranging decisions as *Elmore vs. Rice, Smith vs. Allwright, Brown vs. Topeka Board of Education,* and *Baker vs. Carr.* In three far-reaching civil rights acts, the United States Congress broke old patterns and realigned southern political and economic society. No longer could traditional southern policies be followed or relied upon to reverse the tide of revolution. So badly disturbed were some of the old system's supporters that they sought refuge behind the façade of the Republican party. They did this without changing their basic attitudes or philosophy of the South's approach to the future, and at a time when that party's central leadership was all but admitting that it too would have to accept the very facts of change. These were the ones which proved so irritating to old-line southern guardsmen of the traditional clichés.

Southerners had believed there was a distinct peculiarity about their way of life, and that this had set them apart from the rest of the nation. In specific terms, this meant a culture that centered on family and historical background, embraced the higher values of a mature society, reflected refinement and gentility, and found a way of life apart from a hard-driving, impersonal and all-absorbing money-grubbing commercial economy. In its more negative aspects it meant a willingness to follow policies which tolerated racial injustices and a failure to recognize the social and political liabilities involved in such attitudes. An older southern society was irritated when earlier travelers visiting the region made adverse comparisons between conditions prevailing in slave and free territories. Statisticians also upset defenders of the region; beginning with Hinton Rowan Helper and the publication of his *Impending Crisis* in 1857 and continuing down to publication of the latest edition of the annual *Statistical Abstract*, the South has been subjected to unfavorable comparison with other parts of the United States.

New Deal economists and sociologists produced volumes of materials substantiating the statement that the South was the nation's number one economic problem. Scores of southern scholars have found that the southern way of life cannot meet the bare objective test of statistics. The public press has perhaps done as much as scholars to show how far behind the South has lagged. This has been true especially of the agricultural press, which has crusaded so diligently for change in farming procedures.

Much less precise in their understanding of the South's accomplishments than the statisticians, political and social extremists have used emotional assertions as means of defending the southern way of life. Following *Brown vs. Topeka Board of Education* decision they were emphatic in their pledges to fight to the last ditch to sustain white supremacy as the central fact of southern history. They made these commitments after the foundations of the kind of life they defended had been eroded. Lowering of barriers to Negroes on public accommodations; admitting Negroes, often by force of court orders, to colleges and universities across the region, and desegregation of more and more public schools were proof that this part of the traditional southern way of life had all but passed along with lien laws, cotton tenantry, and hookworm. This was clearly apparent in 1965, when the United States Commissioner of Education required local school districts and state departments of education to file positive and workable plans for the desegregation of classrooms before allotting them federal funds. Federal support of public education, a step denied in the 1880's by the defeat of the Blair Educational bill, had in the latter half of this century become more vital to the operation of public schools than the policy of segregation. Opponents of federal aid in this age reckoned with the forces of necessity for education if the South was to survive and compete economically.

No area of southern life was more certainly disturbed by the weight of moral conscience over racial and social issues than the churches. Though a majority of local churches were unrelenting barriers against social change, they could hardly bar the forces of revolution which operated in the streets before them. Congregations found it increasingly difficult to reconcile the doctrine of brotherhood of man within segregated church bodies. Thus pressure from the larger administrative organizations, and sometimes from local sources, made defense of the status quo difficult.

With something like ritualistic fidelity, everyone who has discussed the South has felt obliged to define its regional limitations in geographical terms. The fact that so much variation prevails within the states themselves makes precise definition of the term "South" oftentimes little more than academic. To discuss the modern South of the later twentieth century in terms of traditional or even faintly historical solidity is to deal in myth. If there ever was in fact a "New South" in December 1886, when Henry W. Grady gave such wide publicity to the term, then it was long ago submerged under a wave of rising modernism of global dimensions. In every phase of life the South has, in the past half-century, undergone a revolution. Landmark dates can be ascribed to the rise of the textile industry, the introduction of hydroelectricity generation, and the crusade to achieve diversification of southern agriculture. Industrialism itself is not a new fact in the economy of the South; it dates from English foundations in the new world, and has had a continuing impact upon the region somewhat in proportion to industrial change in the nation itself. But industry was not a central fact in the southern economy until after the depression of the 1930's. Disaster resulting from boll-weevil infestation, two world wars and a depression, and subsequent international revolutions have wrought changes.

Despite the criticisms of its lack of industrial development, the South never existed in industrial isolation, and certainly it does so less at present than at any time in its history. Debates in Congress over two decades, and the quieter rulings of federal courts have drafted blueprints for a "New South" which neither Grady nor his immediate successors could have believed possible. Indicative of how definite shifting attitudes were was the tone of an address delivered in April 1964, at the University of Alabama by Luther Hodges, Secretary of Commerce and former governor of North Carolina. Secretary Hodges could hardly have been clearer in outlining the forces of change. Speaking to a symposium engaged in discussing the role of the social sciences in the development of the modern South, he revealed how far conservative southerners could go in revising their thinking. As governor of North Carolina, he had struggled with problems created by the Supreme Court's decision of 1954. As Secretary of Commerce in 1964, and part of a liberal Administration, he viewed the South and its problems from entirely different perspectives than from those of the governor's office in Raleigh when he was trying to maintain the status quo of segregation. "We are witnessing," he told the Alabamians, "a social revolution centering on the demands of Negro rights, and given the whole history of this nation and of the world itself, the ultimate outcome cannot be in doubt. The Negro in America cannot forever be denied equal opportunity and the full dignity without abandonment of everything America has stood for in the history of civilization. The Negro deserves better treatment, and he must surely get it. Our good sense will not permit us to continue to sanction the waste of the talents of our Negro citizens."

This and a lot more was said almost at the very threshhold at which Governor George F. Wallace had taken his stand to deny two Negro students admission to the University of Alabama. In part Secretary Hodges seemed to speak as though Booker T. Washington's ghost stood beside him. He admonished fellow southerners not to train Negroes with great care and expense only to waste their talents in labors far beneath their capabilities to be productive men. In plainer words he said if the South hoped to approximate the level of national personal income within the next decade, it would have "to run at least twice as fast as that." He was saying perhaps more than he knew. To equalize southern personal income would be to push up demands of the lower half of the region's population far beyond what Harry Ashmore called the "fat back and hominy level." For a century it had been clear to southerners that low personal incomes meant both low and inferior consumer demands, and, except for large-scale agriculture and consumers of southern goods beyond the region, low profits and services for everybody. Efforts to equalize wages actually meant making a complete break with most existing economic practices. American business pressure to develop in the South a profitable market for consumer goods did almost as much in the last half-century to thrust the region into revolution as did the courts, Congress, and American technology. State governments, partly in attempts to attract the location of industry, and partly to protect traditional concepts of wage levels, have enacted right-to-work laws. Repeatedly these laws have caused vigorous discussions in Congress, and have often been threatened by federal legislation nullifying them. They have also been aimed at organized labor, which since 1920 has become a more active force in southern economic life. Much southern labor is still unorganized, but management of the new industry realizes, whatever its public expressions, that this situation will almost certainly undergo a change as urbanization and industrialization increase.

Whether or not the South succeeds in closing the gap in average personal income in the latter part of this century depends upon the kind of educational effort it makes. Thus in 1964 in Tuscaloosa the Secretary of Commerce was repeating once again the old axiom that Southerners could not hold an important economic segment of their people down in the ditch of low income without getting down in the ditch with them. In August 1965, the Congress acted as though it had read the message of Secretary Hodges and finally swept away the last great legal bastion of political resistance when it enacted the voter rights bill. In the enactment of this law the long-dormant philosophy of the Fifteenth Amendment was revived as an active fact in American history. Almost the last vestiges of Populist-imposed restrictions against voters in the South were in a fair way of being nullified. Only a shadow of the past remained in the exception made in regard to the poll tax, and the way was left open for this ancient shibboleth to be brought into the courts for final ajudication.

Equally important, the Supreme Court's decision in *Baker vs. Carr*, an action originally begun by the city of Nashville, promised to weaken materially the last hold of the old agrarian oligarchy on southern politics and economy. Statehouses now sheltered legislators who were instructed to erase by their own action the old lines of political manipulations which had kept their kind in office for so many decades. Now legislators had to take cognizance of the realities of southern population shifting from rural areas to suburban centers. Whether or not the modern South would see masses of voters rush to the polls bent on realigning the power structure or seizing control of political machines which had operated so freely since 1890 would be determined by the application of the new ruling. One thing, however, seemed clear at the outset; a second, sweeping emancipation now confronted the South as an accomplished fact.

Viewed from saner perspectives than from the center of a brainless and vicious mob, or even from the long lines of chanting freedom marchers, the wave of change had already broken over southern history. The South actually entered its new age with far less dramatic fanfare than was indicated by disorderly, violent upheavals. These, perhaps, were the least significant facts associated with the revolution. Conditions of the times were indicated in the small areas of regional social and economic intercourse as well as in the larger ones of agricultural and industrial re-direction.

The Southern Governors' Conference in 1959 confronted history directly. Considering statistics then available to them, the governors realized that their section was rapidly becoming an urban industrialized one in which people would make new and more varied demands on their government. Even more impressive were the statistics based on the 1960 census report. As measured against its past industrial accomplishments, the South had made phenomenal economic progress. Since 1930 per capita wages and earnings had risen, new and different types of industries had moved south, a complex system of improved highways now linked every part of the region in a fairly efficient system of transportation, southerners had left farms in droves and gone to town, and the fresh statistics revealed an impressive increase in the number of standard metropolitan centers, numbers which were still growing. Banks were either able to supply large amounts of capital so necessary for financing the new industry or they could readily procure it from outside sources. The southern farm was already mechanized far beyond the most extravagant prediction of the dreamiest-eyed prophet of the 1930's and 1940's. A broader diversity of farm crops, and tremendous gains in the new livestock grazing industry bore little if any relationship to farm economy in 1920. Even the cotton industry itself had felt the impact of revolution, and no longer was the little farmer of sun-ridged-neck fame a worn and broken servitor of the land. An eloquent southern governor might have been prompted by parts of the census report to recall the oratorical prophecies of Henry W. Grady, and to proclaim to his colleagues and the press that indeed the age of a new South had arrived. In all this optimism, however, there was one overwhelming fact: although the South had made phenomenal progress over its own past record, it actually had not kept pace with that made in the nation as a whole. In 1914 there were 852,857 wage-earners engaged in manufacturing in the South as compared with 11,907,000 nonagricultural workers in 1963. This contrasted to the nation as a whole, where the comparable figures were 7,036,337 in 1914 and 57,174,000 in 1963. Arkansas and Mississippi employed slightly more laborers in manufacturing in the latter year than did the whole South a half-century earlier.[1]

This was achieved despite the fact that five states, Mississippi, Alabama, Arkansas, North Carolina, and Georgia suffered heavy population losses in the 1950's.

The economic image of the southern farm contrasted sharply with that of manufactuing when income from the two economies are compared. Farm income in 1965 was $10,115,030,000 as compared with value added by manufacturing in 1962 of $31,063,000. In 1953 there were 202,735,000 acres of forest lands in the South as compared with 772,000,000 acres in the nation, and southern timber acreage was increasing annually. The timber increase also affected manufacturing, since paper products were an important southern industry. Southern farmers cultivated 311,104,000 acres in crops as compared with 1,123,508 acres in the nation. Thus the depth of change became more clearly discernible. In the 1960's, however, the discrepancy between southern and national achievements was clearly defined. It was in these areas that the South had been most seriously challenged not only to maintain a status quo relationship with national economy, but to surpass

(1) In 1904 the region added in value from manufacturing, $949,534,000, and in 1963, $31,063,000,000. Mississippi alone in the latter year added approximately the same value as did the entire South sixty years earlier. Southern gains from manufacturing in 1904, out of a national added value of $9,293,695,000, was slightly less than one-sixth of national value. The national value in 1962 was $179,290,000,000, and the South's share was again less than one-sixth of this amount.

national gains. With its resources of water, labor, and raw materials, the test of southern capacity was to capitalize on its assets to close the yawning gap between national and regional per capita incomes.

In order to make progress the South had first to educate the mass of its labor supply to perform efficiently at both production and management levels. There still remains a large reservoir of common laborers who could be employed at minimum wages. These people are willing to work, well oriented in their communities, and have excellent dexterity skills, but they do not have the education to compete fully with comparable grades of laborers in other sections of the country. The best inducements which the South could offer many highly technical and specialized industries was a supply of well-trained personnel who could manage and operate plants producing highly sophisticated goods and services. This was especially true in the new age of physics, chemistry, and the generation and distribution of large volumes of electrical energy. The South struggled to achieve these objectives by relatively heavy expenditures on education. It appropriated approximately $4.3 billion for public schools in 1964 as compared with a national expenditure of over $21 billion. In the field of higher education the South made a less favorable showing by spending only about $1.3 billion against a national expenditure of $6.6 billion.

The new industrial age and the shrinking significance of agriculture as a central fact in southern economy caused a considerable shift in the base of regional culture. Universal distribution of cheap rural electrical current brought almost every southerner into instantaneous communication with the world about him. Radio and television facilities broadcast news of national and international events to the humblest backwoods cabin as well as to the modern split-level urban home. For the first time in southern history a love of rowdy and raucous country music was shattered, if not repulsed, by the broadcasting of different if not better music. Conversely, popular southern tastes were as debased by the popular media as were those of the rest of the nation. Southerners could view events on television as they occurred, including the racial disturbances in New Orleans, Little Rock, Clinton, Jackson, and Selma. Even illiterate Ku Klux Klansmen could themselves play a role on television and in the press. Not only could they proclaim themselves bigots, but they could and did conduct tirades against everyone who failed to agree with them. Perhaps no one in the second half of this century knew precisely what effects all of this publicity had either on shaping southern political and social opinion, or in further maturing regional cultures. It was certain that the Negro had found a national platform from which to indicate to the white man his strong determination to destroy barriers in his way to full participation in national life. Thus it was self-evident that the southern frame of reference was vastly broadened. A by-product no doubt was a readier acceptance of less provincial ideas, especially those relating to politics and the new sciences.

Of greater importance to modern southerners was the fact that they now had a dependable basis for the common man to compare his own accomplishments with those of Americans generally. Through daily papers, television and radio, and popular magazines they had, for instance, opportunities to view the interiors of homes in other areas and to compare them with those of their own communities. At the same time southerners more readily became fair game for national advertisers. If the so-called regional way of life was threatened from no other quarter, popular advertising alone would have been sufficient to have wrought a revolution. Even southerners' cherished food tastes were assaulted by the promotion of foods of standard flavors and grand mediocrity. Regional foods themselves were advertised as retaining their particular flavors, even though they were mass-produced in industrial kitchens which sacrificed flavors to maintain volume of production. Old racial bastions were assailed and taken by co-racial advertising and popular musical and dramatic performances. Much of the white South took genuine pride in the success of Eartha Kitt, Leontyne Price, Marion Anderson, and other Negro artists. Manufacturers and merchants followed Congress and court and came to view customers more and more in terms of one-man-one-customer, rather than as racial and regional entities.

If racial barriers were swept away subtly by entertainment and advertising features, the pillars of southern theology itself were threatened by an invasion from the "outside." Devout but illiterate fundamentalists sat by their firesides and heard calm and logical ministers deliver well-prepared and thoughtful sermons, and they heard trained church choirs sing sacred songs that were dignified and inspiring. These were in sharp contrast to the old emotional and ill-prepared ministerial offerings which were more impressive in sound and fury than in logic and learning. It is doubtful indeed whether today fundamentalists anywhere in the South could mount a crusade such as that which embarrassed the region in the mid-1920's over evolution, for confrontation by more learned biblical scholars with access to such powerful news media as radio and television have revealed the fundamentalists' ignorance and bigotry.

With considerable apprehension the South has lost many of its major literary figures by death or by the attrition of changing times since 1945. A question which remained unanswered was whether or not future southern writers could attune themselves to an urban industrial South. It seemed the region in transition would offer the richest sort of materials for creative writers. People caught in the process of change revealed their innermost humanity. Dispossession brought about by mechanization of agriculture, and the rise of towns and industrial centers, and the relocation of sources of political power were rich materials for fresh regional approaches by both fiction writer and dramatist. While modern southern dispossession was much less harsh in many ways than that of the 1920's and 1930's so dramatically presented by John Steinbeck's *Grapes of Wrath*, Erskine Caldwell's *Tobacco Road*, and William Faulkner's *The Sound and the Fury*, it was socially as pertinent. Much later Harper Lee in *To Kill a Mockingbird* revealed both the fact and subtlety of change. A good portion of American writing has come from the cities, and the rapid rise of standard metropolitan centers in the South could well mean the change of locale and emphases of southern writers.

Brown vs. Topeka Board of Education stimulated the production of a large volume of southern writing which should be labeled "no-literature." It was extreme in its point of view, and uninformed and misleading in its interpretation of anthropology and history. Everybody who had a bitter prejudice or a deep-seated hate rushed to a printer's office to have a leaflet or pamphlet printed for wide distribution. A decade later there was a slight let-up by the hate authors and publishers, but the ever-rising stream of southern materials was now fed by crusaders for reform and "I saw it happen" writers. Few if any of these went much beneath the surface to determine the nature of the forces which influenced conditions of the moment.

It was not without significance that the South found itself confronted with upheavals after 1954. Clashes between the segregationist

Citizens' Councils and the civil rights groups exposed conditions in the South to the world. Not even in the Civil War had southerners been so prominently featured in the press both at home and abroad. Every feverish incident brought reporters and photographers running, hungry for sensational news.

Of more importance, however, was the fact that restless American youth, especially college and university students across the nation, found in the problems of the South an opportunity to identify themselves in positive terms with the changing world in which they lived. In doing this they could snatch at a moment of history by engaging actively in all sorts of direct actions such as freedom marches, sit-ins, lie-ins, summer seminars, teaching in freedom schools, working with family improvement groups, taking special courses in political science, sociology, anthropology, and history. Practicing a form of neo-abolitionism, the rebelling college students found in both the Negro and southern poor cause enough to harness their energies, and reason enough not only to provoke searching reappraisals but to stir the reactionaries of the South to do likewise.

In this revolt there was a frantic search in southern history for some deep underlying causes for extremist reaction. Armed with W. J. Cash's *Mind of the South* and C. Vann Woodward's *Reaction and Reunion, The Strange Case of Jim Crow,* and the *Burden of Southern History,* college students went forth to battle the old southern guard at the steps of its courthouses and polling places. They even dug into Populist history, charging those earlier crusaders on the one hand with being the masterminds of white supremacy, and on the other with being liberal revolutionists who had snatched power out of the hands of the old order. Much of this youthful activity was indeed adolescent in nature, and often missed the mark, but it nevertheless had behind it the genius of the American university student for organization and his will for direct action. This movement baffled and confounded the old southern standpatters who had always dealt with politicians and reformers from the North on a more indirect level; they now realized that they faced forces with the strength to achieve their objective to remake the social South by helping the Negro and the poor get on with their efforts to participate in the region's society and economy.

While students and related social reform groups tugged at the

problems of the South, other groups, many of them extremely conservative if not downright reactionary, were active. No matter whether
liberal and directly activist, or reactionary and angry, everybody
shelled enemy camps with heavy bombardments of words. In fine
American bureaucratic style they brought typewriter and duplicating
machines actively into line of battle, producing a huge volume of
documentary material on the problems of the South as viewed by
almost everybody with a cause. Leaflets, essays, pamphlets, booklets,
and press releases poured forth in profusion. Someday literature on
the South in the mid-twentieth century may come to equal in volume
that written about the French Revolution. It was an irony of history
that the emotionally charged race problem in the South should compete
for authorship and services of printing facilities at a time when North
and South were collaborating on the various observances of the cen-
tenary of the Civil War.

The rise of southern cities and the growing maturity of colleges
and universities have contributed significantly to southern culture. These
institutions have not only trained but acted as patrons for artists. Art
collections such as those assembled in galleries in Louisville, Atlanta,
Miami, Richmond, Houston, Memphis, and Dallas contain works of
high achievement, both regional art and some of the major masterpieces
of western art. In the same way patronage of local symphony orches-
tras and other musical organizations and programs, whether of local
or outside origin, contributes materially to the refinement of artistic
and cultural taste in the South.

The façade of southern history has been a long time in the shaping, and it consists of many divergent elements. A less pleasant aspect
has been that of regional police activities. Unhappily much of this
body has been comprised of poorly educated and badly motivated
men who were the first in the social order to be confronted with
public expressions against traditional patterns and social mores. Some
of this element of southern society felt historically the keenest competition from the Negro. The local police force may even be considered
to be spiritual descendants of the old patrols and overseers of the
period of slavery. The unsavory publicity which law enforcement officers have recently brought the South has as often as not reflected
the social and legal failures of the region. Police excesses and brutalities
and the failure of responsible state officials to insure police restraint

have been costly. Within an overwhelmingly agrarian society, lynchings and other excessive acts could occur without much economic retribution or particular injury beyond bitter charges of moral bankruptcy. This was no longer the case after 1910 when so many positive social and political commitments were necessary to bring about the region's economic improvement. Never before has the basic welfare of the South been so effectively linked with national standards of conduct.

A further challenge to today's South is the need to restructure the state governments. Though outwardly the South was represented at the national level by many men elected to office, who reflected in their responses, at least, the will of the majority of their constituents, they did not reflect the full range of southern opinion. As late as 1960 there was not a single state constitution which did not need a complete overhaul. These documents, drafted between 1890 and 1910, represented a philosophy of government no longer tenable today. Populism as an active fact in southern politics may have passed out of existence, but its skeletal hand still strangles more liberal political approaches to southern problems. The state constitutions still contain legal and philosophical conflicts which arose in an era of economic failure and abject fear. Not all of the constitutional shortcoming, however, can be charged to Populists and the conditions of their times. In subsequent years scores of amendments have been added to these documents with the purpose of preserving southern life from racial equality.

In the latter half of the twentieth century the South had again come to the point of repeating some of the questions raised by Robert Latham, editor of the Charleston *News and Courier*, in his Pulitzer Prize-winning editorial. Following the Presidential election of 1924, there were many voices crying out in one place or another about the South, but the question of who spoke for the South went unanswered. Times have indeed changed for the region, pressures have been heightened, and questions have become more insistent and demanding for clearer answers than in 1924. Latham's observations, however, are still pertinent:

> The plight of the South in these respects would be perilous at any time; in a period when political currents are deeper and swifter than ever before, with more violent whirlpools, more dangerous rocks

and shoals, ours is truly a perilous position. Changes which used to be decades in the making now sweep over us almost before we know they are in contemplation. It is true everywhere. In all the countries of Europe the pendulum is swinging, now far to the left, now far to the right. Center parties have lost their power. They are in a very bad way.

And the South has belonged to the school politically which sought as a rule the middle of the road, eschewing ultra-conservatism on the one hand and radicalism on the other. With labor organized and in deadly earnest, with conservatism organized and drawing the lines sharply, what is the South to do, what course shall she take, where do her interests lie, what is due to happen to her?

These are the questions which already press for answers. Who is to speak for the South? How many of her citizens are prepared to help formulate her replies?

Some questions raised by the Charleston editor have been answered. Many other questions now had national and even international connotations. The leadership question, however, was still an open one. Since the Civil War there has seemed to prevail in southern history a notion that the region stood apart from the nation, that there were regional spokesmen who represented it in the fields of religion, economics, social movements, and politics. More frequently than not these spokesmen spoke in negative voices. Examples of such failures of southern leadership in moments of deep challenge were the filibusters against the civil rights acts, and the Congressional manifesto signed by Congressmen and Senators in 1956. Equally reflective of gross failure of leadership at the state level was the enormous amount of energy expended by governors and legislators on the doctrine of interposition and the search for other ways to circumvent decisions of the federal courts at a time when the South was confronted with its greatest challenges to turn the force of change into a constructive gain for the region.

In his Tuscaloosa address Governor Hodges warned of major failures by southern leadership when he said:

> We cannot maintain the employment traditions of a plantation economy and expect to be a leader or even a full participant in a highly technical national and international economy. But even if the South could afford this waste, it would not be possible to maintain in an open, democratic society practices and traditions which an overwhelming majority of the people know in their hearts to be unfair,

intolerable, and morally wrong. This is the reality we must face, if we are to make the difficult adjustments and accommodations that are necessary to prevent a rending of our social fabric by extremists on both sides.

As Governor Hodges so well knew, conditions of the times and the burden of history itself spoke for a region as well as a nation, and leadership which gave voice to contemporary moments had to reckon realistically with the past. Since 1945 the South has faced the problem of trying to develop a formula by which its people can be launched into the mainstream of modern America without creating a crisis at every turn of events.

Politically the New Deal, while making the South a chief beneficiary of its program, also brought a revolt against the past. Even though Franklin D. Roosevelt was reluctant to deal directly with race problems which would irritate southern politicians, and especially those men on whom he depended to secure passage of his legislative program by Congress, he helped initiate a revolution. Mrs. Roosevelt, however, was outspoken in the area of human rights, and so were many members of the Roosevelt adminstration.

Today it is clear that some kind of restructuring of political forces in the South is a certainty. No longer can a minority of strategically placed white rural voters hope to dominate southern politics to the exclusion of other whites and Negroes. In 1965 Governor Paul Johnson campaigned in Mississippi for a constitutional amendment which would greatly liberalize the registration of voters, not to make it easier for Negroes to register but to encourage and enable more white voters to register. In states where unusually complex technicalities had either prevented people from registering or had slowed down the process of registration, the federal government sent civil service agents to act for registrars.

It appears that the center of political control would soon shift from the unyielding black belt to industrial-urban population centers. And if federal legislation in favor of Negroes upset the old bedrock areas of political solidity, then another alignment would inevitably take place. A rapid urbanization and increased urban voter interest in political direction of the South promised tremendous changes. By 1950 it seemed clear that old-style redneck farmer voters and their demagoguic political heroes who for more than a half-century had conducted noisy campaigns which appealed more to prejudice and hate than to reason were nearing the end of their influence. As fundamental political controls shifted away from the past, and came to be centered more on Congress and the courts, the so-called solid South faced grave difficulties in maintaining both a national position of power and control over problems of purely regional concern.

A century has elapsed since the end of the Civil War and the beginning of reconstruction. In this period the South experienced one crisis after another. Every decade since the surrender of General Lee's army promised a revolt against either the old system or pressures imposed upon the region by special interests.

It might well be contended that in the past the South lived in expectancy of change without actually experience it. This might well be a fact, but not for the past few decades. Change has come fast, and, more important, it has come with firm assurance of being permanent. Up until the beginning of the Great Depression there had been promise of change without its actual realization. The post-World War II era, however, brought a revolution. Scarcely a single phase of southern life went untouched. Changes cut deeply into traditional southern policies and institutions. By holding out so strongly against a revision of the old systems, southerners such as Orval Faubus, Leander Perez, Ross Barnett, and George F. Wallace no doubt did as much or more to hasten desegregation as did most of the direct actionists. They brought the region enormous publicity, and helped to formulate a determined national opinion in favor of drastic legal action.

Changes have now been made permanent by court decision and the enactment of federal laws in Congress. These at last helped all southerners to exercise the rights of full citizenship and to have a voice in the South's future planning. In the broad field of economics the region largely loosed the shackles of colonialism and moved closer to the mainstream of American commercial life, despite the fact it still had to advance at least twice as fast as the rest of the nation merely to catch up. There was no longer any profit in continuing to irritate and harass the large Negro segment of the population by seeking in legislative assembly and the courts for ways to maintain a way of life which had been so thoroughly negated by law, judicial decision, and an aroused national public opinion. No historian can say precisely when an era ends and a new one begins, if in fact there really is a discernible demarcation between the past and the future, but at least the South which faces the future today is not the South which a special New Deal committee branded as a region virtually without hope and populated by defeated people. Above the shouting of extremist and crusader there can be heard the voice of a sturdier South already committed to the acceptance of change thrust upon it by all the forces which stirred the Western world after World War II.

It may be that the "South" of history and nostalgia has disappeared altogether. In 1965 schools opened all over the region with few or no incidents. Certainly there were no wild stampedes as in Clinton, Tennessee, about Central High School in Little Rock, or in New Orleans. Still there are elder sons and daughters who cry out in vain for a return to the past. There no longer is a southern past to which either the economic or social South can return. Nor since the civil rights legislation of 1965 and subsequent voter registration activities is there much if any of a political past left to the region.

Speaking before the Southern Governors' Conference in Sea Island, Georgia, on September 13, 1965, Governor John Connally of Texas told his colleagues:

> As you and I well know, the South is often considered in public consciousness as a region apart, an area which has stayed still while other areas move forward, a section contemplating its past rather than aggressively seeking its future. . . . There is no doubt that the South is forced to play catch-up in several fields. . . . We have a role to play in the future of our country. It can be a voice for progress, stability and freedom, or only a voice in the wilderness.

Bibliography

I The New South—A Perspective in Change

Southern historical bibliography has become extensive, and there is no indication of a let-up in the production of regional studies. The South presents a most confusing challenge to authors who deal with broad chronological scopes of its history. Does the region present a distinct and consistent enough character to justify special treatment inside the context of national history, or in a long-term analysis do regional peculiarities become insignificant? The past century opened with Reconstruction, and because of this fact E. Merton Coulter, *The South During Reconstruction* (Baton Rouge, 1947) takes on basic importance as does James G. Randall, *Civil War and Reconstruction*, (Boston, 1937). C. Vann Woodward, *Origins of the New South, 1877–1913* (Baton Rouge, 1951), is a penetrative study of the South in its period of redemption. Much less capably done from points of view and research are the essays by a group of scholars in J. A. C. Chandler *et al.*, *The South in the Building of the Nation*, 13 vols. (Richmond, 1909–13). These essays are usually too brief to be more than suggestive of the problems in the New South. Articles in the *Journal of Southern History* are more searching, and they have come under the scrutiny of capable editors. No student of southern history can afford to overlook the extensive bibliographical appraisals in Arthur S. Link and Rembert W. Patrick (eds.), *Writing Southern History: Essays in Honor of Fletcher Melvin Green* (Baton Rouge, 1965). The postwar South attracted hundreds of travelers, American and foreign, and in time they produced accounts of highly varying quality. Thomas D. Clark (ed.), *Travels in the New South*, 2 vols. (Norman, 1962), lists and appraises the worth of most of these.

Southerners have searched for answers to their many questions about their region during the past century. One of the earliest of these background studies is John Crowe Ransom (ed.), *I'll Take My Stand: The South and the Agrarian Tradition* (New York, 1930). In 1934 the symposium under the editorship of W. T. Couch, *Culture in the South* (Chapel Hill, 1934), took an altogether different view of the region from that of the Agrarians. Virginius Dabney, *Liberalism in the South* (Chapel Hill, 1932), and Wilbur J. Cash, *The Mind of the South* (New York, 1941), make able and extensive explorations into the philosophical and intellectual reactions of the region. C. Vann Woodward, *The Burden of Southern History* (Baton Rouge, 1960), is an erudite discussion of the major forces shaping southern reactions to the modern period. Gunnar Myrdal, *An American Dilemma,* 2 vols. (New York, 1944), is a discussion in depth of Negro culture in social transition, starting with its historical background and ending with its emergence into American culture in general. In two provocative books, *The Southern Heritage* (New York, 1958) and *Who Speaks for the South* (New York, 1965), James M. Dabbs takes soundings of the southern mind and commitments. A group of scholars in the allied social studies look at the more recent South in Allan P. Sindler (ed.), *Change in the Contemporary South* (Durham, 1963).

II Political Reconstruction

Travelers from the North and from abroad during Reconstruction left colorful and sometimes penetrating accounts of conditions in the South. Among the best of these accounts are: Sidney Andrews, *The South Since the War* . . . (Boston, 1866); Edward King, *The Great South* . . . (Hartford, 1875); Charles Nordhoff, *The Cotton States in the Spring and Summer of 1875* (New York, 1876); Whitelaw Reid, *After the War: A Southern Tour* . . . (New York, 1866); and Robert Somers, *The Southern States Since the War, 1870–71* (London, 1871). Other valuable contemporary accounts are: Myrta L. Avary, *Dixie After the War* (reprint, Boston, 1937); Frances Butler Leigh, *Ten Years on a Georgia Plantation Since the War* (London, 1883); Hilary A. Herbert, *et al., Why the Solid South?* (Baltimore, 1910); and Alexander K. McClure, *The South: Its Industrial, Financial and Political Condition* (Philadelphia, 1886). There are two collections of Reconstruction documents: Edward McPherson, *The Political History of the United States of America during the Period of Reconstruction* (Washington, D.C., 1875); and Walter L. Fleming (ed.), *Documentary History of Reconstruction* . . . , 2 vols. (Cleveland, 1906–7). It should be noted, however, that these are excerpts, taken out of context, and seem designed to discredit the Negroes, carpetbaggers, and scalawags.

Probably the best of the general accounts of Reconstruction is James G. Randall and David Donald, *The Civil War and Reconstruction* (Boston, 1961). The traditional conservative view of Reconstruction is given in

William A. Dunning, *Reconstruction, Political and Economic, 1865–1877* (New York, 1907). A contrasting view is that of W. E. B. DuBois, *Black Reconstruction* (New York, 1935). Other valuable studies are: John Hope Franklin, *Reconstruction After the Civil War* (Chicago, 1961); E. M. Coulter, *The South During Reconstruction, 1865–1877* (Baton Rouge, 1947); and Paul H. Buck, *The Road to Reunion 1865–1900* (Boston, 1937). Best of the individual state studies are: W. L. Fleming, *Civil War and Reconstruction in Alabama* (New York, 1905); J. W. Garner, *Reconstruction in Mississippi* (New York, 1901); F. B. Simkins and Robert H. Woody, *South Carolina During Reconstruction* (Chapel Hill, 1932) which sets a new tone of objective appraisal of the Radical regimes; Ella Lonn, *Reconstruction in Louisiana after 1868* (New York, 1918); and Thomas B. Alexander, *Political Reconstruction in Tennessee* (Nashville, 1950). Of special importance for the overthrow of the Reconstruction governments is C. Vann Woodward, *Reunion and Reaction: The Compromise of 1877 and the End of Reconstruction* (Boston, 1951).

Worthy of special note in the periodical literature are: Howard K. Beale, "On Rewriting Reconstruction History," *American Historical Review*, XLV (1940); William A. Russ, Jr., "Registration and Disfranchisement Under Radical Reconstruction," *Mississippi Valley Historical Review*, XXI (1934); Francis B. Simkins, "New Viewpoints of Southern Reconstruction," *Journal of Southern History*, V (1939); D. D. Wallace, "The Question of the Withdrawal of the Democratic Presidential Electors in South Carolina in 1876," *Journal of Southern History*, VIII (1942); Thomas B. Alexander, "Whiggery and Reconstruction in Tennessee," *Journal of Southern History*, XVI (1950); Jack B. Scroggs, "Southern Reconstruction: A Radical View," *Journal of Southern History*, XXIV (1958); Bernard A. Weisberger, "The Dark and Bloody Ground of Reconstruction," *Journal of Southern History*, XXV (1959); Jack B. Scroggs, "Carpetbagger Constitutional Reform in the Atlantic States, 1867–68," *Journal of Southern History*, XXVII (1961); Allen W. Trealease, "Who Were the Scalawags?" *Journal of Southern History*, XXIX (1963); William A. Russ, Jr., "The Negro and White Disfranchisement During Radical Reconstruction," *Journal of Negro History*, XIX (1934); Horace Mann Bond, "Social and Economic Forces in Alabama Reconstruction," *Journal of Negro History*, XXIII (1938); Patrick W. Riddleberger, "The Radicals' Abandonment of the Negro During Reconstruction," *Journal of Negro History*, XLV (1960); Robert H. Woody, "Franklin J. Moses, Jr., Scalawag Governor of South Carolina, 1872–74," *North Carolina Historical Review*, X (1923); John M. Mecklin, "The Black Codes," *South Atlantic Quarterly*, XVI

(1917); Agnes S. Grosz, "The Political Career of Pinckney Benton Stewart Pinchback," *Louisiana Historical Quarterly*, XXVII (1944); Francis B. Harris, "Henry Clay Warmoth, Reconstruction Governor of Louisiana," *Louisiana Historical Quarterly*, XXX (1947); and Hilda T. McDaniel, "Francis Tillon Nicholls and the End of Reconstruction," *Louisiana Historical Quarterly*, XXXII (1949).

III   Agrarian Revolt

Most of the general works mentioned earlier concern themselves with politics in the post-Reconstruction period. C. Vann Woodward, *Origins of the New South, 1877–1913* (Baton Rouge, 1951), gives a brilliant insight into post-Reconstruction politics. Other standard works are: Solon J. Buck, *The Granger Movement* (Cambridge, 1913) and *The Agrarian Crusade: A Chronicle of the Farmer in Politics* (New Haven, 1921); and J. D. Hicks, *The Populist Revolt* (Minneapolis, 1931). Special studies with political emphasis for the "Bourbon" period are: Theodore Saloutos, *The Farmer Movements in the South, 1865–1933* (Berkeley, 1960); V. P. DeSantis, *Republicans Face the Southern Question: The New Departure Years, 1877–1897* (Baltimore, 1959); R. B. Nixon, *Henry W. Grady, Spokesman of the New South* (New York, 1943); A. J. Going, *Bourbon Democracy in Alabama, 1874–1890* (University, Ala., 1951); J. F. Doster, *Railroads in Alabama Politics, 1875–1914* (University, Ala., 1951); Albert D. Kirwan, *Revolt of the Rednecks: Mississippi Politics, 1876–1925* (Lexington, 1951); and Paul Lewinson, *Race, Class, and Party: A History of Negro Suffrage and White Politics in the South* (New York, 1932).

Francis B. Simkins, *The South Old and New: A History, 1820–1947* (New York, 1947), devotes much attention to politics in this period. So does Benjamin B. Kendrick and Alex M. Arnett, *The South Looks at Its Past* (Chapel Hill, 1935). Wilbur J. Cash, *The Mind of the South* (New York, 1941), is a penetrating analysis of southern society by a journalist who was a keen student of politics. C. Vann Woodward, *Tom Watson: Agrarian Rebel* (New York, 1938), and Francis B. Simkins, *Pitchfork Ben Tillman, South Carolinian* (Baton Rouge, 1944), are excellent studies of agrarian rebels. So is Robert C. Cotner's lengthy biography of the more moderate Texan, *James S. Hogg* (Austin, 1959).

Periodical literature is rich in political studies of the period. Especially valuable are: *The Nation*, (1890–91); Anonymous, "The New South and the Old South: Myths and Mythmakers," *Tyler's Quarterly*, VII (1926); Vincent P. DeSantis, "Republican Efforts To 'Crack' the Solid

South," *Review of Politics*, XIV (1952); Herbert J. Doherty, Jr., "Voices of Protest from the New South, 1875–1910," *Mississippi Valley Historical Review*, XLII (1955); Vincent P. DeSantis, "President Garfield and the Solid South," *North Carolina Historical Review*, XXXVI (1959); William A. Mabry, "Disfranchisement of the Negro in Mississippi," *Journal of Southern History*, IV (1938); Vincent P. DeSantis, "The Republican Party and the Southern Negro, 1877–1897," *Journal of Negro History*, XLV (1960); Patrick W. Riddleberger, "The Radicals' Abandonment of the Negro during Reconstruction," *Journal of Negro History*, XLV (1960); Thomas B. Alexander, "Persistent Whiggery in the Confederate South, 1860–1877," *Journal of Southern History*, XXVII (1961); James F. Doster, "Were Populists Against Railroad Corporations? The Case of Alabama," *Journal of Southern History*, XX (1954); Vincent P. DeSantis, "President Arthur and the Independent Movements in the South in 1882," *Journal of Southern History*, XIX (1953); Frank B. Williams, Jr., "The Poll Tax as a Suffrage Requirement in the South, 1870–1901," *Journal of Southern History*, XVIII (1952); George B. Tindall, "The Campaign for the Disfranchisement of Negroes in South Carolina," *Journal of Southern History*, XV (1949); Albert D. Kirwan, "Apportionment in the Mississippi Constitution of 1890," *Journal of Southern History*, XIV (1948); Willie D. Halsell, "Republican Factionalism in Mississippi, 1882–84," *Journal of Southern History*, VII (1941); W. D. Halsell, "The Bourbon Period in Mississippi Politics, 1875–1890," *Journal of Southern History*, XI (1945); W. D. Halsell, "James R. Chalmers and Mahoneism in Mississippi," *Journal of Southern History*, X (1944); Vincent P. DeSantis, "President Hayes's Southern Policy," *Journal of Southern History*, XXI (1955); William B. Hesseltine, "Economic Factors in the Abandonment of Reconstruction," *Mississippi Valley Historical Review*, XXII (1935); and James A. Barnes, "The Gold Standard Democrats and the Party Conflict," *Mississippi Valley Historical Review*, XVII (1930).

IV   Farmers on the Land

The agricultural history of the South since 1865 has been varied and complex. The past century of agricultural change and expansion has involved a diversification of crops, methodology, politics, international economy, and education. A good background study is Lewis Gray, *History of Agriculture in the Southern United States*, 2 vols. (Washington, D.C., 1933). The reinstatement of southern agriculture after 1865 is covered in the late volumes of *DeBow's Review*. Authors of the articles in these post Civil War volumes reflected eloquently the hopes of both farmers

and merchants that cotton could be restored to its estate of supremacy.
Matthew Brown Hammond's *The Cotton Industry—An Essay in American
Economic History* (Ithaca, 1897) is a sound treatise on the role of cotton
on the southern farm. In much more abbreviated form, Henry W. Grady
discussed the plight of cotton and farmers in "Cotton and Its Kingdom,"
Harper's Magazine, Oct. 1881, LXIII, 122. In a more recent and more
scholarly study Nannie May Tilley, *The Bright Tobacco Industry,
1860–1929* (Chapel Hill, 1948), discusses the history of a second staple
crop, with chapters treating growth, manufacture, and distribution. A second and broader study is Joseph C. Robert, *The Story of Tobacco in
America* (New York, 1949). A highly competent study of the sugar industry is J. Carlyle Sitterson, *Sugar Country: The Cane Sugar Industry
in the South, 1753–1950* (Lexington, 1953). John Norman Efferson
has presented a view of the modern rice industry in *The Production
and Marketing of Rice* (New Orleans, 1952).

The personal side of the southern way of life before 1900 is treated
in Henry W. Grady, *The New South* (New York, 1890); Francis Butler
Simkins, *Pitchfork Ben Tillman* (Baton Rouge, 1944); Stuart Noblin,
Leonidas LaFayette Polk (Chapel Hill, 1949); Alex Arnett, *The Populist
Movement in Georgia* (New York, 1922); Daniel M. Robison, *Bob Taylor
and the Agrarian Revolt in Tennessee* (Chapel Hill, 1935); C. Vann Woodward, *Tom Watson, Agrarian Rebel* (New York, 1938).

Selective treatments of agrarian experiences in the South include: Clar-
ence Poe, "The Farmer and His Future," W. T. Couch (ed.), *Culture
in the South* (Chapel Hill, 1934); C. Vann Woodward, *Origins of the
New South* (Baton Rouge, 1951); Thomas D. Clark, *The Southern Country
Editor* (Indianapolis, 1948) and *The Rural Editor and the New South*
(Baton Rouge, 1948); Rupert B. Vance, *Human Geography of the South*
(Chapel Hill, 1932). Several essayists treat various aspects of agriculture
in *The South in the Building of the Nation*, Vol. VI (Richmond, 1909);
Benjamin B. Kendrick and Alex Arnett, *The South Looks at Its Past*
(Chapel Hill, 1935); A. E. Parkins, *The South, Its Economic-Geographic
Development* (New York, 1938); Fred A. Shannon, *The Farmer's Last
Frontier* (New York, 1945); John H. More, *The South Today* (New
York, 1916); R. B. Brooks, *The Agrarian Revolution in Georgia* (Madison,
1914); Enoch Banks, *The Economics of Land Tenure in Georgia* (New
York, 1905); John B. Clark, *Populism in Alabama* (*Auburn*, 1927).

Failure of the southern agrarian system has stimulated a massive
amount of appraisal. Some of these sources are: Charles Otken, *Ills of
the South or Related Causes Hostile to the General Prosperity of the
Southern People* (New York, 1894); George R. Holmes, "Southern Peon-

age," *Annals of the Academy of Political Science and Social Sciences*, Vol. IV, p. 64; W. H. Skaggs, *The Southern Oligarchy* (New York, 1924); Arthur Raper, *Tenants of the Almighty: A Tale of Two Blackbelt Counties* (New York, 1943); *Preface to Peasantry* (Chapel Hill, 1936) and, with Ira De A. Reid, *Share Croppers All* (Chapel Hill, 1941); Rupert B. Vance, *The Human Factors in Cotton Culture* (Chapel Hill, 1929); Carl Kelsey, *The Negro Farmer* (Chicago, 1903); J. O. Nall, *The Tobacco Night Riders of Kentucky and Tennessee* (Louisville, 1939); Edwin R. Embree, Charles S. Johnson, and W. W. Alexander, *The Collapse of Cotton Tenancy, 1933–1935* (Chapel Hill, 1935), is brief but highly reflective of the depth of the Depression in the cotton belt. The most disturbing of the Depression reports was that prepared by the Committee on Economic Conditions in the South under the chairmanship of Lowell D. Mellett. In this slender pamphlet (1938) was introduced the phrase, "The South, the Number One Economic Problem of the Nation." Frank Freidel, *FDR and the South* (Baton Rouge, 1965), gives insight into the southern farmer's plight in the late 1920's. A discussion of the southern credit and furnishing system is contained in Thomas D. Clark, *Pills, Petticoats and Plows* (Indianapolis, 1944). Howard W. Odum, *Southern Regions of the United States* (Chapel Hill, 1936), contains an excellent statistical analysis of southern agriculture as reflected by the United States Census, 1930. A serious consideration of the status of agricultural is contained in the reports of the Southern Commercial Congresses. The report of 1911, entitled *The South's Physical Recovery Described in One Hundred Addresses* (Washington, D.C., 1911), is an especially good report.

Modern views of the status of southern agriculture are contained in: John Leonard Fulmer, *Agricultural Progress in the Cotton Belt Since 1920* (Chapel Hill, 1950), which contains a splendid bibliography, especially on experiment stations and extension service bulletins. *Types of Farming in the United States from the Fifteenth Census* (Washington, D.C., 1933); Calvin B. Hoover and Benjamin U. Ratchford relate agriculture to southern industrialization in *Economy of the South, Report of the Joint Committee on the Economic Impact of Federal Policies on the South* (Washington, D.C., 1951) and in their more extensive study, *Economic Resources and Policies of the South* (New York, 1951). The impact of modernization on southern agriculture is discussed in Thomas D. Clark, *The Emerging South* (New York, 1961). An account of the struggle to improve plant types, which led to modern production, is George Lee Simpson, Jr., *The Cokers of Carolina* (Chapel Hill, 1956).

Both the United States Department of Agriculture and the state experiment stations and extension services have published great quantities of revealing historical materials. Especially useful are the *Yearbooks* of the U.S. Department of Agriculture, and of these, *Farmers in a Changing World* (Washington, D.C., 1940) is most useful. State publications include: J. P. Montgomery, *Louisiana Farm Production* (Baton Rouge, 1952); G. H. Aull, *Rural Landholding in South Carolina* (Clemson, 1940); *Farm Land Ownership in the Southeast*, pub. 4, S. E. Regional Land Tenure Committee (Clemson, 1940); and *Base Book of Mississippi Agriculture, 1866–1953* (Jackson, 1955).

V   Demagoguery and Reform

C. Vann Woodward's revisionist classic, *Origins of the New South*, extends its coverage into the early years of the twentieth century. Solon J. Buck, *The Agrarian Crusade* (Cambridge, Mass., 1913), traces the connection between the Populist movement and the progressive reforms of the early 1900's. Theodore Saloutos, *Farmer Movements in the South, 1865–1933* (Berkeley, 1960), a more general synthesis of the agrarian movement in the South, devotes major attention to the early decades of the twentieth century. Eric F. Goldman, *Rendezvous with Destiny* (New York, 1952), emphasizes the somewhat ironic relationship between liberal economic reform and demagogic racism. This theme is substantiated at the state level by Albert D. Kirwan, *Revolt of the Rednecks* (Lexington, 1951). Richard Hofstadter, *The Age of Reform, From Bryan to F.D.R.* (New York, 1955), depicts the agrarian revolt as stemming from the same acquisitive ambitions as those of the industrial leaders.

The most thorough study of twentieth-century southern politics at both state and regional levels is V. O. Key, *Southern Politics in State and Nation* (New York, 1959). Key, while emphasizing the role of the black belt as the core of southern sectionalism, points out that socio-economic divisions have had great influence on the politics of the South. This view is supported by Rupert B. Vance, *Human Geography of the South: A Study of Regional Resources and Human Adequacy* (Chapel Hill, 1932). Dewey W. Grantham, *The Democratic South* (Athens, 1963), is a brilliant analysis of the origins of the one-party system in the South. It also suggests possible developments of a two-party system, as also does Alexander Heard, *A Two-Party South?* (Chapel Hill, 1952).

Arthur S. Link was the first historian to discover the southern progressive movement of the early twentieth century. His article, "The Progressive Movement in the South, 1870–1914," *North Carolina Historical Review*, XXIII (1946), was further developed in numerous articles which were summarized in the first volume of his *Wilson: The Road to the White*

House (Princeton, 1947). Link further develops this theme in two subsequent volumes: *Woodrow Wilson and the Progressive Era, 1910–1917* (New York, 1954) and *Woodrow Wilson: The New Freedom* (Princeton, 1956), and in "The South and the 'New Freedom': An Interpretation," *American Scholar,* XX (1951). Scholarly biographies of a few reform governors have thrown light on the reform movements in individual states. The best of these is Dewey W. Grantham's *Hoke Smith and the Politics of the New South* (Baton Rouge, 1958). Another excellent biographical study is Joseph L. Morrison's *Josephus Daniels Says . . . : An Editor's Political Odyssey from Bryan to Wilson and F. D. R., 1894–1913* (Chapel Hill, 1962). Insights into grass-roots politics are given in Thomas D. Clark, *The Southern Country Editor* (Indianapolis, 1948), and *Pills, Petticoats and Plows: The Southern Country Store* (Indianapolis, 1944).

Southern demagogues have been the subjects of numerous studies. Among the best are: Reinhard H. Luthin, *American Demagogues: Twentieth Century* (Boston, 1954); Gerald W. Johnson, "Live Demagogues or Dead Gentlemen," *Virginia Quarterly Review,* XII (1936); Daniel M. Robinson, "From Tillman to Long: Some Striking Leaders of the Rural South," *Journal of Southern History,* III (1937); T. Harry Williams, "The Gentleman from Louisiana: Demagogue or Democrat," *Journal of Southern History,* XXVI (1960); Allan P. Sindler, *Huey Long's Louisiana: State Politics, 1920–1952* (Baltimore, 1956). Other items of interest are: William G. Carleton, "The Conservative South—A Political Myth," *Virginia Quarterly Review,* XXII (1946); W. G. Carleton, "The Southern Politician—1900 and 1950," *Journal of Politics,* XIII (1951); George E. Mowry, "The South and the Progressive Lily White Party of 1912," *Journal of Southern History,* VI (1940). A. Elizabeth Taylor, in a series of articles and one book, has given the most complete coverage of the woman suffrage movement in the South. See especially her *Woman Suffrage Movement in Tennessee* (New York, 1957). T. Harry Williams has an excellent essay on the period in his *Romance and Realism in Southern Politics* (Baton Rouge, 1966).

VI   The Path to Industrialization

Like other phases of southern history industrialization has produced a broad literature. This subject is treated generally in a series of essays in A. C. Chandler, *et al.,* "Economic History, 1865–1909," *The South in the Building of the Nation* (Richmond, 1909). A background study of worth is Victor S. Clark, *History of Manufactures in the United States* (New York, 1929). This work gives a glimpse of the beginnings of post Civil

War industry. Broadus Mitchell and George S. Mitchell, *The Industrial Revolution in the South* (Baltimore, 1931), is a good preliminary view of the spread of industry. Rupert B. Vance, *Human Geography of the South: A Study in Regional Resources and Human Adequacy* (Chapel Hill, 1932), A. E. Parkins, *The South: Its Economic-Geographic Development* (New York, 1938), and Edwin D. Mims, *The Advancing South* (Garden City, 1926), give a background of southern industry in the context of the old agrarianism.

Specific industries are treated in Ethel Armes, *Story of Coal and Iron in Alabama* (Birmingham, 1910); Nannie May Tilley, *The Bright Tobacco Industry, 1860–1929* (Chapel Hill, 1948); Joseph C. Robert, *The Story of Tobacco in America* (New York, 1949); John K. Winkler, *Tobacco Tycoon: Story of James B. Duke* (New York, 1942); J. Carlyle Sitterson, *Sugar Country: The Sugar Cane Industry in the South, 1753–1950* (Lexington, 1953).

There is considerable historical literature treating the rise of the cotton mills. The best works are: B. Mitchell and G. S. Mitchell, *The Industrial Revolution in the South* (Baltimore, 1931); Broadus Mitchell, *William Gregg: Factory Master of the Old South* (Chapel Hill, 1928) and *Rise of the Cotton Mills in the South* (Baltimore, 1921); Clarence Heer, *Income and Wages in the South* (Chapel Hill, 1930); Harriet L. Herring, *Welfare Work in Mill Villages: The Story of Extra-Mill Activities in North Carolina* (Chapel Hill, 1929); Lois McDonald, *Southern Mill Hills* (New York, 1928); J. J. Rhyne, *Some Southern Cotton Mill Workers and Their Villages* (1930); James A. Morris, *Woolen and Worsted Manufacturing in the Southern Piedmont* (Columbia, 1952).

Unfortunately there are no histories of any scope of the coal industry in the South. A. C. Mcfarlan, *Geology of Kentucky* (Lexington, 1943), gives a geological background of this industry. Malcolm Ross, *Machine Age in the Hills* (New York, 1933), gives a human view of the mines and their villages. Thomas J. Crawford, *Compilation of Coal and Petroleum Data for Kentucky* (Lexington, 1958), is a helpful statistical source. Howard Beers (ed.), *Kentucky: Designs for Its Future* (Lexington, 1945), deals with the social background for a part of the mining industry. The clearest study of social conditions in the coal-mining industry is Harry M. Caudill, *Night Comes to the Cumberland: A Biography of a Depressed Area* (Boston, 1963). H. H. Chapman, *et al.*, *The Iron and Steel Industries of the South* (Tuscaloosa, 1953).

Labor is treated in: John Van Sickle, *Planning for the South: An Inquiry into the Economics of Regionalism* (Nashville, 1943); Abraham Berryman, George T. Starnes, and Frank T. DeVyver, *Labor in the Indus-*

trial South: A Survey of Wages and Living Conditions in the Major Industries of the New Industrial South (Charlottesville, 1930); George T. Starnes and John E. Hamm, *Some Phases of Labor Relations in Virginia* (New York, 1934); Calvin B. Hoover and Benjamin U. Ratchford, *Economic Resources and Policies of the South* (New York, 1951); John L. Johnson, *Income in Kentucky* (Lexington, 1955).

The struggle to adjust southern freight rates is treated in: William H. Joubert, *Southern Freight Rates in Transition* (Gainesville, 1949); Clyde C. Carter, *State Regulations of Commercial Carriers in North Carolina* (Chapel Hill, 1952); Robert A. Lively, *The South in Action: A Sectional Crusade Against Freight Rate Discrimination* (Chapel Hill, 1949).

A reflection of change during the post World War II period is contained in the social and economic study by John M. Maclachlan and Joe S. Floyd, Jr., *This Changing South* (Gainesville, 1956). Thomas D. Clark, *The Emerging South* (New York, 1961), discusses the many industrial changes after 1920. The new timber industry is treated in: Nollie Noble Hickman, *Mississippi Harvest: Lumbering in the Longleaf Pine Belt, 1840–1915* (Oxford, 1962); and Jonathan Daniels, *The Forest of the Future* (New York, 1957). The petroleum industry is treated in: C. C. Rister, *Oil! Titan of the Southwest* (Norman, 1949); Gerald Forbes, *Flush Production: The Epic of Oil in the Gulf-Southwest* (Norman, 1942); James A. Clark and Michel T. Halbouty, *Spindletop* (New York, 1952); and John O. King, *The Early History of the Houston Oil Company of Texas, 1901–1908* (Houston, 1959).

VII   Education the Central Challenge

The history of southern education since 1865 has not received an adequate general treatment. Numerous special studies present many facets of the subject, but few deal with its full scope. A general study which presents a brief outline of the subject down to the 1920's is Edgar W. Knight, *Public Education in the South* (New York, 1922). A much more complete consideration is to be found in Charles W. Dabney, *Universal Education in the South*, 2 vols. (Chapel Hill, 1936). Like Dabney, Edgar Gardiner Murphy was an active crusader for educational advancement. *The Present South* (New York, 1909) considers the movement for universal education in a fuller context of southern economic and social life. A scholarly treatment of early phases of education reinstatement in the South is Henry Swint, *The Northern Teacher in the South, 1862–1870* (Nashville, 1941). Carter G. Woodson viewed the subject from another point of view in his *Miseducation of the Negro* (Washington, D.C., 1933). Edgar

W. Knight dealt specifically with the Reconstruction period in *The Influence of Reconstruction in Education in the South* (New York, 1913). The basic story of universal education after 1865 lies buried in the voluminous annual reports of the state superintendents of public instruction of the various states. Histories of education in the states include: M. D. S. Noble, *A History of the Public Schools of North Carolina* (Chapel Hill, 1930); Dorothy Orr, *A History of Education in Georgia* (Chapel Hill, 1950); Cornelius J. Heatwole, *A History of Education in Virginia* (New York, 1916); Nita Katharine Pyburn, *Documentary History of Education in Florida* (Tallahassee, 1951); Barksdale Hamlett, *History of Education in Kentucky* (Frankfort, 1914); H. M. Bond, *Negro Education in Alabama* (Washington, D.C., 1939); Henry T. Thompson, *The Establishment of the Public School System in South Carolina* (Columbia, 1927); Edward Mayes, *History of Education in Mississippi* (Washington, D.C., 1899); Charles E. Jones, *Education in Georgia* (Washington, D.C., 1889); Thomas H. Harris, *The Story of Public Education in Louisiana* (New Orleans, 1924); Oscar W. Harris, *Development of Secondary Education in Alabama Prior to 1920* (Nashville, 1933); and Edwin W. Fry, *History of Education in Louisiana* (Washington, D.C., 1899).

Documentary studies of background importance are Edgar W. Knight (ed.), *Documentary History of Education in the South before 1860*, 5 vols. (Chapel Hill, 1949–53); and L. D. Rubin (ed.), *Teach the Freedmen: The Correspondence of Rutherford B. Hayes and the Slater Fund for Negro Education, 1881–1892*, 2 vols. (Baton Rouge, 1959).

General discussions of post Civil War education are contained in: C. Vann Woodward, *Origins of the New South* (Baton Rouge, 1951); Burton J. Hendricks, *The Training of An American: The Earlier Life and Letters of Walter Hines Page, 1855–1913* (Boston, 1928); Josephus Daniels, *Tar Heel Editor* (Chapel Hill, 1939); Gunnar Myrdal, *An American Dilemma*, 2 vols. (New York, 1944); and W. T. Couch (ed.), *Culture in the South* (Chapel Hill, 1931).

Biographical studies include: Edwin A. Alderman and Armistead C. Gordon, *J. L. M. Curry, A Biography* (New York, 1901); Booker T. Washington, *Up from Slavery: An Autobiography* (Garden City, 1901); Basil J. Matthews, *Booker T. Washington: Educator and Interracial Interpreter* (Cambridge, 1948); Robert D. W. Conner and Clarence Poe, *Charles Brantley Aycock* (Garden City, 1912); Dumas Malone, *Edwin A. Alderman: A Biography* (New York, 1940).

STATISTICAL CONSIDERATIONS: One of the most direct and meaningful commentaries on the failure of the South to nurture education is Charles L. Coon, *Facts about Southern Educational Progress, A Present-Day Study in Public School Maintenance for Those Who Look Forward* (Raleigh 1905). A modern source, which reveals in detail the education position of the South, is Rupert B. Vance *et al., High Schools in the South: A Fact Book* (Nashville, 1966).

VIII   An Ever-Broadening Educational Challenge

Many of the sources listed in the bibliography for Chapter VII are applicable here also. In recent years statistical methods have been greatly improved, thus giving a more precise picture of what has actually happened in educational expansion. Truman Pierce *et al., White and Negro Schools in the South* (Englewood Cliffs, 1955), is a rather thorough survey by professional educationists. A more general consideration of southern cultural and educational approaches is Edwin Mims, *The Advancing South: Stories of Progress and Reaction* (Garden City, 1926). The same author viewed some earlier southern educational history in *Chancellor Kirkland of Vanderbilt University* (Nashville, 1940). A more searching biographical account is Dumas Malone, *Edwin A. Alderman,* (New York, 1940). The struggles of a university president at a state university in the New South is contained in Marcus Wilkerson, *Thomas Duckett Boyd* (Baton Rouge, 1935). Frank L. McVey, *The Gates Open Slowly* (Lexington, 1949), presents a similar picture.

John M. Maclachlan and Joe S. Floyd, Jr., reflect the basic challenges and failures of southern education in *This Changing South* (Gainesville, 1956). An earlier and more revealing study of the plight of education in the 1930's is Howard W. Odum, *Southern Regions of the United States* (Chapel Hill, 1936). Redding S. Sugg, Ernest Swanson, and John A. Griffin, *Public Education in the South Today and Tomorrow, A Statistical Survey* (Chapel Hill, 1955), is a more modern survey.

Some of the special aspects of southern education are treated in: Joseph Cannon Bailey and Seaman A. Knapp, *Schoolmaster of American Agriculture* (New York, 1945); Katharine Dupre Lumpkin, *The South in Progress* (New York, 1940); Allan Sindler (ed.), *Change in the Contemporary South* (Durham, 1963); Charles A. True, *A History of Agricultural Extension Work in the United States, 1785–1923* (Washington, D.C., 1925); George Hilton Jones, *The Southern Regional Education Board: Ten Years of Regional Co-operation in Higher Education* (Baton Rouge, 1960); Redding S. Sugg, Jr., and George Hilton Jones, *The Southern Regional Educational Board: Ten Years of Regional Co-operation in Higher Education* (Baton Rouge, 1960).

Histories of southern universities and colleges reveal much of the story of the rise of education in the South at all levels. Among these are: Walter L. Fleming, *Louisiana State University, 1860–1896* (Baton Rouge, 1936); Philip A. Bruce, *History of the University of Virginia, 1819–1919,* 5 vols. (New York, 1920–22); James F. Hopkins, *The University of Kentucky: Origins and Early Years* (Lexington, 1951); Charles G. Talbert, *The University of Kentucky: The Maturing Years* (Lexington, 1965); Dan Hollis, *University of South Carolina,* 2 vols. (Columbia, 1956); John Bettersworth, *Peoples College* (Tuscaloosa, 1953); Nora Chaffin, *Trinity College, 1839–1892: The Beginnings of Duke University* (Durham, 1950); and Elizabeth Peck, *Berea's First Century, 1855–1955* (Lexington, 1955).

The *Brown vs. Topeka School Board* decision in 1954 stimulated a flood of southern educational studies. One of the most important of these is Harry S. Ashmore (ed.), *The Negro and the Schools* (Chapel Hill, 1954). There was organized in Nashville, Tennessee, a southern educational reporting service which has issued a monthly summary of educational news under the title *Southern School News.* This service has issued annually a summary of the changing situation in the South, *Statistical Summary of School Segregation-Desegregation in the Southern Border States,* a major source of statistical information for all phases of educational change. Accounts of southern communities making progress toward accepting the Court's mandate are contained in Omar Carmichael and Weldon James, *The Louisville Story* (New York, 1957); and Don Shoemaker (ed.), *With All Deliberate Speed: Segregation-Desegregation in Southern Schools* (New York, 1957). Three views of the traumatic experience of desegregating the University of Mississippi are contained in James Silver, *Mississippi: The Closed Society* (New York, 1964), Russell Barrett, *Integration at Ole Miss* (Chicago, 1965), and James H. Meredith, *Three Years in Mississippi* (Bloomington, 1966).

There is almost no limit to the special educational projects, self-studies, statistical summaries, and general comment on southern education. Since 1954 regional and national newspaper presses have published hundreds of thousands of words on this subject.

IX The Mightier Sword

There is no general history of Southern literature from 1865 to 1965. This is a highly complex subject which involves many aspects of human change and reaction. The early years represent the transitional period when southern writers fell under the impact of war and reconstruction. Many of them exhibited a deep nostalgia for the past and faced the future with uncertainty. Jay B. Hubbell, *The South in American Literature, 1607–1900* (Durham, 1954), covers this earlier period of the postwar years in a half dozen chapters. W. T. Couch (ed.), *Culture in the South* (Chapel Hill, 1934), contains several penetrating essays on this subject. There are various exploratory essays in J.A.C. Chandler *et al.*, *The South in the Building of the Nation*, 13 vols. (Richmond, 1909). Even more extensive coverage is contained in *The Library of Southern Literature*, 17 vols. (New Orleans and Atlanta, 1908–23). This work is a combination of biographical sketches and selections from the writings of southern authors. A specific consideration of southern writing is contained in William T. Lynn, *Southern Literature* (New York, 1932). Robert Spiller (ed.), *Literary History of the United States*, 2 vols. (New York, 1963), treats many of the southern writers as they contributed to a national literature.

There is a paucity of southern newspaper history. Some of the better works are: Josephus Daniels, *Tar Heel Editor* (Chapel Hill, 1939); Joseph Frazier Wall, *Henry Watterson, Reconstructed Rebel* (New York, 1956); Arthur L. Krock (ed.), *The Editorials of Henry Watterson*, 2 vols. (New York, 1923); Thomas D. Clark, *The Southern Country Editor* (Indianapolis, 1948) and *The Rural Editor and the New South* (Baton Rouge, 1948); R. B. Nixon, *Henry W. Grady* (New York, 1943); Joel Chandler Harris (ed.), *Life of Henry W. Grady, Including His Writings and Speeches* (New York, 1890); Burton J. Hendricks, *The Training of An American: The Earlier Life and Letters of Walter Hines Page, 1855–1913* (Boston, 1928); Sam Acheson, *35,000 Days in Texas: A History of the Dallas News and Its Forebears* (New York, 1938); E. L. Bell, *The Augusta Chronicle: Indomitable Voice of Dixie, 1785–1960* (Athens, 1960); T. E. Dabney, *One Hundred Great Years: The Story of the Times-Picayune from Its Founding to 1940* (Baton Rouge, 1944); W. W. Ball, *The State That Forgot, South Carolina's Surrender to Democracy* (Indianapolis, 1932).

Biographies of southern writers are numerous. Among the best are: Grant C. Knight, *James Lane Allen and the Genteel Tradition* (Chapel Hill, 1935); Louise M. Field, *Ellen M. Glasgow: Novelist of the Old and New South* (Garden City, 1923); Aubrey H. Starke, *Sidney Lanier* (Chapel Hill, 1932); Carl Van Doren, *James Branch Cabell* (New York, 1925); Julia Harris, *The Life and Letters of Joel Chandler Harris* (Boston, 1918); Ed Winfield Parks, *Charles Egbert Craddock (Mary Noailles Murphree)* (Chapel Hill, 1941); Arlin Turner, *George W. Cable* (New York, 1962); Earl Rovits, *Herald to Chaos* (Lexington, 1964); Hyatt H. Waggoner, *William Faulkner: From Jefferson to the World* (Lexington, 1959); C. Hugh Holman, *Three Modes of Southern Fiction: Ellen Glasgow,*

William Faulkner, Thomas Wolfe (Athens, 1966); James B. Merriwether, *The Literary Career of William Faulkner: A Bibliographical Study* (Princeton, 1961); Cleanth Brooks, *William Faulkner: The Yoknapataw-pha Country* (New Haven, 1963); Richard S. Kennedy, *The Window of Memory: The Literary Career of Thomas Wolfe* (Chapel Hill, 1962); and Louis D. Rubin, Jr., *No Place on Earth: Ellen Glasgow and James Branch Cabell and Richmond-in-Virginia* (Austin, 1959).

The modern period of southern literature is treated in H. L. Mencken, "The Sahara of the Bozarth," *American Mercury Magazine* (*Prejudices*, second series, pp. 136–54, 1924). This article stirred the literary South in much the same way that the Economic Commission's report on economic conditions did the economic South in the late 1930's. Three studies that deal with the southern literary renascence with major contemporary emphasis are: John M. Bradbury, *Renaissance in the South: A Critical History of Literature* (Chapel Hill, 1963); Louis M. Rubin, Jr., *The Faraway Country: Writers of the Modern South* (Seattle, 1963); and Louis D. Rubin, Jr., and Robert D. Jacobs, *South: Modern Southern Literature in Its Cultural Setting* (New York, 1961). Donald Davidson, *Southern Writers in the Modern World* (Athens, 1958) deals with southern authors after 1920. The Fugitives, who operated around Vanderbilt University in the 1930's, are discussed in Louise Cowan, *The Fugitive Group, A Literary History* (Baton Rouge, 1959). Some of the Fugitives were among the Agrarians who produced, John Crowe Ransom (ed.), *I'll Take My Stand: The South and the Agrarian Tradition* (New York, 1930).

X   Depression and the New Deal

Historians have been remarkably timid about venturing into the period after 1930. John Samuel Ezell's *The South Since 1865* (New York, 1963) treats generally of the period, as also does the most recent edition of Francis B. Simkins's *A History of the South* (New York, 1963). Thomas D. Clark's *The Emerging South* (New York, 1961) explains social and economic changes in the region and is helpful in understanding political changes. Frank Freidel's essay *F.D.R. and the South* (Baton Rouge, 1965) explains the complex reactions of the South to the New Deal. Of value also are: Avery Craven, "Democratic Theory and Practice," *Virginia Quarterly Review*, XIX (1943); E. David Cronon, "A Southern Progressive Looks at the New Deal," *Journal of Southern History*, XXIV (1958); and Fletcher M. Green, "Resurgent Southern Sectionalism, 1933–1955," *North Carolina Historical Review*, XXXIII (1956).

Scholarly work on this period by social scientists is impressive. The best analysis of southern regionalism is Howard W. Odum's *Southern*

Regions of the United States (Chapel Hill, 1936). Its counterpart in the area of economics is Calvin B. Hoover and B. U. Ratchford, *Economic Resources and Policies of the South* (New York, 1951). Special monographic studies of importance are: Abraham Berglund, *et al.*, *Labor in the Industrial South* (Charlottesville, 1930). Liston Pope's *Millhands and Preachers: A Study of Gastonia* (New Haven, 1942) is a comprehensive analysis of the social and cultural history of a North Carolina milltown which was the center of the labor disturbances of the late 1920's. Harriet L. Herring's *Welfare Work in Mill Villages: The Story of Extra-Mill Activities in North Carolina* (Chapel Hill, 1929); and Herbert J. Lahne's study of *The Cotton Mill Worker* (New York, 1944), are also valuable sociological studies. Other labor studies of importance are Tom Tippett, *When Southern Labor Stirs* (New York, 1931); and Marion D. Irish, "The Proletarian South," *Journal of Politics*, II (1940). Two pamphlets that are helpful are Lucy Randolph, *Standards for Workers in Southern Industry* (National Consumers League, 1931) and Robin Hood, *Industrial Social Security in the South* (Chapel Hill, 1936).

Good sociological studies of the rural South are abundant. Among the best are: Charles S. Johnson, Edwin R. Embree, and W. W. Alexander, *The Collapse of Cotton Tenancy: A Summary of Field Studies and Statistical Surveys, 1933–35* (Chapel Hill, 1935); Arthur F. Raper, *Preface to Peasantry: A Tale of Two Black Counties* (Chapel Hill, 1936); and Morton Rubin, *Plantation County* (Chapel Hill, 1951).

Political scientists have made the greatest contribution to an understanding of contemporary southern politics. Taylor Cole and John H. Hallowell (eds.), *The Southern Political Scene, 1938–1948* (Gainesville, 1948), is a collection of important studies published earlier in the *Journal of Politics*. Other good studies are: Jasper B. Shannon, *Toward a New Politics in the South* (Knoxville, 1949); Joseph L. Bernd, *Grass Roots Politics in Georgia: The County Unit System and the Importance of the Individual Voting Community in Bifactional Elections, 1942–1954* (Atlanta, 1960); Alexander Heard and Donald S. Strong (eds.), *Southern Primaries and Elections, 1920–1949* (University, Ala., 1950); Cortez A. M. Ewing, *Primary Elections in the South: A Study in Uniparty Politics* (Norman, 1953); L. M. Holland, *The Direct Primary in Georgia* (Urbana, 1949); and Frederick D. Ogden, *The Poll Tax in the South* (University, Ala., 1958).

XI The South in the Electrical Age

Much of the literature relating to the generation and distribution of electricity in the South consists of corporate reports, pamphlets, and brochures.

A central theme has been utilization of the region's water resources to generate electrical current. In 1911 the Southern Commercial Congress considered this subject seriously, and its report, *The South's Physical Recovery Described in One Hundred Addresses* (Washington, D.C., 1911), is one of the earliest explorations of this source for power. General works relating to the subject in part are Calvin B. Hoover and Benjamin U. Ratchford, *Economic Resources and Policies of the South* (New York, 1951). This study deals with both the Tennessee Valley Authority and the private utility companies. In 1909, Emory R. Johnson in "Water Transportation and the Progress of the South," *The South in the Building of the Nation*, vol. VI (Richmond, 1909), discussed transportation without so much as giving a hint that he knew about the hydroelectrical potential. Almon E. Parkins's *The South Its Economic-Geographic Development* (New York, 1928) contains valuable background information on the growing importance of electrical power. Rupert B. Vance's *Human Geography of the South* (Chapel Hill, 1932) contains a brief background section on this subject. A popular treatment of hydroelectrical pioneering is contained in J. W. Jenkins, *James B. Duke, Master Builder* (New York, 1927). Howard W. Odum, in *Southern Regions of the United States* (Chapel Hill, 1936), discusses the early phases of the development of the Tennessee Valley.

THE TENNESSEE VALLEY AUTHORITY: By far the best source on the background of the Tennessee Valley Authority is Preston J. Hubbard, *Origins of the Muscle Shoals Controversy 1920–1932* (Nashville, 1961). This work contains an impressive bibliography, especially of articles appearing in a wide variety of periodicals. An unfavorable view of the Authority and its relationship to the valley is contained in Donald Davidson, *The Tennessee*, 2 vols. (New York, 1946–48). A good source describing the multiple purposes of the Authority is Joseph Ransmeier, *The Tennessee Valley Authority: A Case Study in the Economics of Multiple Purpose Stream Planning* (Nashville, 1942). A first-hand description of the harnessing of the Tennessee is David Lilienthal, *TVA-Democracy on the March* (New York, 1944). A sequel to this is Gordon Clapp, *The TVA: An Approach to the Development of a Region* (Chicago, 1951). James A. Dahir's, *Region Building: Community Development Lessons from the Tennessee Valley* (New York, 1955) treats the sociological aspects of regional planning. Norman I. Wengert, *Valley of Tomorrow: The TVA and Agriculture* (Knoxville, 1952), is an examination of one of the major purposes of the Authority. Gilbert E. Govan and James Livengood, *The Chattanooga Country, 1940–1951: From Tomahawks to TVA* (New York, 1952). Roscoe C. Martin (ed.), *TVA, The First Twenty Years: A Staff Report*

(Tuscaloosa, 1956), examines the great experiment from the viewpoint of its political and administrative functions. A popular view of the early phases of the reclamation of the Valley is R. L. Duffus, *The Valley and Its People* (New York, 1946). W. H. Droze's, *High Dams and Slack Waters, TVA Rebuilds a River* (Baton Rouge, 1965), is a modern study of the Valley. John H. Kyle, *The Building of TVA: An Illustrated History* (Baton Rouge, 1958).

Important sources of information about electrical power development in the South are the annual reports of the various power companies, and the annual reports of the Tennessee Valley Commission. These publications give the details of power generation and distribution. There are at least a dozen publications issued by the Tennessee Valley Authority, issued in pamphlet form, which treat individually the multiple purposes of the Authority.

XII The Tide of Industrial Progress

Transportation has been a key to the modernization of the South, yet historians have not considered this as a major fact in their economic studies. Railways formed the backbone of southern transportation to 1930. An over-all study is John F. Stover, *The Railroads of the South, 1865–1900* (Chapel Hill, 1955). James F. Doster, *Railroads in Alabama, 1875–1914* (Tuscaloosa, 1957), treats the operation of railroads in a single state. A further treatment is contained in the brief specialized essays in Julian A. C. Chandler (ed.), *The South in the Building of the Nation*, Vol. VI (Richmond, 1909). The early expansion of the Illinois Central into the South is discussed in Thomas D. Clark, *A Pioneer Southern Railroad from New Orleans to Cairo* (Chapel Hill, 1936).

The nearest thing to a history of highway building in the South is *History, Organization and Functions of the Department of Highways* (Virginia), (Richmond, 1942). The United States Department of Commerce published *Highways Statistics for 1955* (Washington, D.C., 1957) with many comparative tables. There are no more revealing sources than the annual reports of state highway commissions. Among the more general sources discussing highways are: Thomas D. Clark, *The Emerging South* (New York, 1961) and *The Southern Country Editor* (Indianapolis, 1948). Howard W. Odum, *Southern Regions of the United States* (Chapel Hill, 1936), reflects statistically the slowness of the South to build and improve its highways. Calvin B. Hoover and Benjamin U. Ratchford, *Economic Resources and Policies of the South* (New York, 1951), deals briefly with highways. The politics of highway management at the political level is discussed in V. O. Key, Jr., *Southern Politics in State and Nation* (New York, 1949); Albert D. Kirwan, *Revolt of the Rednecks, 1876–1925* (Lexington, 1951); and Allan P. Sindler, *Huey Long's Louisiana: State Politics, 1920–1952* (Baltimore, 1956).

The southern states spend a good sum of money annually to attract tourists into the region. Much of the published material is booster in nature. Lewis C. Copeland, *Estimating Tennessee's Tourist Business* (Nashville, 1954) is more objective. *Know Florida, A Narrative and Graphic Guide to the Sixty-seven Counties of the State* (Tallahassee, 1955) is an informational bit of boosterism. Historians tend to ignore the state guides published by the Federal Writers' Project in the 1930's and 1940's. Nevertheless these have real value. They contain materials not readily available elsewhere.

Material relating to the location of new industry is voluminous. Much of it is in the form of special surveys and articles. Some is public, official reports, for example. Among these are: Robert M. Atkins, "A Program for Locating the New Plant," *Harvard Business Review*, Nov.–Dec. 1952; John O. Tomb, "Should Industry Move South," *Harvard Business Review*, Sept.–Oct. 1953; Henry V. Allen, Jr., *Survey of Mississippi as a Location for a Chemical Industry* (Jackson, n. d.); Stefan H. Robock, "The Negro in the Industrial Development of the South," *Phylon, the Atlanta University Review of Race and Culture* (3rd quarter, 1953); Robert Cassell, *Industrial Tennessee, 1954–1955* (Nashville, 1955); Louisiana's *Industrial Expansion, 1946–1954* (Baton Rouge, 1955); and *Louisiana Invests in Industry* (Baton Rouge, 1954).

XIII   The Great Crusade and After

The politics of the contemporary South are analyzed in several popular regional studies. The following are of special importance: Harry S. Ashmore, *An Epitaph for Dixie* (New York, 1958); James McBride Dabbs, *The Southern Heritage* (New York, 1958); Ralph McGill, *The South and the Southerner* (Boston, 1963); and Virginius W. Dabney, *Below the Potomac: A Book About the New South* (New York, 1942).

There are many special topical studies. One multi-authored volume of real merit is Allan P. Sindler (ed.), *Change in the Contemporary South* (Durham, 1963). Two book-length studies on foreign policy and the South are: Alfred O. Hero, Jr., *The Southerner and World Affairs* (Baton Rouge, 1965); and Charles O. Lerche, Jr., *The Uncertain South: Its Changing Patterns of Politics in Foreign Policy* (Chicago, 1964). Supplementing these are two scholarly studies, one by E. Malcolm Jewell, "Evaluating the Decline of Southern Internationalism Through Senatorial Roll Call

Votes," *Journal of Politics*, XXI (1959); the other by Alexander De Conde, "The South and Isolationism," *Journal of Southern History*, XXIV (1958).

The periodical literature on politics in the contemporary South is voluminous. The Dixiecrat movement is analyzed in: Emile B. Ader, "Why the Dixiecrats Failed," *Journal of Politics*, XV (1953); in William G. Carleton, "The Fate of Our Fourth Party," *Yale Review*, XXXVIII (1949); and in Sarah McCulloh Lemmon, "The Ideology of the 'Dixiecrat' Movement," *Social Forces*, XXX (1951). Republican growth in the South at mid-century is covered in: Donald S. Strong, "The Presidential Election in the South, 1952," *Journal of Politics*, XVII (1955); D. S. Strong, *Urban Republicanism in the South* (University, Ala., 1960); Paul T. David, Malcolm Moos, and Ralph M. Goldman (eds.), *Presidential Nominating Politics in 1952: The South*, 5 vols., III (Baltimore, 1954); James W. Prothro, Ernest Q. Campbell, and Charles M. Grigg, "Two-Party Voting in the South: Class vs. Party Identification," *American Political Science Review*, LII (1958); Max Lerner, "The Outlook for a Party Realignment," *Virginia Quarterly Review*, XXV (1949); Allan P. Sindler, "The Unsolid South," in Allan F. Westin (ed.), *The Uses of Power* (New York, 1962); and Bernard Cosman, "Presidential Republicanism in the South, 1960," *Journal of Politics*, XXIV (1962).

The influence of increased Negro voting in the South is discussed in Margaret Price, *The Negro Voter in the South* (Special Report of the Southern Regional Council, 1957); H. D. Price, *The Negro and Southern Politics: A Chapter of Florida History* (New York, 1957); Louis E. Lomax, *The Negro Revolt* (New York, 1962); and a symposium on the southern Negro voter published in *Journal of Negro Education*, XXVI (1957).

Other special studies worth noting are: Manning J. Dauer, "Recent Southern Political Thought," *Journal of Politics*, X (1948); Robert J. Harris, "States Rights and Vested Interests," *Journal of Politics*, XV (1953); Joseph G. La Palombora, "Pressure, Propaganda, and Political Action in the Elections of 1950," *Journal of Politics*, XIV (1952); Alden L. Powell, "Constitutional Growth and Revision in the South," *Journal of Politics*, X (1948); Howard W. Odum, "Social Change in the South," *Journal of Politics*, X (1948); and William G. Carleton, "Why Call the South Conservative?" *Harper's Magazine*, CXCV (1947).

XIV The Negro

A monumental classic on the American Negro is a collaborative work under the direction of Gunnar Myrdal, *An American Dilemma: The Negro Problem and Modern Democracy*, 2 vols. (New York, 1944). There is scarcely a phase of Negro life that is not covered in Myrdal's two volumes. John Hope Franklin, *From Slavery to Freedom: A History of American Negroes* (New York, 1956), is an excellent survey of the history of the Negro. A superior sociological study is E. Franklin Frazier, *The Negro in the United States* (New York, 1949). W. E. B. DuBois, *The Souls of Black Folk* (Chicago, 1928); *Dusk of Dawn* (New York, 1940); and *Black Folks, Then and Now* (New York, 1939), are works of special interest by the militant Negro leader. Booker T. Washington's autobiography, *Up From Slavery* (New York, 1901), is a contrasting work.

The volumes of the *Negro Yearbook,* published by Tuskegee Institute, contain vital information on all aspects of Negro life, particularly on relations with the white race. A major development in Negro historiography occurred in 1916 when Carter G. Woodson founded *The Journal of Negro History.* This soon developed into a standard scholarly quarterly, and its issues contain valuable information on Negro life in America. Important monographs on special geographical areas are: Joel Williamson, *After Slavery: The Negro in South Carolina During Reconstruction* (Chapel Hill, 1965); George B. Tindall, *South Carolina Negroes 1877–1900* (Columbia, S.C., 1952); Alrutheus A. Taylor, *The Negro in Tennessee, 1865–1880* (Washington, D.C., 1944); Frenise A. Logan, *The Negro in North Carolina, 1876–1894* (Chapel Hill, 1964); and Vernon L. Wharton, *The Negro in Mississippi, 1865–1890* (Chapel Hill, 1947).

Paul Lewinson's *Race, Class, and Party: A History of Negro Suffrage and White Politics in the South* (New York, 1932), emphasizes southern preoccupation with the race problem in all its political behavior. Negro migratory movements are dealt with in: Carter G. Woodson, *A Century of Negro Migration* (Washington, D.C., 1918); Frenise A. Logan, "The Movement of Negroes from North Carolina, 1876–1894," *North Carolina Historical Review,* XXXIII (1956); Joseph H. Taylor, "The Great Migration from North Carolina in 1879," *North Carolina Historical Review,* XXXI (1954); George B. Tindall, "The Liberian Exodus of 1878," *The South Carolina Historical and Genealogical Magazine* (1952); and Donald H. Henderson, "The Negro Migration of 1916–1918," *Journal of Negro History,* VI (1921).

Articles dealing with other special phases of Negro history are: Ashby M. Jones, "The Negro and the South," *Virginia Quarterly Review,* V (1927); Gilbert T. Stephenson, "Education and Crime Among Negroes," *South Atlantic Quarterly,* XVI (1917); G. T. Stephenson, "The Segregation of the White and Negro Races in Cities," *South Atlantic Quarterly,* XIII (1914); and Elsie M. Lewis, "The Political Mind of the Negro, 1865–1900," *Journal of Southern History,* XXI (1955). Benjamin Brawley discusses Negro intellectuals in *The Negro Genius* (New York, 1937); and August Meier treats of Negro attitudes in *Negro Thought in America, 1880–1915: Racial Ideologies in the Age of Booker T. Washington* (Ann Arbor, 1963).

There is no fully satisfactory work on the darker aspects of Negro subjection, but several accounts of lynching have been written. Among these are: James Elbert Cutler, *Lynch-Law: An Investigation into the History of Lynching in the United States* (New York, 1905); Arthur F. Raper, *The Tragedy of Lynching* (Chapel Hill, 1933); and Walter Francis White, *Rope and Faggot: A Biography of Judge Lynch* (New York, 1929). An outstanding contribution to an understanding of the development of modern segregation in the South is C. Vann Woodward's *Strange Career of Jim Crow* (New York, 1955).

XV   Urbanization of the South

The rise of the urban community has brought a new element into southern history. The most comprehensive work on this subject is Rupert B. Vance and Nicholas J. Demerath (eds.), *The Urban South* (Chapel Hill, 1954), a symposium of papers by sociologists and historians. Rupert B. Vance's, *All These People: The Nation's Human Resources in the South* (Chapel Hill, 1954). Howard W. Odum, *Southern Regions of the United States* (Chapel Hill, 1936), considers urbanization in the South and its bearing upon old institutional patterns. *This Changing South* by John M. Maclachlan and Joe S. Floyd, Jr., (Gainesville, 1956) reflects both population and economic changes. Population shifts and changes are discussed in Joseph J. Spengler, "Demographic and Economic Change in the South, 1940–1960," Allan P. Sindler (ed.), *Change in the Contemporary South* (Durham, 1963), pp. 26–63. The human effects of industrialization are discussed in W. H. Nicholls, *Southern Traditions and Regional Progress* (Chapel Hill, 1960). S. Kuznets, *et al., Population Redistribution and Economic Growth, United States, 1870–1950: Analysis of Economic Change* (Philadelphia, 1957), includes the redistribution of southern population. Thomas Ford (ed.), *The Southern Appalachian Region: A Survey,* (Lexington, 1962), is a revealing analysis of the drainage of the human resource from this part of the South.

Studies relating to specific cities and communities are: Gilbert E. Govan and James W. Livengood, *The Chattanooga Country, 1540–1962* (Chapel Hill, 1963); Gerald Capers, *The Biography of a River Town, Its Heroic Age* (Chapel Hill, 1939); William D. Miller, *Memphis During the Progressive Era, 1900–1917* (Memphis, 1957); and Shields

McIlwaine, *Memphis Down in Dixie* (New York, 1948); John Ballenger Knox, *The People of Tennessee: A Study of Population Trends* (Knoxville, 1949); Harry M. Caudill, *Night Comes to the Cumberland: A Biography of a Depressed Area* (Boston, 1963); Melvin Clyde Hughes, *County Government in Georgia* (Athens, 1940); William Weltner, *Southerner* (New York, 1966); Weldon Cooper, *Metropolitan County, A Survey of Government in the Birmingham Area* (Tuscaloosa, 1949); William K. Boyd, *Durham: City of the New South* (Durham, 1925); Thomas J. Wertenbaker, *Norfolk: Historic Southern Port* (Durham, 1962).

Urban and industrial communities are discussed in Harriet L. Herring, *Southern Industry and Regional Development* (Chapel Hill, 1940). Specifically this author deals with the industrial village in *Welfare Work in Mill Villages: Revolution in a Southern Institution* (Chapel Hill, 1949). Additional cotton mill studies are Marjorie A. Potwin, *Cotton Mill People of the Piedmont: A Study in Social Change* (New York, 1927), and Jennings J. Rhyne, *Some Southern Cotton Mill Workers and Their Villages* (Chapel Hill, 1930). The coalfields have had their chroniclers. Among them are Thedore Dresier, *A Harlan Miner Speaks* (New York, 1931) and Malcolm Ross, *Machine Age in the Hills* (New York, 1933).

The following studies relate the race problem to the rise of southern suburbia: John Dollard, *Caste and Class in a Southern Town* (New York, 1937); Hortense Powdermaker, *After Freedom: A Cultural Study in the Deep South* (New York, 1939); M. Elaine Burgess, *Negro Leadership in a Southern City* (Chapel Hill, 1962); Arnold M. Rose, *The Negro's Morale* (Minneapolis, 1949); and Gunnar Myrdal, *An American Dilemma*, 2 vols. (New York, 1944).

XVI   Enter the Supreme Court

Many works listed in the bibliography of Chapter XIV are helpful here. School segregation in the South has been treated also in L. R. Harlan, *Separate and Unequal: Public School Campaigns and Racism in the Southern Seaboard States, 1901–1915* (Chapel Hill, 1958); R. P. Warren, *Segregation, the Inner Conflict of the South* (New York, 1957); A. P. Blaustein and C. C. Ferguson, *Desegregation and the Law: The Meaning and Effect of the School Segregation Cases* (New Brunswick, 1957); Don Shoemaker (ed.), *With All Deliberate Speed, Segregation-Desegregation in Southern Schools* (New York, 1959); Robert J. Steamer, "The Role of the Federal District Courts in the Segregation Controversy," *Journal of Politics*, XXII (1960); and Carl B. Swisher, "Dred Scott One Hundred Years After," *Journal of Politics*, XIX (1957).

The daily press and news magazines must be relied on for current developments. Especially helpful are: New York *Times;* Washington *Post;* Louisville *Courier-Journal; Time Magazine; Newsweek; Life;* and *United States News and World Report.*

XVII   Exit Jim Crow

In addition to many of the works noted in previous chapters, background for the Negro revolution of the mid-twentieth century may be obtained from: Leo Alilemas, "Legal Restrictions on the Negro in Politics," *Journal of Negro History,* XXV (1940); J. L. Bernd and Lynwood M. Holland, "Recent Restrictions upon Negro Suffrage: The Case of Georgia," *Journal of Politics,* XXI (1959); Loren P. Beth, "The Case for Judicial Protection of Civil Liberties," *Journal of Politics,* XVII (1955); Virginius Dabney, "Civil Liberties in the South," *Virginia Quarterly Review,* XVI (1940); Carl M. Frasure, "Charles Sumner and the Rights of the Negro," *Journal of Negro History,* XIII (1928); James W. Garner, "Recent Agitation of the Negro Question in the South," *South Atlantic Quarterly,* VII (1908); R. W. Hainsworth, "The Negro and the Texas Primaries," *Journal of Negro History,* XVIII (1933); Charles S. Johnson, *Patterns of Segregation* (New York, 1943); Louis C. Kesselman, "The Fair Employment Practices Commission Movement in Perspective," *Journal of Negro History,* XXXI (1946); Leonard W. Levy and Harlan B. Phillips, "The Roberts Case: Source of the 'Separate but Equal' Doctrine," *American Historical Review,* LVI (1951); Louise Overacker, "The Negro's Struggle for Participation in Primary Elections," *Journal of Negro History,* XXX (1945); Hugh D. Price, "The Negro and Florida Politics, 1944-1954," *Journal of Politics,* XVII (1955); Carl B. Swisher, "The Supreme Court and the South," *Journal of Politics,* X (1948); Julius Turner, "Primary Elections as the Alternative to Party Competition in 'Safe' Districts," *Journal of Politics,* XV (1953); John G. Van Deusen, "The Negro in Politics," *Journal of Negro History,* XXI (1936); and Rayford W. Logan, *What the Negro Wants* (Chapel Hill, 1944).

Current developments must be followed in the news media referred to in the previous chapter's bibliographical note. The following accounts are also helpful: Louis E. Lomax, *The Negro Revolt* (New York, 1962); and James W. Silver, *Mississippi: The Closed Society* (New York, 1964).

XVIII   The Evolving South

Within a century there has been considerable revision of southern history. No subject has been examined more assiduously than the impact of Reconstruction upon the region. Within the centennial years immediately ahead no doubt other revisions will be made. Such studies will have pertinency to a consideration of the modern South.

W. D. Workman, *The Case for the South* (New York, 1960), is largely a plea for the status quo *circa* 1910, while Harry Ashmore, *Epitaph for Dixie* (New York, 1958), viewed the region four years after the *Brown vs. School Board* decision and immediately after the Little Rock crisis as incapable of change. In calmer and more considered tones are Brooks Hayes, *A Southern Moderate Speaks* (Chapel Hill, 1959) and Robert Penn Warren, *Segregation: The Inner Conflict* (New York, 1956). In a new departure, Howard Zinn analyzes the innermost conflict between white and black southerners in *The Southern Mystique* (New York, 1964). A revealing group of essays is contained in Robert B. Highsaw (ed.), *The Deep South in Transition* (Tuscaloosa, 1964). The authors of these essays in large part speak a philosophy that is foreign indeed to that of Alabama officials and voters. A thoughtful and dynamic book is Wilma Dykeman and James Stokely, *Neither Black Nor White* (New York, 1957). Some of the most valid books about the South are those which reflect personal experiences and views. Among these are: Jonathan Daniels, *A Southerner Discovers the South* (New York, 1938); Virginius Dabney, *Below the Potomac: A Book about the New South* (New York, 1942); Clarence Cason, *90° in the Shade* (Chapel Hill, 1935); William A. Percy, *Lanterns on the Levee* (New York, 1941); Ellis G. Arnall, *The Shore Dimly Seen* (Philadelphia, 1946); Carl T. Rowan, *South of Freedom* (New York, 1952); Hodding Carter, *Southern Legacy* (Baton Rouge, 1950); Ben Robertson, *Red Hills and Cotton: An Upcountry Memory* (New York, 1942); Katharine Dupre Lumpkin, *The Making of a Southerner* (New York, 1947); James Silver, *Mississippi: The Closed Society* (New York, 1964); James H. Meredith, *Three Years in Mississippi* (Bloomington, 1966); Ralph McGill, *The South and the Southerner* (Boston, 1963); Martin Luther King, Jr., *Stride Toward Freedom* (New York, 1958); Charles Longstreet Weltner, *Southerner* (New York, 1966); Alfred O. Hero, Jr., *The Southerner and World Affairs* (Baton Rouge, 1965).

The precise sources for determining the depth of changes in the South are, of course, statistical ones. Among these are the annual editions of the *Statistical Abstract of the United States*, the *Statistical Summary of School Segregation-Desegregation in the Southern Border States*, and the annual reports of the various state industrial commissions.

Index

Abbott, Edward, 177
Abbott, Lyman, 207
Abolitionists, 17, 203
Adams, Herbert Baxter, 226
Adams, Louis, 190
Addams, Jane, 327
Aderholt, O. F., 233, 234
Aeneas Africanus, 216
Agrarian society, and negativism, 14; versus industry, 19; ravages of war on, 23; and Southern Alliance, 68; Great Depression, 193, 227; school funds for, 349
Agricultural Adjustment Act, 95, 235, 238, 241, 242, 324
Agricultural experimental stations, 96, 100, 101
Agricultural Extension Service, 96
Agriculture, in the New South, 1, 3; mechanization of, 7, 18, 104, 160, 209, 338; "forty acres of land," 13; decline in, 53, 67, 163; lien law, 88, 89; diversification of, 84, 89, 92, 102, 106; scientific advancement in, 100, 194; education in, 187, 193; staple crops, 211, 254, 285, 296; during depression, 227, 280; need for fertilizer, 252; subsidized, 239, 249; Tennessee Valley Authority, 260; soil conservation program, 269; industrial revolution, 269, 308; war boom in, 324
Agriculture, Department of, 86, 96, 105, 250, 274
Aiken, William, 170
Alabama, Negroes in, 23, 77; and Fourteenth Amendment, 35; issues railroad bonds, 38; radical rule in, 46; corruption in, 55; Alliance movement in, 69; disfranchisement, 79; iron mines in, 156, 157, 160
Alabama, University of, 198, 200, 358
Alabama and Chattanooga Railroad, 39
Alabama Men of Justice, 42
Alabama Polytechnic Institute, 197, 199
Alabama Power Company, 249, 250

Alabama State Normal School, 180
Alcorn, James L., 37, 44
Alden, Henry Mills, 217
Alderman, Edward A., 164, 197
Aliens, 133–5; *see also* Immigration
All the King's Men, 223
Allen, James Lane, 217, 219
Alliance and Populists, 73
Allwright Case, 288–91
America First Committee, The, 286
American Academy of Political and Social Science, Annals of, 92
American Book Company, 122
American Claimant, 216
American Commonwealth, The, 1
American Federation of Labor (AFL), highly conservative, 133; on strikes, 232, 233; discrimination, 314
American Historical Review, 226
American Tobacco Company, 146, 147
Amnesty Bill, 44
An American Dilemma, 191, 280
Anderson, Marion, 386
Anderson, W. T., 209
Antioch College, 259
Appalachian Power Company, 257
Appomattox, 24, 26, 136
Arkansas, devastation in, 22; political reconstruction, 26; ratifies Fourteenth Amendment, 35; issues railroad bonds, 38; radical rule in, 46; illiteracy in, 183; school crisis, 257, 285
Arkansas Educational Commission, 5
Armed Forces, *see* Federal troops
Armstrong, Samuel C., 178, 189, 190
Arp, Bill, 212
Arthur, Chester B., 65
As I Lay Dying, 222
Ashe, W. W., 251
Ashford, Bailey K., 182
Ashland Oil and Refining Company, 162
Ashmore, Harry, 381
Aswander Case, 257

Atkinson, Edward, 83, 148
Atlanta, Georgia, 20
Atlanta *Constitution*, 98, 148, 205–7, 210, 216
Atlanta *Herald*, 206
Atlanta *Journal*, 208
Atlanta Riot, 323
Atlanta University, 326
Atlantic Monthly, 218
Atomic power, 264, 267
Automation, 147
Automobile, 140, 271, 275
Avery, B. F., 160
Aycock, Charles B., 111, 112, 307

Bailey, Josiah, 241
Baker, Newton D., 250, 257
Balance Agriculture Law, 283
Baldwin, James G., 213
Balloting, see Elections
Bankhead, William B., 242
Bankhead-Jones Farm Tenant Act, 236, 238
Banking, post Civil War, 3, 6, 53; limited facilities, 12, 88, 89; war measures, 32; farm credit charges, 61, 91; Greenback movement, 65; prosperity of, 67; trusts, 68; rural economy, 112, 333, 383; legislature on, 122; see also Finances
Baptists, 114, 197, 355; see also Religion
Baptist Recorder, 356
Barkeley Dam, 267
Barker, Eugene C., 226
Barkley, Alben, 156
Barkley, G. W., 144
Barksdale, Ethelbert, 59
Barnett, Ross, 356, 358, 360, 393
Barren Ground, 219
Bass, Ross, 302
Bassett, John S., 226, 227
Battles and Leaders of the Civil War, 225
Beal, Fred, 233, 234
Beale, Howard K., 43
Beauregard, Pierre G. T., 58
Beckworth, Byron de la, 371
Benedict, George, 177
Benjamin, Judah P., 24
Berea College, 192
Beverages, Coca-Cola, 162, 163
Beyond Dark Hills, 224
Bigotry, lack of education, 8, 197; Ku Klux Klan, 19; extremism, 121, 122, 126; in literature, 217
Bilbo, Theodore G., 111, 112, 123–9, 243, 292
Bingham, Barry, 210
Birmingham, Alabama, iron industry in, 158; riots in, 367, 368

Birmingham *Age-Herald*, 209
Birmingham *News*, 208, 209
Birthright, 220
Black, Hugo, 242, 291, 352, 360
Black April, 221
Black Belt, voting in, 63, 135, 292; agrarian revolt in, 74; cotton raising in, 105; in Alabama, 117, 118; demonstrations in, 297, 372; Negro population in, 325, 331
Black codes, in deep South, 29, 30; and integration, 349
Black Patch War, 95, 223
Blackwell, William T., 145
Blaine, James G., 77
Blair, Henry W., 176, 380
Blease, Cole, 124–6
"Bloody Mingo," 155
Blossom, Virgil T., 357
Blue Grass and Rhododendron, 218
Blue Grass Region of Kentucky, The, 217
Blue laws, 114
Boggs, Hale, 303, 355
Boll weevil, cotton scourge, 11, 380; during depression, 103; in Texas, 100; campaigns against, 194
Bonaparte, Charles F., 159
Bonaventure, 218
Bonsack, James A., 144, 146
Bossism, political, 39, 40; Democratic party, 72; in South Carolina, 124; Huey Long, 129
Boswell Amendment, 290
"Bourbon" rule, incipient revolutions, 54, 69; and public lands, 57; downfall of, 73; demagogues in, 120
Boycotts, see Sit-ins
Boyd, William J., 226
Boys' Clubs, 195
Bradford, Roark, 221
Bradley, Joseph P., 49
Brazier, James, 319
Bridges, 273, 275
Broken Battalions, 214
Brooks, Cleanth, 222
Broward, Napoleon B., 111
Brown, John C., 57
Brown, Joseph E., 54, 120, 125
Brown, Oliver, 353, 354, 358
Brown, William G., 6, 225
Brown vs. Topeka Board of Education, 281, 353, 378, 379, 387
Browning, Gordon, 294
Bruce, Blanche K., 36
Bryan, William Jennings, 72, 73, 126, 132
Bryce, James, 1
Bulloch, Rufus B., 58, 205, 206
"Bummers," 20, 21

Bunche, Ralph, 328
Burden of Southern History, 388
Burkitt, Frank, 121
Burleson, Albert, 132
Buses, 271, 363
Butler, Matthew C., 47, 54, 59, 176
Byrd, Harry, 241, 294, 299
Byrnes, James, 281, 355

Cabell, James Branch, 219
Cable, George Washington, 218, 220, 325
Caldwell, D. J., 208
Caldwell, Erskine, 221, 387
Calhoon, S. S., 75
Calhoun, John C., 5, 356
Calvert City, 284
Camp, Lawrence, 241
Camp Meetings, 43; *see also* Religion
Campbell, George W., 190
Campbell, John C., 254
Candler, Allan D., 179
Candler, Asa G., 162, 163
Cape Kennedy, 277
Capital, 136, 137; *see also* Banking
Carey, James F., 46
Carnegie, Andrew, 191
Carpetbaggers, exploited Confederacy, 33, 36–40; and Ku Klux Klan, 41; controlled voting, 60; opposed integration, 349
Carr, Julian Shakespeare, 145
Carroll, E. M., 198
Carver, George Washington, 192, 198
Cash, Wilbur J., 54, 134, 280, 388
Cash crops, 89
Caste system, 219, 306, 309, 326
Catawba Power Company, 247
Catchings, Thomas, 56
Catholics, 126, 133, 134, 217, 235, 356
Cattle Raising, 104, 153, 338, 342
Celanese Corporation of America, 284
Central Railroad (Georgia), 270
Century Magazine, 215
Chalmers, James L., 66
Chamberlain, Daniel H., 46–9
Chambers of Commerce, 281, 282, 338, 360
Chandler, A. B., 156
Chandler, J. A. C., 227
Charleston, South Carolina, 21
Charleston *News and Courier*, 179, 203, 206, 307, 390
Charlotte (N.C.) *Observer*, 78, 208
Chase, Harry Woodburn, 197, 200, 233
Chattanooga, Tennessee, 204
Chattanooga and St. Louis Railroad, 270
Chattanooga *Free Press*, 256
Chattanooga Medicine Company, 162

Chattanooga *News*, 256
Chattanooga *Times*, 204
Cherokee Indians, 253, 255
Chesapeake and Ohio Railroad, 154, 270
Chicago *Tribune*, 30
Child labor, laws on, 70, 108, 125; in factories, 111, 147, 231, 237; crusade against, 152
Choir Invisible, The, 217
Churches, for migrant workers, 106; and integration, 309, 355, 380; freedmen, 317; rural areas, 334, 335, 344, 345; burned, 371; *see also* Religion
Cigarette industry, 95, 144–6
Cincinnati Southern Railroad, 154
Citizens' Council, 355, 357, 388
Citizenship, *see* Suffrage
Citrus crop, 340
Civil liberties, 5, 31
Civil rights, and Democratic party, 126; and presidential elections, 302
Civil Rights, President's Committee on, 292, 293, 308
Civil Rights Act, of 1866, 36; passed by Congress, 42; and President Andrew Johnson, 30, 31; authorized martial law, 43; in the South, 185, 302, 303; Supreme Court on, 307; and discrimination, 315; 342, 348; of 1962, passage of, 369, 370; social revolution, 376, 378
Civil War, end of the Old South, 2, 3, 10; veterans of, 20, 21, 25, 31, 44; ravages of, 20–24, 87, 206, 213, 269; expatriates, 24; heritage of, 52; education after, 187, 188; historians of, 225
Civil War and Reconstruction in Alabama, 227
Civilian Conservation Corps (CCC), 142
Clark Hill Dam, 267
Classic Case, 288
Clay, Cassius Marcellus, 45
Clemens, Samuel L., 215
Clemson College, 358
Clergy, 31, 134; *see also* Religion
Cleveland, Grover, 72, 73, 78, 124
Climate, effect on agriculture, 1, 13, 90; rainfall, 84, 100, 103, 251, 253
Clinchfield, Virginia, and Norfolk and Western Railroad, 154
Clingman, Thomas, 66
Coal industry, origin of, 12, 153–5; transportation problem, 269; labor, 280, 311, 312; location of, 336
Cobb, Rufus, 57
Coca-Cola, 162–3
Code duella, 320

Codes, *see* Black Codes
Coker, Caleb, 101
Coker, James L., 101
Colleges, post Civil War, 4; agricultural, 62, 68, 193; independent movement, 65, 67; state, 124; discrimination in, 179, 188; expansion of, 184, 199; land-grant, 187, 195–7; Negro, 352; *see also* Education
College of Veterinary Medicine, 199
Collier's Magazine, 221
Colquitt, Alfred H., 53, 54, 59
Columbia, South Carolina, 20, 182
Columbia (South Carolina) *Record*, 281
Columbia (South Carolina) *State*, 179, 208
Columbus (Georgia) *Enquirer*, 87, 209
Colyar, Arthur S., 57, 159
Comer, Braxton B., 54, 111
Command of the Army Act, 32
Commercial Congress, 7
Commonwealth and Southern, 255
Communism, 133, 200, 234
Compendium of the History of the United States, A, 225
Conciliatory policy of Lincoln and Johnson, 26–8
Confederacy, 31, 33
Congress, United States, and reconstruction, 26, 27, 30, 52; and Fourteenth Amendment, 34, 35; passes Civil Rights Act, 42; election of 1876, 48
Congress for Racial Equality (CORE), 328
Congress of Industrial Organization (CIO), 313, 314
Congressional Joint Committee on Reconstruction, 22, 28
Connally, John, 394
Connor, Eugene "Bull," 367
Conservation, land, 100; natural resources, 138; erosion, 209, 251; water, 280
Conservatism, resists industrialization, 14; fostered by religion, 18; in reconstruction period, 27; and economic progress, 57; and elections, 40, 45; political retirement of, 73; disfranchisement, 76; opposed to reform, 117, 121, 128; in rural areas, 132, 197; and Negro education, 191; strikes, 234; on Supreme Court, 242; and New Deal, 287, 294; leaders of, 307; on integration, 349, 357
Constitution, state, 6, 8, 33, 75, 76, 290, 291; conventions on, 14, 25; federal, 27, 31, 35, 41, 75, 290, 346; in Georgia,

59; reconstruction, 62, 63, 349; on education, 165
Constitutional View of the War between the States, A, 225
Conventions, on constitutions, 14; at St. Louis, 73; state, 110; for educations, 164; national 293, 294
Convicts, leasing of, 55, 56, 69, 75, 112; *see also* Penal system
Cooke, John Esten, 212, 213
Coolidge, Calvin, 250
Coons, Charles L., 174, 175
Corn crop, 23, 96, 98, 99, 102
Corruption, in reconstruction period, 36–40; under carpetbaggers, 46; at polls, 47; Negroes, 50; in Georgia, 54; in state funds, 55; conventions, 79
Cotton, mills, 1, 147–50; culture of, 11, 12, 239; declining prices, 60, 90, 91, 103, 229; production of, 60, 101, 153, 261; in small supply, 83, 89; balanced farming, 97, 102; boll weevil, 100, 103, 104; labor, 236, 310, 311; transportation of, 270; importance of, 338
Cotton Exchange, 125, 230
Cotton Exposition, 149, 192
Coulter, E. M., 198
Council of Federated Organizations, 371
Country Life Commission, 182
Courts, post Civil War, 7; federal, 16, 343; military, 33, 34; during reconstruction period, 38; reforms in, 50; and law enforcement, 151; on discrimination, 307, 320, 323, 348; *see also* Supreme Court
Craddock, Charles E., 217
Credit, to farmers, 60, 61, 88, 89; interest rates, 98; and agriculture, 106
Crédit Mobilier, 39
Crime, 318, 336, 340, 346
Crops, staple, 96, 261, 338; citrus, 106
"Crossroads" merchandising, 88
Crump, Ed, 294
Culberson, Charles A., 111
Cultural revolution, 280, 296, 342; in New South, 9; folklore, 17, 19; in education, 188; of Negroes, 191; in Old South, 202, 203; in newspapers, 211; in literature, 216; urbanization, 337
Curry, Jabez L. M., 173, 174, 177, 178

Dabbs, James McBride, 14, 17, 18
Dabney, Charles W., 172, 179, 184
Dabney, Robert Lewis, 167, 168
Dabney, Virginius, 210, 220
Dams, for water power, 248; construction of, 260, 267; hydroelectric, 272; attract tourists, 278

Daniels, Josephus, 111, 208, 210
Davidson, Donald, 222
Davis, David, 48
Davis, Jackson, 180
Davis, Jefferson, 58, 225, 372
Dawe, G. Grosvenor, 4
Dawson, Francis W., 148, 203, 204, 206
Day, David F., 161
Dyer Anti-Lynching Bill, 327
DeBardeleben, Henry, 157–9
DeBow's Review, 3, 82, 86, 213
Debts, Confederacy, 27, 31; state, 37, 38, 57, 67; repudiation of, 54; farm, 87–90; road building, 276
Defeatism, 137
Delta Pine Land Plantation, 101
Demagoguery, conservatives, 117, 118, 121; techniques of, 124–6; newspaper propaganda, 212; political, 221, 392; oppose integration, 356, 357
Democratic party, allegiance of masses to, 15, 25, 32; and Negroes, 44, 53, 66, 67, 295; national elections, 49, 293, 301, 303; railroad conflict, 39; independence movement, 64, 65; Alliance movement, 69; Populists, 73; in South Carolina, 76; and New South, 81; reforms in, 111; dominates South, 115, 116, 127, 229, 240; on education, 165; and New Deal, 287
Democratic National Convention (1948), 293
Depressions, affect southern economy, 11, 103, 104, 338; agriculture, 102, 122, 280; fear of, 142, 158; labor market, 156, 230; and conservatives, 235; see also Panics
Desegregation, see Integration
Dewey, John, 327
Dewey, Thomas E., 294, 299
Dillard, James Hardy, 180
Dingell, John, 370
Dirksen, Everett M., 370
Discrimination, in unions, 314; Negroes, 327, 361; in education, 346
Disease, see Health
Disfranchisement, of Negroes, 6, 50, 109, 118, 124, 291, 292, 315; of poor whites, 34; during reconstruction period, 74–6; demonstrations against, 78, 319
Diversification, in agriculture, 106, 195
Dixie, 4, 293
Dixiecrats, 294–6
Dixon-Yates contract, 267
Dobie, J. Frank, 198
Dodd, William E., 226
Doolittle, James R., 34
Double Dealer, 221, 222
Douglass, Frederick, 326

Dred Scott decision, 348
Dreher, Julius, 177
Dreiser, Theodore, 156
Drew, George F., 47, 48
DuBois, W. E. B., militant Negro leader, 61, 120, 191, 311, 326, 327, 362
Dudley, Thomas, 177
Duke, Benjamin N., 145
Duke, George Washington, 144–6
Duke, James Buchanan, 145, 146, 245, 247
Duke Power Company, 267, 268
Duke University, 197, 198, 284
Dukesboro Tales, 214
Dunning, William A., 226
Dwinnell, Melville, 206

Early, Jubal A., 24, 58
Eastland, James, 370, 374
Eastman Kodak Company, 284
Eaton, John B., 177
Economic Resources and Policies of the South, 16, 266, 271
Economic revolution, 136, 207, 243, 269, 316, 324, 331, 378; in New South, 2, 6, 13; and conservatives, 57; in agrarian society, 82, 88–91, 99, 102, 107; reforms in, 111; and Negro, 187; affects newspapers, 212; during depression, 224, 227; rural electricity, 240; in transportation, 275, 279
Economics Council, 377
Edison Company, 245
Education, post Civil War, 4, 5, 14, 18, 19, 38; under "Bourbon" rule, 50, 54; independent movement, 64; Alliance program, 69; and the Negro, 81, 291, 309, 327, 346; compulsory, 108; reforms in, 111, 117; prison, 112; taxes for, 122, 164; under Huey Long, 128; discrimination in, 166, 167, 176, 306, 317, 352; Peabody Fund, 170; vocational, 179, 189, 190, 192, 196, 343; high school, 183; federal support, 379; see also Colleges
Education, Federal Commission of, 185
Education, United States Commission of, 177, 379
Edwards, Harry Stillwell, 216
Eisenhower, Dwight D., 265, 298–301, 355, 357
Eighteenth Amendment, 114
Elections, congressional, 31, 71; fraudulent, 40, 74, 75, 80, 117; Negro vote, 44, 77, 373–6; campaigns, 45; in Louisiana, 46, 47; Hayes-Tilden, 47, 48, 349; procedures of, 56, 121; in Black Belt, 63, 64; reforms in, 68, 69; primaries, 109, 110, 120, 288; national,

115, 116, 119, 131–4, 235, 301–3; federal intervention, 130, 131; state, 375
Electric power, rural, 107, 240, 262–4, 268; need for, 244, 245; availability of, 338
Electric Power Board of Chattanooga, 258
Emancipation, problems created, 23, 30, 176, 305, 309, 310
Emory University, 197
Emotional revolution, 137, 214, 281, 317; post Civil War, 2, 5, 8; on lynching, 122; in literature, 223; regional, 228; in religion, 334, 335; integration, 348
Employment, on plantations, 29, 279; industrial, 111, 150, 186, 341; of teachers, 170; during depressions, 230, 231; in lumbering industry, 284; Negro, 312, 313, 344; discrimination in, 314, 328, 360, 362; see also Labor
Endowments, see Philanthropy
English Corporation at Newport, Tennessee, 142
Ensley, Enoch, 157
Erosion, 90, 100, 101, 251; see also Conservation
Etheridge, Mark, 209, 210
Evarts, William M., 170
Evers, Medgar, 371
Evolution, teaching of, 196, 197
Expatriates, 58, 324
Experimental Stations, 193, 261
Extension services, 194
Extremism, 121

Factories, industrial revolution, 138; child labor, 237; expansion of, 285, 340
Fair Deal, 108
Fair Employment Practices Act, 292; 329; see also FEPC
Fair Labor Standards Act, 238
Fantus Report, 284
Farm Bureau, 118
Farm Security Administration, 238, 241
Farmers' Alliance movement, 99, 307
Farmers' Union, 313
Farming, mechanization of, 11, 195, 279; homestead legislature, 32; Negroes, 44, 308, 310; depressed conditions, 60, 124; financing of, 67, 88, 89; one-crop system, 90; tobacco, 95, 97, 102, 143; education in, 187, 254, 339; subsidized, 236, 384; rural electrification, 263; see also Agriculture
Farmers and Southern Alliance, 68
Farragut, David G., 170
Faubus, Orval, 356, 357, 361, 393
Faulkner, William, 222, 223, 387

Fayetteville, North Carolina, 166
Federal Bureau of Investigation (FBI), 318
Federal Cotton Pool, 236
FEPC, 287, 288, 314, 329
Federal Emergency Relief Administration, 237
Federal Highway Act, 276
Federal Troops, during reconstruction period, 46–8; to secure integration, 49, 314, 357, 358; at strikes, 233; segregation in World War II, 286
Ferguson, Joe T., 377
Fertilizer, lack of, 11, 13, 61; manufacture of, 90, 250, 252, 256, 265, 342; corn production, 97, 98; chemical, 99, 102, 107, 284; from cottonseed oil, 153; Tennessee Valley Authority, 195, 261
Fever ticks, 105
Few, William P., 197
Field, James G., 71
Fifteenth Amendment, suffrage, 35, 74, 131; states' rights, 36; violated, 81, 109, 114; repeal advocated, 122; and Supreme Court, 287, 382
Fifth Amendment, 200
Finances, of industry, 86, 151, 283, 285; see also Banking
Fink, Albert, 157
First Reconstruction Act, 32–5
Fish, Hamilton, 170
Fisk University, 198
Fitzhugh, George, 227
Flagler, H. M., Jr., 207
Fleming, Walter L., 198, 226, 227
Florida, ratified Fourteenth Amendment, 35; treatment of Negroes, 43; under Republican control, 46; grants public lands, 57
Florida, University of, 199
Flute and Violin, The, 217
Folk culture, 17, 19; see also Culture
Folsom, Jim, 118
Ford, Henry, 249, 250
Foreigners, see Aliens
Forests, see Lumber industry
Forge, The, 220
Forrest, Nathan Bedford, 41, 42, 59, 157
"Forty acres of Land," 13
Fourteenth Amendment, civil liberties, 5, 31; ratified, 35, 36; reinstated Confederate veterans, 44; disfranchisement, 74; disregard of, 81, 122; Supreme Court, 346, 353, 354
Foster, L. H., 280
Fox, John, Jr., 155, 218
Free Joe, 216
Free silver, 69–72, 132

Freedmen, post Civil War, 3, 4, 23; need for education, 5, 349; laws for, 29–35; Fourteenth Amendment, 31; elections, 39, 63, 326; agricultural lien law, 88; education of, 165; in industry, 204; status of, 306, 326; join fraternal orders, 317

Freedmen's Bureau, voting rights, 34; dissolution of, 44, 192; and education, 167, 190

Freeman, Douglas Southall, 210

Freight, tobacco industry, 148; water transportation, 245; cotton industry, 261; rate differentials, 270, 271

Frick, Henry Clay, 159

Frissell, Hollis B., 177, 190

Fugitive, The, 221

Fulbright, J. William, 294, 355, 370

Fundamentalism, 10, 114, 134, 196; *see also* Religion

Gaines Case, 353

Garfield, James A., 65, 148

Garner, John Nance, 241

Garrison, William Lloyd, 326

Gas industry, 161

Gastonia, North Carolina, 233, 234

General Education Board, 184, 185, 195

Geography, influence of, 10, 12, 18, 117, 340, 380; along political lines, 52; U. S. Geological Survey, 161; in literature, 219

George, James Z., 45, 54, 59, 66, 70

George, Walter F., 119, 241, 243

Georgia, Sherman's march, 21, 22; and Fourteenth Amendment, 31, 35; issues railroad bonds, 38; voting, 63, 76; banking, 88; Negro population, 119; integration, 359

Georgia, University of, 173, 193, 198, 205, 358

Georgia Institute of Technology, 358

Georgia Power Company, 267

Germans, in Texas, 1; in New Orleans, 47

Gerry, Elbridge, 159

Gerrymandering, 126

Gilmer, Frank, 157

Glasgow, Ellen, 219, 220

Glass, Carter, 241, 243

God's Little Acre, 221

Gold standard, 132

Golden Triangle, 284

Goldwater, Barry, 300–303

Gordon, John B., 45, 54, 58, 59, 70, 120, 125

Gore, Albert, 302, 355, 369

Government, federal, 16, 24

Governors, provisional, 26

Grady, Henry W., militant journalist, 71, 84, 97–9, 148, 205–10, 308, 380, 381, 384

Graft, *see* Corruption

Graham, Frank K., 197, 200

Grain production, 83, 96, 101, 102, 104, 204, 244

"Grandfather clause," 75, 78, 108

Grandissimes, The, 218

Grange, 97, 98

Grant, Ulysses S., 32, 35, 37, 39, 40, 43, 45, 170

Gray, G. A.,. 148

Great Bowater Paper Company, 266

Great Depression, social revolution, 114, 163; and agrarian system, 193, 230; economic reaction, 286, 393; *see also* Depressions

Great Meadow, The, 220

Great Society, 108

Green, John R., 145

Greenback-Republican fusion, 65, 71

Greensboro, North Carolina, *News,* 208

Greenville *Southern Enterprise,* 42

Gregory, Thomas W., 132

Gretny People, 221

Griffin, John, 101

Grovey Case, 288

Hagar, 220

Haldeman, W. N., 203

Hall, Basil, 216

Hall, Grover, 209

Halleck, Henry W., 21

Hamilton, James D., 226

Hammett, H. P., 148, 149

Hammond, M. B., 83, 85

Hampton, Wade, 21, 47, 53, 54, 59, 124

Hampton Institute, 178, 180, 189–92

Hancock, Winfield Scott, 148

Hardy, Thomas, 217

Harlan, John M., 348

Harlan County, Kentucky, 156

Harlan Miners Speak, 156

Harney, John Hopkins, 203

Harper's Magazine, 99, 217

Harriman, E. H., 159

Harris, Cora, 220

Harris, George W., 213

Harris, Isham G., 59

Harris, Joel Chandler, 207, 209, 212, 216, 217, 220

Harris, Julia Collier, 209

Harris, Julian, 209

Harrison, Benjamin, 77

Harrison, Pat, 235, 241

Hartzog, Henry S., 5, 6

Hayes, Rutherford B., 47–9, 65

Hayes-Tilden election, 349

Hays, Brocks, 294
Haynes, Paul H., 144, 145, 212–4
Health, hospitals, 124, 128, 256, 316; patent medicines, 162; of Negroes, 181–3; education in, 187, 210; Tennessee Valley Authority, 259; urbanization, 264, 340; spread of disease, 342, 354
Health, Education, and Welfare, Department of, 360
Helper, Hinton R., 3, 379
Hemmingway, William L., 55
Henderson, Richard, 253
Herty, Charles T., 142
Heyward, DuBose, 221, 222
Hill, Daniel H., 225
Hill, George Washington, 36, 131, 146
Hill, Lister, 242, 355, 369, 370
Hillbillies, 11
Hodges, Luther, 381, 382, 391, 392
Hogg, James S., 69, 70, 111, 112
Hogs, 105, 124, 153
Holden, W. W., 44
Holmes, George K., 92
"Home rule," see States' rights
Homestead legislation, 32
Hookworm, 182, 379
Hooper, Johnson J., 213
Hoover, Herbert, 131, 134, 135, 250
Horses, 104
Hospitals, 124, 128, 256, 316; see also Health
Housing, rural areas, 15; for Negroes, 344; discrimination in, 354, 360, 362, 365
Houston, Texas, 7, 340
Houston, George S., 57
Houston Chronicle, 208, 210
Howard, Perry, 131
Howell, Clark, 208
Howell, Evan, 208
Howells, William Dean, 327
Hubbell, Jay B., 198
Huckleberry Finn, 215, 216
Hugh Swinton Leagaré, 214
Humphrey, Hubert, 293
Hunter, A. B., 177
Huntsville, Alabama, 264

I'll Take My Stand, 224
Illinois Central Railroad, 270
Illiteracy, Negroes, 16, 19, 181, 349, 352; poor whites, 86, 175; educational problem, 91, 128, 169; in Arkansas, 183; in literature, 221; among unskilled workers, 280; voting qualification, 290; in agrarian society, 331, 335
Immigration, from Europe, 1, 155, 330;

in Tennessee Valley, 255; white, 339; rural areas, 344
Impeachment, 45, 127
Impending Crisis, 379
In Night Rider, 223
Independent movement, and liberal programs, 64, 65; election factor, 66, 67; against trusts, 68; and white farmers, 81
Indian Head Shoals, 247
Industrial revolution, 120, 244, 385; in New South, 1, 3, 8, 12; fears of, 13, 14, 18; expansion of, 19, 104, 155, 336, 337; and planters, 56, 128; prosperity of, 67, 324; agriculture, 101, 269; textile mills, 113; tariffs, 130; Ku Klux Klan, 133; labor problems, 135, 231; water power needed, 150; affects schools, 185; and unions, 232; Tennessee Valley Authority, 256; transportation, 275, 279; financing of, 282, 283
Inflation, 6, 7, 70
Inman, John H., 159, 207
Integration, Populist movement, 74; in education, 169, 177, 192, 306, 349, 359, 360, 361; newspapers, 209; difficulties of, 281; at Little Rock, Ark., 357; Martin Luther King, 365
Intermarriage, 306
Interior, Department of, 278
Internationalism, 286
Interstate Commerce Commission, 270, 271, 343
Iron industry, capitalization needed, 12; origin of, 153, 156; during depression, 230; transportation required to move ore, 269

Jackson, Mississippi, burned, 20; oil industry, 161; segregation, 358, 385
Jackson, Stonewall, 167, 189
Jackson Convention, 294
Jackson (Mississippi) Daily News, 209
Jarrell, Randall, 222
Jeannes, Anna T., 180
Jefferson, Thomas, 165
Jeffersonian tradition, 97, 98, 114, 197
Jews, 126, 134, 333, 344
Jim Crowism, 307, 346, 362, 367
Johns Hopkins University, 226
Johnson, Andrew, and Fourteenth Amendment, 31, 32; opposed by Congress, 26, 27, 30, 52
Johnson, Charles S., 198
Johnson, Herschel V., 24
Johnson, Lyndon B., nominated for Presidency, 52; southern liberal, 243; election of 1964, 299–303; on dis-

crimination, 255; Civil Rights Act, 370; on Ku Klux Klan, 373
Johnson, Paul B., 301, 377, 392
Johnson Yuba Dam, 212
Johnston, Mary, 220
Johnston, Olin B., 295, 370
Johnston, Oscar, 236
Johnston, R. Malcom, 213, 214
Journal of Southern History, 227
Juries, 319, 353, 354
Justice, see Courts
Juvenile delinquency, 345

Keating, Kenneth, 302
Kefauver, Estes, 294, 355, 369
Kelley, Florence, 327
Kellogg, William P., 36, 46, 47
Kennedy, John F., 299, 368
Kennedy, John Pendleton, 212, 213
Kennedy, Robert F., 291, 302
Kentucky, tobacco state, 144; coal fields in, 154; iron mining in, 156
Kentucky, University of, 198, 284
Kentucky Dam, 284
Kentucky Utilities Company, 247, 255, 267
Kephart, Horace, 254
Kerner, Otto, 302
Key, V. O., 61, 81, 117
King Cotton, tribute to, 5, 18; see also Cotton
King, Edward, 136
King, Martin Luther, at Philadelphia, Miss., 361; opposition to discrimination, 364-7, 369, 372, 373
Kirby, Thomas B., 204
Kirkland, J. H., 197
Kitchen, William B., 111
Kitt, Eartha, 386
Knapp, Seaman, A., 97, 99-102, 194, 195, 261
Knight of the Cumberland, 218
Knights of Labor, 70
Knights of the Black Cross, 42
Knights of the Rising Sun, 42
Knoxville (Tennessee) *Journal*, 209
Knoxville Summer School, 172
Kolb, Reuben, 70, 72
Ku Klux Klan, bigotry of, 19, 385; organizational chart of degrees, 41; lawless activities of, 42, 43, 373; opposition to, 45, 113, 206, 281; and clergy, 134; unions, 313

Labor, shortage of manpower, 1, 3, 23, 83, 87, 89, 137, 156; child, 70, 108, 113, 114; skilled, 82, 191, 283; factory, 99, 150, 154, 155, 283, 285; farm, 107, 279; railroad, 112; regulation of, 125, 128, 129; organized, 134, 314, 382; un-

skilled, 141; cigarette industry, 147, 148; job training, 151, 152; during depression, 230; building highways, 273; and Negroes, 306, 309, 311, 312
LaFollette, Robert M., 121
Lake Murray, 248
Lamar, Lucius Q. C., 24, 45, 54, 59, 66, 120
Lamb in His Bosom, 221
Land, abundance of, 12, 137; and railroads, 57; management of, 97, 99, 100, 259
Land We Love, The, 225
Landlords' agricultural lien laws, 88
Landon, Alfred, 299
Lanier, Sidney, 97, 213, 214
Last Year of the War, The, 225
Latham, Robert, 390
Law, enforcement of, 320-24; see also Courts
Lea, Luke, 132
Leach, S. M., 66
Lee, Harper, 387
Lee, Robert E., 136, 167, 393
Lee, W. S., 247
Legacy of the Civil War, 224
Legends and Lyrics, 214
Lesinski, John, 370
Lewis, John L., 155
Libby Prison, 145
Liberalism, contributions of, 220; and New Deal, 287, 294
Liberalism in the South, 220
Liberia, 324
Libraries, 112, 198, 202, 352
Lien notes, 91, 106
Life and Labor in the Old South, 226
Life of Jefferson Davis, 225
Life on the Mississippi, 215
Lilienthal, David, 258
"Lily-white" movement, election primaries, 109; Republican party, 129, 131; and unions, 313
Lincoln, Abraham, reconstruction policies of, 26, 27, 32
Lippincott's Magazine, 218
Literacy, voting test requirement, 75, 108, 109, 132, 289
Literature, regional, 9; Old South, 202; and newspapers, 212; on Civil Rights, 389
Little Rock, Arkansas, 357, 385
Little Shepherd of Kingdom Come, 218
Liuzzo, Viola, 373
Lives of Robert Young Hayne, 214
Livestock, 82, 91, 100, 104, 194, 277, 383
Lodge, Henry Cabot, 71
Lodge Force Bill, 71
Logan, Rayford W., 280

Long, Earl, 356
Long, Huey P., political demagogue, 111, 116, 117, 126–9, 235
Long, Russell, 370
Longstreet, A. B., 213
Look Homeward Angel, 222
"Lost Cause," legend of, 43, 49, 51, 57; and Confederate heroes, 59; familiar campaign slogan, 126
Louisiana, Scotch-Irish in, 1; political reconstruction, 26; ratifies Fourteenth Amendment, 35; under Republican control, 46; corruption in, 40, 55, 117; grants public lands, 57; lottery, 59; Negroes, 77, 356; banking center, 88; rice culture, 100; oil in, 161, 162
Louisiana Knights of the White Camelia, 42
Louisiana Land Reclamation Company, 99
Louisville *Courier-Journal*, 203, 210, 256
Louisville *Daily Journal*, 202, 205
Louisville *Democrat*, 203
Louisville Gas and Electric Company, 247, 248
Louisville *Herald*, 209
Louisville and Nashville Railroad, 39, 57, 58, 154, 157, 270
Love, Robert, 176
Lower South in American History, The, 6
Lowry, Robert, 56
Lucas, Anthony, 161
Lumber industry, a natural resource, 12, 57, 86, 103; waste of timber lands, 139, 140, 282; during depression, 230; and water power, 244; growth of, 254, 340; Tennessee Valley Authority, 259; transportation, 269; labor in, 284, 311; established, 333, 336
Lupton, J. T., 165
Lynch, John R., 36, 131
Lynching, crime of, 16; vigilante committees, 80, 178; emotionalism, 122, 124; reaction to, 210, 281, 289; laws against, 293; violence of, 317, 319
Lytle, Andrew, 222

McAdoo, William G., 132
McCarthy, Joseph, 354
McCleod, Daniel, 281
McCombs, William F., 132
McDow, T. B., 204
McElwain, W. S., 157
McGill, Ralph, 210
McGowan, John E., 205
McKeithen, John J., 301
McKellar, Kenneth, 119, 294
McLaughlin and Robock, 282, 283
McLaurin, Anselm J., 56, 124

McMath, Sidney, 294
McMillan, Benton, 111
McVey, Frank L., 196
Machine Age in the Hills, 155
Machinery, cigarette industry, 145, 147
Macon *Telegraph*, 209
Mahone, William, 57, 65
Malone, Vivian, 359
Man with a Bull-Tongue Plow, 224
Manhattan Project, 264
Mann, Horace, 171, 173
Mann, Woodrow, 357
Mansion, The, 222
Manufacturing, prosperity of, 67, 277; industrial revolution, 151, 269; employment in, 186; and unions, 232; Negroes, 312; growth of, 341
Markets, colonial, 12; foreign, 139, 337
Marshall, Burke, 368
Martial law, 43; *see also* Federal troops
Martin, James W., 198
Martin, Thomas S., 133
Maury, Matthew Fontaine, 24
Maverick, Maury, 243
Mayo, Amory, D., 177
Mebane, A. D., 101
Mechanization, in tobacco industry, 144
Medicine, 61, 316, 333; *see also* Health
Mellett, Lowell D., 103
Memphis, race riots in, 32
Memphis, Birmingham, and Atlanta Railroad, 59
Memphis *Commercial-Appeal*, 209
Memphis Power and Light Company, 247, 250, 255
Mencken, Henry L., 220, 224
Mercer Academy, 214
Merchants, post Civil War, 53, and agrarian society, 60, 61; unscrupulous, 90, 91; and tourist trade, 277
Meredith, James H., 199, 358
Methodists, 114; *see also* Religion
Mexicans in Texas, 1
Miami *Herald*, 210
Migration, agrarian society, 104, 106, 342; of Negroes, 230, 242; to the cities, 324, 325; of the poor whites, 331, to industry, 337
Militia, Negro, 45; *see also* Federal troops
Miller, Caroline, 221
Milligan, J. P., 33
Mills, employ child labor, 114; result of industrial revolution, 133, 335; sites of, 140, 333; in New South, 147, 148, 150; cotton textiles, 151, 152, 204
Mind of the South, 281, 388
Minerals, 1, 13
Mingo and Other Sketches in Black and White, 216

Mining, 154
Minor, John B., 168, 176
Missionaries; see Religion
Mississippi, elections in, 29, 30, 63, 301; corruption in, 55, 56; convention system, 121; discrimination, 209; industries in, 283; black belt, 325
Mississippi, University of, 358
Mississippi Constitutional Convention, 56, 74
Mississippi Plan, disfranchisement, 46, 48, 75
Mississippi Power Company, 267
Mississippi River, 272
Mississippi Society of the White Rose, 42
Mitchell, Broadus, 149
Mobile and Ohio Railroad, 270
Moderates, 349, 374
Money, 68; see also Finances
Montague, Andrew, 111
Montgomery (Alabama) Advertiser, 76, 208, 209, 304
Montgomery, Alabama, demonstrations in, 363, 364, 372
Montgomery Improvement Association, 364
Mooney, C. P. J., 209
Moore, James, 217
Moore, Jerry, 97
Moore, John H., 93
Moore, Merrill, 222
Moore and Schley Steel Company, 159
Morgan, Arthur E., 258
Morgan, Harcourt, 259
Morgan, J. Pierpont, 159, 207
Morgan, John Tyler, 176
Morin, Relman, 186
Moses, Franklin J., Jr., 37, 46
Motow, Robert R., 192
Mountain of the Lovers, The, 213
Murphree, Mary N., 217-19, 254
Murphy, Edgar Gardner, 113, 172, 225
Murphy, Isaac, 22
Muscle Shoals, 248-50, 261
Myrdal, Gunnar, 191, 280, 351, 352

Nashville, Tennessee, 270
Nashville, University of, 171
Nashville American, 57
Nashville Banner, 208, 210
Nashville, Chattanooga, and St. Louis Railroad, 57
Nashville Tennesseean, 210
Natchez, Mississippi, 161
Nation, 80
National Association for the Advancement of Colored People (NAACP), on Negro crime, 318; organized

lobbies, 327, 329; aggressiveness of, 328; activities curbed, 356
National Child Labor Committee, 113
National Cotton Planters' Association, 99
National Emergency Council, 103
National Farmers' Alliance and Co-operative Union, 68
National Industrial Recovery Act (NIRA), 127, 236-8
National Labor Relations Act, 237
National Negro Conference, 327
National Road Parliament, 274
National Textile Workers' Union, 233
National Union Convention, 31
National Urban League, 317, 328
Nationalism, in Old South, 3
Native sons of the South, 42
Nativism, 135, 215
Natural resources, 137, 141
Negativism, in southern writing, 9; caused by social conditions, 14, 15; Supreme Court decisions, 16
Negro, suffrage, 6, 27, 33, 34, 44, 47, 72, 77, 115, 121, 287, 298, 302, 303, 344, 373-6; discrimination against, 9, 314, 362; domination of, 15, 16, 51, 54, 79, 118; migration of, 23, 29, 230, 242, 342; terrorized, 39, 41-5; local militia, 45; white fear of, 49, 66, 75, 76, 81, 115, 229; penal system, 55, 56; political pawns, 62, 64, 68, 71, 74, 108, 131; and education, 81, 166-9, 174, 178, 180, 185-9, 191, 343, 346, 350; agrarian society, 91, 92, 101, 308-10; literacy tests, 109, 181; in Georgia, 119; colleges for, 192, 193; in literature, 221; emancipation of, 305; share of taxes, 307; and labor unions, 312, 313; family life of, 317
"Negrophobia," 120
Neo-Populists, 111
New Deal, reforms of, 108, 229; opposed by Huey Long, 127; social and economic revolution, 156, 235, 286, 379, 392, 394; as a welfare program, 220, 221, 235; opposition to nationally, 241; and unions, 313; labor, 328
New Deal-Fair Deal Democrats, 299
New Frontier, 108
New Orleans, race relations, 32, 43, 80; Germans in, 48
New Orleans Picayune, 208, 210
New Orleans States, 208
New Orleans Times-Democrat, 78, 208
New South, newspapers in, 6, 7, 211; from 1930, 7; occupation of, 24; industrialization, 58, 123, 147; philosophy of, 71; natural resources of, 138; cultural revolution, 204; phrase

coined by Grady, 205, 207; literature on, 215, 216, 220, 224; violence in, 320

Newspapers, in New South, 6, 7, 211; as a political force, 31, 125; Negroes, 80, 326; propaganda of, 86, 192, 210, 245; influence of, 98, 163; organization of, 202, 203, 333; suffered ravages of Civil War, 206; on civil rights, 387, 388

Nicholls, Francis T., 47, 48, 53, 54

Nineteenth Amendment, 115

Nixon, Herman C., 198

Nixon, Richard M., 298, 299

Noble, M. S. C., 167

Norfolk and Western Railroad, 270

Norris, George, 121, 250, 251

Norris Act, 256

Norris Dam, 260

North Carolina, ratifies Fourteenth Amendment, 35; issues railroad bonds, 38; and Independent movement, 66; Populists, 73; mills in, 113; banking in, 88

North Carolina, University of, 167, 171, 197, 201, 284

North Carolina Advisory Committee for Equal Protection of the Law in Education, 185

North Carolina Board of Health, 182

North Carolina Council of Safety, 42

North Carolina State University, 284

North Carolina White Brotherhood, 42

Nullification, 52

Oak Ridge, Tennessee, 264, 277

Ochs, Adolph, 204–6

Odom, Howard, cultural observations of, 9, 15; social-historian, 103, 105, 227; at University of North Carolina, 197; quoted, 262, 331; on Negroes, 305

Of Time and the River, 222

Ogden, Robert C., 172, 177–9, 183

Ohio River, 272

Oil industry, growth of, 12, 137, 161, 162, 341; taxes on, 127; transportation, 269, 277; strikes in, 338

Oklahoma, University of, 353

Old Creole Days, 218

Old Dominion, The, 215

Old South, post Civil War, 1–5, 13; myth of, 51, 52; caste system of, 133; tradionalism, 202, 214, 320

Ole Virginia, 215

One-crop system, agrarian society, 90, 97, 175, 221; failure of, 98, 102; cotton economy, 103, 104

One-party program, political monopoly of, 80, 108, 109, 115, 117–20, 132, 242

Operation Dixie, 314

Orr, Gustavus, 349

Oscar, 162

Otken, Charles H., 85, 90

Owsley, Frank L., 198

Oxford, Mississippi, 358

Packard, Stephen B., 46, 48, 49

Paducah, Kentucky, 253, 255, 277

Page, Thomas Nelson, 132, 215

Page, Walter Hines, 132, 164, 177, 208

Panic of 1873, 39

Panic of 1893, 72, 159; *see also* Depressions

Paper manufacturing, 142, 143

Parker, Alton B., 132

Parker, Mack, 322

Parks, Rosa, 363, 366

Paternalistic humanism, 133

Patronage, 130, 202, 301; *see also* Corruption

Patterson, William B., 180, 377

Payne-Aldrich tariff, 131

Peabody, George F., 170, 177

Peabody Fund, 170–73, 179, 182

Peabody Normal College, 172, 173

Peake, Mary S., 189

Pemberton, John S., 162

Penal system, during reconstruction period, 38; reform in, 54; corruption in, 55, 56; and Independent movement, 67; leasing of convicts, 69, 75, 112; paroles and pardons, 112, 124

Peonage, 11, 92; *see also* Sharecroppers

People's party, 70

Pepper, Claude, 243, 294

Percy, Charles, 302

Percy, Leroy, 123

Perex, Leander, 393

Perkins, George W., 7

Pershing, George, 233, 234

Peterkin, Julia, 221, 222

Petrie, George, 197

Petroleum, *see* Oil industry

Phelps-Stokes, Caroline, 180

Philadelphia Centennial Exposition, 146

Philanthropy, in education, 170–73, 179, 180, 188, 192

Phillips, Ulrich B., 226, 227

Pinchback, P. B. S., 36, 46

Pinchot, Gifford, 251

Pinckney, Josephine, 222

Plant Industry, Bureau of, 195

Planter class, post Civil War, 2, 3, 6, 11, 23, 29, 53; political activities, 44, 47, 71, 112, 117; in industry, 56, 128,

139; agrarian society, 85, 89; break-up of, 92; and Ku Klux Klan, 133
Plessy vs. Ferguson, 192, 307, 308, 348, 353, 354
Poe, Edgar Allan, 212
Political Prisoners, National Committee for the Defense of, 156
Political revolution, post Civil War, 2, 3, 7, 8, 24; and the Negro, 50; agrarian society, 107; spurred by Woodrow Wilson's election, 132; and newspapers, 211; the New Deal, 229; racial unrest, 281
Polk, James K., 55
Polk, Leonidas, 55, 69
Polk, Marshall T., 55
Poll tax, and Negroes, 29; repeal of, 65; Mississippi Plan, 75; qualification for voting, 79, 109, 110, 132, 297; and education, 168, 169; unconstitutional, 375; *see also* Taxation
Pollard, Edward, 225
Poor whites, post Civil War, 3; social problem, 11, 117; democratic political system, 50; education for, 349, 350; *see also* Sharecroppers
Popular History of the United States, 225
Population, immigration, 1, 155, 330; Negro, 23, 324, 350; urban, 296, 343; indigenous, 330, 332
Populist party, and Alliance movement, 70, 71; reforms of, 72; reactions to, 77, 81; ruthlessness of, 111; Negroes, 131; in progressive period, 239
Porgy, 221
Porter, James D., 57
Porter, Walter, 100, 195
Poteat, William L., 197, 233
Pratt, Daniel, 157, 158
Prentice, George Dennison, 202–6
President's Committee on Farm Tenancy, 238
President's Island, 272
Press, *see* Newspapers
Price, Leontyne, 386
Prisoners, *see* Penal system
Pro Bono Publico, 145
Progressivism, post Civil War, 9; and Democratic party, 74, 132; reforms of, 111, 113, 117, 118; legislation of, 125, 128; Populist movement, 239; and Farmers' Alliance, 307
Prohibition, 108, 114
Propaganda, during reconstruction, 32; on "lost cause," 51; by newspapers, 86, 192, 210, 245; racial, 287
Property, war losses in, 23, 25; voting qualification, 34, 109, 138; taxes on, 123, 274, 282; confiscation of, 249;

Civil Rights Act of 1866, 315; private, 353
Protestants, 134, 356; *see also* Religion
Public Works Administration (PWA), 258, 352
Pulitizer Prize, 209

Race Relations Report, 280
Racism, post Civil War, 2, 9, 10, 18, 19; economic problems, 16, 297; riots, 32, 327, 360; during elections, 135, 344; discrimination, 281, 356, 376, 377; operation Dixie, 314; Civil Rights Act, 348
Radical movement, fears of, 17; in reconstruction period, 27, 30, 31, 60; election campaigns, 40, 45; acts of violence, 43, 46, 81; influence wanes, 44, 49; and Huey Long, 128; Negro education, 191; in strikes, 234
Railroads, post Civil War, 3, 53; ravaged by Civil War, 20, 269; and radical Congress, 32; during reconstruction period, 38; labor problem, 55–7, 311, 312; financing of, 67, 68, 270; and Alliance movement, 70; importance of, 112, 338; mergers of, 123; aid lumbering industry, 141; construction of, 154–8, 204, 207; Jim Crowism, 307
Raleigh *Chronicle*, 208
Raleigh *News and Observer*, 208
Raleigh *State Chronicle*, 208
Randall, James G., 40
Randolph, Virginia, 180
Ransom, John Crowe, 198, 222
Ratchford, Benjamin U., 15, 266, 270
Rayburn, Sam, 242
Reactionaries, 356
Reaction and Reunion, 388
Readjustment movement, 65
Rebel, 203
Reconstruction, political, 10, 20, 26, 74, 204; controlled by carpetbaggers, 40; agrarian revolt, 51; in education, 166, 168, 189; in literature, 214, 227
Recreation, 277, 278, 334, 335, 345, 354
Red Bean Row, 221
Red Jackets, The, 42
"Red Menace," 133
Red Mountain Iron and Coal Company, 157
Redemption, of Old South, 53–8, 60, 71, 111, 115, 121, 306, 320
Redevelopment Housing Act, 345
Rednecks, 11, 98, 392
Redstone Arsenal, 264, 277
Reform, post Civil War, 7, 62; in Independent movement, 65; in Alliance movement, 69, 70; elections, 69, 109;

of Populist party, 72–74; Great Society, 108; among progressives, 111, 117, 118; trusts, 113; social, 121, 122, 229, 388; of Supreme Court, 241; in New Deal, 243; integration, 352

Relief, *see* Welfare

Religion, in Old South, 8, 51; evolution, 18; agrarian society, 91; and Ku Klux Klan, 134; fosters education, 165–7, 180, 188, 191; in urban areas, 334, 335; and integration, 356, 386

Report of the Dreiser Committee, 156

Republican party, post Civil War, 25; radicals in, 27–31; railroad conflict, 39; and Negroes, 44, 66, 67, 74; use of federal troops, 46; national elections, 49, 301, 64, 65, 301, 303; fusion with Populists, 73; and New South, 81; and Nineteenth Amendment, 115; minority group, 129, 131, 297; in Great Depression, 229; and social revolution, 292, 378

Revels, Hiram R., 36

Review of Reviews, 251

Reviewer, The, 221

Reynolds, Robert J., 144–6, 241

Rice crop, 23, 89, 97–100, 239

Richmond, Virginia, 20

Richmond *Dispatch,* 203

Richmond *Examiner,* 203

Richmond *News-Leader,* 209, 210

Richmond *Times-Dispatch,* 208, 210

Right-to-work Law, 382

Riots, 323, 371; *see also* Violence

Rise and Fall of the Confederacy, 225

River House, 220

Rivers, navigable, 154; aid from federal government, 248; ports on, 272

Rives, William Cabell, 170

Roads, and Alliance movement, 69, 70; state, 123, 124; in Louisiana, 127; aid lumbering industry, 139; to rural schools, 183; inadequate, 211; federal government, 248; freight on, 272–4; and urbanization, 276

Roanoke College, 177

Robert E. Lee, Man and Soldier, 215

Roberts, Elizabeth Madox, 220

Robinson, Joseph T., 134, 135, 235, 241

Rockefeller, John D., Jr., 178, 182, 184

Rome *Commercial,* 206

Roosevelt, Eleanor, 392

Roosevelt, Franklin D., National Emergency Council, 103; opposed by Huey Long, 127; New Deal program, 235–7, 240, 241; secured Negro vote, 242, 287, 292, 296, 298, 299; on discrimination, 329, 392

Roosevelt, Theodore, "lily-white" program, 130, 131; and trust-busting, 159;

friend of Booker T. Washington, 191, 192, 212; Muscle Shoals, 248, 251

Rosenwald, Julius, aid to education, 180, 181

Ross, Malcolm, 155

Rubin, Louis D., Jr., 219

Ruffin, Edmund, 24

Ruffner, William H., 167, 174

Rural Electrification Authority, 107, 262, 263

Rural free delivery, 125

Russell, Richard B., 241, 293, 355

Rhyne, Daniel, 148

Sage, Russell, 207

Sala, George A., 137

Sale, William H., 177

Sales tax, 129

Sanctuary, 222

Sanitary Commission for the Eradication of Hookworm Disease, 182

Sartoris, 222

Sass, Herbert Ravenal, 222

Savannah, Georgia, 20

Savannah *News,* 208

Scalawags, local Southern whites, 33, 36, 40; terrorized by Ku Klux Klan, 41; overthrown, 60; patronage, 130; integration, 349

Scarlet Sister Mary, 221

Schools, in New South, 1; during reconstruction period, 37; funds for, 75, 122; for migrant workers, 106; compulsory, 108; evening, 128; for agrarian society, 124, 151, 332, 334, 335, 344, 345; public, 165, 166, 174, 196; church-sponsored, 168; Tennessee Valley Authority, 256; integration, 349, 359, 362; *see also* Education

Schurz, Carl, 28

Scott, Robert K., 37, 46

Screw worm, 105

Screws, Claude, 319

Screws, W. W., 209

Seaboard Airline, 270

Sears, Barnas, 171, 173, 174

Secession, problems created by, 10, 25, 37, 203; opposition to, 44, 76; political issues involved, 52, 53, 205

Secret History of the Southern Confederacy, A, 225

Sectionalism, 7

Segregation, 224

Segregation, use of federal troops, 286; Supreme Court ruling on, 292; Lyndon B. Johnson, 301; humiliation in, 304, 306, 307, 309; and lynchings, 322; urbanization, 342; Civil Rights Act, 348; in education, 352, 354; Martin

Luther King, 368; at Birmingham, 368
Sellers, Clyde, 364
Selma, Alabama, ravaged by war, 20; Negro population in, 23; demonstrations in, 372, 373, 376, 385
"Separate but equal" doctrine, 348, 353, 354
Sewanee Review, 225
Shannon, Jasper, 241, 287
Sharecroppers, and agrarian radicalism, 61, 69; income of, 79; white tenancy, 85, 89, 98; Negroes, 92, 310; social revolution, 133, 135, 236; Farm Security Administration, 241
Share-the-Wealth program, 128
Shaw, Albert, 172
Sherman, William T., 20, 21, 207
Shipping, 130, 138, 340
Shuttleworth, Fred, 367
Silent South, 218
Silver, James W., 320
Simms, William Gilmore, 212, 213, 215, 225
Single-crop farming, see One-crop system
Sit-ins, 363, 366, 367; see also Riots
Skaggs, William H., 92
Slack Barrett, 162
Slater, John F., 180
Slave codes, see Black codes
Slavery, subservient labor, 2, 3, 23; created race problems, 10; abolishment of, 27, 29, 176; political overtones, 52, 63; agrarian society, 82, 92; in Virginia, 181; in defense of, 213; literature on, 226; degradation of, 305, 306
Sloss, J. W., 157
Smathers, George, 370
Smith, Alfred, 134, 235
Smith, Ellison D., 125, 241, 242
Smith, Hoke, 76, 111-13, 307
Smith, Howard W., 241, 329, 370
Smith, J. Russell, 251
Smith, Lamar, 323
Smith, Z. F., 183
Smith-Hughes Act, 195
Smith-Lever Act, 195
Smith vs. Allwright, 288
So Red the Rose, 220
Social Life in Old Virginia, 215
Social revolution, post Civil War, 2, 3, 11, 17, 24: reforms of, 4, 10, 16, 111, 121, 122, 229, 243; and negativism, 14, 133, 137, 224; agrarian society, 52, 107; "Bourbon" program, 54; in education, 164, 165, 168, 188, 192; and Negro, 187; newspapers, 209, 211; strikes, 232; cultural attainments,
280; the Great Depression, 286; caste system, 306, 324, 378; discrimination, 316; crime, 321
Social Security Act, 238
Socialism, and Populist party, 73; and Huey Long, 126; Tennessee Valley Authority, 256, 265, 266
Sociology for the South, 227
Soil conservation, Domestic Allotment Act, 95; erosion, 251; and agriculture, 266
Solid South, 130, 134, 229, 297
Sound and the Fury, 222
South Atlantic Quarterly, 226
South in the Building of the Nation, The, 227
South Carolina, Sherman's march through, 21; rice crop in, 23; ratifies Fourteenth Amendment, 35; government corrupt, 37, 38; martial law in, 43; under Republican party control, 46; disfranchisement, 76; banking in, 88; "lily-white" primary, 109; cigarette industry, 144; and education, 165, 168
South Carolina Farmers' Association, 91
South Carolina Gas and Electric Company, 267, 268
South Carolina Tax Study Commission, 264
Southern Alliance, 68, 69
Southern Association of Schools, 200
Southern Baptists Convention, 355
Southern Christian Leadership Conference, 366
Southern Commercial Congress, 4, 97
Southern Education Board, 172, 174, 179, 182
Southern Educational Conference, 178, 179
Southern Governors' Conference, 293, 383
Southern Historical Association, 227
Southern History of the War, 225
Southern Literary Messenger, 213
Southern Pacific Railroad, 270
Southern Planter and Farmer, 168
Southern Power and Light Company, 247
Southern Railroad, 270
Southern Regions of the United States, 15, 103, 105, 142, 262
Southern Regional Education Board, 199
Southern Schools: Progress and Problems, 186
Sparkman, John, 118, 355, 369, 370
Spindletop Research Center, 284
Sports, see Recreation
Sprague, 162

Standard Oil Company, 127, 128, 161
State normal schools, 171–3
States' rights, and Old South, 7; "home rule," 36; and conservatives, 57; campaign shibboleth, 125; Dixiecrats, 294
Stearns, Marcellus L., 47
Steffens, Lincoln, 327
Steinbeck, John, 387
Stephens, Alexander H., 225
Stevens, Thaddeus, 30, 31
Stevenson, Adlai, 298, 299
Stiles, Charles Wardell, 182
Stone, Alfred H., 101
Stone, John M., 45
Store, The, 220
Strange Case of Jim Crow, The, 388
Strikes, in textile industry, 152; and unions, 155; during depression, 232; in oil industry, 338; buses in Birmingham, 365
Stribling, Thomas S., 220
Stuart, Alexander H. H., 24, 349
Stuart, Jesse, 222, 224
Student Nonviolent Co-ordinating Committee (SNCC), 328, 366
Suffrage, Negro, 6, 27, 31–4, 44, 47, 72, 77, 115, 121, 287, 298, 302, 313, 326, 344, 373–6; during reconstruction, 34, 38; Independent movement, 64; "ballot box," 80; women, 108, 115; Fifteenth Amendment, 131; integration, 326
Sugar cane, 97, 102
Sullens, Frederick, 209
Supreme Court, on voting, 6, 374; decisions of, 16, 33, 108, 145, 288, 382; rules on Agricultural Adjustment Act, 95; Plessy vs. Ferguson, 192, 307; education, 199, 281; on New Deal program, 236, 237, 241; voided National Industrial Recovery Act, 238
Supreme Court, reform of, 241; and Fifteenth Amendment, 287; and Fourteenth Amendment, 246; on integration, 353, 354, 356, 358, 360
Surgeon-General, United States, 95
Sydnor, Charles S., 198

Taft, Robert, Jr., 302
Taft, William Howard, 4, 131
Talmadge, Gene, 116, 241
Talmadge, Herman, 295, 377
Taps for Private Tussie, 224
Tariffs, 32, 60, 130, 296
Tate, Allen, 222
Taxes, post Civil War, 5, 9, 14; during reconstruction period, 37, 38; exemptions, 57, 59, 117; for education, 122, 164, 166, 169, 179, 361; reforms in, 123; sales, 129; Tennessee Valley

Authority, 256, 265; property, 274; on industry, 282; paid by Negroes, 308
Taylor, Robert Love, 111
Teachers, lack of, 170, 171; salaries of, 174; Peabody Fund, 179; training of, 180, 190, 350; in agriculture, 194; and social revolution, 211; Negroes, 316, 349
Technological revolution, post Civil War, 2; in agriculture, 85, 96, 101, 283; in lumbering industry; 139; in education, 185; need for skilled labor, 312
Temperance, 114
Tenantry, sharecroppers, 85, 89; agrarian society, 92, 221; cotton growing, 101; migrant workers, 104; social revolution, 133, 236, 251; Farm Security Administration, 241; Negroes, 310
Tennessee, political reconstruction, 26; corruption in, 55; and Republican party, 131; coal fields in, 154, 160; iron mining, 156, 160; Civil Rights Act in, 302
Tennessee, University of, 179, 259
Tennessee Alliance, 69
Tennessee Coal, Iron and Railroad Company, 57, 159
Tennessee Electric Power Company, 250, 257
Tennessee Pale Faces, 42
Tennessee Power and Light Company, 263
Tennessee River, source of power, 251, 253; navigational management of, 259, 260
Tennessee River Valley, 250
Tennessee Valley Authority, source of industrial power, 199, 248, passim, 280, 284
Tenure of Office Act, 31
Terrorism in the Kentucky Coalfield, 156
Texas, German element in, 1; political reconstruction, 27; rejected Fourteenth Amendment, 31; radical rule in, 46; "redeemed," 46; grants public lands, 57; banking in, 88; oil in, 161, 162; opposed Fifteenth Amendment, 287
Texas, University of, 198
Texas and Pacific Railroad, 57
Textile industry, location of, 99; cheap labor in South, 113, 148, 149; financing of, 151, 152, 280; growth of, 153, 154, 335, 336; during depression, 230; South's source of water power, 244; favors high tariff, 295

Thirteenth Amendment, 36
Thomas, Ben F., 163
Thurmond, Strom, 294, 295, 298, 370
Tick eradication, 100
Tilden, Samuel J., 48
Tillman, Benjamin R., champion of the common man, 59, 124-6; and Tennessee Alliance, 69, 70; Democratic party, 76; opposed Negroes, 80, 307; on agriculture, 91; liberal views of, 111-13; opposed lynching, 323
Timber, a natural resource, 138, 139, 141, 154; increased acreage of, 266, 384; see also Lumber Industry
Time of Man, The, 220
Timrod, Henry, 212
Tobacco, growing of, 12; cash crop, 89-91, 97, 103; regulation of, 95, 96, 239, 245; scientific seed selection, 102; manufacture of, 143-5, 147; transportation of, 270; Negro labor, 313; importance of to South, 338
Tobacco Road, 221
Tom Sawyer, 215, 216
Tompkins, D. A., 148, 208
Toombs, Robert, 24, 59
Tourist business, 277-9
Tower, John, 299
Trade, post Civil War, 4; regional, 12; foreign, 139, 337
Tradesman, 13
Traditionalism, restrictions of, 8, 12; largely myth, 18, 19; and "lost cause" legend, 43
Trail of the Lonesome Pine, 218
Transportation, in New South, 1; produce to market, 105, 270; freight rates for, 112; in Louisiana, 128; lack of, 137; importance of, 139, 210, 342; for industry, 148-50, 269; water travel, 154, 245, 249, 265, 272; improvement in, 277; see also Roads
Transylvania Land Company, 253
Treason, in Confederacy, 28
Trent, William P., 215, 225
Trials, see Courts
Trinity College, 197, 225, 226
Trowbridge, J. T., 28
Truman, Harry S., on civil liberties, 292-9
Trusts, agrarian society, 61, 67; and Independent movement, 67, 68; tobacco industry, 113; legislation against, 125, 208; oil industry, 126, cotton seed industry, 153
Tuck, William N., 294
Tulane, University of, 197, 199
Tuskegee High School, 359
Tuskegee Institute, 180, 181, 190-92, 198
Twain, Mark, 216

Tweed Ring, 39
Twenty-fourth Amendment, 303
Two Little Confederates, 215
Two-party system, 52, 115, 120, 229
Tydings, Millard, 242

Uncle Remus, 208, 216
"Uncle Toms," 64
Underwood, Oscar W., 132, 133
Unemployment, post Civil War, 22; during depressions, 156, 230, 231; Federal Emergency Relief Administration, 237; see also Labor
Unfinished Cathedral, The, 220
Union League, 42
Unionists, 27
Unions, organized, 232, 234, 382; Negroes barred, 312-4; wages paid, 343
United Mine Workers, 155, 313
United States Geological Survey, 161
United States Office of Public Roads, 274
United States Steel Company, 159, 160
United States vs. Butler, 95
United Textile Workers, 232, 233
Universal Education in the South, 184
University presses, 201
Urban League, 317, 328
Urban South, The, 345
Urbanization expansion of, 19, 23, 133, 334, 335, 337, 339, 345

Vagrancy laws, black codes on, 29
Valleau, W. D., 198
Vance, Rupert B., 152, 197, 227, 345
Vance, Zebulon, 70
Vandenbosch, Amry, 198
Vanderbilt, George, 254
Vanderbilt University, 197-9, 222
Vardaman, James K., on social reform, 111, 112, 116; a demagogue, 121-6; for the common man, 129; emphasized "separate but equal" doctrine, 192, 307; opposed lynching, 323
Vein of Iron, 219
Veterans, Confederate, 53, 82, 136, 152, 225; organizations for, 70; bonus, 128; see also Civil War
Vicksburg, Mississippi, 20
Vicksburg Herald, 56
Vigilante committees, 16, 321
Villard, Oswald Garrison, 327
Vincent, Isaac H., 55
Vinson, Fred M., 352
Violence, strikes, 152, 155, 232-4, 338; during reconstruction period, 311; lynchings, 319, 323; integration, 355, 357, 365
Virginia, political reconstruction, 26; corruption in, 55, 56; banking, 88;

coal fields in, 154; iron mining, 156; and education, 174; road-building program, 276; integration, 356, 360
Virginia, University of, 176, 197, 205
Virginia Polytechnic Institute, 226
Virginia Power and Light Company, 267
Vocational training, 189, 192, 196, 343
Voice of the People, The, 219
Voting, Supreme Court decisions on, 6; Confederate veterans, 27; black codes, 29; buying of influence, 40, 44; Negroes, 66, 77, 121, 135, 287, 302, 303, 344, 373–6; literacy tests, 109; election process, 112; poll tax, 289; *see also* Suffrage

Waddell Academy, 173
Wade-Davis Bill, 26, 27
Wages, farm laborers, 89, 92; during depressions, 103, 230; legislature on, 128, 241; in industry, 150, 284; inequities of, 201, 279, 318; to Negroes, 308–10, 313
Wagner Act, 242
Wake Forest College, 197, 233
Walker, Gilbert C., 57
Wall Street, 125, 159, 234
Wall Street Journal, 281
Wallace, George C., influence on 1964 national election, 301, 304; on integration, 356, 359, 372, 381, 393
Wallace, Henry, 294, 295
Walthall, E. C., 59
Waring, J. Waties, 288
Warmoth, Henry Clay, 36, 37, 46, 54
Warren, Earl, 354
Warren, Robert Penn, 52, 222, 223
Wartegg, Ernest von Hesse, 216
Washington, Booker T., and President T. Roosevelt, 130; on education, 190–92; compared to Robert E. Lee, 226; advocated vocational training, 311, 381; on crime, 318; pacifistic reformer, 326, 327, 351
Washington College, 167
Washington and Lee College, 197
Water power, exploitation of, 13, 137, 138, 158, 280, 335; industrial revolution, 148–50, 244; in transportation, 154, 245, 249, 265, 272
Wateree-Catawba Basin, 247
Watson, E. J., 97, 126
Watson, Tom, 73–6, 121, 125
Watterson, Harvey, 26
Watterson, Henry, 203
Weather, *see* Climate
Weaver, James B., 71
Web and the Rock, The, 222
Webb, George, 144

Webb, Walter Prescott, 198
Weeks, Stephen B., 225–7
Welfare, as bribery for votes, 41; to farmers, 62; programs of, 117, 127; for factory workers, 235, 236; for indigent families, 238
Weltner, Charles L., 370
Western and Atlantic Railroad, 58
What the Negro Wants, 280
Wheat crop, 99
Wheeler Dam, 250, 259
Whigs, as conservatives, 27; scalawags, 36; and James L. Alcorn, 44; in Florida, 47; slavery crisis, 53
Whiskey Ring, 39
White, Hugh, 133
White League, 48
White Man's party, 53
Whitehead, Joseph B., 163
Whitener, M. C., 245
Whites, myth of supremacy, 15, 16, 66, 80, 308, 348; and the conservatives, 44; literacy tests, 75, 109, 175; on voting, 78, 79, 291; sharecroppers, 92; solidarity of, 120; *see also* Poor whites
Why Industry Moves South, 283
Wiggins, Ella Mae, 234
Wilkins, Roy, 318, 374
Willkie, Wendell, 257, 258, 299
Wilson, James H., 157, 195
Wilson, W. L., 176
Wilson, Woodrow, 52, 132, 226
Wilson Dam, 249–51, 256, 257, 259
Winston-Salem Conference, 178, 179
Winston-Salem *Daily Sentinel,* 178
Wisconsin Public Service Commission, 258
Wise, Harry, 13, 349
Withers, W. T., 86
Wolfe, Thomas, 222
Women, working, 114, 147
Woodward, Baldwin, and Company, 151
Woodward, C. Vann, 51, 52, 56, 388
Woofter, J. T., Jr., 331
Works Progress Administration (WPA), 156, 237, 240, 313
World Enough and Time, 223
Wright, Fielding, 292, 293
Wright, Wesley A., 145
Wylie, W. Gill, 245

Yarborough, Ralph, 369, 370
You Can't Go Home Again, 222
Young, Stark, 220
Young, Stephen, 302
Young, Whitney M., Jr., 328